Daniel Bros. , Ethel Z Bailey

Daniels Bros. Ltd. materials

Daniel Bros. , Ethel Z Bailey

Daniels Bros. Ltd. materials

ISBN/EAN: 9783741196010

Manufactured in Europe, USA, Canada, Australia, Japa

Cover: Foto ©knipser5 / pixelio.de

Manufactured and distributed by brebook publishing software
(www.brebook.com)

Daniel Bros. , Ethel Z Bailey

Daniels Bros. Ltd. materials

Price —

Estd · 1844·

Entd Sa Hall

DANIELS BROS'

Illustrated GUIDE for

ROYAL · NORFOLK · SEED · ESTABLISHMENT
SPRING 1896

AMATEUR GARDENERS

The Royal Norfolk Seed Establishment,

NORWICH,

Seed Warehouses.
EXCHANGE STREET
AND BEDFORD STREET.

Chief Offices.
BEDFORD STREET.

ENGLAND.

Seed Grounds.
IPSWICH ROAD AND EATON.

Nurseries.
THE TOWN CLOSE NURSERIES
NEWMARKET ROAD.

TO OUR CUSTOMERS.

WE have much pleasure in submitting a copy of our "ILLUSTRATED GUIDE FOR AMATEUR GARDENERS for Spring, 1896," at the same time thanking you for your kind and liberal support in the past.

It is a source of much gratification to us, that while year by year steadily adding to our very large number of customers we still retain the confidence of so large a number of our older clients, some of whom have honoured us with their patronage for more than a quarter of a century; this assures us that our efforts to supply them with Seeds and Plants of the best quality at fair and moderate prices are fully appreciated.

The severe and protracted frost of the winter of 1895, followed by the prolonged drought, was highly detrimental to the crop of many kinds of Seeds, and in some few instances it has been found necessary to make a slight advance in prices; we are, however, pleased to state that we have secured an ample supply of Seeds of the choicest quality for our trade of 1896, whilst our prices have been fixed at the lowest rates consistent with reliable stocks and good growing quality.

Soliciting the favour of your obliging commands, which shall have our best and most careful attention,

We are,

Your obedient Servants,

Daniels Bros.

January, 1896.

DANIELS' IMPROVED
WHITE SPANISH ONION

This fine variety, which has been specially selected and grown by ourselves, is undoubtedly the finest type of White Spanish Onion in cultivation. It grows to a large size, is of beautiful even shape, and of excellent flavour. A first-class variety for Exhibition or general use.

Per oz., 2s. 6d. ; per packet, 1s.

NEW POTATO: DANIELS' EARLY QUEEN

– Price per lb. 6d., 7 lb. 2/6 –

NEW POTATOES FOR 1896.

NEW POTATO—MAJOR NEVE. (*From a Photograph.*)

NEW POTATO—MAJOR NEVE.

This fine Potato now offered for the first time, we can highly recommend as one of the best introductions of late years. It is a white round variety, very robust in habit, and a heavy cropper. The skin is slightly rough, eyes few and shallow, season late; the flesh, which is white, is dry and mealy when cooked, and of excellent flavour. We have grown this variety on our own seed farm this season, and have no hesitation in recommending it as a first class late variety, suitable both for market and the private grower.

On account of its excellent cropping and cooking qualities, it was awarded a First Class Certificate by the Royal Horticultural Society of England.   Price, per 7 lb. 2s.; 14 lb. 3s. 6d.; 56 lb. 12s. 6d.

DANIELS' EARLY QUEEN.

(*See Coloured Plate.*)

This splendid variety sent out by us last year has amply sustained the high recommendation we then gave it, viz., a grand early variety, of extra fine quality and enormous productiveness. It is kidney-shaped, somewhat inclined to oblong: the eyes few and almost even with the surface. The skin is white, suffused with a delicate shading of pink. The flesh which is very fine grained is beautifully white and mealy when cooked, and of superior flavour. The tubers are of handsome appearance, and very uniform in size, growing compactly round the haulm which is only fifteen inches in height. It is a fine variety for exhibition, and has with us this season again yielded a heavy crop of fine tubers.

Price, per lb. 6d.; 7 lb. 2s. 6d.; 14 lb. 4s. 6d.; 56 lb. 16s.

EVIDENCE OF QUALITY.

KITCHEN GARDEN SEEDS.

NEW AND SELECT VARIETIES FOR 1896.

We have much pleasure in drawing the attention of Amateurs and others to the special varieties of Vegetables, &c., mentioned on these pages, and which we can recommend as of sterling merit in the production of really fine specimens for Exhibition and other purposes.

ONION—ALLAN'S RELIANCE. (*From a Photograph.*)

ONION—ALLAN'S RELIANCE.

We have much pleasure in introducing this fine Onion to the notice of our Customers. It has been grown and selected by Mr. Allan of Gunton Park Gardens for many years past, and, as will be seen from our illustration, is now brought up to the very highest type of a White Spanish Onion, and which, besides its splendid size and keeping qualities, is unsurpassable for exhibition or general crop. We cannot do better than by giving the description of Mr. Allan and others, who have grown it of late years.

Price 1s. 6d. and 2s. 6d. per pkt.

Mr. Allan says:—" Allan's 'Reliance' Onion was a very fine stock when I took it in hand twenty-six years ago, even then winning prizes whenever shown. Selecting the bulbs for seed for the above number of years, I have fixed the shape and colour. No stock in existence can surpass it for trueness; it keeps well, owing to its firmness and density, and may be grown to the largest size it is possible to grow an Onion, if sown early and given special cultivation. Under ordinary cultivation, other kinds which have been grown on the same piece of ground are a long way behind it in weight of crop and size of bulb."

Mr. John Crawford, Coddington Hall Gardens, a well-known authority on Onion growing, says: "I have been a grower and exhibitor of Onions for many years, and am acquainted with most of the best strains in cultivation. By far the best is one which recently came under my notice at Gunton Park. Its size, weight and general symmetry is all that can be desired, and throughout a large plot which I saw growing at Gunton last Autumn, it was difficult to discern the least difference between the bulbs, so true were they. One striking feature of this choice strain is the exceptionally small neck, which is always a sure guarantee for early maturity and long keeping."

Mr. F. Hanson, The Gardens, Somerleyton Hall, says:—"I am highly pleased with the 'Reliance' Onion, and consider it one of the very best varieties in cultivation, its size and form being all that can be desired, and its heavy cropping and good keeping qualities will commend it to every one."

Mr. H. G. Oglee, Blickling Hall Gardens, says:—"I have grown your 'Reliance' Onion for several years, and can safely say it is the best type of White Spanish I have ever grown, both for size and keeping qualities."

New & Select Garden Seeds for 1896.

NEW PEA—
DANIELS' DWARF PROLIFIC.

A second early dwarf wrinkled marrow, growing about 1½ ft. high; it is enormously prolific, bearing a profusion of dark green, slightly curved pods four inches long, well filled with eight to nine peas of excellent flavour. It is a very compact grower, and will be an acquisition to all gardens where space is limited, on account of the little room it occupies as compared with its heavy cropping qualities. We have had this Pea under trial for several years, and consider it one of the best of the dwarf marrows, and have no hesitation in recommending it to our customers.

Per pint 1s. 6d.; per quart 2s. 6d.

"The Peas gave me great satisfaction last year. I had an abundant crop of excellent colour and flavour."—**Mr. H. COOPER**, Alton.

"I take this opportunity of informing you that I have never had such a satisfactory crop of **Peas**. I shall certainly adopt the same sort next year."—**Mr. J. CLARKE**, King's Lynn.

"I am highly pleased with the Seeds I have had from you. My **Peas** are a splendid crop."—**Mr. W. BLACKWELL**, Seadon.

"I got some **Peas** from you last Spring, and they have done wonderfully well."—**Mr. G. THOMPSON**, Bolton.

"Your **Peas** were excellent last year."—**Mrs. BROWNRIGG JAY**, Ascot.

NEW PEA—GRADUS.

A new large-podded first early wrinkled variety. First Class Certificate from the Royal Horticultural Society after trial at Chiswick. Without doubt this is the greatest advance yet achieved in early Peas, for although it ripens with *William I.*, the deep green coloured pods are of the size and as well filled as those of *Duke of Albany*, with large wrinkled Peas of the *Ne Plus Ultra* colour and of quality quite equal to that famous variety. Gradus is also the most distinct early Pea yet raised, and is alike good for table and for show. Height 2 ft.

In sealed half-pint packets 1s. 6d.

PEA. DANIELS' DWARF PROLIFIC.

NEW PEA—ALDERMAN.

Received the highest award from the Royal Horticultural Society after trial at Chiswick, 1891. The raiser claims that this is in advance of all the Peas of the *Telephone* and *Duke of Albany* type. In habit it is stronger and more branching, averaging in height 5 ft., and producing, a few days later than *Duke of Albany*, an enormous weight of very large handsome, straight, deep green and well filled pods, many of which contain twelve large wrinkled blue peas of the richest *Ne Plus Ultra* flavour and quality, whilst nearly every pod is fit for show.

In sealed half-pint packets 1s.; per pint 1s. 9d.

NEW CLIMBING KIDNEY BEAN.

First Class Certificate, Royal Horticultural Society. This Bean combines the best features of the two types—Dwarf French and Scarlet Runner. It crops earlier than the Runners and has all the delicate flavour and quality of the Dwarfs. The pods are very long, narrow, fleshy, and brittle, and very fine in the grain. They are borne freely from the bottom to the top of the haulm, which grows up to six or seven feet high. The abundance of handsome pods strikes every one who sees them.

Per pint 1s. 3d.; per quart 2s.

NEW MELON—BISHOP'S FAVOURITE.

Award of Merit, Royal Horticultural Society, June 25th, 1895.

The following is the raiser's description:—"This Melon is very handsome in appearance, being beautifully netted, with a magnificent golden yellow skin; it has a white flesh of great depth, remarkably tender, with a most luscious flavour, the fruit reaching six and seven pounds in weight. I have grown it over four years, and find its constitution most vigorous and robust. I feel confident it will become one of the standard varieties."

Per packet 1s. 6d.

NEW TOMATO—FORDHOOK FIRST.

A grand new variety from America, said to be one of the earliest Tomatoes yet introduced, and has the great advantage over most early sorts now in commerce, in being perfectly smooth and of good shape. It is recommended as a free-setter and a very heavy cropper. The fruit which are of a beautiful crimson colour are smooth, solid, and very handsome; the flavour is all that can be desired.

Per packet 1s.

BROCCOLI—METHVEN'S JUNE.

This is a splendid stock, and one of the latest Broccolis in cultivation, producing fine pure white heads till nearly the end of June. It is very hardy, standing the Winter better than any other sort. Sow in April, and plant out as soon as ready. Per packet 1s.; per oz. 2s. 6d.

FLORAL NOVELTIES FOR 1896.

NEW DWARF SWEET PEA—CUPID.

A SINGLE PLANT OF CUPID. *Grown in a pot, engraved from a Photograph.*

NEW SWEET PEA- CUPID. Per packet of 20 seeds, 1s. Per packet of 10 seeds, 8d.

This new and remarkable variety, which hails from the United States, promises to be one of the very best floral novelties of recent years. The habit of the plant is dwarf and compact, and it does not exceed five inches in height, the individual plants spreading to ten or fifteen inches diameter. The foliage is dark green, the flower stems about four inches long, and bear near the end two or three blossoms of the purest white, and quite as large and as deliciously scented as those of the Eckford class. It is a wonderfully free bloomer, the plant being literally covered with the pure white flowers. It is said to commence blooming in May, and to continue till November, and will undoubtedly prove a plant of splendid effect as an edging for massing, or for mixing with other flowers in the garden.

DANIELS' NEW GODETIAS.

(*See Coloured Plate.*)

We beg to draw particular attention to the two following superb varieties raised by ourselves, which are now offered for the first time, and which will prove valuable and welcome additions to this popular and splendid class of hardy annuals.

GODETIA—MARCHIONESS OF SALISBURY. A quite new and charmingly effective variety, growing only about one foot in height, and bearing a profusion of very large beautiful flowers ; colour, a bright carmine-crimson, the petals having broad, clearly-defined light margins, giving the plants, when in bloom, a fresh and lovely appearance. A variety of exceptional beauty. **Award of Merit, Royal Horticultural Society, 9th July, 1895.** Per pkt. 2s. 6d.

„ **CARMINEA AUREA (Crimson and Gold).** A very distinct and beautiful variety, and quite a new break of colour amongst Godetias. The plants grow about one foot in height, and the numerous medium-sized flowers are of a bright deep rosy-crimson colour, the petals being beautifully edged with bright pale yellow, at times approaching a deeper or golden shade. Grown in a mass at our Seed Grounds during the past Summer, the effect was at once novel, rich, and pleasing. Per pkt. 2s. 6d.

ASTER, GIANT COMET—"THE BRIDE."

A very fine new variety of the Comet Aster, the colour of which may be best described as white changing to rose, the flowers being firstly pure white, then white changing to delicate rose and finally of a beautiful rose tint. It is the same variation of shades already seen in the Victoria and Mignon sections, and which lends to the plant such a peculiar charm, and which is most effective in the Giant Comet Aster with its long wavy petals, like those of the Japanese Chrysanthemum. Per pkt. 1s.

CROTOLARIA RETUSA.

This is described as a new golden yellow flowering Pea. The flowers of this beautiful annual are of a rich golden yellow colour of the true Sweet Pea form, and as large as those of the Eckford varieties. It is a low growing, branching plant, every branch and branchlet ending in racemes, six to ten inches long, of handsome golden Sweet Pea like flowers. The leaves are oval, smooth, of darkest green, and the plant blooms profusely throughout the Summer. The seeds are best started in a gentle heat, first soaking them for some hours in warm water.

Per pkt. 1s.

PANSY—PRESIDENT CARNOT.

A charming new variety of French origin. The flowers are large, of splendid form, and each of the five pure white petals is adorned with a deep violet blotch, which covers the greater part of its surface. The two colours stand out in sharp contrast to each other, and form a very handsome combination. Per pkt. 1s.

NASTURTIUM LILIPUT—
(Tropæolum lobbianum compactum).

An entirely new class of Dwarf Nasturtiums, and one which deserves the greatest attention. The plant is in every respect smaller than the Tom Thumb, and the pretty little flowers, produced in the greatest profusion and standing up well above the small-cut and bushy foliage, make it one of the prettiest annuals imaginable. The blossoms appear in the most various and showy colours, and it is especially noteworthy that some quite new shades appear among them, such as are not represented in the old class. This feature, and the further one that the seed is much smaller than in the Tom Thumb Nasturtiums and similar to that of the Lobbianum section, are the best evidences that we have here to do with an entirely new break in the Tropæolum family. Excellent for groups and borders. Per pkt. 1s.

FLORAL NOVELTIES FOR 1896.

NEW SWEET PEAS (Eckford's).

CROWN JEWEL. Pale standard, tinted and veined with violet rose, the wings creamy, slightly tinted with rose, a most profuse bloomer, the rows, the past season, having been literally bedecked with bloom from bottom to top. In sealed packets 2s. 6d.

ALICE ECKFORD. Rich cream tinted cerise standards, white wings, a refined beautiful flower, the most chaste variety ever offered. First Class Certificate, Shrewsbury and Wolverhampton, 1894. In sealed packets 2s. 6d.

COUNTESS OF ABERDEEN. White, margined with pale pink, finely formed standards, a distinct charming flower, very lovely. In sealed packets 2s. 6d.

CAPTIVATION. Rosy purple self, finely expanded, shell-shaped standard, a charming novelty, quite distinct and beautiful. In sealed packets 2s. 6d.

LITTLE DORRIT. Carmine, tinted pink, standard of finest form, large white wings, the colours beautifully harmonised, a superbly lovely variety. In sealed packets 2s. 6d.

MIKADO. Deep orange cerise ground, striped white, of exquisite form and good size, a very pleasing and desirable novelty. In sealed packets 2s. 6d.

MIGNONETTE, GOLDEN MACHET.

All the excellencies peculiar to the justly popular Machet Mignonette, recognised by every raiser as the best for forcing and pot culture, are possessed also by this new variety. The plants are of strong compact habit, with the large crinkled leaves peculiar to the Machet, and bear long massive spikes crowded with golden yellow blossoms. This novelty is as valuable as it is distinct and cannot fail to attain a great popularity. Per packet 1s.

MIGNONETTE, GIANT MACHET.

This fine variety is a great improvement on the well-known and popular *Machet*, sent out some few years ago. The plants are of the same vigorous compact habit of growth, but slightly taller, whilst the very large spikes of finely-scented flowers are much superior to those of the old variety. The seed we offer has been carefully saved from pot plants only, and may be depended on for good results. Per packet 6d. and 1s.

WALLFLOWER, RUBY GEM.

WALLFLOWER, RUBY GEM.

This grand Novelty is certainly the most brilliant and effective variety of Single Wallflower hitherto sent out. The colour is a beautiful clear shade of ruby violet, with a bluish satin-like sheen (quite unlike the old purple Wallflower, which is much more dark and dull in colour), and when seen in a mass the effect produced is very striking. It has the habit of the ordinary dark Blood Wallflower, of medium height, and the flowers are extra large and of good substance. Per packet 1s.

TECOMA SMITHI.

One of the finest seed novelties yet introduced, and an exceedingly beautiful addition to our Autumn and early Winter flowering greenhouse plants. The handsome pinnate leaves, surmounted by the large terminal corymbiform heads of orange-coloured blossoms are most charming and effective. The seed may be sown at any time. It is as easily managed as a Chrysanthemum, the flowers lasting in perfection upwards of a month. The individual flowers are about two inches long, tubular, of a rich lemon and dark orange combined, the mouth of the tube being about one inch in diameter. Per packet 2s. 6d.

CARNATION, "URIAH PIKE."

We have secured a supply of seed saved from this grand crimson perpetual flowering Carnation, which is thus described:—This is undoubtedly the grandest crimson Carnation ever offered, at the same time the most decided acquisition to the Tree or Perpetual flowering class that has ever been raised; an ideal Carnation, faultless in form and colour. It is possessed of an extremely robust and vigorous constitution such as no other Perpetual Flowering Carnation can boast, and no collection will, in future, be complete without it. In point of colour this noble Carnation reigns supreme, being a veritable glowing crimson velvet self and in this respect absolutely unique. The flowers which are produced abundantly and continuously for a long period, are perfect in form, and emit a powerful clove fragrance; and measure 2½ inches to 3 inches across, the petals forming a complete rosette. It is consequently a model "button-hole" flower, and High-Class Florists regard it as indispensable. The calyx is faultless, always remaining intact. Per packet 1s. 6d. and 2s. 6d.

With reference to **New Sweet Pea, Cupid**, quoted on opposite page, the REV. W. T. HUTCHINS, the eminent Sweet Pea specialist, says of it: "A novelty it certainly is. It is the only genuine dwarf Sweet Pea, and has sported so at one jump. By some freak of nature it has lost the habits of a vine, and makes a low tuft of short branches which hug the ground, showing no tendency either to trail or climb. But it has not lost the free-blooming habit, and thus its blossoms, which are uniformly the purest possible white, form a low, crowded mass that nearly hide the foliage."

NEW CACTUS-FLOWERED DAHLIAS.

MAHALA SHERIFF. A splendid new pure white Cactus Dahlia, with broad, beautifully curled and twisted petals. Very free flowering, and throws its blooms well above the foliage; a capital exhibition variety, and exceedingly useful for cutting.

Each 1s. 6d.; 3 for 4s.

MAHALA SHERIFF. A splendid new pure white Cactus Dahlia, with broad, beautifully curled and twisted petals. Very free flowering, and throws its blooms well above the foliage; a capital exhibition variety, and exceedingly useful for cutting.

Each 1s. 6d.; 3 for 4s.

[NEW CACTUS-FLOWERED DAHLIA, MAHALA SHERIFF.

The following, which are of the true Cactus type, we can confidently recommend as being a decided advance on most other varieties hitherto sent out.

EARL OF PEMBROKE. Florets very long, quite three inches in length, beautifully and regularly arranged porcupine-like. A fine large flower, the colour a bright plum, deeper and more velvety towards the centre. Height, 3 feet. Each 2s.

MARQUIS. Deep rich velvety maroon or crimson, a colour seldom seen, except in a good coloured *Reynolds Hole* Rose, towards the outside the petals are lighted up with a tinge of fiery crimson, giving to the whole flower a very rich effect; in form nothing could be better, the long pointed petals, which have a slight curl inwards, show off the richness of colouring to good advantage. Height, 4 feet. Each 2s.

MRS. BARNES. Lovely pale primrose, gradually shading towards the outside of the flower and towards the tip of each petal with the palest tint of rosy pink, the blend of colours being exactly that found in a *Macie Van Houtte* Rose; a large flower of exquisite shape, with long, twisted, pointed petals. Height, 3½ feet. Each 2s.

HARMONY. Reddish bronze, rather more yellow towards the centre, florets long, curled, and very pointed; very free flowering, the flowers being of a splendid Cactus shape and of fair size. This may be considered an improved *Countess of Gosford.* Height, 3 feet. Each 2s.

MAYOR HASKINS. The brightest glowing crimson imaginable; a large bold flower of true Cactus type, reminding one of *Gloriosa*, but much deeper in colour, the back of the petals is of a very pale red, and as the petals twist, especially towards the outside of the flower, they show this pale tint, and give the flower quite a tipped appearance. Height, 3½ feet. Each 2s.

MRS. A. BECK. This variety is very similar in form and shape to the now well-known *Mrs. A. Pearl*, but of a rich reddish salmon colour. The petals are very long and beautifully twisted, forming a flower which is not unlike a Japanese Chrysanthemum in appearance. The plant is of dwarf habit, the flowers are of medium size, and borne very freely. Each 2s.

One of each above six superb varieties ... 10s.

SALISBURY WHITE.

(See illustration, page 105.)

THIS is a flower of the purest snow white, having short pointed petals of the decorative type. We introduce this not as an exhibition Cactus Dahlia, but one which on account of its small pure white flowers, borne in the greatest profusion on long wiry stems, will prove invaluable to florists for wreaths, bouquets, and decorations of all kinds. Height, 5 feet. Each 1s., or 3 for 2s. 6d

GRAND NEW IVY-LEAVED PELARGONIUM.

IVY-LEAVED PELARGONIUM—QUEEN OF ROSES.

QUEEN OF ROSES
(See illustration).

We have much pleasure in introducing this superb variety, which we feel sure will soon become highly popular. It is a cross between *Gloire d'Orleans* and *Madame Thibaut*, and combines the high-class qualities of both those varieties. The flowers are very large, 2½ to 3 inches across, perfectly double, of splendid form and substance, and of the most beautiful rosy crimson carmine colour. The flowers retain their beauty for a much longer period than most other varieties, as the petals do not fall, but gradually wither and dry on the plants, when they are easily picked off. It is very free flowering, and being of a strong vigorous habit of growth is admirably suited for training on trellises, hanging baskets, pots, vases, &c. Some cut blooms of this were exhibited at the Royal Horticultural Society's Show, London, in July last, and were very much admired.

Strong young plants.

Each 1s. 6d., or 3 for 4s.

From THE GARDEN,
13th July, 1895.

"Messrs. Daniels Bros., Norwich, showed a quantity of an Ivy-leaved Pelargonium named 'Queen of Roses.' The trusses compact, the flowers large, very double, and of a deep rose colour."

NEW ZONAL PELARGONIUMS OF 1895.

DONALD BEATON. Clear bright orange, with a decided tint of yellow in it; a most telling colour, and a distinct advance in this class, through which we hope eventually to reach a real yellow: the plant has a good habit, and is very free. Each 2s. 6d.

DR. MACDONALD. Rich glowing crimson scarlet, a splendid flower in the style of *John Forbes*, which we distributed last year, but deeper in colour than that variety. Each 2s. 6d.

GEORGE GORDON. Bright rosy scarlet, a perfect florist's flower, the pips being 2½ inches in diameter, and beautifully formed, perfectly circular, with each petal gracefully reflexing: a charming variety. Each 2s. 6d.

HILDA. Clear salmon, darker towards the centre, where it is shaded with bright orange, and also a distinct tint of pink in the upper petals; the flower is well formed, and the largest we have raised in this class, being 2½ inches in diameter; the habit of the plant is good, and the foliage distinctly marked with a dark zone. Each 2s. 6d.

KITTY. Soft cherry red, with white eye, and a paler blotch on the two upper petals; flowers very large, perfectly circular in outline. The colouring of this variety is lovely, and it is altogether one of the most charming varieties we have ever sent out. Each 2s. 6d.

MRS. D'OMBRAIN. Pale blush at the margin of pips deepening to rich salmon in the centre, an immense flower of exquisite form; in fact we consider this variety so near perfection that we feel hopeless of raising anything better in its colour. The plant is good in habit, and wonderfully free blooming. Each 2s. 6d.

PRINCESS ALIX. Clear pale rose, a distinct and beautiful shade; the flower is immense, single pips measuring up to 2½ inches in diameter, though not quite so perfect in form as some of its companions; a fine acquisition. Each 2s. 6d.

ST. CECILIA. A beautiful warm shade of salmon deepening towards the centre, the deeper colour forming a ring round the eye; the flower is large both in pip and truss, and the plant remarkably free flowering; a charming novelty. Each 2s. 6d.

SEAGULL. White, not absolutely pure, having a faint blush shade; the bloom is grand in size and substance, far ahead of any previous introduction. Each 2s. 6d.

SNOWDROP. Snow white, absolutely pure under all conditions; a distinct advance upon all our previous introductions, the flowers being of perfect form, and very large for a white, single pips measuring 2½ inches in diameter; habit very dwarf and free. Each 2s. 6d.

One of each the above ten varieties, 21s.

Six varieties, our selection, 12s. 6d.

NEW AND SELECT PLANTS FOR 1896

SUPERB EXHIBITION CHRYSANTHEMUMS.

Plants ready in March.

CHARLES H. CURTIS (Incurved). Most splendid variety. The flowers are extra large, well incurved, and of good depth, the petals slightly pointed, a fine grower, and of medium height; colour a deep rich yellow. First Class Certificate. Each 2s. 6d.

EDITH TABOR (Japanese). The flowers are large and handsome, with long broad drooping florets, curled at the tips, the colour is a very fine lemon-yellow, and is quite distinct from the colour of any other variety, the whole flower is suffused with the faintest tinge of green. The plants are of strong vigorous habit, medium height, and easy to grow. First Class Certificate Crystal Palace and Royal Aquarium. Each 7s. 6d.

MADAME CARNOT (Japanese). A splendid flower of large size, and of the purest white, long drooping florets, a vigorous grower. First Class Certificate. Each 1s. 6d.

MRS. E. S. TRAFFORD (Japanese). Bronzy-rose, quite distinct, a beautiful sport from Wm. Tricker, and a fine exhibition flower. First Class Certificate. Each 1s. 6d.

MUTUAL FRIEND (Japanese). One of the finest exhibition varieties; immense flowers with long florets, white, tinted lilac; good dwarf habit. First Class Certificate. Each 2s. 6d.

MRS. CHARLES BLICK (Japanese). Without doubt one of the finest white Japanese yet introduced; the flower is made up of a deep, dense, but graceful spreading mass of long florets, which incurve slightly at their tips. The habit is very compact and dwarf, the foliage being an extraordinary size, indicating that the plant is very robust. All who have seen this variety pronounce it to be a grand acquisition, and will no doubt be grown extensively this coming season. It will prove a grand exhibition variety. First Class Certificate National Chrysanthemum Society; Award of Merit, Royal Horticultural Society. Each 5s.

MRS. W. H. LEES (Japanese). One of the largest and most beautiful flowers known; has been grown nine inches across and the same in depth; colour a beautiful soft blush, lighter in the centre, with long curly drooping florets; a splendid exhibition flower. First Class Certificate. Each 1s. 6d.

PHILADELPHIA (Incurved Japanese). An Incurved Japanese of the finest form, six inches in diameter, and of the most delicate creamy-white colour, the tips tinged with sulphury yellow; very distinct. Has received awards wherever shown. Each 1s. 6d.

LORD PENZANCE'S HYBRID SWEET BRIARS.

A NEW AND CHARMING CLASS WHICH WILL BECOME HIGHLY POPULAR.

AMY ROBSART. Lovely deep rose, robust and free. Ea. 5s.

ANNE OF GIERSTEIN. Dark crimson, followed by an abundance of pretty clustered bunches of hips; graceful habit. Each 5s.

BRENDA. Maiden's blush or peach, dainty in colour and shade. Each 5s.

FLORA McIVOR. Pure white, blushed with rose, perfect for cutting. Each 5s.

LADY PENZANCE. Beautiful soft tint of copper, with a peculiar metallic lustre; delightfully scented. Each 5s.

LORD PENZANCE. Soft shade of fawn or écru passing to a lovely lemon-yellow, sometimes toned with a most delicate pink. Each 5s.

LUCY ASHTON. Pretty white blooms with pink edges, free flowering; foliage very sweet. Each 5s.

MEG MERRILIES. Gorgeous crimson, very free flowering; seeds abundantly. Each 5s.

ROSE BRADWARDINE. Beautiful clear rose, perfect in shape; very profuse, strong, robust habit. Each 5s.

PAUL'S NEW CARMINE PILLAR ROSE.

Large single flowers 3½ to 4 inches across, and of the brightest possible rosy-carmine, which are produced so abundantly that the last year's shoots, some ten to twelve feet long, were covered from base to top with large bunches of flowers breaking from every eye, the flowers in the bunches opening in succession. It seems absolutely hardy, and in every way admirably suited for planting in shrubberies and rosaries for effect. It is a great acquisition to Climbing Roses on account of its colour, its free, bold growth, and the sweet scent of its bloom. Each 7s. 6d.

CHINA ROSE—DUKE OF YORK.

The flowers are variable in colour between rosy-pink and white: sometimes pale with deep red centres, sometimes white edged and tipped with deep rosy-pink, in the way of *Homer*, but the pink shade deeper than in that variety, and the contrast of colour therefore more striking; always beautiful, and quite distinct from any other Rose; it is of vigorous growth and good habit; a splendid constantly flowering decorative Rose. Each 7s. 6d.

NEW AZALEA—Mollis X Sinensis.

ANTHONY KOSTER. A splendid, perfectly hardy hybrid of *Azalea Mollis* and *Azalea Sinensis*. The flowers are individually large, the petals broad, robust, and of a brilliant orange-yellow shade, shot with rose. It is a useful plant for flowering early under glass, and is altogether a superb type, brilliant in colour, and remarkably free, simply covering itself with blooms. It is one of the handsomest Azaleas in cultivation, and should be included in every collection. Each 7s. 6d.

NEW CANNA—KOENIGIN CHARLOTTE (Pfitzer).

A superb variety. Very vigorous, with enormous and massive foliage; the spikes, on which the individual blooms are arranged bouquet-wise, are very large, and stand out well around the foliage; the flowers are large with well-rounded petals, bright red, edged one-eighth of an inch wide with gold, the contrast of colour giving a novel and effective appearance to the plant. Award of Merit, Royal Horticultural Society. Also Highest Awards at Antwerp, Paris, Lyons, Mayence, &c. Strong plants, each 2s. 6d.

Daniels' Superior Lawn Grass Seeds.

DUNSTON HALL, NEAR NORWICH.

HINTS TO AMATEURS
IN MAKING A NEW LAWN OR TENNIS GROUND.

A WELL-KEPT, rich green velvety lawn, or grass plot, adds a great charm to the house and garden, and is perennial in its freshness and beauty, but in sowing seeds for these, it must be borne in mind that to obtain a really good close turf, the seeds must be sown thickly, in fact, grass seeds can never be fairly sown too thickly for making a new or improving an old lawn, as it is found that the thicker the seed is sown, the finer will be the turf. Where it is desired to form a turf quickly, as much as two or three pounds a rod should be sown. As many varieties of small birds are very fond of grass seeds, it will be well, when sown, to give some protection for a short time till the plants are up.

In constructing a new Lawn or Tennis Court, the ground should be carefully prepared. An open level piece of ground, naturally well-drained, should, if possible, be selected; but where a good natural position is not to be obtained, the soil must be removed from the higher to the lower parts until the surface is perfectly level; and if the ground be too moist or retentive, it should be thoroughly well drained. Let the ground selected be well dug to the depth of eighteen inches or two feet, and an equal depth of soil obtained. If poor, a good coating of well-decayed manure should be incorporated with the soil. After digging, rake down level, and roll or beat the surface to an equal firmness all over. A frequent mistake is made in carting the soil on to the plot to be laid down, instead of having it wheeled on planks put down for the purpose. The cart-rut so made is much harder than the surrounding ground, and when the natural subsidence takes place a very uneven surface is left. The surface soil to the depth of three inches should also be as nearly as possible of equal richness, in order that the grass should grow evenly and of the same colour. April and September are the best months for sowing, and the quantity of seed from a pound to the rod, or six bushels to the acre. All weeds should be removed as soon as they make their appearance, and when the grass has grown to the height of three or four inches it should be cut and rolled. Frequent cutting and rolling are of great importance where a fine, close, and soft turf is required, and an occasional dressing of Daniels' Eureka Manure will also be found of great service in promoting a healthy growth of the young sward. The renovating and improving of old lawns is also a work of importance at the proper season—say, in April. Daisies and other weeds should be eradicated. The holes that these weeds are taken from should be filled up with soil, which should be beaten hard into them; and the surface of the lawn ought then to be sown over moderately thick with Finest Lawn Mixture, and covered with another heavier sowing of sifted soil, the whole being rolled down. This rolling should be done when no fear exists of the soil adhering to the roller. It is surprising what good can be effected (to say nothing of the pleasure derived from the improved appearance) from a small outlay annually, by employing cheap labour for a short time each year, and by giving an annual surface-dressing.

DANIELS' MIXTURES OF LAWN GRASS SEEDS
FOR TENNIS LAWNS, CROQUET AND CRICKET GROUNDS, &c.
Carriage Free in quantities of not less than 2 lbs.

	per lb.		per bush.	
Mixture of Dwarf Grasses, for producing a fine close turf	1s. 0d.		20s.	
Fine Mixture of Dwarf Grasses, for producing a dark green velvety turf	1s. 6d.	,,	25s.	
Finest Mixture of Dwarf Evergreen Grasses, extra choice	2s. 0d.	,,	30s.	

Our Lawn Grass Mixtures can be supplied with or without Clover as required.

DANIELS' COMPLETE COLLECTIONS
OF
KITCHEN GARDEN SEEDS.

The great value of an abundant supply of Fresh Fruit and Vegetables, in the maintenance of good health in the household, cannot be fairly over-estimated, and every one having a garden of any extent, should grow, as far as possible, an ample supply for their own requirements, bearing in mind that a comparatively small occupation, by judicious sowing, planting, and cultivation, will yield a long and valuable succession of Choice Fruits, Vegetables, and Salads.

Daniels' Complete Collections.
ALL PACKAGE AND CARRIAGE FREE.

No. 1.	Contains 28 quarts of Choice Peas	And		£5 5 0
No. 2.	Contains 20 quarts of Choice Peas	all		£4 4 0
No. 3.	Contains 16 quarts of Choice Peas	other	...	£3 3 0
No. 4.	Contains 10 quarts of Choice Peas	Seeds in		£2 2 0
No. 5.	Contains 8 quarts of Choice Peas	proportion	... ...	£1 11 6

These Collections are carefully made up with seeds of finest quality in best varieties from each class, with a view of furnishing an ample supply of Choice Vegetables throughout the year, and will be found extremely valuable for those who have not sufficient time nor experience for making their own selection.

N.B.—Our Collections will be made up in the same liberal manner as heretofore. Intending purchasers will kindly bear in mind that it is only by having Seeds specially grown, and by preparing the packets in large numbers that we can be so liberal in the quantity of the Seeds supplied for the amount charged, and that by ordering our selections, instead of making their own, they will reap an advantage of at least 25 per cent. below the general Catalogue prices. We therefore wish it to be understood that no reduction, alteration, or substitution can be allowed in any of the collections. When ordering please quote Number and Price.

No. 6. Daniels' Complete Collection, £1 1 0

Package and Carriage Free. All the best kinds for succession for a Villa Garden.

14 pints -	Peas, Early, Medium, and Late	2 pkts. -	Celery, Red and White	1 pkt. -	Parsley, Fine Curled
3 pints -	Broad Beans	1 pkt. -	Couve Tronchuda	2 ozs. -	Parsnip, Hollow-crowned
1½ pint -	French Beans	8 ozs. -	Cress, Plain & Curled		
1½ pint -	Runner Beans	2 pkts. -	Cucumber, Ridge and Frame	4 ozs. -	Radish, Long and Turnip
1 pkt. -	Beet, Dark-leaved	1 pkt. -	Endive, Curled	4 ozs. -	Spinach, Round and Prickly
1 pkt. -	Borecole, Curled	2 pkts. -	Gourd or Pumpkin		
1 pkt. -	Brussels Sprouts	1 pkt. -	Leek, Giant	3 ozs. -	Turnip, Snowball, &c.
3 pkts. -	Broccoli, Early & Late	3 pkts. -	Lettuce, Cos and Cabbage	4 pkts. -	Herbs, Sweet and Pot
3 pkts. -	Cabbage, Choice sorts			2 pkts. -	Tomato
½ oz. -	Savoy, Drumhead	6 ozs. -	Mustard, White	1 pkt. -	Capsicum
3 ozs. -	Carrot, Intermediate, &c.	1 pkt. -	Melon, Choice		
2 pkts. -	Cauliflower, Choice	4 ozs. -	Onion, White Spanish &c.		

No. 7. Daniels' Complete Collection, 12s. 6d.

Package and Carriage Free. All the best kinds for succession for a Small Garden.

7 pints -	Peas, Early, Medium and Late	1 pkt. -	Cauliflower, Choice	1 pkt. -	Melon, Choice
1 pint -	Broad Beans	1 pkt. -	Celery	1 pkt. -	Parsley, Fine Curled
1 pint -	French Beans	4 ozs. -	Cress, Plain & Curled	1 oz. -	Parsnip, Hollow-crowned
1 pint -	Runner Beans	2 pkts. -	Cucumber, Ridge and Frame		
1 pkt. -	Beet, Dark-leaved	1 pkt. -	Endive, Curled	2 ozs. -	Radish, Long and Turnip
1 pkt. -	Borecole, Curled	1 pkt. -	Gourd or Pumpkin	2 ozs. -	Spinach, Round and Prickly
2 pkts. -	Brussels Sprouts	1 pkt. -	Leek, Giant		
2 pkts. -	Broccoli, Choice Sorts	2 pkts. -	Lettuce, Cos and Cabbage	2 ozs. -	Turnip, Snowball, Orange Jelly
1 pkt. -	Cabbage, Choice Sorts				
1½ oz. -	Savoy, Drumhead	3 ozs. -	Mustard, White	1 pkt. -	Vegetable Marrow
	Carrot, Intermediate, &c.	2 ozs. -	Onion, White Spanish, &c.	3 pkts. -	Herbs, Sweet and Pot
				2 pkts. -	Tomato

No. 8. Daniels' Complete Collection, 7s. 6d.

Package and Carriage Free. All the best kinds for succession for a Cottage Garden.

4 pints -	Peas, Early, Medium, and Late	1 oz. -	Carrot, Intermediate	1 pkt. -	Parsley, Fine Curled
1 pint -	Broad Beans	1 pkt. -	Cauliflower, Autumn Giant	1 oz. -	Parsnip, Hollow-crowned
½ pint -	French Beans	1 pkt. -	Celery, Red and White	1 pkt. -	Pumpkin
½ pint -	Runner Beans	2 ozs. -	Cress, Plain	2 ozs. -	Radish, Long and Turnip
1 pkt. -	Beet, Dark-leaved	1 pkt. -	Cucumber, Ridge		
1 pkt. -	Borecole, Curled	2 pkts. -	Lettuce, Cos and Cabbage	1 oz. -	Spinach, Summer
1 pkt. -	Brussels Sprouts			1 oz. -	Turnip, Snowball
1 pkt. -	Broccoli	1 pkt. -	Leek, Musselburgh	1 pkt. -	Vegetable Marrow
1 pkt. -	Savoy, Drumhead	1 oz. -	Mustard, White	2 pkts. -	Herbs
1 pkt. -	Cabbage	1 oz. -	Onion, White Spanish	1 pkt. -	Tomato

No. 9. Daniels' Cottager's Collection, 5s. 0d.

Package and Carriage Free. Containing Three packets of Peas, One packet each Broad, French, and Runner Beans, and a choice selection of the best sorts for succession. This collection is of exceptional value.

No. 10. The Cottager's Packet, 2s. 9d. Post Free.

Containing sixteen varieties of choice Vegetable Seeds, including fair quantities of Peas, Onion, Radish, Lettuce, Carrot, Cabbage, &c. This is a very cheap collection which can be highly recommended.

Peas.

Cultivation.—The Pea is one of our most important crops, and to be successfully grown, must be liberally treated. A deep rich soil, well pulverized and incorporated with a fair allowance of well-decayed manure, should be chosen for the principal crop in summer. For early Peas the ground does not require to be so rich. Sowings of William the First, Gem of the Season, and other first early varieties should be made in November, December, and January. The second early sorts, including Lye's Favourite, Supreme, and Gladiator, three splendid varieties, may be sown in February, and others including Daniels' Matchless Marrow, Yorkshire Hero, Veitch's Perfection, Ne Plus Ultra, and Maincrop Marrow for main crops, from March to the end of May. For last crop sow a few of the first early varieties in June or July.

In sowing Peas those of ordinary height should be in drills three or four feet apart; the taller varieties five or six feet. They can also be grown to advantage in rows twelve feet apart, and some other crop between them, as by this means both sides of the row get the full benefit of light and air, and yield a greater abundance of pods. When a crop is grown between the rows, the rows should run, if possible, from north to south, to give both the Peas and the intervening crop free access to the sunlight.

Staking up should be commenced when they are three inches high. The dwarf varieties may be grown without sticks, but all are benefited by being kept from the ground. Peas, when making their appearance above ground, are very subject to the depredations of sparrows, &c.; this may be easily prevented by placing a short stout stick at each end of the row, and then leading from one to the other a single *black* thread or cotton at a distance above the ground of two or three inches. We have found this by experience to be at once the most simple and efficacious remedy that will apply with equal benefit to *any kind of seed* subject to the depredations of birds, whether sown in drills or seed beds; if the latter, the threads should be stretched from end to end at intervals of about nine inches.

Section I.—Earliest Varieties.

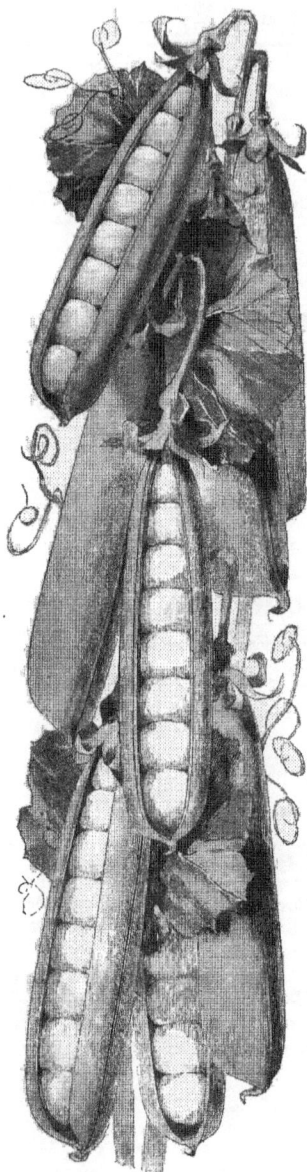

DANIELS' GEM OF THE SEASON. The earliest Pea in cultivation. Height three feet, and very prolific. This magnificent early Pea is the most valuable for general use ever sent out. Is always the earliest, whether sown in Autumn, Winter, or Spring. Is also the hardiest, resisting frost better than any other kind, and is not affected by mildew. Being very prolific and of a most delicious flavour, will be found most desirable for marketing, and invaluable for the private garden. New selected stock ...   . per quart 2s.

"I have been very fortunate with Pea, **Gem of the Season,** for notwithstanding the intense of the season and dry weather, I gathered first lot 13th of June."—**Mr. L. B. LOVELACE,** Rickinghall.

"Your Pea, **Gem of the Season.** did so well with us last year that I should like to try them again."—**The Rev. C. KNOWLES,** Doncaster.

Exonian. A First Early Wrinkled Marrow; very productive. The haulm, which is thickly covered with pods containing six to eight peas of fine flavour, is rather light and pale green in colour. Awarded a First Class Certificate, Royal Horticultural Society. Height 3 feet.

Per pint 1s. 3d., quart 2s.

"The Peas sent me last Spring were excellent. **Exonian** is the best early quality I have ever tried, and is a good cropper."—**Mr. Z. INGOLD,** Frampton.

	ht.	pr quart.
	in ft.	s. d.
English Wonder (new). A great improvement on the well-known American Wonder, in earliness, productiveness, length of pod and flavour, and being somewhat dwarfer than that variety cannot fail to become a general favourite	1	2 3
American Wonder. A first early Pea, some days in advance of William the First. For small gardens it is unsurpassed, owing to its earliness, productiveness, and the small space it occupies	1	1 6
Dillistone's First Early. Very early. Known also as **Carter's First Crop** and **Sutton's Ringleader** ...	3-4	0 9
Early Sunrise. Very hardy and prolific	2½	1 3
Earliest of All. A round blue-seeded Pea of excellent and rich flavour; is dwarfer than Ringleader, more prolific ...	2½	1 4
Early Paragon. A blue wrinkled Marrow of fine flavour. It is the earliest of the large wrinkled marrows	4-5	1 0
Kentish Invicta. A fine early blue Pea	2½	1 0
Sangster's No. 1 Improved. Extra select stock	3	1 0
William Hurst. An early blue wrinkled variety, similar to American Wonder. An abundant bearer, of first-rate quality: as an early Pea it should be grown in every garden ...	1	2 0
William the First. Selected stock. One of the finest early green Marrows, combining flavour, earliness, and productiveness	3	1 6

DANIELS GEM OF THE SEASON.

Peas *(continued).*

Section II.—Second Early & Main Crops.

NEW PEA.—DANIELS' MATCHLESS MAR-ROW.

Height four feet, bearing a profusion of handsome well-filled pods, each containing ten to twelve large marrow peas of the most delicious flavour. For use late in the season this Pea is unequalled, and cannot fail to become a leading kind for market purposes, possessing as it does all the good qualities of Ne Plus Ultra and Veitch's Perfection combined

per pint 1s. 6d., per quart 2s. 6d.

"I feel it my duty to inform you I have taken First Prize with your Pea, **Matchless Marrow.** I have ten long rows of Peas on trial, all cultivated the same, and **Matchless Marrow** is by far the finest throughout."—Mr. GEORGE HURRELL, Southminster.

"There are some very fine sorts of Peas out, but have more confidence in your **Matchless Marrow Pea** than I have in any one sort else. It is a real, good, profitable, hardy Pea, and still A 1 for exhibition; can always grow them eleven to twelve in a pod."—Mr. W. HILL MOORE, Barton.

"Among the Seeds purchased from your firm this season I am especially pleased with your **Matchless Marrow.** At the Headley Horticultural Annual Show, held last Tuesday, I was awarded First Prize with that Pea grown from your Seed. They have been much admired, and are very prolific; all who require an Exhibition Pea should grow them for they are excellent."—Mr. E. DAVID, Headley.

"I have just had five stones of beautiful peas from the pint of Seed supplied by your firm of the **Matchless Marrow.**"—Mr. W. DOWNING, Harthill.

"My gardener says he has never had anything so fine as your **Matchless Peas.**"—Mrs. FRIEND, Preston Park.

"I planted half-pint of your **Matchless Marrow Peas** last April, in a row thirty-six feet long in a four acre field. Although the sharp June frost severely punished them they turned out splendid, literally covered with pods 5 to 5½ inches long, and ten to twelve beautiful peas of exquisite flavour; as to quantity, all who saw them were of opinion they exceeded your coloured plate, which certainly was no exaggeration."—Mr. JOHN HOLMES, Borrowash.

NEW PEA.—THE DANIELS.

This grand new Pea is the result of a cross between Best of All and Alpha, and is quite distinct. The haulm is robust, and grows about four feet in height, is of light green colour, up to the present it has exhibited no trace of mildew. The pods are long and handsome, averaging five to six inches in length, and filled with ten to twelve delicious marrow peas of exquisite flavour; it is a main-crop variety, and will take a high place for exhibition purposes, while its heavy cropping qualities will recommend it to the market grower. Owing to the excessive drought during the past Summer, our crop of this fine Pea is very limited　　　　　per pint 2s., per quart 3s. 6d.

"The Daniels New Pea secured several First Prizes, being the best in the neighbourhood."—Mr. W. WEBSTER, Newball.

"The New Pea, The Daniels, on my ground astonish every one that sees them, one and all want to know the name, &c. The pods are enormous."—Mr. W. H. SAVILLE, Newmarket.

	ht. in ft.	pr quart. s.	d.
Daniels' Dwarf Prolific *(see Novelties).*	1½	2	6
Daniels' Early Long-pod. A fine early variety; pods five inches long and well filled with fine-flavoured peas. A useful variety alike to the market gardener and private grower	4	1	6
Duke of Albany. A fine long-podded variety. One of the best for exhibition, and of very fine flavour	4-5	2	0
Gladiator. The plant is very robust and vigorous, stem branched, growing about three feet in height, exceedingly productive, bearing in pairs an abundance of long, curved, handsome pods, which are very closely filled with medium-sized peas of excellent quality. First Class Certificate, Royal Horticultural Society	3	1	6
Nelson's Vanguard. A fine second early wrinkled Marrow; haulm densely covered from the bottom with fine handsome pods, well filled with peas of excellent flavour	2½	1	6
Stratagem. This is a splendid variety, with pods five to six inches in length, containing eight to ten large fine-flavoured peas. First Class Certificate, R.H.S.	2	2	0
TELEGRAPH. A valuable market variety of first-class quality	4	1	9

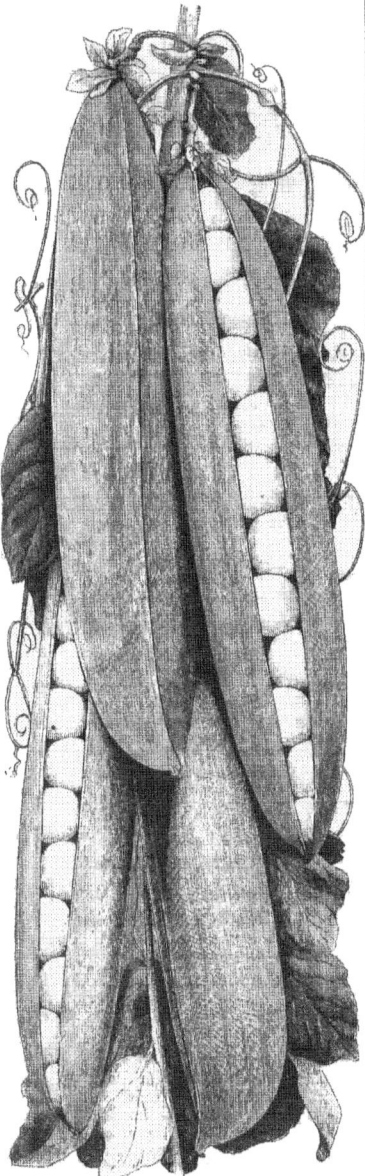
DANIELS' MATCHLESS MARROW.

Peas (*continued*).

Section II. Second Early and Main Crops (*continued*).

	ht. pr quart. in ft.	s.	d.
LYE'S FAVOURITE. This magnificent Pea was raised by Mr. James Lye, Clyffe Hall, Market Lavington, Wilts. It is a second early variety, bearing a profusion of handsomely curved pods, well filled with delicious marrow peas. Ten to eleven peas in a pod. Awarded a First Class Certificate, Royal Horticultural Society	3½	1	6
Champion of England or **Fortyfold**	5	1	0
Harrison's Glory. Large blue variety	3	0	9
Fillbasket (Laxton). Very prolific	3	1	6
Supreme (Laxton). This is a first-class blue round Pea, and an enormous bearer	4	1	0
Prize-taker. Good market variety	4	1	0

Section III.—Main Crop and Late.

DANIELS' MAIN CROP MARROW. We have great pleasure in stating that this splendid Marrow Pea has stood the test of several years and has become a favourite. It is of the same flavour as the old Ne Plus Ultra; but the pods are longer. It is very prolific, and should be largely grown as a Main Crop Pea for all purposes **per pint 1s. 6d.**	4	2	6
Autocrat. First Class Certificate, Royal Horticultural Society. Is of exceedingly robust habit, much branched, foliage of a dark lustrous green. Owing to its strong constitution, it is perfectly free from mildew, and is the best late Pea in cultivation	4	2	
Dr. Maclean. A blue wrinkled Marrow, of vigorous growth, wonderfully productive, flavour of the first quality	3½	1	6
Maclean's Wonderful, or Prince of Wales	3	1	6
Queen (Sharpe). A blue wrinkled Marrow Pea of sturdy branching habit. It requires to he sown thinly. The pods are large, dark green, slightly curved, and well filled; the peas are of delicious flavour when cooked	2-2½	2	6
Yorkshire Hero. A fine dwarf Marrow Pea of the Veitch's Perfection type, is very prolific, bearing a profusion of well-filled pods, containing six to eight large peas each; flavour first-class	3	1	3
Triumph (Sharpe). A blue wrinkled Marrow, of exquisite flavour; the pods are long and well filled, each containing nine to eleven large peas. In constitution it is robust and hardy	2-3	1	6
Telephone. First Class Certificate, Royal Horticultural Society. This fine variety is good either for exhibition or market purposes	4½	2	0
NE PLUS ULTRA. Delicious Marrow Pea, very prolific, quality first-class, fine for general crop	6	1	3
NE PLUS ULTRA. Extra select stock	6	2	0
British Queen (Oxford Tom). Very long pods, productive, quality first-class, a great bearer	6	1	6
Veitch's Perfection Marrow	3	1	3
Veitch's Perfection Marrow. Extra select stock	3	2	0

EVIDENCE OF QUALITY.

"I took First Prize in Amateurs and Professionals Classes with the **Matchless Marrow** Pea which you supplied me with last year."—Mr. **E. T. DUCK**, Robertsbridge.

"I think perhaps you would like to know that for the last five years I have taken First Prize with your Matchless Marrow Pea, at our Ealing Show, in Amateur and Open Class. The name is thoroughly descriptive of this fine Pea. I may say at the last Show, on July 3rd, my dish of Peas in the Open Class measured 5½ inches long, and contained eleven and twelve in a pod."—Mr. **E. TATLER**, Ealing.

"I am glad to tell you I took First Prize at St. Giles' Show with your **Matchless Marrow Peas**."—Mr. **W. SHEARS**, Chalbury.

"I took Special Prize at Thurlow Show for the twenty best pods of Peas, **Matchless Marrow**; and First Prize for Continuity Lettuce."—Mr. **D. MAYES**, Great Thurlow.

"I received some Daniels' Long-pod Peas from you this year, and I have found them to be a splendid Pea to grow as a main crop."—Mr. **C. RANNER**, Newmarket.

DANIELS' MAIN CROP MARROW.

PARROTT'S PROLIFIC MARROW.

A remarkably fine wrinkled Marrow Pea of the Veitch's Perfection type, but more sturdy in its habit of growth and rather shorter in the straw, is also about three weeks earlier than that fine old variety. It is wonderfully prolific, being covered with quite a profusion of well-filled, rich green pods, with six to eight large peas in each, and of the most delicious Marrow flavour. Height about 2½ feet. One of the very best dwarf Peas in cultivation. Price 2s. per quart.

PARROTT'S PROLIFIC MARROW. Price 2s. per quart.

EVIDENCE OF QUALITY.

" I have sent you a photo of a row of your **Parrott's Prolific Pea** grown in my garden, which has been much admired by a great many people, they persuaded me to have it taken as they never saw such a crop before, they hung so thick, and were a perfect sight; as for eating, I must own I never tasted a better Pea."—**Mr. E. BROWN,** Martock.

"I am pleased to say that all the Seeds have done remarkably well. I have never had such a crop of Peas, in particular, **Parrott's Prolific.**"—**Mr. J. H. ASKEW,** Dodston Hill.

"I may say the Pea I had from you, **Parrott's Prolific Marrow,** is a splendid Pea, the produce is remarkable, there is scarcely a single pod amongst them; they are all doubles, and a splendid marrow when cooked."—**Mr. G. H. KIDD,** Willingham.

New Pea—Duke of York. This is the most distinct and valuable Pea that has been introduced for many years, as it combines earliness with good appearance and fine flavour; is of the most useful height both for market and private gardens, and in robustness of habit, size of pod, and productiveness will satisfy the most exacting. It may best be described as an earlier and dwarfer form of the "Duke of Albany," possessing all the good qualities of that standard variety but maturing two or three weeks earlier. Height 3½ to 4 feet. Per quart 2s. 6d.

Superabundant. This is a dwarf Marrow Pea, deep green in colour, an immense cropper. Fine market Pea of the finest quality. Height 2½ feet. We can recommend this as a very superior variety. Per pint 1s. 6d., per quart 2s. 6d.

New Pea—The "Daisy." The Daisy Pea is a dwarf wrinkled Marrow, coming in after the first early varieties. The haulm grows to a length of fifteen to eighteen inches, and is practically covered with handsome pods five inches in length, containing eight to ten deep-coloured peas of the most exquisite flavour. Per pint 2s., per quart 3s. 6d.

Epicure. Awarded Full Marks by the Royal Horticultural Society. A green wrinkled Marrow, producing an abundance of large, deep green, pointed pods, containing from nine to twelve large peas of the highest quality, which retain their beautiful green colour when cooked, a Pea of very great merit. Height 5 feet. Per pint 1s. 6d., per quart 2s. 6d.

EVIDENCE OF QUALITY.

"From one gallon of **Duke of York Potatoes** I have lifted twelve gallons of fine tubers, which speaks well. I also took First Prize with it in the kidney class at our Annual Show. Also First Prize for your **Giant White Cos Lettuce,** and First for **Matchless Marrow Pea;** they were much admired by all, some having eleven large peas in a pod."—Mr. H. SAYERS, Chessington.

"I am pleased to tell you I took fifteen Prizes at Clydach and seven at Swansea Show with Vegetables grown from your Seeds last year."—**Mr. T. THOMAS,** Swansea.

"I won First Prize with your **Duke of Albany Pea,** Norfolk Giant Beans, Beet Root, Leeks, and Parsnips last year."—**Mr. J. PURTON,** Aberystwith.

Broad Beans.

Cultivation.—These succeed best in a deep, stiff, loamy soil, moderately enriched, and once the seed is sown require little attention, beyond earthing the plants up well by drawing the soil freely against them on either side, when the young plants are a few inches high. Immediately the plants have ceased blooming pinch off the points beyond the blooms, and should the weather prove very dry it will conduce to more quick cropping to damp the blooms over with water from a syringe, or otherwise. Early Mazagan and Long-pod varieties should be sown in November and again in February and March for early crops. Sow also at the same time during the latter months Daniels' Norfolk Giant, the best of all Broad Beans, Windsor, and Seville Long-pod, or other main crop varieties. Draw drill rows about three inches deep, with a wide hoe, and plant the seeds in two rows, at about half-a-foot distance in each row apart, and each two rows at about two feet apart. Sow the dwarfs in rows eighteen inches apart, and the tall varieties thirty inches apart.

		per quart—s.	d.
DANIELS' NORFOLK GIANT LONG-POD. The longest-podded Bean known, growing from twelve to eighteen inches in length, of a handsome uniform shape. First-class for exhibition, obtains first prize wherever exhibited per pint 1s. 3d.		2	0
Beck's Green Gem. Excellent for small gardens ...		1	3
Broad Windsor (Taylor's). Fine selected stock ...		0	8
Emperor Long-pod. A fine selected variety, much superior to the old Long-pod		1	0
Giant Seville Long-pod. A very fine long-podded variety First Class Certificate, R.H.S.		1	6
Green Long-pod. Fine flavour and delicately green		0	10
Green Windsor (or Nonpareil). Abundant bearer		1	0
Harlington Windsor. Larger and finer pods than the old Windsor		1	0
Johnson's Wonderful (Mackie's Monarch). ...		0	8
Mazagan. Small, early, and hardy		0	6
Minster Giant Long-pod. Large and prolific ...		0	10

The following First Prizes, besides many others, have been won by NORFOLK GIANT LONG-POD BEAN during the past few years.

FIRST PRIZE.	Fowey	...	1888
FIRST PRIZE.	Shrewsbury	...	1888
FIRST PRIZE.	Sherborne	...	1888
FIRST PRIZE.	St. Ives	...	1888
FIRST PRIZE.	Tunbridge Wells	...	1888
FIRST PRIZE.	Banbury	...	1889
FIRST PRIZE.	Bloxwich	1889 &	1890
FIRST PRIZE.	Cuckfield	...	1889
FIRST PRIZE.	Clapham	...	1889
FIRST PRIZE.	Market Drayton	...	1889
FIRST PRIZE.	New Barnet	1889 &	1890
FIRST PRIZE.	North Tawton	1889 &	1890
FIRST PRIZE.	Parbold	...	1889
FIRST PRIZE.	Strabane	...	1889
FIRST PRIZE.	Luton	1889 &	1891
FIRST PRIZE.	Tillingbourne	...	1889
FIRST PRIZE.	Wingate	1889 &	1890
FIRST PRIZE.	Worlaby	...	1889
FIRST PRIZE.	Alfreton	...	1890
FIRST PRIZE.	Birchover	...	1890
FIRST PRIZE.	Blagdon	...	1890
FIRST PRIZE.	Bingham	...	1890
FIRST PRIZE.	Burton-on-Trent	...	1890
FIRST PRIZE.	Royal Horticultural Society, Chiswick	...	1890
FIRST PRIZE.	Royal Oxfordshire Horticultural Society	...	1890
FIRST PRIZE.	Castle Bromwich	...	1890
FIRST PRIZE.	Croydon	...	1890
FIRST PRIZE.	Ferndale	...	1890
FIRST PRIZE.	Great Bookham	...	1890
FIRST PRIZE.	Gretton	...	1890
FIRST PRIZE.	Lea and Holloway	...	1890
FIRST PRIZE.	Scarcliffe	...	1890
FIRST PRIZE.	Wigan	...	1890
FIRST PRIZE.	Worksop	...	1890
FIRST PRIZE.	Berkswell	...	1891
FIRST PRIZE.	North Carlton	...	1891
FIRST PRIZE.	Pilsley	...	1891
FIRST PRIZE.	Radstock	...	1891
FIRST PRIZE.	Reynoldston	...	1891
FIRST PRIZE.	Llangollen	...	1892
FIRST PRIZE.	Norwell	...	1892
FIRST PRIZE.	New Barnet	...	1893
FIRST PRIZE.	Rye	...	1893
FIRST PRIZE.	Chertsey	...	1894
FIRST PRIZE.	Ealing	...	1894
FIRST PRIZE.	Glanamman	...	1894
FIRST PRIZE.	Velindre	...	1895

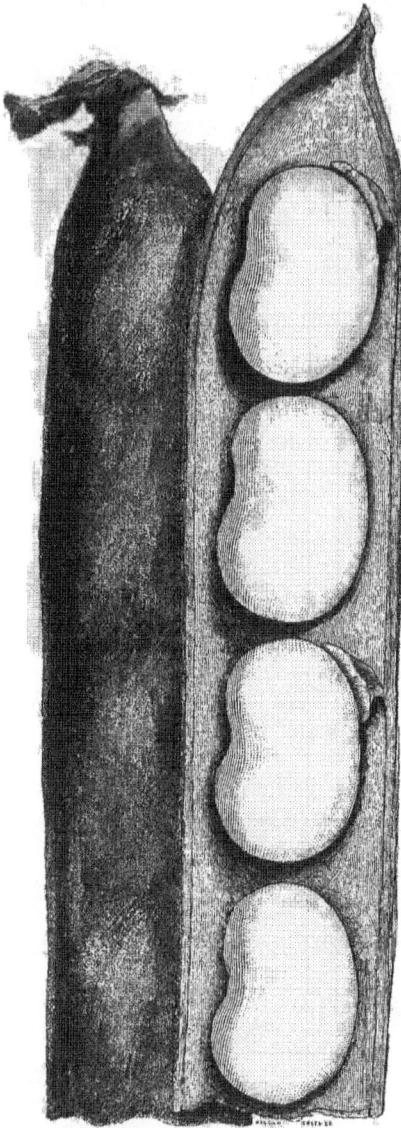

DANIELS' NORFOLK GIANT LONG-POD.

Dwarf French or Kidney Beans.

DANIELS' GIANT WHITE RUNNER.

Cultivation.—Sow from 1st of May to 1st July, in drills two feet apart; thin out the plants to nine inches or one foot apart. They may also be sown earlier under glass, in boxes or pans, and afterwards transplanted when three inches high where intended to stand. A light rich soil and warm situation suit them best, and frequent hoeings and thoroughly clean culture are highly essential.

	per quart—s.	d.
DANIELS' FIRST EARLY. The finest first early Kidney Bean in cultivation; an extraordinary cropper. Pods medium length, unstained, of excellent quality and particularly tender (scarce) ... ... per pint 1s. 3d.	2	0
Buff. Very early; one of the most useful	0	10
Canadian Wonder. Abundant bearer, very fleshy and tender	1	0
EARLY BLACK WONDER. The hardiness and productiveness of the plant, the size and appearance of the pods (rich light green in colour), show that both quality and quantity are together combined in this excellent variety ...	1	6
Early Golden Butter (dwarf). Pods thick and fleshy, nearly transparent, and of a bright yellow colour, which is retained when boiled	2	0
Early Prince Albert. One of the earliest and most prolific	1	6
Fulmer's Early Forcing	1	0
Negro. Long-pod	1	0
NE PLUS ULTRA. It is enormously productive both in doors and out. First Class Certificate R.H.S.	1	6
Newington Wonder (or Nonsuch). Early	1	0
Robin's Egg (or Chinese)	1	0
"The Monster" Negro. First Class Certificate, R.H.S.	1	6
Williams' Early Prolific	1	6
All kinds mixed	1	0
NEW CLIMBING KIDNEY BEAN (*see Novelties*) ... ... per pint 1s. 3d.	2	0

Runner Beans.

Cultivation.—Plant from end of April to middle of June, on well-manured land, in rows four feet apart; mould and stake up when three or four inches high, and frequently pinch as they surmount the stakes.

	per quart—s.	d.
DANIELS' GIANT WHITE. This is without doubt the finest type of Runner Bean extant, bearing in profusion long, green, thick, fleshy pods, upwards of twelve inches in length, and nearly two inches in breadth. This variety, besides the best for culinary purposes, will also be found a grand exhibition kind ... ... per pint 1s. 6d.	2	6
TITAN (new). No other Scarlet Runner approaches this in appearance, size, and productiveness; the pods, which are broad, straight, and handsome, are produced in clusters, and are very fleshy and almost stringless. This variety is very hardy, and most useful to grow, either for table or market, while for exhibition purposes it is unequalled ... per pint 1s. 6d.	2	6
CHAMPION or GIANT. Excellent variety, pods nearly double the size of the old Scarlet Runner; an abundant cropper and highly recommended	1	6
GIRTFORD GIANT. This is an immense variety of the Scarlet Runner; pods exceedingly thick, fleshy, and of extraordinary size	2	0
Mont d'Or or Golden Wax Runner. Very early and productive, tender and fleshy. First Class Certificate, Royal Horticultural Society	2	0
Painted Lady. Scarlet and white blossom, very ornamental	1	3
FILLBASKET. Pods from twelve to fourteen inches in length, of a bright green colour. It was awarded a silver medal at the Hamburg Exhibition, September, 1887 per pint 1s. 6d.	2	6
NE PLUS ULTRA (Neal's). A fine variety for Exhibition and main crop, producing an enormous quantity of extraordinary pods of splendid form, from ten to fourteen inches long, and quite straight. To grow it to perfection each bean should be planted one foot apart in the row ...	1	9
Scarlet. Best for general crop	0	10
White Dutch or Caseknife. Very prolific and of good quality	1	0

Asparagus.

EARLY GIANT PURPLE.

Cultivation.—This, one of the finest vegetables in creation, is a general favourite, and were its medicinal qualities fully known would, considering its easy culture, be more extensively grown, and the wonder is, why all who possess any form of garden, short of an allotment, do not grow it plentifully. Nor does the preparation, and subsequent support required by the bed exceed that of other crops, if, indeed, it is nearly so much, whilst the bulk of the produce, if taken account of, perhaps exceeds that of most kinds, and that of a quality we need not accord words of praise to here. We would most impressively urge our customers to make Asparagus the first and most important consideration in planting a kitchen garden.

Asparagus likes a moderately consistent soil, and one both moisture absorbing and transmitting, or such as does not retain an excess of latent moisture. In view of this a good drained quarter is best for it, and that on a site both open and sunny. To work the bed properly, it should be deeply trenched, adding manure of any green or coarse kind plentifully to the bottom of the trenches, and such as is more decomposed and shorter, near to the upper soil. If the bed becomes somewhat elevated in the operation, so much the better. Where good subsoil exists, and the necessary labour referred to above cannot be afforded, even then, rather than have no Asparagus bed, we advise all to thoroughly manure and dig the site most approved, and make a plantation at once. Even so treated, it will afford much and fairly good useful produce.

Asparagus plants are easily grown from seed. A rich nursery bed should be made for them, and if it can be made upon a firm bottom, and where it can be kept well manure-watered, so much the better. Sow the seeds in thin drill rows at from one to three feet apart, according to the desire that exists to grow very strong young plants. Thin the seedlings out well when they are up, and keep them free from weeds. Seeds may be sown to form plants permanently upon the beds whereon they are to stand and grow. It is best, however, to plant one year old seedlings.

The young plants may be planted during March and the first week in April, either upon beds which have been formed some four feet wide, having alleys of two feet in width between, or in rows from three to five feet apart across the whole piece, but not less than the former. Plant them in trenches or deep drill rows shovelled out, and somewhat thickly in the rows, covering them over with about three inches of soil. Always so manipulate the soil as to be able to spread the roots out straight all around.

In the Autumn, as soon as the stems turn quite yellow, cut them off below and remove them, well hoeing the ground and raking all litter off neatly. In January of the following year give a thorough good dressing of decayed manure, and a sprinkling of salt. With good cultivation till the plants are three years old, they are fit to cut from. Cut all the "blades" both large and small as they form. Cease cutting each year as soon as a fair supply has been obtained, as to do so proves a material guarantee for subsequent fine produce.

							per oz.—s.	d.
Asparagus (True Giant)	...	...	...	...	...	...	per lb. 3s.	0 4
Connover's Colossal. A very large variety			...	...	...	...	" 6s.	0 6
EARLY GIANT PURPLE (Argenteuil). As grown by the celebrated French growers for Paris Market;								
robust variety of the most delicious flavour	...	...	...	...	per lb. 7s.			0 8

Borecole or Kale.

Cultivation, *see Cabbage.*

DANIELS' DWARF EXQUISITE

	per pkt. s. d.	per oz. s. d.
DANIELS' DWARF EXQUISITE. A dwarf compact-growing variety, leaves exquisitely curled and fringed, most valuable for garnishing, it is also well adapted for culinary purposes, presenting a pleasing appearance when cooked ...	0 6	1 6
DANIELS' MOSS CURLED. Of medium height, very hardy, with foliage beautifully curled	0 6	1 6
Cottagers'. Exceedingly hardy	0 3	0 8
Dwarf Green Curled. Very hardy, dwarf-stemmed, flavour very mild, colour dark green when cooked, the best for general crop	—	0 6
Tall Green Curled. The Tall Scotch Kale ...	—	0 6
Variegated or Garnishing. A fine curled-leaved variety, beautifully variegated, very useful and ornamental for garnishing, also valuable for Winter gardening	0 4	1 0

"I may mention that I was again very successful during the past season with Seeds, &c., supplied by your firm, winning 16 Prizes at Axminster District Show, 13 at Shute and District Show, and 4 at the Devon and Exeter Summer Show,—in all 33 Prizes."—Mr. S. E. ENTICOTT, Shute.

Couve Tronchuda, or Portugal Cabbage.
Per packet 4d., per ounce 1s.

Brussels Sprouts.

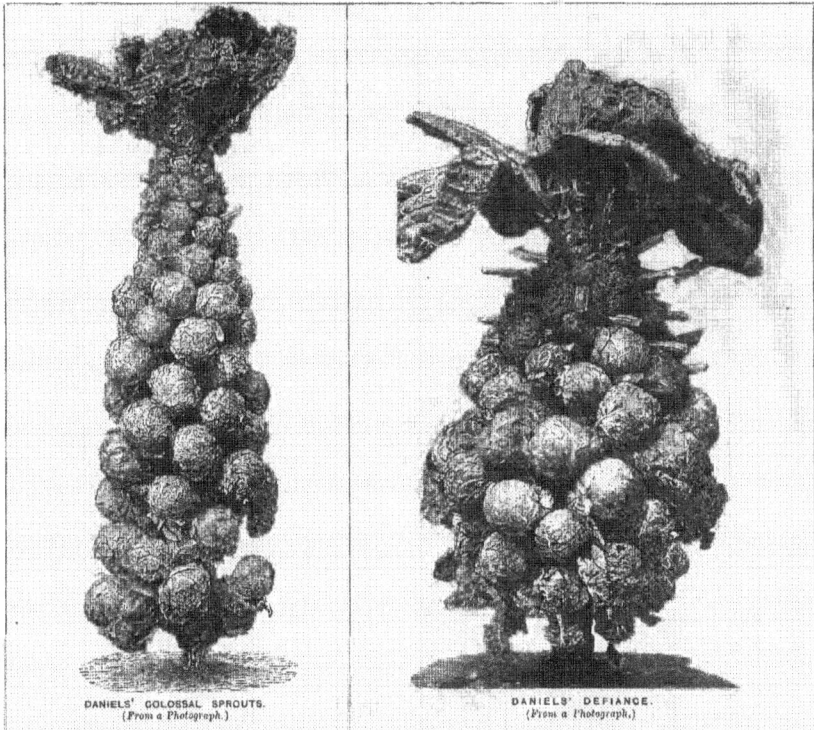

DANIELS' COLOSSAL SPROUTS.
(From a Photograph.)

DANIELS' DEFIANCE.
(From a Photograph.)

Cultivation.—Few comestibles have a finer flavour than that of the better kinds of Brussels Sprouts; and we have much pleasure in stating that we possess the finest stock in cultivation of this delicious vegetable. Daniels' Colossal, a truly magnificent variety, a most abundant cropper, of mild flavour, and the best for general use, should be grown by everyone who has a garden. To ensure really good sprouts it is necessary to grow medium-sized by contrast with the very large ones, which are invariably somewhat strong-flavoured. They delight in a deep, rich, and somewhat light or moderately stony soil. Sow seeds during the early part of March, and by way of succession early in April also. The plants should be planted in drill rows, drawn two feet apart, and about twenty inches from plant to plant in the rows. Earth the plants up well when active growth has commenced. In the Autumn when the lower leaves turn yellow, and commence to ripen off, remove all such as show these symptoms, and hoe and rake neatly between the plants. Do not, as is too frequently done, cut the crowns off the plants until February, as they serve us a necessary protection to the young sprouts, and, indeed, the plants generally. They delight in Summer waterings, manure water in particular.

per oz.—s. d.

DANIELS' COLOSSAL. One of the finest and best in cultivation, of very vigorous growth, bearing sprouts of a large compact globular shape all the way up the stem; these will be found of a more delicate and fine flavour than any of the Cabbage tribe ... ... per pkt. 9d. 2 0

DANIELS' DEFIANCE. An extra select variety, half dwarf, and exceedingly productive, the stem being covered with fine compact sprouts of excellent quality ... ... per pkt. 9d. 2 0

Aigburth. Extra fine ... ... „ 4d. 1 0

Dalkeith. Extra fine, select stock ... ... „ 6d. 1 4

Imported. Good variety for general use 0 6

Scrymger's Giant. A good tall variety; stems well covered with fine sprouts ... ... per pkt. 3d. 0 9

EVIDENCE OF QUALITY.

Beet.

Cultivation.—This is one of our most valuable vegetables, and takes a high place amongst them. The culture is extremely simple. A free open soil suits it best; and to grow it well a shallow bastard trench should be worked sixteen to twenty inches deep, at the very bottom of which a layer of well decayed manure should be laid. Do not manure the layer of soil above, but fork it over just before sowing the seeds. Make an early sowing about the 10th of April, and a main sowing about the 5th of May. Sow in shallow drill rows twenty inches apart, or even less if a short-top kind is chosen, as by this means the ground is better protected from the too scorching rays of the sun. The seedlings should be thinned out to about six or eight inches apart, or even more if large kinds are grown, which is not advisable. Hoe them occasionally during the whole Summer to ensure both the destruction of weeds and that a free soil exists around them. The earlier sown might be drawn for use as soon as they have become large enough. Take the main crop up within a week of October 1st, and during a dry day. Every root must be taken up carefully and with a fork, so as not to break off a single fibre, which is essential to their future merits both as regards colour and flavour when cooked. Never cut the leaves off; but twist them off with the hands. We would direct special attention to Daniels' Crimson Perfection Salad, which will be found a most useful and splendid variety. Also Dracæna-leaved; this latter, a highly desirable variety for the Flower Garden.

	per oz.—s.	d.
DANIELS' CRIMSON PERFECTION SALAD. A new dark-leaved variety with crimson flesh, of excellent quality. An acquisition in the way of ornamental Beet, having deep blood red foliage with metallic hue; fine for flower-garden decoration and for salads ... ... per pkt. 6d.	1	6
Daniels' Black Queen. Fine new dark-leaved variety per pkt. 4d.	1	0
Dark Red Salad	0	6
Dell's Black. A fine dark-foliaged variety ... per pkt. 3d.	0	9
Egyptian Dark Red Turnip-rooted. One of the best for Summer Salads, as it comes into maturity very early ... per pkt. 3d.	0	10
Eclipse. A fine early Turnip-rooted variety ... „ 4d.	1	0
Henderson's Pine Apple. Dark-leaved ... „ 3d.	0	9
Nutting's Dwarf Red. Fine dark foliage ... „ 3d.	0	10
Omega. A useful variety ... ... „ 4d.	1	0
Dracæna-leaved. A highly ornamental variety for the Flower Garden. The leaves are fine, long, and of a deep rich crimson. The root is of fine quality and excellent colour. A most desirable variety, both for ornamental and culinary purposes ... ... per pkt. 4d.	1	0
Ornamental Chilian. Non-edible; a strikingly handsome variety; invaluable for subtropical and ornamental gardening per pkt. 6d.	1	6
Silver Sea Kale or Spinach Beet. The leaves make an excellent substitute for Spinach	0	6

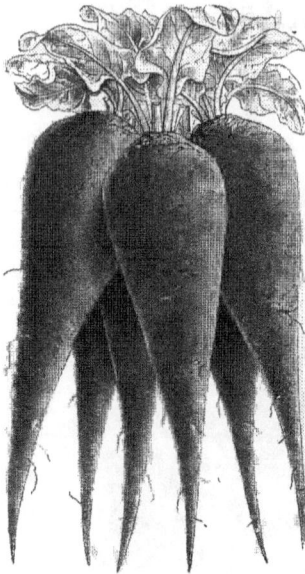

DANIELS' CRIMSON PERFECTION.

"I have had very great success with the Seeds which you sent me last Spring. The Beet, **Daniels' Black Queen**, is much admired by my friends and neighbours."—Mr. F. KEER, Hounslow.

Broccoli.

Cultivation.—As the aim of every cultivator should be to grow as constant a succession of this very valuable vegetable as possible, hence it will be necessary not only to make occasional sowings, but also to choose several distinct varieties so to treat. The first sowing should be made early in March in a gentle heat, and this should consist of Snow's Winter White, and also, if possible, Daniels' New Year. Make other and successional sowings about once a fortnight, commencing about April 10th. In regard to culture these require a peculiar kind of soil, viz., one that is at once consistent and somewhat stiff, yet such as does not hold moisture in any great degree. The site these are to be planted upon cannot be worked too deeply, or manured too heavily, and it should always, where practicable, be trenched a month or two before the time for planting arrives. Take advantage of damp weather upon which to forward all transplanting work. The seedlings should be transplanted thickly on to what is termed nursery beds, at distances of about five inches apart. Thin out the strongest plants to treat thus, permitting the smaller ones to remain in the seed bed until they become large enough for final transplanting. So soon as the early sown plants become large enough for the latter purpose, transplant them into drill rows previously drawn for them at distances of three feet apart, and allowing a similar distance between each plant in the row. The later Winter crops should be planted a foot less apart all ways. No opportunity should be missed to give them good waterings during all subsequent dry periods, and manure water will aid them greatly. Always take care to cut the heads for use immediately the "flower" is seen through or between the apices of the leaves. It is a commendable practice to cut the top or chief head off all "sprouting" kinds so soon as it is seen to have produced the necessary bulk. The late Autumn kinds should always be protected by means of bracken fern, straw, or any similar material at the approach of frost, or if the "heads" are fit for use the plants may be drawn bodily and hung up in any cool shed until required for use. Our own specialities in this class, viz., Daniels' Norfolk Giant, a splendid kind, which has been grown to the enormous weight of 28 lbs., should be sown in March and April for cutting the following Spring; whilst Daniels' King of the Broccoli, the best late variety in cultivation, should be sown in April and May for cutting in May and June the following season.

EVIDENCE OF QUALITY.

"Your **Norfolk Giant Broccoli** are the finest stock I ever grew. The heads large, white, and solid, and stand well through the severest weather. Out of 2000 plants I only lost about 30 during the past winter, when most other varieties were destroyed. They came in very regular, and I did not have one bad one in the whole lot."—Mr. J. CATTON, The Gardens, Saxlingham Hall.

Broccoli (*continued*).

DANIELS' NORFOLK GIANT.

First Division.

Sow in April, May, and June for cutting in September, October, and November the same year.

	per pkt. s. d.	per oz. s. d.
Early Purple Cape	0 4	1 0
Walcheren (true). Sow in succession every three weeks from February till October ...	0 6	1 6
White Cape. A valuable variety ...	0 4	1 0
White Sprouting	0 6	1 6
VEITCH'S SELF-PROTECTING AUTUMN. Extremely valuable to grow as a succession to "Autumn Giant" Cauliflower	0 6	1 0

Second Division.

Sow in April, May, and June, for cutting in January and February the following Spring.

	per pkt. s. d.	per oz. s. d.
DANIELS' NEW YEAR. A vigorous, compact, dwarf-growing variety, with self-protecting foliage over-lapping snow-white heads, which are fit to cut from Christmas to end of January	1 0	2 6
Adams' Early White. A fine white variety ...	0 3	0 9
Osborn's Winter White	0 6	1 6
Penzance Early White ...	0 4	1 0
Snow's Winter White. May be cut from Christmas to end of January	0 6	1 6
St. Hilary. A splendid Broccoli of hardy, vigorous constitution, dwarf, compact growth, and large white heads, coming into use the second week in January	0 6	1 6

Third Division.

Sow end of March and beginning of April for cutting in March and April the following Spring.

	per pkt. s. d.	per oz. s. d.
DANIELS' NORFOLK GIANT. A magnificent variety of robust and compact habit, stem short, the flower-heads exceedingly large and beautifully white, being well protected with luxuriant over-lapping foliage. Have been grown to the enormous weight of twenty-eight pounds each	1 0	2 6

	per pkt. s. d.	per oz. s. d.
Dilcock's Bride. Heads pure white ...	0 4	1 0
Easter Day or Springtide. A fine variety of dwarf, compact habit and vigorous growth, one of the best kinds for the main crop in the Spring	0 6	1 6
Knights' Protecting	0 4	1 0
Leamington. Heads large and solid ...	0 4	1 0
Purple Sprouting. Very hardy Winter variety	0 4	1 0

Fourth Division.

Sow in May and June for cutting in May and June the following season.

	per pkt. s. d.	per oz. s. d.
DANIELS' KING of the BROCCOLI. This splendid variety comes in for cutting from the beginning of May to the first week in June, and as a late kind cannot be surpassed. It is of a fine dwarf habit, and being well protected is exceedingly hardy. Its heads are remarkably fine, close, and white, and of large size	1 0	2 6

	per pkt. s. d.	per oz. s. d.
Daniels' Latest White or Summer. One of the best kinds for filling up the gap or period that occurs between Broccoli and Cauliflower	0 6	1 6
Chappell's Large Cream	0 3	0 9
Queen. Very fine	0 6	1 6
Methven's June (*see Novelties*) ...	1 0	2 6

EVIDENCE OF QUALITY.

"The Walcheren Broccoli was an excellent crop, also the King of the Cauliflowers, never have had better quality."—Mr. J. H. CLEMENTS, Overstrand.

"I am glad to say that I have had plenty of good Cauliflowers, and have a splendid supply at present. The Autumn Giant are very good, and also the Autumn Broccoli are coming in very fine heads, which I think are very handy to grow, with a little protection they will stand till Christmas."—Mr. S. JEFFRIES, Ditchingham Hall.

"I have great pleasure in stating that I am now cutting Veitch's Self-protecting Broccoli from Seed supplied by you, and they are giving great satisfaction."—Mr. C. W. FIELD, Ely.

"The Kitchen Garden Seeds supplied by you this Spring, all have proved very good, Cauliflowers excellent, viz.—Veitch's Autumn Giant, Walcheren, and Early London. Veitch's Self-protecting Broccoli is promising to be very good and true, just forming."—Mr. J. CLARKE, The Gardens, Shadwell Court.

Cabbage.

DANIELS' DEFIANCE GIANT EARLY MARROW.

Cultivation.—Although Cabbages would appear to occupy quite a second-rate position among the list of comestibles of the vegetable garden, Spring Cabbages are nevertheless universally appreciated for their tenderness and unquestionably delicious flavour. In the culture of them, a constant succession of quickly grown and hence tender heads should always be aimed at in preference to an undue quantity. Cabbages, as do all the tribe, delight in a deeply-worked, well enriched soil; one however that has been brought into good order by constant manuring and manipulation in the past, rather than such as has been recently so treated. They will succeed best in well-worked and fertilized open or stony soil. It is only necessary in these regards to study one particular in regard to such, viz., if any soil is very light, it should have been well enriched, and be allowed a month or two to settle down subsequently before the crop is planted out upon it. By such means we have carried the finest possible crops upon very light stony soils, by transplanting the Autumn sown plants intended for the Spring crop upon the previously used Onion bed. This be it understood without digging it over following the Onion crop; but in fact only hoeing it over deeply, drawing the drill rows, and planting the young plants thereon. All heavy, stiff, retentive, and damp soils, it were needless to remark, must be well worked up for the crops, or they will not succeed thereon. The first sowing in the year should be made about the middle of March. These, if transplanted on in patches as they become large enough, will afford the late Autumn and Winter supply. For the main or Spring crop sow about August 11th. These must be transplanted on to an open sunny aspect, so soon as large enough for the purpose. Sow the seeds upon prepared and finely raked soil, and where practicable transplant into nursery beds, there to grow the plants on to become large enough for final planting out. Good Cabbages should be thirty inches apart in the rows. A sowing of Rosette Colewort, made about the middle of July and during showery weather, will often form very excellent and useful stuff for the early Autumn months, and prove useful away into the Winter.

DANIELS' DEFIANCE GIANT EARLY MARROW.

A magnificent variety, growing to the weight of from ten to twenty pounds. Remarkably early, short-legged, and compact, and of the most delicious marrow flavour. Invaluable for the market gardener or the private grower. Our own unequalled stock, grown on our Seed Farms under personal supervision. The true and original stock of this fine Cabbage can only be supplied by us.

Per pkt. 6d.; per oz. 1s. 6d.

EVIDENCE OF QUALITY.

"I grew your **Defiance Cabbage** last year, some of them weighed twenty pounds; the best in the village."—**Mr. F. H. MALKIN,** Halmerand.

"It will perhaps interest you to hear I took First Prize at our Show yesterday with your **Defiance Cabbage.**"—**Mr. H. PICKTHORN,** Ashby-de-la-Zouch.

"I grew last year a Cabbage, **Daniels' Defiance,** that weighed 19½ lbs. without stalk or leaves; and another close upon 18 lbs., grown with very ordinary cultivation."—**J. H. TURNER, Esq.,** St. Austell.

"I was much pleased with the Cabbages grown from your Seed, **Daniels' Defiance,** one of them weighed over seventeen pounds."—**Mr. F. PAGE,** Andover.

"I grew some splendid Cabbages last year from your **Defiance Cabbage** Seed, weighing seventeen pounds.". **Mr. A. G. SELF,** Clay Cross.

"I am very pleased with the **Defiance Cabbage** grown from your Seed last year, I cut some sixteen pounds without stalk or outside leaves."—**Mr. F. LEVERIDGE,** Tonbridge.

	per oz.—s.	d.
DANIELS' LITTLE QUEEN. A finely selected stock, dwarf, compact, and early. First-class variety, highly recommended ... per pkt. 6d.	1	6
Ellam's Early Dwarf. A first-class Early Cabbage in all respects. Being very compact, they can be planted close together, thus growing double the quantity of plants on the same space than most kinds. A fine early market kind ... per pkt. 4d.	1	0
Daniels' Improved Enfield Market per pkt. 4d.	1	0
Early Dwarf York. Dwarf and compact	0	6
Early Large York. Very useful variety ...	0	6

	per oz.—s.	d.
Enfield Market. Excellent main crop variety ...	0	6
Ewing's No. 1. A very fine, early, Dwarf Cabbage per pkt. 3d.	0	9
Early Rainham. Excellent	0	6
Heartwell Early Marrow. A dwarf compact variety of excellent quality ... per pkt. 4d.	1	0
Nonpareil Improved Dwarf. Early variety per pkt. 3d.	0	10
Nonpareil. Large	0	6
Rosette Colewort	0	8
St. John's Day. A fine, dwarf, very early variety ...	0	6
Wheeler's Imperial. Extra select stock per pkt. 3d.	0	9

Savoy Cabbage.

DANIELS' VICTORIA SAVOY.

Cultivation.—This, like all of its class, delights in deep, rich, moderately consistent soil, and it must be the chief object of the grower to grow good plants that may become well-established, large, and leafy by the Autumn. Sow early in March, and again about April 10th, and thinly, into a well-enriched and finely-worked soil. We are very partial to the Dwarf Ulm, Tom Thumb, or Daniels' Extra Early, as they produce such neat firm heads, and may be planted more thickly than is ordinarily requisite. Transplant the larger kinds out permanently in drill rows two feet apart, and from eighteen to twenty inches apart in the rows. The dwarfer kinds may be planted eighteen inches apart in the rows, and fifteen inches asunder in the run. To prevent clubbing, deep and good culture, and frequent changing of crops is beneficial, often besides it proves a powerful preventive to dip the roots of all young plants into a lye formed of cow-dung, wood ashes, &c., just before planting them out into the permanent Winter quarters. If a sprinkling of lime or soot be thrown amongst the seedling plants upon the seed beds when very young, this often deters the pest from attacking them, as it sometimes does at this early date. For late use, and northern and cold climates, "Norwegian" cannot be surpassed.

	per oz.—s.	d.
DANIELS' NONPAREIL. Splendid variety for early use, quite distinct; the most delicately flavoured Savoy grown ... ... per pkt. 4d.	1	0
Drumhead (Selected Stock). The largest variety	0	6
Dwarf Green Curled. Very compact ...	0	8
Dwarf Ulm. Early, very dwarf ... per pkt. 3d.	0	8
Golden Autumn. A distinct and beautiful variety per pkt. 3d.	0	9
Green Globe. A good hardy variety	0	6

	per oz.—s.	d.
VICTORIA. Extra large and fine quality per pkt. 4d.	1	0
Norwegian. Excellent variety for late use, extremely hardy, and well suited for northern and cold climates per pkt. 4d.	1	0
Tom Thumb. The most compact variety in cultivation per pkt. 3d.	0	8
DANIELS' EXTRA EARLY. Fortnight earlier than Dwarf Ulm, very dwarf and compact per pkt. 4d.	1	0

DANIELS' GIANT RED DRUMHEAD.

Red or Pickling Cabbage.

	per oz.—s.	d.
DANIELS' GIANT RED DRUMHEAD. Very fine, grows to a large size, the finest Red Cabbage known ... ... per pkt. 4d.	1	0
Erfurt Blood Red. Dwarf, compact, small heads ,, 3d.	0	9
Manchester Large Red. Fine, large, firm heads ...	0	8
New Early Red Nonpareil. It has a pointed head; its main feature, however, is its dark red colour throughout, besides being the earliest of all the Red Cabbages per pkt. 4d.	1	0
Red Dutch. Useful variety, well-known	0	6

EVIDENCE OF QUALITY.

"I took First Prize for your **Giant Red Drumhead Cabbage** at Campsey Ash Show, and First for Continuity Lettuce, and several other Prizes from your Seed."—Mr. J. THURSTON, Blaxhall.

"I feel it my duty to bear testimony to the value of your unsurpassed Seeds. Last December I cut a splendid Savoy Cabbage which I grew from your **Victoria Savoy** which turned the scale at twenty-eight pounds. Last Monday I cut a Cabbage grown from your **Defiance** Seed of excellent quality and shape which, when the rough leaves and stem were taken off, it turned the scale at thirty-two pounds."—Mr. F. JOHNSON, Great Bowden.

"I am pleased to inform you that the collection of Seeds you sent me last year produced excellent crops. I had **Savoy** Cabbages from eight to ten pounds."—Mr. S. CANN, Alderney.

"The **Giant Red Drumhead Cabbage** are the best I have ever seen. I have won First Prize with it at Welshpool on August 9th, and First Prize at Newtown on August 23rd."—Mr. T. H. PUGH, Newtown.

Cauliflower.

DANIELS' KING OF THE CAULIFLOWERS.   Per packet 1s. 6d. and 2s. 6d.

Cultivation.—In the Cauliflower we possess at once the tenderest and sweetest delicacy that we can boast of amongst vegetables and one universally appreciated. To grow it well it requires the richest of soils, with no stint of root moisture throughout its whole growth. Hence to insure this, deeply worked, heavily manured ground is of the first importance. To keep up a successional supply during as much of each year as possible, considerable care and attention is requisite. Advantage must be taken of many kinds of frames, handlights, &c., to grow young seedling plants under throughout the Winter months. A sowing should be made in a moderate warmth about February 12th, and as soon as the plants are large enough they should be pricked off in boxes, trays, &c., and placed in a cool frame. When the plants are somewhat stronger transplant into frames or under handlights, give air during mild weather, and about the middle of May remove the covering entirely. Sowings in the open air, to produce a crop to succeed the above, should be made about the 10th of April, May, June, and July successively. Transplant on good soil and water constantly, draw the soil up to and around them freely. As it is necessary not only to maintain moisture over the roots, but also to ward off the somewhat too direct rays of the sun during hot dry weather, when practicable, mulch with some rich moisture-retaining materials. The Autumn crop, which consists of Walcheren and Veitch's Autumn Giant, must be looked through daily, to see if any need gathering, and all that are ready should be pulled up and laid in, in a cool situation till wanted. For Spring work the Early Snowball and Daniels' Dwarf Mammoth are good, and to sow in Spring for Summer culture Daniels' King of the Cauliflowers is the best. Spring sowings are particularly liable to the depredations of White Fly, which cluster on them or destroy their centres, and so cause what is termed "blindness." To prevent this, sprinkle the leaves over when damp with soot, or the hearts with tobacco powder. Finally take care to use the heads when young, white, and solid; and to insure the production of such, the fewer sudden changes the plants are subject to the better. Irregularities in culture cause them to button or "bolt," as they sometimes do at the earliest stage of growth.

	per oz. s. d.
DANIELS' KING OF CAULI-FLOWERS. New and distinct variety; heads large, firm, and first-class to sow for early Spring and Summer work; good exhibition variety per pkt. 1s. 6d. and 2s. 6d.	—
DANIELS' SNOWBALL. Invaluable, *ready to cut in four months from the time of sowing* per pkt. 2s.	—
DANIELS' DWARF MAMMOTH. A very superior early dwarf variety, the best for early forcing; heads white and compact per pkt. 1s.	2 6
Eclipse. This is an excellent large Autumn Cauliflower, and very useful for Market purposes. By successional sowings it can be had from August to Christmas per pkt. 9d.	2 0

	per oz. s. d.
Early London White per pkt. 6d.	1 6
Self-protecting Autumn Giant. A fine variety, coming into use directly after Veitch's Autumn Giant, the large white flowers being well protected from the Autumn frosts by overlapping leaves; may be had in good condition up to Christmas per pkt. 6d.	1 9
Veitch's Autumn Giant. An extremely valuable late variety, perfectly distinct from any other sort, heads magnificent, beautifully white, large, firm, and compact per pkt. 6d.	1 6
Walcheren (the true kind). Sow under glass in February, to succeed the Spring Broccoli, and in beds from May to July for succession per pkt. 6d.	1 6

EVIDENCE OF QUALITY.

"I think I may say I am able to give a very favourable account of the Cauliflower crop; this season suited them. I had a very good plant, and they all came up well, and the flower was very good and free from leaf; in fact, the heads were perfect, and they came well together."—Mr. E. S. TAYLOR, Soham.

"The **Veitch's Autumn Giant Cauliflower** I had from you in the Spring has turned out a splendid crop, the best for miles around. You must use very great care in selecting your stocks."—Mr. J. W. CHURCH, Bracomish.

Carrot.

Cultivation.—Few subjects delight more in a free, open, sandy loam, of good depth. In preparing the ground for them it will be well to bastard trench it over, if possible, a few months before the seeds are sown. Place good decomposed manure ten inches deep for all long and intermediate kinds, and four inches deep for Short Horns of whatever variety. Whilst the soil cannot well be too open, free, and rich, wherein the roots form and swell, it will be important to make it so by working it up, and manuring it the season previously, as if it be too rich, caused by the presence of actual manure, it will have a tendency to cause the produce to become forked, and as regards symmetry and real usefulness, of inferior merit. Sow always in drill rows and but moderately deep. To promote a vigorous youthful growth, and enable the young plants to grow freely, the drills may be drawn deep enough to enable a small quantity of well-rotted manure to be placed at their bottom and covered over with a little fine soil, into which the seeds are to be sown. They must be kept scrupulously clean by frequent hoeings. Sow Horn Carrot early in August and about the 4th of September for Winter and early Spring use, in rows about eight inches apart, drawing for thinning, so soon as large enough. Make the early Spring sowings of Short Horn upon a sunny aspect in March, and the main sowings about April 10th.

Daniels' Telegraph Carrot is the best to grow for general crop for market or exhibition, and is becoming a general favourite with market gardeners. It has gained First Prizes many seasons wherever exhibited. Daniels' Scarlet Perfection or Main Crop is a most useful kind for general use, as it attains a large size in a short space of time.

per oz.—s. d.

NEW MAIN CROP CARROT, DANIELS' SCARLET PERFECTION. This is well adapted to shallow soils, being intermediate and stump-rooted *(see accompanying illustration)*; is easily raised. Its symmetrical shape and its colour of bright orange-scarlet, make it a most desirable variety for the exhibition table, and also for market purposes .. ... per pkt. 4d. 1 0

DANIELS' TELEGRAPH. The best form of intermediate we know of. Carefully grown from selected roots; it is early, of good colour and shape *(see accompanying illustration).* A fine exhibition variety, and invaluable for market use per pkt. 4d. 1 0

LONG RED ST. VALERY. A very choice stock, and a great improvement on the Long Surrey. Fine for exhibition 0 8

DANIELS' LONG RED WITHOUT HEART. Flesh bright red, without the core usually found in the Carrot 0 9

Daniels' New Early Forcing Horn. One of the earliest Carrots yet introduced. In shape it is nearly round. They can be left thickly in the row, and drawn for use as required 0 0

Altringham Improved per lb. 4s. 6d. 0 4
Early French Nantes. Dwarf, stump-rooted ... 0 8
Early Scarlet Horn. For first early crop ... 0 6
Giant White. Much larger and of finer quality than Belgian White. Highly recommended ...) 0 6

JAMES' SCARLET (Intermediate) Fine selected stock ... per lb. 6s. 0 6
Long Red Surrey or Long Orange 0 6
Studley. A fine intermediate variety 0 6

EVIDENCE OF QUALITY.

"As for your **Scarlet Perfection Carrot** I never saw a better one. I took First Prize at our August Show; that splendid Carrot was the admiration of all who saw it; the best I ever saw."—**Mr. FINCH**, Newmarket.

"I am perfectly satisfied with the **Scarlet Perfection Carrot** Seed that I had of you. I have had an extraordinary crop of them, and some measuring eighteen inches round, free from fangs, and of excellent quality."—**Mr. W. BARBER**, Ditchingham.

"I am glad to inform you that the **Daniels' Telegraph Carrots** took First Prize at the Velindre Show; very fine carrots, everybody said they had never seen their equal."—**Mr. W. JONES**, Wern Nowydd.

"I took First Prize for your **Scarlet Perfection Carrot** at our Show on August Bank Holiday. They were admired by all that saw them."—**Mr. J F. COTTIS**, Halstead.

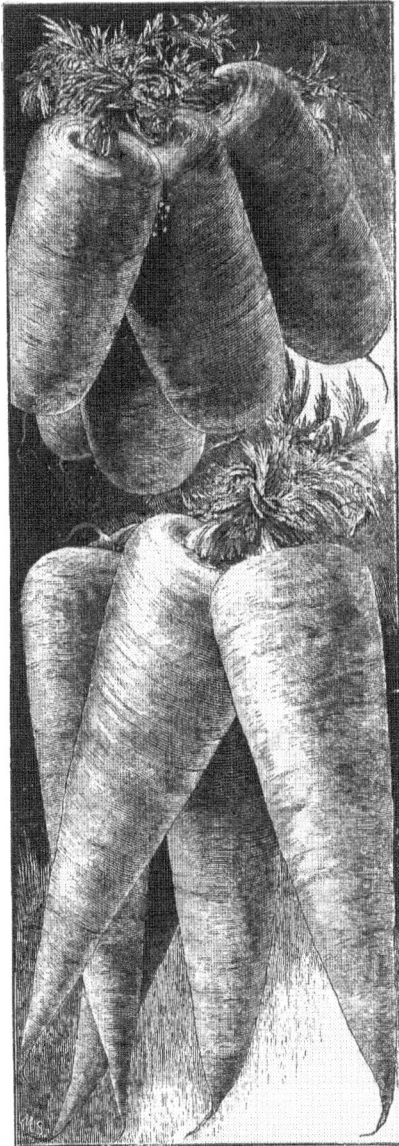

DANIELS' SCARLET PERFECTION.
DANIELS' TELEGRAPH CARROTS.

Capsicum or Chili.

Cultivation.—Seeds should be sown between the beginning of March and April 20th : but the sooner the better within the above dates. Their culture is very simple, as seeds may be sown in pots or pans, and placed in moderate heat. Sow more nearly in the latter date under some kind of frame protection, or in the open border, where the above convenience does not exist. Seedlings must be transferred to single small pots, or two plants in each, as soon as they are fit to handle, and he thus grown on until the first week in June. At this date plant them out at the foot of a full South aspect wall, keeping them well watered. It is safest during all the changes of seasons to grow the crops in pots under glass, where convenience exists so to do. Even half-a-dozen pots so grown often prove very serviceable, besides coming in earlier than the general crops out of doors. The smaller kinds or Chili variety is more dwarf in its habits than the other varieties, though it is always more profitable to grow the larger ones.

	per pkt.—s.	d.
CELESTIAL. Very ornamental and useful 6d. and	1	0
Chili or Bird Pepper. Small	0	4
ELEPHANT'S TRUNK. A new and distinct variety, with very fleshy scarlet fruits of an extraordinary length, viz, ten to twelve inches long, and three to four inches broad, resembling in shape an elephant's trunk. The flavour is very mild. This will also make an excellent decorative plant for the conservatory	1	0
Long Red. Large, the best for general use	0	4
Long Yellow. A very useful variety	0	4

	per pkt.—s.	d.
Procopp's Giant. Superior variety 6d. and	1	0
MONSTREUSE. Pods of enormous size	0	6
RUBY KING. Valuable as a decorative plant for the conservatory, besides being exceedingly useful for stews, pickles, &c. 6d. and	1	0
SWEET GOLDEN DAWN. Very useful as a decorative plant, also for stews and pickles, having the flavour of the Capsicum, without the hot piquancy of the Chili or Cayenne Pepper	1	0
Mixed. All kinds	0	6

Cress.

Cultivation.—The several varieties of Cress, consisting of the Australian, American, and commoner, not to omit that known as Watercress, all delight in a damp or moist situation ; and as such is known and acted upon in practice, so is their simple growth enhanced, and the size of their leaves, &c., and more delicate piquancy increased. It is only necessary to sow the common kinds about five or seven days before they are required for use, and to keep them moderately moist, to insure a crop. The Australian, on the contrary, should be sown from early in the month of April to July, and for the Winter crop about August 20th and September 4th. The American variety sown at similar dates also comes in most usefully, and is a moderate substitute for our own popular Watercress. This latter may be produced from seeds sown upon a shady north aspect border. It is better to make a shallow basin-like bed for the seeds, and after these are sown to keep the same as constantly and copiously watered, artificially during dry weather, as possible.

	per oz.—s.	d.
DANIELS' GARNISHING or PARSLEY-LEAVED. Useful alike for salads and garnishing	0	6
American or Land. Eaten as Water-cress in Winter	0	4
Australian or Golden. This valuable Cress is a most desirable addition to all salads	0	4
Curled. For salads in the second leaf per quart 1s. 9d., per pint 1s.	0	2

	per oz.—s.	d.
Plain. For early salads, best for garden use per quart 1s. 9d., per pint 1s.	0	2
Sorrel-leaved. The largest-leaved of all, dark green colour, and good flavour. A most useful salad	0	6
Water. Sow in a moist, shady place per pkt. 6d. and 1s.		

Gourd or Pumpkin.

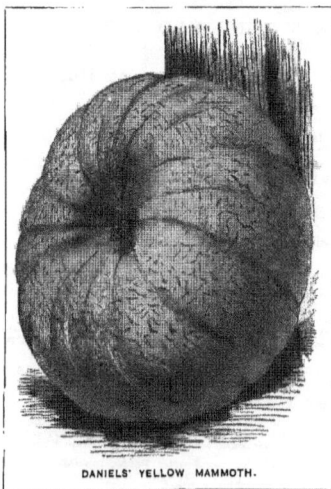

DANIELS' YELLOW MAMMOTH.

Cultivation.—Though these often succeed sown upon very rich soils in the open ground, and especially if a handlight or *cloche* be placed over ; yet it is a far better way to sow seeds about April 25th, and so soon as the seedlings assume the third or rough leaf, pot them off into about four-inch pots : one plant only of the large kinds should be placed in each pot. The best place to plant them is in a good thickness of soil placed upon a mound of manure. If a slight warmth exist in the latter so much the better. Plant them out about May 26th or soon after, and place some kind of protection over or around them. Do not plant them less than six or eight feet apart. The smaller-fruited kinds are best trained to upright rods or trellis-work, and are very ornamental. An abundance of liquid manure should be given to them constantly, and especially to the young plants when they commence growing freely. The fruit of the large sorts when ripe is useful for mixing with apples for pies, tarts, &c., and they keep well throughout the Winter months when stored in dry places, &c.

	per pkt.—s.	d.
DANIELS' YELLOW MAMMOTH. Seed from large, handsomely netted fruit, weighing one hundredweight and upwards 6d. and	1	0
Bottle-shaped. Green, very ornamental	0	4
Common Pumpkin. Very useful for pies and preserves in Winter	0	3
Pear-shaped. Green and yellow, pretty	0	4
Potiron Jaune or Mammoth. A giant variety, frequently attains one hundredweight 6d. and	1	0
Small Orange. Strongly resembling an orange	0	4
Variegated Turk's Cap. An exceedingly handsome variety, striped orange, green, and white 6d. and	1	0

Celery.

Cultivation.—Few vegetables exhibit more prominently the features which result from good culture than does Celery. If it receives any check during its entire growth, the invariable result is that the produce becomes either stringy, or bolts, and indeed, not infrequently both; and the latter sometimes happens at a very early date in the Autumn. Too early sowing also causes the latter to happen sometimes, following very arid Summers; hence it is not advisable to sow but sufficient for a few first rows when the earlier sowing has to be made. As regards the date of sowing, the grower must determine this according to the date when the earlier supply is in demand. In some establishments it is required by the beginning of September, or before; though generally consumers like it to remain until cold nights and a little frost have given to it less of that strong natural taste which it invariably has, at such times as the leaves are young, active, and in full growth. For the first crop sow in February, in pans, boxes, or upon a slight hotbed, if time and the opportunity exist to do the latter. So soon as the young plants, the produce of this sowing, become large enough for handling, prick them out thickly on to nursery beds formed upon a slight hotbed. Make another successional sowing in March, and in a like manner, and as soon as the plants, the produce of such, are large enough, prick them out in turn, either upon a warm aspect, under handlights, or any kind of protection that may exist. Make yet another sowing, out of doors, on a warm sheltered site, and in a very rich mellow soil, about the last week in April. The produce of this sowing will form excellent late sticks, and may come in useful besides for soups, &c. When the plants assume fair proportions, trenches must be prepared to finally plant them into. The trenches should be from nine to twelve inches deep, and from fourteen to eighteen inches wide, according to the earliness of planting, &c. Throw out the soil to this required size and depth, packing it up neatly on either side. Then procure, and dig in four or five inches of thoroughly decomposed rich manure; turn this over, and knock it about, so as to mix it freely together, and proceed to plant the plants therein directly. The principal attention they will require for the next month or two will consist of watering, &c., and both clear water and rich liquid manure should be given to them as frequently as it may be possible to do so. The earthing-up process should commence early in July, or previously, when a very early supply is in demand. When it is in contemplation to proceed with this process, first go over all the plants, remove all the small leaves from around their base, and any young side or sucker shoots which are seen to form; then upon a fine dry day, chop down some of the soil from the sides of the trenches, breaking it up fine, and with the hands, aided by a trowel, place the soil in around the base of each plant neatly with the right hand, whilst each plant or stick is held firmly in position with the other. It is better to mould up at three successional times. Take care not to press the soil too firmly around the hearts, and avoid letting crumbs of soil fall into the hearts of the plants beside, as if carelessness be permitted in either case, there will be great danger that the "sticks" will grow crooked, or become "seated" as it is commonly called. All successional crops must be earthed up in rotation, and at studied intervals apart, but each should, at the advent of Winter, have sufficient soil placed around to protect all from severe frosts. Daniels' Golden Heart, Daniels' Giant White, and Daniels' Giant Red are the best, being extra selected stocks of superior merit.

			per pkt.—s.	d.
DANIELS' GIANT RED. The largest grown, splendid colour, very solid, and of fine flavour			1	0
DANIELS' GIANT WHITE. The largest white in cultivation, very solid, crisp, and of excellent flavour			1	0
DANIELS' GOLDEN HEART. An excellent, sturdy, dwarf variety, very quick-growing, solid, and of fine nutty flavour, and when blanched the heart is of a pure yellow			1	0
Hatch's Conqueror. An exceedingly fine variety; grows to a good size, heads very solid and crisp, and of a fine nutty flavour. It has been exhibited with great success during the past three years, and will be found the best Red Celery for market purposes.			1	0
Manchester Fine Red		3d. and	0	6
Sandringham Dwarf White		3d. and	0	6
Seymour's Superb White		3d. and	0	6
Silver Plume. A fine white-leaved variety. It blanches well by simply tying up the plants with matting		6d. and	1	0
Sulham Prize Pink		3d. and	0	6
Williams' Matchless Red		3d. and	0	6
Standard Bearer, extra fine Red		6d. and	1	0
Wright's Grove Red		6d. and	1	0
Wright's Grove White		6d. and	1	0
Mixed Red and White. Useful for Cottagers ...		3d. and	0	6
Soup Celery		per lb. 2s.	—	

EVIDENCE OF QUALITY.

"Your **Giant Red and White Celery** turned out the very best I have ever grown. I could not wish for cleaner or finer roots. In addition to this, all your Seeds (Flower and Vegetable) have turned out admirably."—Mr. W. WITHAM, Gardener to J. W. Rose, Esq.

"I have had my seeds from you for twenty years, and have always found them of the same good quality. I have been a regular exhibitor at Pennyford and Mold Shows, and have taken a large number of Prizes. At Mold Show last August, I took twelve Prizes, including seven First, four Second, and one Third. I have taken five First Prizes the last two seasons with your Matchless Marrow Peas, and find it grand for show or table use. I won First Prize with two Lettuces, **Daniels' Giant White Cos.** The two weighed 9½ lbs.—Mr. JOHN BECK, Buckley.

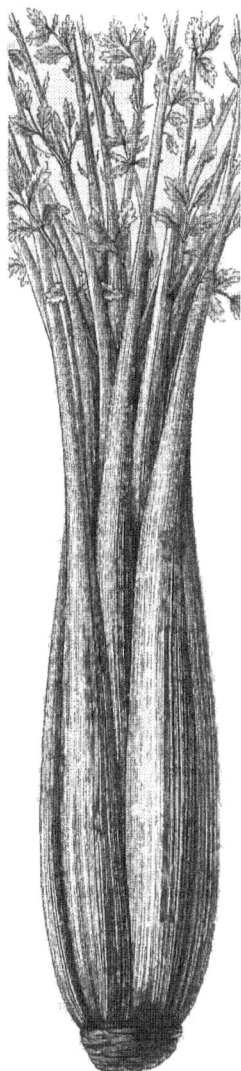

DANIELS' GIANT WHITE.

"I like your **Giant White Celery** very much, in fact I consider it second to none both for exhibition and general purposes."— Mr. F. ATKINSON, Gardener to E. S. Trafford, Esq.

Cucumber.

Cultivation in Glass Houses.—The essential points in the successful cultivation of Cucumbers under glass may be summed up in their having a light and rich soil, and plenty of light and heat with abundant moisture and good drainage. Those who grow Cucumbers for market and profit, use well heated span-roofed houses, with large panes of glass, and long experience has shown these to be the most useful. Excellent results, however, may be had with differently constructed and smaller houses, provided the conditions are favourable, and a fair amount of attention is given. Make a first sowing of seeds towards the end of January, and, for succession, sow again in February, March, and April. Sow the seeds singly in small pots, and plunge in a good heat, keeping as close to the light as convenient, and when the plants have made the first pair of rough leaves shift into larger pots, and in about four or five weeks from the seed being sown they will be ready for planting on the mounds. In preparing the house for Cucumbers, it should first be thoroughly cleaned, and fitted with a wire trellis placed about one foot from the glass. Cucumbers delight in a light rich soil, and one of the best composts consists of light turfy loam, not broken too small, with about one half the quantity of well-decayed manure. Let the soil be placed in heaps and well warmed before the plants are inserted; about a yard apart is far enough, and a stick should be placed to each at starting. As the plants advance in growth, a temperature of seventy to seventy-five degrees, or more on bright days, with a night temperature of at least sixty degrees, should be maintained, and they should be syringed morning and evening with tepid water, the walls and footways being kept moist, but air should only be given on warm days. As the roots force themselves through the mounds, fresh soil should be added, and care should be taken, after stopping the main shoot, to train the laterals a good distance apart, and to thin out from time to time, so as to get the full benefit of light. When the plants have set the first lot of fruit, liquid manure may be given twice or three times a week, and this may be continued whilst the plants are in bearing. Excellent crops may also be obtained in limited space by growing in large pots and training up, giving the plants a good top-dressing and liquid or artificial manure.

Cultivation in Pits and Frames.—Where stable manure, leaves, and litter are plentiful, a good supply of Cucumbers may be had during the summer months without fire heat. Mix the fermenting materials well together, and turn over occasionally a week or two before using, wetting it to cause fermentation if too dry. For a pit, a bed of three feet, or a little more, in thickness will be sufficient, whilst for a frame, the bed should be quite a foot thicker, and should extend a foot beyond the frame all round. Tread down firmly and evenly, and place a small mound of soil under each light, nine inches or so from the glass and leave the sashes partly open for a few days, to let off any rank heat or steam. When the heat has subsided to eighty or ninety degrees, the plants may be inserted, and as growth advances, they should have air on warm days, and the shoots should be stopped and thinned to induce fruitfulness. Should there be an insufficiency of heat in the frame, it will be necessary to remove the outer portion of the bed, and replace with fresh fermenting material.

Cultivation in the Open Air.—The seeds for this purpose should be sown about the first week in April. Plant out about the middle of May in a warm sunny position; a few days before planting, dig holes or trenches about eighteen inches deep and three feet wide, and fill them with fermenting material to about a foot above the level; tread down firmly, and cover with about nine inches of light rich soil. When the plants are inserted, they should be watered with tepid water, and covered with handlights, gradually admitting air as the plants become established, and removing the handlights altogether, if the weather is favourable, towards the end of June.

DANIELS' DEFIANCE.

CUCUMBER—DANIELS' DEFIANCE (early prolific).

A white-spined variety of hardy, robust constitution, producing in great abundance very short-necked and elegant fruit of a rich dark green colour, from 18 to 24 inches in length, straight and uniform, and of the same thickness throughout; a magnificent variety for early Spring and Summer work, and first-class for market purposes and general use; is also a grand exhibition kind.

W.S., sealed packets, 1s. 6d. and 2s. 6d.

EVIDENCE OF QUALITY.

"The Seeds I had from you last year gave great satisfaction. The **Defiance Cucumber** was a complete success."—Mr. J. LAWRENCE, Pitlake.

"The **Duke of Edinburgh Cucumber** Seed I had from you last year did remarkably well, and fruit thirty inches long was very common. A friend of mine to whom I gave two plants took First Prize at our Local Show with very fine fruit."—Mr. G. WATWOOD, Cannock.

"The **Duke of Edinburgh Cucumber** last year was excellent. I grew them in a pig's house, and produced them over two feet in length, and they were unrivalled at our Local Hermitage Show."—Miss BRAND, Hampstead Norris.

"Please send me a 1s. 6d. Packet of **Daniels' Improved Telegraph Cucumber** Seed, as my servant highly approved of it."—R. V. GOREHAM, Esq., Yoxford.

Cucumber (*continued*).

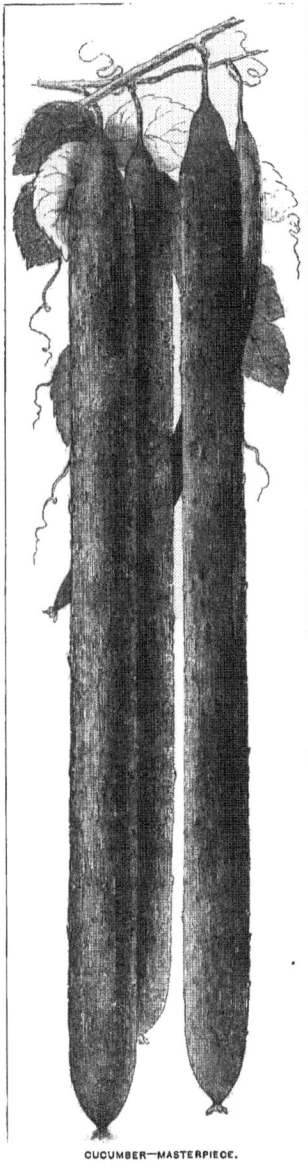

CUCUMBER—MASTERPIECE.

per pkt.—s. d.

DANIELS' MASTERPIECE. The fruit are slightly spined, and of a rich dark emerald green, twenty to thirty inches long. For colour, quality, constitution, and prolificness, it cannot be surpassed, while at the same time it is A 1 for exhibition, and will be found invaluable for market purposes ... ... W.S. 1s. 6d. and | 2 6

DANIELS' DUKE OF ALBANY. Since its introduction a few years ago, this remarkable Cucumber has obtained First Prize wherever exhibited. It is a long, straight, dark green fruit, averaging from twenty to twenty-six inches in length, bearing sometimes as many as three or four at a joint. Few can equal this Cucumber for exhibition purposes ... ... W.S. 1s. 6d. and | 2 6

DANIELS' DUKE OF EDINBURGH. A beautiful white-spined variety sent out by us, and pronounced by all competent judges to be the finest Cucumber in cultivation. It is of a fine robust constitution and habit, its fruit growing rapidly to the length of thirty to thirty-six inches, being at the same time of the most beautiful proportions, and of a fine rich green colour, which it retains to the last. A first-class variety for general use, and unrivalled for exhibition. W.S.
Our own fine selected stock in sealed packets 1s. 6d. and | 2 6

THE ROCHFORD. A most prolific bearer. The fruit are smooth, slightly spined, 18 to 20 inches in length, of a beautiful fresh green colour, and of the most handsome form. It is a wonderful cropper, producing two and three fruit at a joint, and is one of the best flavoured and most profitable sorts with which we are acquainted 1s. 6d. and | 2 6

DANIELS' IMPROVED TELEGRAPH. A great improvement on the old Telegraph, bearing clean straight fruit twenty to twenty-four inches long, an abundant bearer ... B.S. 1s. 6d. and | 2 6

DANIELS' RELIABLE. This magnificent variety is a cross between Daniels' Duke of Edinburgh, and Tender and True, combining the extra fine qualities of each. The plants are strong and robust growers, and extraordinarily prolific bearers, two and three fruit 20 to 30 inches long at a joint, and are of a dark green colour, and very symmetrical and handsome. For exhibition and market work it is unsurpassable
1s. 6d. and | 2 6

LOCKIE'S PERFECTION. The fruit are produced in great abundance; medium in length, quite straight, short-necked, with no ribs, and only a few black spines, and are very uniform in size. It has received seven First Class Certificates ... ... B.S. 1s. and | 2 0
Manchester Prize. Good market variety ... W.S. 6d. and | 1 0
Rollisson's Telegraph (true) ... ... B.S. 6d. and | 1 0
Tender and True. Superior quality and flavour ... ... W.S. | 1 6

B.S. Black Spine.   W.S. White Spine.

EVIDENCE OF QUALITY.

"It is a pleasure to grow your **Masterpiece Cucumber**. It is so hardy, and quite a picture in growing. They are bound to be First Prizetaker, the colour and quality are excellent."—**Mr. W. HILL**, Moore Barton.

"Your **Masterpiece Cucumber**, which I grew this year, turned out everything I could wish, having taken First Prize at Chesham Show; one measuring twenty-two inches long, and weighed 2 lbs. 10 ozs.; admired by all."—**Mr. H. SEAR**, Chesham.

"Kindly send me, at earliest convenience, 150 Seeds of Rochford Cucumber, you will perhaps be gratified to hear that my former order has produced very satisfactory results."—**Mr. R. QUINN**, Sutton.

"The **Masterpiece Cucumber** which I got were very fine."—**Mrs. PITCAIRN**, South Yeo.

Cucumbers for Ridge Cultivation.

per pkt.—s. d

DANIELS' PERFECTION RIDGE. A very hardy and prolific variety of extra fine quality, length fifteen to twenty inches, very straight and few seeds ... ... 6d. and | 1 0

NEW JAPANESE CLIMBING. This new Cucumber is said to be a very useful variety, and succeeds well for outdoor cultivation, being quite as hardy as the Ridge varieties. The plant is a very vigorous and free grower, and can be grown either on poles, trellis work, or any suitable place—a south aspect is best. It will be found very useful both for pickling and for table use ... ... 6d. and | 1 0
Cluster Gherkin. For pickling, an immense bearer ... | 0 4
Short Prickly. Very hardy, fine for pickling ... ... | 0 3
Stockwood. Fine selected stock ... ... 3d. and | 0 6
Prolific Pickling. One of the most prolific out-door varieties we know of; very hardy ... ... 6d. and | 1 0

Endive.

Cultivation.—This crop is not so greatly appreciated as it should be; we think, nevertheless, that it is "growing in favour." When well grown, the curled varieties are greatly appreciated by some, when cooked as other green crops are. To grow it well, thoroughly good deep soils are essential, and water in abundance during all dry periods. For an early Spring or Summer crop, sow during the first week in April on a warm sunny situation, and again towards the middle of May. The plants produced from the latter sowing should be thinned out, and stand where sown to produce thin crops. The best crops are the Autumn, Winter, and very early Spring, which are produced from successional sowings made between the last week in July and the end of August. The seedlings resulting therefrom should be transplanted successionally on to every conceivable space of good, rich soil. Some will be forward enough to blanch by means of tying them up, or placing a slate upon them, for August and subsequent uses. Others must, if at all large, be removed into a shed or frame, or be otherwise protected from sharp frosts. The lesser and later seedlings will stand out during the Winter on a warm aspect.

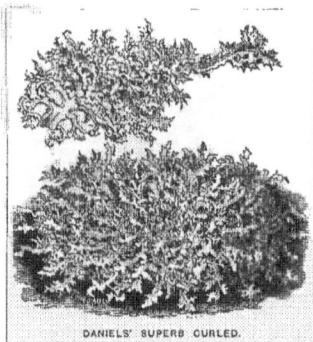

	per oz.—s.	d.
DANIELS' SUPERB CURLED. The best of all the Curled Endives, it bleaches well, and is of first-class quality ... per pkt. 6d.	1	6
Batavian Green. Broad-leaved, very hardy, and desirable for Winter cultivation, tie up for blanching	0	8
Green Curled. Extra	0	8
EXTRA BROAD-LEAVED. An excellent variety, highly recommended ... ... per pkt. 4d.	1	0
Digswell Prize. A fine variety, beautifully curled, hearts well ... ... per pkt. 4d.	1	0

	per oz.—s.	d.
Moss Curled. Very fine ... ... per pkt. 4d.	1	0
White Curled. Excellent variety „ 3d.	0	9

Herbs (Sweet and Pot).

Per packet 3d. Per dozen packets, 2s. 6d.

Angelica. The mid-rib may be eaten as Celery, or when candied makes an excellent confection.
Anise. The seeds are much used for medicinal purposes; the leaves for garnishing or seasoning.
Balm. For making balm tea, which is invaluable in cases of fever; makes also a fine-flavoured wine.
Basil, Bush. The leaves and tops impart the flavour of Clove leaves to soups, and are much used for seasoning.
Basil, Sweet. For flavouring salads and soups.
Borage. The young leaves used as salad or pot herb.
Burnet. The young leaves have the flavour of Cucumbers.
Caraway. For flavouring soups.
Chervil, Green Curled Very fine for salads.
Coriander. The tender leaves are used for soups or salads.
Dill. The leaves are used in soups, sauces, and pickles.
Fennel. Used in sauces for fish and for garnishing.
Horehound. Makes an esteemed well-known beverage.
Hyssop. Young shoots used as pot herbs.
Marigold, Pot. The flowers impart a beautiful colour to broths and soups.
Marjoram, Pot } Aromatic and sweet flavour,
Marjoram, Sweet, or Knotted } used in soups and stuffings.

Lavender. Cultivated for its flowers, which are very aromatic.
Purslane, Green } The shoots and succulent leaves are cooling
Purslane, Golden } when used in Spring as salads.
Rampion. The leaves used as salads; the roots, which have a pleasant nutty flavour, used as Radish.
Rosemary. The leaves make a drink esteemed for relieving headache.
Rue, Broad-leaved. Leaves used medicinally; also used as a remedy for croup in fowls.
Sage. Used in stuffing and sauces.
Savory, Summer } The tops being very aromatic are used
Savory, Winter } in salads and soups; they improve the flavour if boiled with Peas or Beans.
Skirret. The tubers when boiled and served up with butter are most delicious.
Sorrel, Broad-leaved } The leaves are used in salads, soups,
Sorrel, Lettuce-leaved } and sauces.
Tansy. Used for colouring and flavouring confections.
Tarragon. The leaves are excellent when pickled.
Thyme. Broad-leaved. Used in stuffings, soups, and sauces.
Wormwood. Fine tonic when taken as tea; and imparts bitterness to drinks.

Mustard.

Cultivation.—Both the White and Chinese are valuable in salads as they assist digestion. Cut close to the ground the young leaves and stalks, before the second or rough leaves appear; in this state they have a delicate and piquant flavour. When a daily supply is required sow every two or three days throughout the year, in the Winter sow under glass in a temperature of 50° to 60° to hasten the growth. Mustard, as with all kinds of salad, the quicker the growth the more tender the produce.

	per oz.—s.	d.
Chinese. Fine salad variety ... ... per quart 3s., per pint 1s. 9d.	0	4
White. For early salads or medicinal purposes ... per quart 1s. 9d., per pint 1s.	0	2

Price of Mustard for Agricultural Purposes may be had upon application.

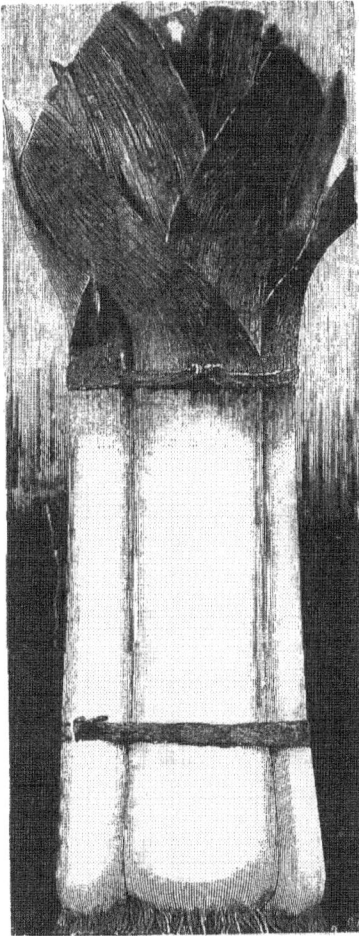

DANIELS' CHAMPION.

Leek.

Cultivation.—The Leek luxuriates in the richest of soils, and the most unctuous of manures only, and such being the case, a thorough preparation must be made for them wherever it is hoped to grow them moderately well. The finest examples are produced in shallow trenches dug out and deeply and thickly manured as for Celery. Here the seedling Leeks are planted either in single, or in double rows, or at right angles with each other. By these means the roots are kept cool during the most arid and hot weather, whilst water can be applied more directly. They like the strongest of manure waters. Sowings may be made very early in the Spring, either in boxes under shelter or on warm borders out of doors, commencing in February; for ordinary main crops sow early in March, in a rich soil and on an open sunny site, and proceed to transplant them so soon as they become large enough so to do. When the plants in either case have made a good growth, some open rich material is often applied to keep additional moisture around them, and to blanch their stems somewhat. Where shallow trenches can be prepared for them during the Winter, seeds may be sown therein early in March, and if the seedlings are subsequently thinned out, a strong and uninterrupted growth is the result.

Our supplies of these being procured from the most noted Musselburgh and other growers, the stocks can be guaranteed of the finest possible quality.

per oz.—s. d.

DANIELS' CHAMPION. A fine broad-leaved variety, highly recommended for exhibition purposes
　　　　　　per pkt. 1s. 6d. —

"I may tell you that the produce of the packet of Champion Leek I had from you last year took Thirteen Prizes at four shows; in fact, they swept all before them, both for weight and quality. I consider it a very long way superior to any Leek in cultivation."—Mr. A. TWIDDLE, Longtown.

		s.	d.
Ayton Castle Giant. Remarkably large and good, may be grown seven inches in circumference, and with one foot of blanched stem ... ... per pkt. 4d.		1	0
CONQUEROR. First-class; very superior either for competition or culinary purposes ... per pkt. 1s.			—
Henry's Prize. Exceedingly large, blanches well, flavour mild, fine for exhibition ... ... per pkt. 4d.		1	0
Large Rouen. A well-known and useful variety ,, 4d.		1	0
London Flag. Large, broad-leaved		0	6
LYON (new). The largest kind grown ... per pkt. 1s.			—
Musselburgh. Extra broad-leaved, blanches to a large size, flavour mild, highly esteemed for soups; grand stock, direct from the Musselburgh growers ... per pkt. 4d.		1	0

Chicory.

per pkt.—s. d.

		s.	d.
Improved Large-leaved. Excellent for blanching ...		0	6
Large-rooted or Coffee		0	6
Whitlœf. Equally good as a salad or boiled. Sow in June ...		0	6

Corn Salad (Lamb's Lettuce)

per oz.—s. d.

		s.	d.
Green Cabbaging. A fine variety, rosette-shaped per pkt. 4d.		0	9
Lettuce-leaved ... ... ,, 4d.		0	9
Large Round-leaved Dutch ,, 4d.		0	9

Dandelion.

per pkt.—s. d.

		s.	d.
Improved Large-leaved. Very valuable for Winter Salads when blanched		0	6
Thick-leaved Cabbaging		0	6

EVIDENCE OF QUALITY.

"The Leeks were very fine indeed. My friends said they had never seen such fine ones. I have some in my garden as thick as a man's wrist."—Mr. J. BOTHARNLEY, Mansfield.

"Your Lyon Leeks answered admirably last year. We have just measured one with the extraordinary circumference of 11½ inches."—Mr. E. BRYANT, Duloe.

"I have grown your Ayton Castle Leek twelve inches in circumference."—Mr. S. WILSON, Dunhampton.

"I am very pleased to inform you that I have had an excellent crop of Leeks from your Seeds, most of them measuring 7½ and several 8½ inches in circumference, a size not often seen anywhere. They have also taken First Prize."—Mr. W. JONES, Velindre.

EVIDENCE OF QUALITY.

"I have almost exclusively used your Seeds, and for twenty-two years have been an exhibitor in all the local shows, during this time I have never failed to take my share of Prizes, on one or two occasions amounting to seventeen, and generally ten or twelve in number. This I consider a fair test of the quality of the Seeds you have supplied."—Mr. W. THOMPSON, Catfield.

Lettuce.

Cultivation.—Of Lettuces, we give particular attention to the growth and selection of two varieties, viz., Daniels' Giant Cos and a capital stock of Daniels' Continuity. The former is the largest Lettuce grown, and very fine for exhibition, being at the same time tender and crisp, and requires no tying. The best Cabbage Lettuce is Daniels' Continuity, which will be found invaluable for Summer use, as it will withstand dry seasons, and continue fit for use after all other kinds have run to seed.

Lettuces are especially partial to an open, deeply worked, and enriched soil, and to an abundant supply of moisture throughout their whole growth. Not only is this necessary to insure a free growth apart from all tendencies to "bolt" or run to seed; but so also is it to ensure such an amount of crispness and natural succulency as alone constitute the higher merits of this important salad plant. Sowings should be made upon a slight bottom-heat, or in boxes, &c., early in February. Make other sowings to follow these during the month of March and again early in April. Sow this time upon warm sunny sites, and transplant a portion of the produce of each sowing only, leaving a sufficient number in the seed beds, and properly thinned, to ensure a supply thereon. For permanent Summer crops sow again during May and June, and this time upon cool, open, airy quarters. Sow the seed in drill rows, and so soon as the seedlings are large enough don't transplant them at this date, but thin out and throw away all but the strongest plants. Too much or too frequent waterings cannot be given them during the hot and arid Summer months. Make a somewhat large sowing or two during the month of July; this for permanent Autumn and Winter uses. The seedlings may be transplanted when the produce of these sowings are thinned out, as by so doing they succeed those which have been permitted to stand. Other sowings should again be made on or about August 11th and 25th, September 5th and 20th, which are likewise to be thinned out and transplanted as necessary for Winter and early Spring supply. Cabbage Lettuces sow in May and August.

CONTINUITY LETTUCE. (*Natural Growth.*)

Price per packet 6d. ; per oz. 1s. 6d.

Daniels' Continuity (or Perpetual).

THE BEST CABBAGE LETTUCE IN THE WORLD.

A bed sown or planted in Spring will keep up a supply of Salad throughout the Summer.

No matter how hot and dry the season they will continue to maintain firm heads long after every other kind has run to seed or gone to decay. One sowing is equal to three or four of any other variety.

A striking example of this was shown during the excessive drought and heat of the past Summer when Continuity stood well throughout the long period of dry weather, and furnished some nice heads when all other varieties failed.

Whatever we have claimed in regard to its most excellent qualities has been more fully borne out in all these respects by the many testimonials we are continually receiving from our customers.

EVIDENCE OF QUALITY.

From *THE JOURNAL OF HORTICULTURE.*

"A good thing which has received much praise this season from many Norfolk Gardeners is Daniels' Continuity Lettuce, a brownish coloured Cabbage kind of good size. In spite of the heat and drought during the past months, it has, wherever grown, developed large solid heads, which stand longer than those of any other known variety."

From *THE GARDENER'S CHRONICLE,*

"Daniels' 'Continuity' Cabbage Lettuce.—I sowed a row of this Lettuce in the Spring, at the same time as Paris Cos, and am very pleased with it. It fully merits the name of Continuity, it came in early, and is as good now, in the middle of August, from one sowing, as it was at first, the Paris Cos and the ordinary Cabbage variety have both bolted long ago, but this does not seem to get any more advanced in that direction at present. It is a brown Lettuce of good flavour, and it grows to a fair size. Ours is a heavy soil, and any Lettuce that shows no disposition to go to seed is an acquisition. The row was thinned, and those that were transplanted at that time have turned out as well as the ones that were left."

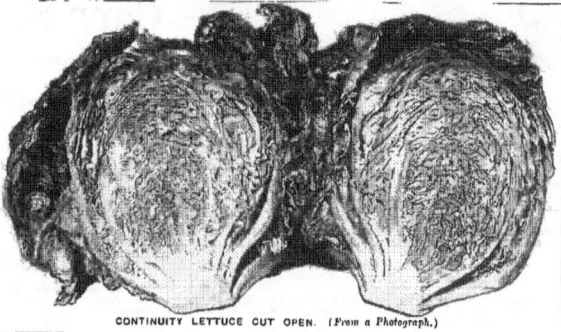

CONTINUITY LETTUCE CUT OPEN. (*From a Photograph.*)

Lettuce (continued)

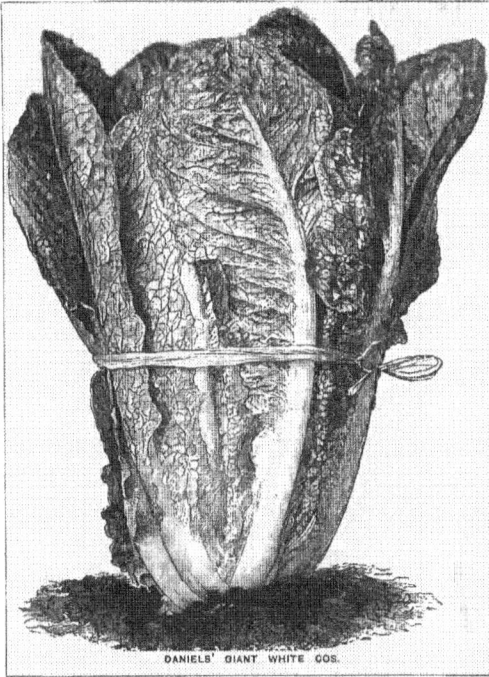

DANIELS' GIANT WHITE COS.

Cos or Upright-growing Varieties.

	per pkt. s. d.	per oz. s. d.
DANIELS' GIANT WHITE. The finest and largest Cos Lettuce in cultivation, very tender and crisp, with fine solid hearts, requires no tying, and will stand a long time without running to seed; should be grown in all gardens; unrivalled for exhibition purposes	1 0	2 6
DANIELS' SOLID BROWN. A medium-sized Lettuce, outer leaves brown, hearts very solid and of a beautiful creamy yellow; very crisp, requires no tying. An invaluable variety for Winter use ...	0 6	1 6
DANIELS' MONSTROUS BROWN. Tender and crisp, requires no tying, the largest grown; fine variety for exhibition ...	0 6	1 6
DANIELS' SELECTED PARIS WHITE. Self-blanching, tender, and mild flavour	0 6	1 6
Hick's Hardy White. A superior variety both for Summer and Winter use	0 4	1 0
Daniels' Black-seeded Bath	0 4	1 0
Daniels' Green Winter. An excellent and hardy kind, valuable for Winter and early Spring work	0 4	1
Daniels' Blood Red Winter. A very handsome and hardy variety; very useful for early Spring use	0 4	1
Paris Green. Blanches well without tying	0 3	0 10
Paris White. Best for general use	0 3	0 10
Mixed Cos vars. All the best for succession	0 3	0 8

Cabbage Varieties.

	per pkt. s. d.	per oz. s. d.
DANIELS' GOLDEN SUMMER (new). This is quite distinct from Buttercup, being more of a bronzy yellow on the outside. The large, firm, solid heads when cut open, are nearly white inside, and exceedingly tender and crisp	0 6	1 6
QUEEN OF SUMMER (new). This is one of the finest Summer Lettuces yet introduced. It is remarkable for its large size, splendid appearance, and for withstanding the drought. It produces fine, crisp, and tender Lettuces in the driest season ...	0 6	1 6
DANIELS' BLACK-SEEDED TEXTER. Large, compact, and solid, one of the most splendid varieties in cultivation, first-class for market gardeners or family use	0 4	1 0
"All the Year Round"	0 4	1 0
DANIELS' ENDIVE-LEAVED (new). The leaves are of a bright rich green colour, and prettily fringed, whilst unlike most of its class, it has a firm, crisp head of fine flavour	0 4	1 0
Brown Dutch. Very large and hardy ...	0 3	0 8
Drumhead or **Malta.** Well known ...	0 3	0 8

	per pkt. s. d.	per oz. s. d.
New York. A very superior American variety. The heads attain a large size, and are very crisp and tender; grand variety for exhibition ...	0 6	1 6
Daniels' Giant White. An exceedingly large and fine variety, crisp and tender, and of fine flavour, stands a long time without running to seed	0 6	1 6
Neapolitan. Leaves beautifully curled and tender, one of the finest Summer sorts, grows very hard and solid	0 3	0 9
American Gathering or **Curled.** Distinct and interesting, intermediate between the Cabbage and Cos kinds	0 4	1 0
Buttercup. This large, handsome variety is remarkable for its tenderness and delicacy of flavour, while its bright citron-coloured foliage renders it perfectly distinct from all existing Cabbage Lettuces	0 6	1 6
Hammersmith Hardy Green ...	0 3	0 8
Large White Winter. The best for Winter use; heads large and solid	0 4	1 0
Tennis-ball. A fine dwarf variety ...	0 4	1 0
Wheeler's Tom Thumb ...	0 4	1 0
Mixed Cabbage vars. All the best kinds for succession	0 3	0 8
Mixed. All kinds, Cos and Cabbage	0 3	0 8

Melons.

Cultivation.—What is generally designated a Cucumber house will prove also an excellent place wherein to grow Melons, and to this fact as opposed to general culturists, is to be attributed much of the success of certain growers. The cultivation of the Melon is very similar to that of the Cucumber up to and a little beyond the full swelling of the fruits. If there exists one thing more than another conducive of or to success, it consists in the maintaining of as equal a temperature as possible throughout their growth; this is not as readily insured in frames as in houses having all convenient hot-water apparatus, &c., hence some allowance must be made for frame growers. The propagation of the Melon is usually by sowing seed, although some do so by cuttings; and certainly, when several sorts are grown in the same structure, and there is a desire to continue the variety pure and unchanged, the latter mode is the best. The seed should be sown in shallow pans instead of in ordinary pots, as the roots coming in contact with the bottom of the pan extend horizontally, instead of perpendicularly, and hence become better furnished with fibres. Sow the seeds during either of the first four months of the year, according as there is a possibility of growing them early or otherwise. Pot them off, &c., in detail similarly with the above, excepting that only one plant must be placed into each pot, and it must be potted more firmly. They delight in deep rich loam, and trodden firmly. The temperature by day should average, with daily ventilation, from seventy-five to eighty-five degrees, according to the warmth of the sun, &c. By night it should not be permitted to exceed seventy-two degrees; an average of seventy degrees being a desirable warmth. Give at all times the freest possible exposure to the full sunlight, as to shade them in any degree is derogatory to their doing well, after once a crop of fruit is "set," and the plants must be kept moderately thin by judicious pruning to insure this. Weak liquid manure may be given to them up to the time of the fruit attaining the size of a hen's egg; after which water more sparingly until the fruit are seen to have commenced netting or to change colour, when it should be withheld by degrees altogether. The water given to Melons, whether superficially or as root-waterings, should always be of the same temperature as the air in any kind of structure in which they may be grown.

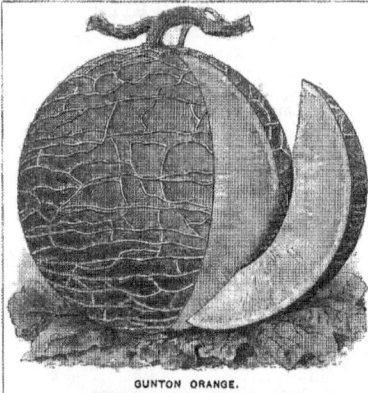

GUNTON ORANGE.

°**NEW MELON, GUNTON ORANGE** (S.F.) per pkt.—s. d.
This unique scarlet fleshed Melon was raised by Mr. Allan, Gunton Park Gardens, and is the result of a double cross from that excellent old variety, Auston's Incomparable. The fruit, which is rather under medium size and nearly round in form, is of a rich golden colour, attractively netted, with flesh of exceptional thickness and exquisite flavour. The plant is of robust constitution and a free setter, and this variety can be highly recommended for its attractive appearance and superb quality. Awarded First Class Certificate, Royal Horticultural Society 1 6

***DANIELS' WESTLEY HALL** (S.F.) This grand new Melon is a cross between Read's Scarlet Flesh and High Cross Hybrid. It has the high quality of the former for flavour, with the free setting qualities of the latter. The skin is beautifully netted, sometimes slightly flushed with yellow towards the ripening period. The flesh is thick, scarlet, and intermixed with streaks of green; with a most sweet and delicious flavour. The fruit slightly oval in shape, weighing 7 lb., are pronounced by those who tasted them to be the best-flavoured and most delicious Melon that has been sent out for years. First Class Certificate, R.H.S. 1s. 6d. and 2 6

Daniels' Green Perfection. This choice new variety is of vigorous habit, and a most prolific bearer. The flesh is very thick and of a pale green, with a rich luscious and melting flavour, and of delicate aroma 1s. 6d. and 2 6

DANIELS' IMPROVED GOLDEN PERFECTION. per pkt.—s. d. A splendid green-fleshed variety, regularly and beautifully netted; thin skin, flesh very thick, firm, of the most exquisite flavour; the plant is of fine robust constitution and a free setter; we confidently recommend this 2 6

***Blenheim Orange** (S.F.). A grand scarlet-fleshed variety, is very prolific and a fine setter; the fruit are beautifully netted, very thin-skinned, and of delicious flavour 1 0

Gunton Scarlet. A fine scarlet-fleshed Melon. Raised by Mr. W. Allan of Gunton Park ... 1 6

Hero of Lockinge (W.F.). Fine exhibition variety; very prolific 1 6

High Cross Hybrid (G.F.). A fine variety; of excellent flavour 1 6

MELTON HYBRID (S.F.). This choice variety will be found a valuable addition to our list of good Melons. The fruit are large and handsome, slightly ribbed, and nicely netted. The flesh is thick, of rich salmon colour, juicy and melting, and of fine flavour 1 6

Royal Ascot. A fine scarlet-fleshed Melon, beautifully netted; fine exhibition variety 1 6

***Read's Scarlet-flesh.** One of the best red-fleshed varieties, a free setter; flesh thick, solid, and of excellent flavour 1 0

Scarlet Premier (S.F.). A useful variety of fine flavour 1 0

***The Countess** (W.F.). A cross between American Musk and Cashmere; of strong constitution, and enormously prolific; clear yellow skin, beautifully netted; flesh thick, tender, juicy, and melting ... 1 0

The following Varieties can also be supplied at 1s. per packet:—

Berkley Castle	Colston Bassett Seedling (G.F.)	*Munro's Little Heath (S.F.)
Ely's Seedling (G.F.)	Monarch (G.F.)	Scarlet Perfection (S.F.)

Abbreviations.—Those marked with an asterisk (*) have received a First Class Certificate from the Royal Horticultural Society. S.F. scarlet flesh, G.F. green flesh, W.F. white flesh.

Onion.

Cultivation.—PREPARATION OF GROUND.—The Onion is what may be termed a gross feeder; and cannot be grown to perfection without a good depth of rich and well pulverised soil and an open situation. Superficially, it would appear the reverse of this, though the roots are known to run downwards many feet where agreeable soil exists, and for which reason very deep and good cultivation is of the first importance. In preparing a bed for Onions, therefore, always endeavour to trench it deeply, adding abundance of manure at the bottom of each trench, and throughout its various strata as the work progresses. The object to be obtained being to thoroughly break up and manure the soil to the depth of twenty to twenty-four inches, we should recommend its accomplishment in the following manner:—In October or November, or as early as possible afterwards, dig out a trench two feet wide and one spade deep, removing the soil where you intend to finish; break up the bottom or subsoil of the trench another spade deep, mixing in a liberal quantity of manure, throw on this the soil from the space of two feet, again mixing in plenty of manure, treat the second and succeeding trenches in the same manner, until the whole plot is completed. It is found that by this means the ground will resist drought much better than when dug in the ordinary way, that heavy soils are rendered less retentive, and light soils greatly improved, and that all soils are much benefited, and will yield much finer crops in successive seasons. By timely sowing, good cultivation, and careful harvesting, Onions can be produced in this country, in size, quality, and mildness of flavour, and for culinary purposes, equal to the finest importations from Portugal or Spain. And the great wonder is that much larger quantities are not grown, as thousands of tons are imported at a cost of more than £100,000 annually, which could be as well produced at home to meet the great demand for this much esteemed article of food, possessing as it does such valuable medicinal and nutritious properties. An occasional dressing of soot during the Winter and Spring will be of great benefit. Daniels' Eureka Manure worked into the soil, or applied in liquid form, is a powerful stimulant to growing crops.

SPRING SOWING.—The early sowing, consisting of such fine sorts as Daniels' Improved White Spanish, Red Wethersfield, and Zittoau Giant Yellow, &c., should be made early in February, and the main one of all kinds early in March. Always where convenient, sow in drill-rows, drawn very shallow, and about nine inches apart. Before sowing the seeds the ground should be well trodden down and raked level. Immediately the seeds are sown, level in the drill-rows neatly, then well tread over the whole surface of the bed, again raking it over to remove all stones, &c. The young seedling plants must be kept quite free from weeds by frequent use of the hoe, and immediately they are large enough, thinning should be performed, carefully drawing all weaklings out without disturbing such as are to remain, and which should be at a distance of from eight to nine inches apart, if any fine produce is aimed at. Where, however, much moderate-sized produce is in demand (and it has become the fashion to garnish with such) it is not desirable to thin nearly so much. In regard to growing " picklers," these should be sown more thickly, and receive no thinning out at all; and it may be necessary, in the case of very good ground, to sow them on to a poor site chosen for its poverty, and stony, or similar characteristics. Irrigation or any kind of artificial waterings, especially if more or less manurial, will prove of great benefit in growing large and fine produce. The maggot, which often attacks the crops, may be "kept off" by sprinkling the young seedlings thinly with fresh slaked lime immediately after thinning, and during showery weather. Watering them with the lime water has also the same effect.

DANIELS' IMPROVED WHITE SPANISH.

EVIDENCE OF QUALITY.

Daniels' Select List of Onions for Spring Sowing.

per oz.—s. d.

DANIELS' IMPROVED WHITE SPANISH. The most perfect type of White Spanish Onion in cultivation, specially selected by ourselves. Grows to a large size, very even, and of good flavour. This variety has been exhibited with marked success for many years past and has given the greatest satisfaction ... ... per pkt. 1s. 2 6

DANIELS' NEW RED GLOBE. The finest red Onion in cultivation. The bulbs are large, of a fine globular shape, and of a beautiful dark crimson. Besides being very attractive in appearance, it has the mild flavour and good keeping qualities of the very best of the White Spanish type per pkt. 6d. 1 6

DANIELS' GOLDEN GLOBE. An excellent variety of true globular shape, skin bright golden yellow, flavour mild; produces a heavy crop and keeps well ... ... per pkt. 6d. 1 6

Daniels' Blood Red. Fine rich colour, very hardy 0 9

ROUSHAM PARK HERO. A magnificent variety of the White Spanish type per pkt. 4d. 1 0

LONGLASTER (Daniels'). This is by far the longest keeping Onion yet introduced. We have had specimens in sound condition eighteen months after being harvested. This variety should be sown early in the season. Can also be sown in Autumn per pkt. 4d. 1 0

AILSA CRAIG. The largest and handsomest exhibition variety in commerce, type not yet distinct, some of the bulbs being almost globe shape, others inclined to a very deep flat oval, either type being excellent for the exhibition table. It has been grown to 26, 28, 30, and 34 lbs. per dozen bulbs per pkt. 1s. 6d. and 2s. 6d. —

Bedfordshire Champion. Selected stock ... 0 9
Brown Globe. Very useful, heavy cropper ... 0 9

per oz.—s. d.

Cranston's Excelsior. A superior variety of the White Spanish type, good keeper, and a fine exhibition variety ... ... per pkt. 6d. 1 6

Early Queen. Remarkably quick-growing, may be sown in July and will ripen same year 1 0

Early White Gem. One of the earliest in cultivation, three weeks earlier than the Queen, and comes to maturity from eight to ten weeks from time of sowing. The bulbs are medium-sized and can be used either for pickling or other culinary purposes per pkt. 6d. 1 6

JAMES' KEEPING. Excellent keeper ... 0 9

New White Globe. First Class Certificate, Royal Horticultural Society. Bulbs of medium size, true globular shape, remarkably firm and solid, with a very white silvery skin; very handsome and distinct ... 1 0

Nuneham Park. Much recommended, a fine variety 0 9

Silver Skin. Of very quick growth, best for pickling 0 9

Strasburgh or Deptford. Well known 0 6

Wethersfield New Red. A capital type of Red Onion for Spring sowing, flesh pure white 0 8

White Globe (straw-coloured). A fine useful variety... 1 0

WHITE SPANISH. Ordinary stock per lb. 6s. 0 6

WHITE SPANISH, Portugal, or Reading. Fine selected stock, best for general use per lb. 7s. 6d. 0 8

ZITTEAU GIANT YELLOW. A magnificent variety, of fine yellow skin, attains a large size, remains sound till June ... per lb. 6s. 6d. 0 8

Mixed, all sorts for Spring sowing 5s. 6d. 0 6

THE LORD KEEPER. One of the finest possible Onions for Show purposes, in type similar to the popular "Rousham Park Hero," very large in circumference, and deep in flesh. It gained the First Prize at the Agricultural Hall, London, in 1893, for "Best Twelve Onions," and again at the Great Onion Competition held at Banbury, 14th September, 1893 per pkt. 1s. 6d. and 2s. 6d.

EVIDENCE OF QUALITY.

"The **Golden Rocca** Onion Seed I received from you last year turned out remarkably well; I have Onions measuring five inches across."—Mr. R. MANLEY, Cruwys Morchard.

"I am pleased to inform you I took First Prize at Ash-next-Sandwich in Competition with your **Golden Rocca** Onion; it is, beyond doubt, the best Autumn Onion yet sent out."—Mr. G. JULL, Sandwich.

ONIONS FOR AUTUMN SOWING.

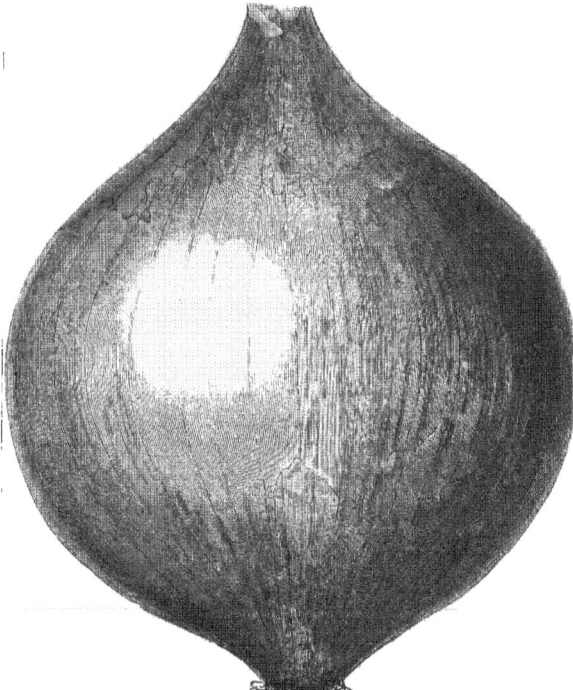

ALTHOUGH most of the varieties recommended for Spring sowing may be sown with advantage in the Autumn, the varieties named below are decidedly superior for this purpose.

AUTUMN SOWING is growing more in favour every year with most cultivators, and the many advantages to be derived from having a plentiful supply of Autumn-sown Onions cannot be well over estimated, as by transplanting they can be grown to double the size and are much milder in flavour, besides a more abundant and heavier crop can be relied on. In these Autumn sowings, the attack by the fly and consequent destruction by maggots is unknown, and if the seed is sown in fairly good time, so as to be well up before the Autumn frosts begin, they will withstand our severest Winter. By thinning the crops, an abundant supply of fresh green Onions can be had for use all through the Spring and early Summer months. Daniels' Golden Rocca, Giant Rocca, and White Elephant Tripoli are amongst the best kinds for Autumn sowing.

TIME OF SOWING FOR STANDING THE WINTER.—Sow any time from the middle of July to the second week in September in moderately rich and well-pulverised soil, in an open situation, in beds four feet wide, (and, where convenient, make two or three sowings at intervals of ten or fourteen days). Before sowing, the ground should be thoroughly consolidated, by treading down with the foot, raked level, and drills carefully made, &c., as recommended for Spring Cultivation. Water and clean from time to time as required. Very fine crops can be obtained in the ordinary way of cultivation by thinning the young plants out to about six inches apart, but where extra fine bulbs are required for exhibition and other purposes, we strongly recommend TRANSPLANTING.

DANIELS' ⟨illustration⟩ GOLDEN ROCCA.

	per oz.—s.	d.
DANIELS' GOLDEN ROCCA. One of the largest and finest Onions ever introduced. Fine globular shape, golden yellow skin, mild flavour, and with careful cultivation comes equal to the imported Portugal Onions, and keeps sound till June. This variety is the best exhibition kind known, and has obtained more Prizes than any other Onion. If sown in Autumn, and kept under first-class cultivation, will grow bulbs two to three pounds each; may also be sown in Spring, and will produce some fine bulbs		
per pkt. 6d.	1	6
DANIELS' GIANT ROCCA (true). A splendid variety, of delicate flavour, large globular shape, and light brown skin	0	9

	per oz.—s.	d.
Daniels' Crimson Rocca. Extra fine variety	1	0
Daniels' White Elephant Tripoli. This new Italian introduction is the largest of the Tripoli sorts, the average diameter of the bulbs being six and a half to seven inches. They are flat in form, with a silvery white skin, and of fine mild flavour. This Onion is unsurpassed as an exhibition variety per pkt. 6d.	1	6
Giant Madeira. Very large, excellent flavour	0	9
Tripoli, Italian Red ⎰ Large handsome varieties. ⎱	0	9
" Italian White ⎱ First-class for Autumn Sowing. ⎰	0	9
White Lisbon. Fine hardy variety; first-rate for drawing green in Spring; also useful for Spring Sowing per lb. 4s.	0	4

PLANTS.—Strong Autumn sown, to plant out for show purposes, can be supplied in Spring of the following kinds only : **White Elephant Tripoli, White Spanish, Golden Rocca,** and **Giant Rocca.**

Each sort 1s. 6d. per 100; 10s. per 1000. Carriage Paid.

EVIDENCE OF QUALITY.

"On August 26th, I took at the North Curry Annual Flower Show First Prize for **Golden Rocca Onions,** and First for **White Spanish.** Last year I got First Prize for **Giant Rocca Onion,** and First for collection of Vegetables grown from Seeds supplied by you."—Mr. C. HOSTE, North Curry.

"I am very pleased to tell you I obtained First Prize with your **Golden Rocca Onion** at the Cuckfield Show on August 15th."—Mr. E. D. MACRO, Haywards Heath.

"Your **Golden Rocca Onion** is a model, I have grown them several years with much success, always taking First Prize with them. If well grown they cannot be beaten on the exhibition table."—Mr. W. HILL, Moore Barton.

"I am pleased to inform you that I took First Prize for your **Golden Rocca Onion** at Welshpool Show against a very close competition of about forty entries. I had twelve Prizes altogether."—Mr. J. O. PRICE, Caerwys.

Parsnip.

Cultivation.—Rarely, if ever, is the Parsnip valued at its proper worth, or are its usefulness and high nutritive properties properly acknowledged. Perhaps there is no crop so remunerative both from the above point of view, and besides from a consideration of the heavy crops that on a system of fairly good culture, very limited space is capable of producing. As this esculent is known as being "dibble-rooted," it may not be necessary to dwell upon the great necessity of deep culture. They delight in fairly stiff soil, moderately moist, and always succeed best upon such soil either trenched, or bastard trenched, and with manure placed not less than eight or ten inches deep and in a goodly layer, and well decomposed. Sow the seeds about March 20th in drill rows fourteen inches apart, thinning out the young seedlings to distances of from eight to ten inches apart in the rows. In cases where it is not possible to insure a regular crop, owing to irregular sowing, germination of seeds, or insect pests, we have seen a fairly good produce, and a better finish given to a bed, by transplanting some of the thickest seedlings during showery weather on to vacant spaces. Hoe frequently during the Summer months, and if a good tender Parsnip is appreciated, never dig up the roots until they are actually required for use.

per oz.—s. d.

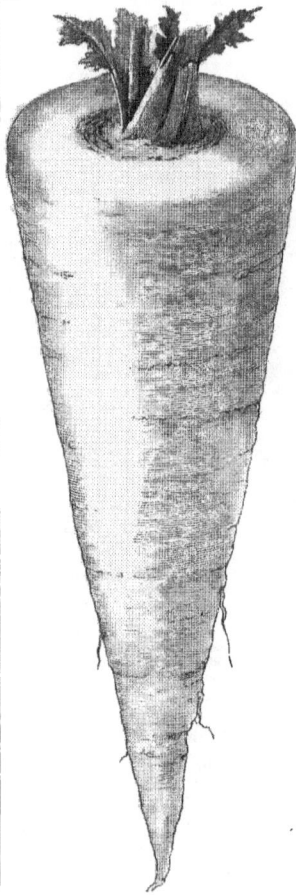

DANIELS' IMPROVED HOLLOW-CROWNED.
A finely selected stock of the true old Hollow-crowned variety. First-class
for exhibition and general use ... ... per lb. 6s. 0 8

"At the Fruit and Root Show I was awarded a First Class Certificate for your
Improved Hollow-crowned Parsnip. The six weighed 20 lbs., one of the largest
weighed 5 lbs."—Mr. W. BAILEY, Lamberhurst.

Elcombe's Improved. Very choice stock, of fine flavour, much
esteemed for exhibition 0 6
Turnip-rooted. Excellent for shallow soils 0 6
Guernsey or **Jersey Marrow.** A fine, large, and heavy cropping
variety 0 6
Hollow-crowned. Largest and best for general use; a fine selected
stock ... ... per lb. 3s. 0 3
The Student. A first-class variety, but requires a good depth of soil ... 0 6

Parsley.

Cultivation.—It is only by thorough and efficient culture that good Parsley can be grown. Hence good, deep, rich soil, should always be prepared for it by trenching, manuring, &c., where practicable. Sowings should be made from about the middle of February until the end of March, according to the demand. For a limited supply only one sowing, made about March 10th, will suffice. Make another sowing about the first week in July, transplant a few seedlings from each sowing, if possible, as finer plants are formed thereby. It is a desirable plan to sow in rows ten inches apart, and to thin the plants out to like distances apart in the rows. By placing frames over some portions of the crop during Winter, or potting up bundles of the roots, and placing them into a gentle warmth, a better supply will be assured at a most acceptable season.
Daniels' Queen of the Parsleys, an improvement upon the Fern-leaved variety, is the most useful for garnishing, and is extremely valuable as an ornamental-foliaged plant for the flower border, &c.

per oz.—s. d.

DANIELS' QUEEN OF THE PARSLEYS.
An extra selected stock of the Fern-leaved variety, carefully grown
on our own Seed Farm. The most useful for garnishing, and extremely
valuable as an ornamental plant for the flower-border   per pkt. 6d. 1 6
Covent-Garden Garnishing. A splendid variety, beautifully curled 0 6
Extra-fine Curled. Fine for garnishing 0 4
Fern-leaved. Distinct foliage, useful for garnishing   per pkt. 3d. 0 3

DANIELS' IMPROVED HOLLOW-CROWNED.

EVIDENCE OF QUALITY.

"I must state that this makes twenty-five years that I have dealt with your firm, and am pleased to say that I have always found your Seeds quite as good as represented, and can always recommend them with confidence."—**Mr. G. BAKER**, Aldershot.

"I am pleased to tell you that I got the First Prize for collection of Vegetables at Laceby Horticultural Show, also First Prize for Cottager's Collection of Vegetables, eight varieties for which I have taken First Prize for six years in succession; I had eighteen entries, and took sixteen Prizes, eleven First, four Second, and one Third, all from your Seeds."—**Mr. G. CAMMACK**, Aylesby.

"Perhaps it may interest you to hear this is the twentieth year I have had Seeds from you, and I have never had reason to complain of any of them."—**Mr. P. F. J. BEESTON**, Wellington.

"I obtained First Prize for the best six kinds of Vegetables grown from your Seeds, **Daniels' King of the Cauliflowers**; better I never saw, and was greatly praised, also the **Scarlet Runner Beans "Titan,"** and the **Duke of York Potatoes**. I must speak very highly of your Seeds and all that I have had from your firm have turned out to be what you have stated them in your catalogue."—**Mr. W. BUCK**, Stoke Ferry.

Radish.

Cultivation.—Grown under favourable conditions, Radishes are ready for use in a very short time from the seed being sown, and when young, crisp, and juicy, are highly popular for salading purposes. For earliest use, a sowing may be made under glass amongst Potatoes or Asparagus that is being forced, or a few may be sown in a frame on a slight bottom-heat made with fermenting materials. The seeds germinate freely, and air should be admitted on all favourable occasions, a temperature of 50° being sufficient in the frame. For later sowings, say in February or March out-of-doors, a deeply dug light and rich soil, and a warm sheltered position are the most favourable. Sow the seeds broadcast, and cover the beds in severe weather, or on frosty nights, with a slight covering of straw, or with mats laid over bended sticks, to be removed during the day, or when the air is sufficiently mild. From March onwards to the end of September, small successive sowings at intervals of about a fortnight will ensure a succession of nice crisp Radishes, care must however be taken to give liberal waterings in dry weather. The China Rose and Black Spanish varieties, for Winter use, should be sown in July and August in shallow drills, six or eight inches apart, and the plants thinned out to four or five inches apart in the drill.

	per oz.—s.	d.
DANIELS' LONG SCARLET. A fine select Stock, beautiful colour, and very crisp, best for general crop per qt. 3s.; per pt. 1s. 9d.	0	4
DANIELS' EARLY SCARLET TURNIP. The finest variety ever introduced, being very early, the roots are firm, solid, and of true globular shape. Colour, rich glowing crimson scarlet. This is unquestionably the earliest forcing Radish extant. It grows very rapidly, is of delicate flavour, and is fit to use in three weeks from time of sowing. The top is short, with leaves few and small per pt. 2s. 6d.	0	6
Daniels' Purple Olive-shaped, White-tipped. This variety is equally as constant and attractive as the French Breakfast. It received the large Silver Medal at Erfurt Exhibition, the sole prize for a vegetable novelty ...	0	4
French Breakfast. Scarlet, tipped white, oval shape, forces well, mild and crisp, highly esteemed in Paris per pint 2s.	0	4
Long Rose, White-tipped. Excellent new sort, attaining an unusual size without becoming stringy. Its pretty rose colour passes to pure white at the end of root, a peculiarity which gives to this Radish a very pleasing appearance ...	0	6
Olive-shaped Scarlet. Early, good forcer, very tender and mild ... ... per qt. 3s. 6d.; per pt. 2s.	0	4
Olive-shaped White. Of quick growth, mild and crisp, handsome shape ... ... per qt. 3s. 6d.; per pt. 2s.	0	4
Olive-shaped Mixed ... ... per qt. 3s.; per pt. 1s. 9d.	0	3
Scarlet Short-top. Best for general crop and market purposes ... ... per qt. 2s. 6d.; per pt. 1s. 6d.	0	3
Turnip, Scarlet, White-tipped. Delicious and handsome per pint 2s. 6d.	0	6
Turnip, Scarlet (For Summer) and (Autumn use.) per qt. 2s. 6d.; per pt. 1s. 6d.	0	6
,, **White**	0	3
,, **Mixed**		
Wood's Early Frame. The best for early crop, forces well ... ... per qt. 3s.; per pt. 1s. 9d.	0	3

Winter Radishes.

Chinese Rose-coloured. Of oblong shape and mild flavour; for Winter use ... ... per pint 2s.	0	4
Black Spanish. For Winter salads; sown in Autumn for Spring use ... ... per pint 2s. 6d.	0	6

EVIDENCE OF QUALITY.

"The Seeds I had of you turned out splendid. I made a few exhibits at our show on August 1st, and won Ten Prizes, including First for Duke of York Potatoes, Matchless Marrow Pea, and Crimson Perfection Beet, for which I have received great praise; they were the best that have been seen about here."—**Mr. DEE,** Leamington.

"I am glad to inform you that I took several Prizes at our show at Horndean from your Seeds. First for Little Queen Cabbage, First for Golden Rocca Onions, First for Snowball Turnip, and First for Collection of Vegetables."—**Mr. G. TARRANT,** Waterlooville.

"I am glad to tell you that I took First Prize with a Collection of your Vegetables, also First Prize for Ne Plus Ultra Beans at Cardiff Flower Show. I also took six First, two Second, and two Third, at Porthcawl Show."—**Mr. T. REES,** Port Talbot.

"I am pleased to tell you that I took Twenty-four Prizes at our Flower Show, held on Saturday, August 18th, at Lysway Hall, London; ten First, nine Second, three Third, and two Extras."—**Mr. R. SCRAGG,** Rugeley.

DANIELS' LONG SCARLET.

DANIELS' EARLY SCARLET TURNIP.

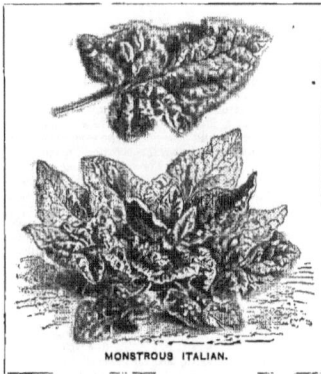

Spinach.

Cultivation.—Round Spinach should be sown for Spring and Summer use at intervals from February to May; Prickly Spinach in July and August for Winter use. The New Zealand variety requires to be raised on a gentle hot-bed in April, and planted out in May on a good rich soil in a warm situation. Sow the Round and Prickly varieties in drills about an inch deep and a foot apart in good rich soil, the richer the better for the Summer crop. Abundance of moisture and an occasional dose of weak liquid manure will improve the crop.

				per oz.—s.	d.
Long Standing. A most valuable variety for Summer use, as it stands the dry weather, and keeps longer fit for use than any other sort ... ... per qt. 3s., per pt. 1s. 9d.				0	4
Monstrous Italian or **Viroflay.** Large and superior; leaves dark green, and extremely thick and fleshy per qt. 2s., per pt. 1s 3d.				0	4
New Zealand. Large and succulent				0	6
Perpetual or **Spinach Beet**				0	6
Prickly. For Winter use ... ... per qt. 1s. 9d., per pt. 1s.				0	3
Round. For Summer use; best for general crop per qt. 1s. 9d., per pt. 1s.				0	3

MONSTROUS ITALIAN.

Salsafy and Scorzonera.

Cultivation.—To grow nice plump, straight roots of Salsafy, the ground should be prepared in Autumn in a similar way to that recommended for Parsnips. Sow in April in drills fifteen inches apart, and thin out the plants to eight or ten inches apart in the row. Keep clean by hoeing, &c., during Summer, and take up for storing in November in same way as Carrots. The roots are scraped and boiled in the same way as Parsnips, and are of a mild sweetish flavour. Much esteemed on the Continent.

Scorzonera will thrive under similar treatment to that recommended for Salsafy, which it somewhat resembles, but should be allowed a little more room in the drill.

	per oz.—s.	d.			per oz.—s.	d.
Salsafy. Common ... ... per pkt. 3d.	0	9	**Scorzonera** ... ... per pkt. 3d.	0	9
„ **Sandwich Island Mammoth.** Splendid variety, lately introduced ... per pkt. 6d.	1	6	„ **Russian Improved** „ 4d.	1	0

Vegetable Marrow.

Cultivation.—This esteemed vegetable is so nearly related to the Gourd that we may say but little in regard to it. Its treatment as regards sowing and the early transplanting, &c., should be identical therewith. Few plants delight more in copious manurial waterings than do these. Too generally the produce is permitted to become much too large before it is cut for use. This is excusable in the case of growers for market. Where, however, persons are enabled to grow their own, it seems strange that the same method should be followed. Every Marrow should be cooked whole, and this fact should alone suggest the most desirable size to grow them to. By cutting young a more abundant supply will be constantly forming than is possible when all are permitted to become more or less "seedy."

	per pkt.—s.	d.
Pen-y-byd (*The best in the World*). Awarded two First Class Certificates. This distinct variety is enormously prolific and a continuous bearer. The vine is extremely short-jointed, setting a fruit at every joint. The fruit is of handsome appearance, almost globular in form, sometimes very slightly ribbed, averaging about six inches in diameter, and is of a delicate creamy white colour, with thick firm flesh, which when cooked is of finest quality and delicate flavour ... ... 6d. and	1	0
DANIELS' GOLDEN CREAM. Very fine and prolific		0 6
DANIELS' LARGE CREAM. Best for general use, fine-flavoured		0 6
Green Bush. Very prolific, compact habit of growth ...		0 6
Custard-shaped. Prolific, ornamental-shaped variety		0 6
Moore's Vegetable Cream. Very prolific, delicious flavour		0 4
Vegetable Marrow and **Squash.** Various sorts mixed		0 3

DANIELS' LARGE CREAM.

	per pkt.—s.	d.
Long Green. Good variety, forms a striking contrast with other kinds	0	4
Long White-ribbed, or **Bush.** Good; a prolific kind	0	4

Tomato or Love-apple.

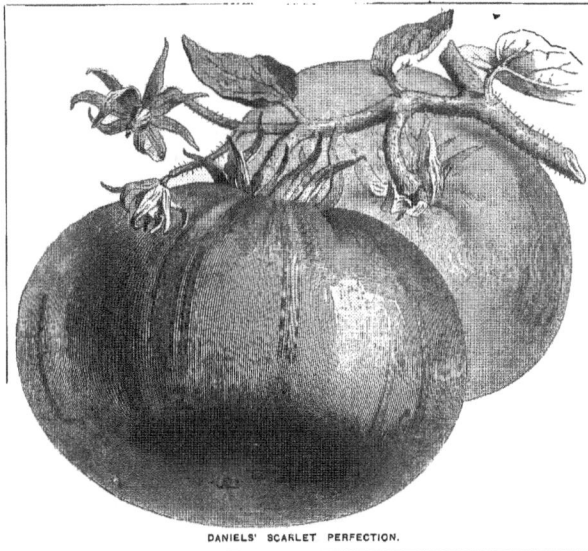

DANIELS' SCARLET PERFECTION.

Out-door Cultivation.
Sow in March on a slight hot-bed, and when two or three inches high pot off singly into three-inch pots. In middle of April place in cool frame or under handglasses to harden off. About this period great care should be taken to keep the young plants shaded from the sun, and well supplied with water. Towards the end of May plant out about four feet apart, in good rich soil, against a south wall, or close to the fence on a warm border. As the plants grow they should be trained up thinly, and nailed up or fastened. Pinch out the young branches from amongst the fruit, as it is highly important they should have the fullest benefit of sun and air to insure their full ripening. Frequent doses of weak liquid manure all through the growing season will be found of great service.

Cultivation under Glass.
They can be easily raised from seed in an ordinary hot-bed or shelf in a greenhouse; when large enough to handle, prick off into pans, &c., when about four inches high, pot into single pots, repotting as required, till they are finally planted out in position where intended to grow them. The chief requirements are a good rich soil composed of two parts loam, one part each leaf mould and manure, see that the drainage is in good order, give air freely, as this materially assists in setting the fruits. Success in Tomato growing depends on constant root moisture combined with good drainage, genial warmth, and ample ventilation. After the fruit is set, frequent waterings of liquid manure will greatly assist in giving them size and colour.

RED VARIETIES.

	per pkt.—s.	d.
'DANIELS' SCARLET PERFECTION. Very handsome, perfectly round and smooth, firm and solid, flavour first-class, and of a beautiful glossy scarlet colour ... ... 1s. and	2	0
Criterion. A most superior red sort, of handsome form and medium size	0	6
Hathaway's Excelsior or Stamfordian. A fine early variety, producing in great profusion a large, smooth, round, and heavy fruit; handsome	0	6
*****Daniels' Dwarf Early Open-Air.** The earliest of all Tomatoes for the open air. Is of dwarf habit, early, and productive ... ... 6d. and	1	0
*****Daniels' Harbinger.** This variety, being very early and a prolific bearer, will be found extremely valuable for growing in the open air. The fruit are round, smooth, solid, and of a bright red	1	0
Torra Cotta. This unique variety is very distinct as regards colour, form, skin, &c. The colour is pure terra-cotta. The skin is lustreless and slightly downy, like that of the Peach. The flesh is very solid and of good flavour, particularly to those who prefer raw Tomatoes. It is very productive, beginning to bear early and lasting a long time 1	0

	per pkt.—s.	d.
DANIELS' CRIMSON QUEEN. A beautiful scarlet crimson variety of extra fine form and delicate flavour, very prolific and early; a magnificent variety for exhibition purposes	1	0
Pondorosa. A new variety from America. Is one of the largest Tomatoes ever introduced. The fruit are handsome, smooth, and very solid; it is a free setter	1	0
*****Laxton's Open-air.** The earliest and hardiest in cultivation ... ... 6d. and	1	0
*****Large Red.** Very prolific and useful	0	4
*****New Early Champion.** Succeeds well both under glass and in the open air. It is of dwarf, compact habit, fruit smooth, solid, and of a bright red 6d. and	1	0
New Peach. Fruit is uniform in size, about as large as a medium-sized Peach, having a delicious fruity flavour not met with in any other ... ... 6d. and	1	0
*****King Humbert or Chiswick Red.** First Class Certificate R.H.S.	0	6
Ham Green Favourite. Very prolific, fine, handsome, smooth variety; first-class for market use 6d. and	1	0
*****Early Ruby.** Very prolific, is of dwarf habit, good shape, colour bright scarlet, flesh solid, succeeds well in the open air ... ... 6d. and	1	0
Mixed. All sorts	0	4

YELLOW OR GOLDEN VARIETIES.

	per pkt.—s	d.
*****Golden Sunrise.** First Class Certificate R.H.S. The fruit are large, round, smooth, and of a bright golden colour, sometimes slightly flushed with crimson; flavour excellent	1	0
*****Golden Eagle.** This is the most prolific variety that we know, and there is none to equal it in flavour 6d.&	1	0
*****Large Yellow Improved.** A fine variety ...	0	4

	per pkt.—s.	d.
Lemon Blush. A quite distinct and splendid variety, the nearest approach to a perfect Tomato yet raised. The skin and flesh are of a bright lemon yellow, with a rosy blush or crimson tint diffused over the surface opposite the stem. The seeds are few, and the flavour exceptionally good, and very superior to that of any other yellow variety	1	0

Those marked thus * are the best for open air cultivation.

Garden Turnips.

Cultivation.—A rich, deep, mellow soil, with a fair amount of moisture, is the most favourable for growing nice, sweet, crisp, and juicy Turnips, but any good soil, well dug and manured, will grow them well. For the first crop sow Daniels' Improved Snowball, and other sorts, on a warm border towards the end of March; sow again in April, and for succession of Summer and Autumn crops, make occasional sowings up to the end of July. For Winter use sow in August or early in September. Turnips, to be of fine quality in Summer, should be grown quick. Sow broadcast, or in drills one foot or eighteen inches apart, and thin out the plants to one foot apart. Keep free from weeds while the plants are small, and give an occasional hoeing, which will greatly facilitate their growth.

WHITE-FLESHED VARIETIES.

per ox.—s. d.

Daniels' Improved Snowball. A distinct and beautiful Turnip. Small, solid, sweet, crisp, and of remarkably quick growth; flesh snow-white and juicy; a variety that cannot be surpassed ... per pint 2s. 0 6

Chirk Castle (Black Stone). Splendid Winter variety ... 0 6

Early Green-top Stone ... per pint 2s. 0 4

Early Milan Red-top. First Class Certificate, Royal Horticultural Society 0 6

Early Munich. First Class Certificate, R.H.S. per pint 2s. 0 6

Early White Strap-leaved. One of the earliest grown ... 0 6

Early White Stone, or Dutch Six Weeks per pint 1s. 0 3

Jersey Navet. Fine variety from Channel Islands ... 0 6

New Scarlet Gem. This is quite distinct; in shape, round and flat; the colour is a rich glowing scarlet, top small and neat; flesh white and of excellent flavour ... 0 8

Paris Market or **Long White** ... per pint 2s. 0 6

Veitch's Red Globe. Useful variety ... „ 2s. 0 6

YELLOW-FLESHED VARIETIES.

per ox.—s. d.

Daniels' Golden Gem. A new and distinct variety. The top is small and neat; the roots are very handsome, with very fine tap-root. The skin and flesh are of a rich golden-yellow, and of excellent quality and flavour ... 0 8

Early Orange Jelly. Very early, fine for late sowing per pint 1s. 6d. 0 4

Golden Ball (selected). Fine stock 0 6

Orange Red-top. Handsome garden Turnip, red top and golden yellow flesh; first-class ... ... per pint 2s. 0 6

DANIELS' IMPROVED SNOWBALL.

Asparagus.

An abundance of fine Asparagus may be grown with less than half the expense usually incurred in making costly "beds," and will succeed admirably on most soils when planted in lines or clumps on the Kitchen Garden borders, or amongst dwarf-growing Fruits where the space will admit, a liberal cultivation being all that is required to ensure the best results. The roots are liable to injury if removed during severe weather in Winter. They are best planted when growth has commenced in Spring, and when they can be carefully taken up and packed so as to travel a long journey, if necessary, without injury. They should, however, in all cases be planted as quickly as possible after receiving them. We consider March and April the best months for planting in the open ground.

Connover's Colossal. Two and three years old

per 100, 5s. and 7s. 6d.

True Giant. Two and three years old ... per 100, 3s. 6d. and 5s.

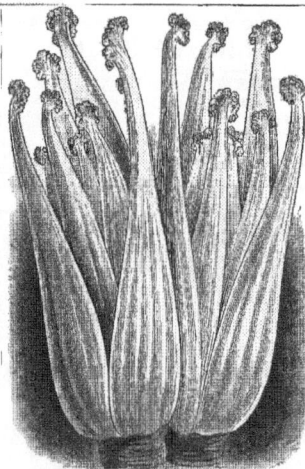

Sea Kale.

This valuable esculent is easily forced if once is taken only to apply heat gradually, as it will not succeed if placed in too high a temperature at starting. Place several crowns a few inches apart in large pots, and stand them in a temperature of about 45 degrees, with an inverted pot placed over each to exclude light and insure blanching, a mushroom house, pit, or cellar, will do well for this purpose. Sea Kale may also be easily forced in the open ground by covering it over with large specially made pots, and applying fermenting material. The heads should be cut when in about the condition shown in illustration, and taken off in the same way.

Strong planting roots per doz. 1s.; per 100, 7s. 6d.

Good strong roots, for forcing per doz. 1s. 6d.; per 100, 10s. 6d.

Extra strong roots, for forcing; very fine per doz. 2s.; per 100, 18s.

Seed ... per pint 2s.; per oz. 6d.

Rhubarb.

Paragon (Kershaw). The most wonderfully prolific kind known; as much as £240 has been made off a single acre for market purposes ... ... each 1s.; per doz. 10s. 6d.

The Queen. A fine new and very early Rhubarb. The stalk is of a beautiful bright red quite through, whilst it is also of a very superior and delicate flavour ... each 2s. 6d.

Strong Plants of the following, each 9d.; per doz. 7s. 6d.

Myatt's Linnæus.   Scarlet Defiance.   Royal Albert.   Myatt's Victoria.

MISCELLANEOUS PLANTS, ROOTS, AND SEEDS

ARTICHOKE—NEW WHITE MAMMOTH.

Artichokes.

NEW WHITE MAMMOTH. This is a pure white skin variety of the Jerusalem Artichoke. The tubers, which are more regularly formed than those of the old variety, are somewhat globular in shape, and of excellent quality. It will prove a great acquisition, and soon displace the present type for market purposes, and also tend to increase the popularity of this useful Winter vegetable.

Per 14 lb. 2s., 56 lb. 7s.

Jerusalem. Good sound tubers
per peck (14 lb.) 1s. 6d., bush. (56 lb.) 5s.
Globe. Strong plants .. .. per doz. 9s.

Cardoons.

per pkt.—s. d.
Smooth Solid. Cultivated for the mid-rib
of the leaf... ... . 0 6
Large Spanish 0 6

Potato Onions.

Bulbs. Fine select stock per lb. 6d.; 12 lb. 5s.

Sweet and Pot Herbs.

WE have a fine collection of these, including the following useful sorts:—

	per doz.—s. d.		per doz.—s. d.		per doz.—s. d.
Balm	... 4 0	Mint, Lamb	4 6	Sorrel, Giant French each 6d.	5 0
Chamomile ...	... 4 0	,, Pepper	4 0	Tarragon ... each 6d.	5 0
Horehound ...	... 4 0	Pennyroyal ... ... each 6d.	5 0	Thyme, Lemon ... each 6d.	5 0
Hyssop ...	... 4 0	Rosemary ... ... each 8d.	6 0	,, Common ...	4 0
Lavender ...	... each 6d. 5 0	Rue	4 0	Wormwood	4 6
Marjoram, Pot ...	... 4 0	Savory, Winter ...	4 0		

The most useful varieties assorted, our selection, per doz. 4s.; per 100, 25s.

Chives and Garlic.

per doz.—s. d.
Chives. Fine strong clumps 5 0
Garlic, Golden Yellow (Seed). Used in same way as Common Garlic; the taste is much milder; excellent seasoning for mutton, sauces, &c. per pkt. 1s. —
Garlic Bulbs 1s. per lb.

Shallots.

(Sow and Cultivate as Onions.)

Far superior to Onions for pickling.

Bulbs. Fine sound bulbs ... ... per lb. 1s.; 7 lb. 6s.
Seed. New Jersey; extra large ... per pkt. 6d. and 1s.

Fruit Seeds, &c.

		per pkt —s. d.
Currant. Fine mixed, from a good collection	...	6d. and 1 0
Gooseberry. Various kinds, mixed	...	6d. and 1 0
Grape. From fine hot-house varieties	...	6d. and 1 0
Strawberry. Mixed varieties, from a fine collection	...	6d. and 1 0
Raspberry. Various kinds, mixed	...	6d. and 1 0
Apple Pips. In great variety, mixed	...	6d. and 1 0
Pear Pips. In great variety, mixed	...	6d. and 1 0

Rhubarb (seed).

	per pkt.—s. d.
Mitchell's Royal Albert	.. 0 6
Myatt's Linnæus	.. 0 6
Myatt's Victoria	.. 0 6
Mixed	.. 0 4

CROSNES (Stachys tuberifera) OR CHINESE ARTICHOKE.

NEW VEGETABLE—CROSNES (Stachys tuberifera). First Class Certificate, Royal Horticultural Society.

This is a new tuberous vegetable introduced from Japan. It is a hardy plant, producing a large quantity of tubers in the same way as the Potato. Its culture is very easy, as it grows well in any good garden soil, and is readily propagated by means of its numerous tubers. They may be left in the ground until required for use, as the severest frost does not injure them in any way. The best and simplest way of cooking this vegetable is to boil in water with a pinch of salt, then fry them. They are of delicate flavour, somewhat resembling boiled Chestnuts.

Fine English grown tubers, per lb. 1/-; 3 lb. 2/6; 7 lb. 4/6.

DANIELS' HOME-GROWN FARM SEEDS
Have Produced some of the Heaviest Crops on Record.

DANIELS' INTERMEDIATE OR GATE-POST.

We have as usual given special care and attention to the selecting and improving of choice stocks of Swedish and other Turnips, and also of Mangolds, which for size, quality, and smallness of top are considered the finest in cultivation. These have been grown expressly for our retail trade, and may be relied upon as being true to name, of the best quality, and saved from selected roots.

Our new Farm Seed Catalogue, published March 1st, will be forwarded gratis and post free on application. Not bound by these prices after March 1st.

Mangolds.

Our stocks of these are all English grown, and can be fully relied on as really first-class. All growers of Mangolds should give our Seeds a trial, as we feel sure the result would be most satisfactory.

per lb.—s. d.

DANIELS' INTERMEDIATE or GATE-POST (*see illustration*). A grand stock; one of the finest Mangolds ever introduced, grows to a great size, with uniform crop of very heavy, handsome, and clean roots, with single tap-roots, and of the finest quality 0 9

DANIELS' IMPROVED MAMMOTH LONG RED. Our stock is very fine and can be highly recommended, having been selected by us for many years 0 8

DANIELS' GOLDEN TANKARD. Specially selected for its yellow or golden flesh, its richness in saccharine matter, and handsome shape 0 9

DANIELS' SELECTED LONG YELLOW. This we can highly recommend as a select stock of Long Yellow 0 8

DANIELS' GOLDEN GATE-POST. The colour and quality of the flesh are equal to the Golden Tankard, being of rich yellow and full of saccharine matter 0 9

DANIELS' CHAMPION ORANGE GLOBE. Our own unequalled stock, highly recommended for its neat top, fine clear skin, and tap root, a heavy cropper of splendid quality 0 9

DANIELS' GOLDEN GLOBE. One of the finest selected stocks introduced of late years 0 10

DANIELS' SELECTED RED GLOBE. Very heavy cropper ... 0 9

Yellow Globe. Good stock 0 8

Special low quotations for large quantities.

Swede Turnips.

DANIELS' NORFOLK GIANT PURPLE-TOP. The success this magnificent variety has met with during the past seasons show it to be superior to most sorts now in commerce, and we have no hesitation in recommending it to our customers. The roots are somewhat oval, and of a deep rich purple. It is a heavy cropper and excellent keeper. All farmers should give it a trial ... ... per lb. 10d.

DANIELS' IMPROVED PURPLE-TOP. A carefully selected and splendid variety ... ... „ 8d.

DANIELS' DEFIANCE GREEN-TOP. A first-class variety for grazing purposes; very hardy ... „ 8d.

Skirving's Purple-top. An old-esteemed variety ... ... „ 8d.

White-fleshed Turnips.

DANIELS' NORFOLK GREEN ROUND. Excellent for main crop, the hardiest of the Globe varieties per lb. 8d.

DANIELS' PURPLE-TOP MAMMOTH. An early Turnip, very heavy cropper, large and handsome roots „ 9d.

Bell or Decanter. Extra selected stock ... ... „ 8d.

Pomeranian or White Globe. Fine for early use ... ... „ 8d.

Stone or Stubble. For late sowing ... ... „ 9d.

Yellow-fleshed or Scotch Turnips.

GREEN-TOP YELLOW SCOTCH or BULLOCK. Grows a heavy crop, flesh solid and juicy, much relished by cattle per lb. 9d.

Purple-top Yellow Scotch or Bullock. A very superior variety, nearly equal to the Swede in quality ... „ 10d.

Carrots for Field Culture.

per lb. s. d.

DANIELS' GIANT YELLOW INTERMEDIATE. Our own stock; grown from selected roots, and the heaviest cropper we know of 2 6

GIANT WHITE BELGIAN. Very large and of fine quality 1 9

ALTRINCHAM IMPROVED. Excellent quality and a heavy cropper 2 6

JAMES' SCARLET or INTERMEDIATE. A heavy cropper, one of the best for shallow soils ... „ 3 0

Prices for larger quantities on application.

Cabbages for Field Culture.

Drill 4 lbs. per acre, or sow at rate of 2 lbs. per acre for Transplanting.

DANIELS' CHAMPION DRUMHEAD.

per lb.—s. d.

DANIELS' CHAMPION DRUMHEAD. A very fine selected variety, producing extraordinarily large heads ... per oz. 4d.   **4 0**

"I have great pleasure in letting you know how pleased I am to see such splendid Cabbages from your improved Champion Drumhead. I cut one weighing forty-two pounds, and have plenty over thirty pounds."—**Mr. J. MAYNARD**, Lochsport.

DANIELS' DWARF DRUMHEAD. Distinct from Robinson's Champion, being dwarf and much earlier, coming into use some weeks before the large Drumhead varieties   per oz. 4d.   **4 0**

Robinson's Drumhead   „   4d.   **3 0**

Thousand-headed Kale. Tall, branching, valuable for early sheep feed, extra stock, improved per oz. 4d.   **2 6**

KOHL RABI.

per lb.—s. d.

Early White Vienna. Best for garden per pkt. 4d. ; per oz. 1s.   **—**

Large Green   { For field culture, makes }   **2 0**
Large Purple   { excellent sheep feed. }   **4 6**

Cleaned Grass Seeds and Clovers,

FOR ALL SOILS AND SITUATIONS, FOR PASTURAGE, ENSILAGE, &c.

Samples and Special Quotations on Application.

GRASS MIXTURES.

per acre.—s. d.

1.—MIXTURES FOR ALTERNATE HUSBANDRY OR ROTATION CROPS.
Rye Grasses and Clovers for one year's lay ...   12s. 6d. to 17 6
Rye Grasses and Clovers for one year's lay, and one year's pasture ...   18s. to 25 0
Grasses and Clovers for one year's lay, and two or three years' pasture ...   20s. to 27 6

2.—MIXTURE FOR PERMANENT PASTURE OR MEADOW.
This comprises a selection of the Finest Perennial Clovers, Cocksfoot, Crested Dogstail, Fescues, Golden Oat Grass, Meadow Foxtail, Poas, Rye Grasses (Italian and Perennial), Sweet Vernal, Timothy, &c. ...   25s. to 35 0

3.—MIXTURE FOR PERMANENT PASTURES IN PARKS, ORNAMENTAL GROUNDS, CEMETERIES, &c.
Made up of Perennial Clovers, Crested Dogstail, Fescues, Golden Oat Grass, Meadow Foxtail, Poas, Evergreen Perennial Rye Grass, Sweet Vernal, &c. ...   25s. to 35 0

4.—RENOVATING GRASSES AND CLOVERS. For improving old or worn-out pastures, mending patches, &c.
Sow 10 to 12 lbs. per acre ...   per bush. 20s. ; per lb. 1s.   **—**

All orders should be accompanied with a description of the nature of the land to be laid down, and the measurement in statute acres.

RYE GRASSES, CLOVERS, &c.

Finest Qualities Selected, and Cleaned by the best Machinery.
Prices subject to the variation of the Market.

per bush.—s. d.

Evergreen Perennial or Devon Eaver   6s. 0d. to 6 6
Italian (*Lolium Italicum*) English ...   4s. 6d. to 6 0
  „   „   Foreign ...   6s. 0d. to 7 6
Perennial (*Lolium perenne*) Scotch ...   5s. 0d. to 6 6
  „   (Pacey's)   ...   ...   4s. 6d. to 6 0
Alsyke or Hybrid (*Trifolium hybridum*)
   per lb. 9d. to 1s. ; 45s. to 60 0
Giant Cow Grass or Perennial Red (*T. perenne*)
   per lb. 9d. to 1s. ; 45s. to 60 0
Red or Broad-leaved (*T. pratense*)
   per lb. 7d. to 9d. ; 35s. to 50 0
Lucerne. Succeeds well on light and chalky soils ; coming into use very early ; requires to be hoed freely, and may be out several times in one season ... per lb. 1s.   **—**

per bush.—s.

White or Dutch (*T. repens*) per lb. 10d. to 1s. ; 55s. to 70 0
Yellow or Trefoil (*Medicago lupulina*)
   per lb. 5d. ; 20s. to 25 0
Yellow or Red Suckling (*T. minus filiforme*)
   per lb. 1s.   **—**
Clover Mixed for Alternate Husbandry
   per lb. 1s. ; 45s. to 65 0
Crimson Clover (*Trifolium incarnatum*) market price   **—**
Perennial Clovers in Mixture   per lb. 1s. 60 0
Sainfoin, Giant. Sow four bushels per acre ; specially adapted for growing on light, dry, chalky soils
   market price   **—**
Sainfoin, Common   ...   „   **—**
Spring Tares or Vetches   „   **—**

GRAND NEW POTATO,
DANIELS' DUKE OF YORK.

DANIELS' DUKE OF YORK. *(From a Photograph.)*

A superb early dwarf-growing variety, producing large, smooth, oval-shaped, handsome tubers. It is quite distinct in appearance, of splendid cooking quality, and by far the most prolific kind with which we are acquainted. First-class exhibition sort, and one that will be in great demand amongst Potato growers. Price, 14 lb. 2s. 6d., 56 lb. 8s. 6d., cwt. 15s.

PRICE PER TON ON APPLICATION.

EVIDENCE OF QUALITY.

"After making a trial of twenty varieties of Potatoes this summer, I am pleased to report most favourably of the following varieties obtained from you. Daniels' Reliable proved a great cropper, and an excellent table variety; and one of the best show Potatoes I have grown; Daniels' Duke of York is a first-rate all round Potato: and the best way of showing my appreciation of the good qualities of these Potatoes is to say that, with the exception of a few trial dishes, I am preserving all of them for seed." W. STANDRING, Esq., F.A.I., Epworth.

"From the stone of Duke of York Potatoes I had of you last year I got 410 lbs. of fine Potatoes."—Mr. J. JONES, Barry Dock.

"I have pleasure to inform you that I am perfectly satisfied with your new Potato, the Duke of York. From the 7 lbs. I had from you in the Spring I raised 196 lbs. Nine tubers took First Prize; I also took First Prize at Harpenden for nine tubers, which weighed 8 lbs. 14 ozs.; they are the finest crop I have ever raised."—Mr. G. W. KENTISH, Redmond.

SEED POTATOES.

For many years past we have devoted great attention to the cultivation and selection of our choice stocks of Seed Potatoes, and have been fortunate in introducing to the public several fine varieties of our own raising that have attained to great popularity. By adopting this system, and by adding to our collection the finest varieties raised by other growers, we are enabled to offer a really first-class selection of the best kinds, and being large growers, we are in a position to offer to large buyers choice Seed Potatoes, true to name and stock, at very moderate prices.

PARCEL POST.—Six pounds of tubers can be sent by Parcel Post to any address in the Kingdom for 1s., and ten pounds for 1s. 6d. *extra for postage*, in addition to the cost of the Potatoes.

POTATO BAGS.—Good strong Bags can be supplied at 4d. each, to hold one bushel; 6d. each, to hold 1 cwt.; 1s. each, to hold 1½ cwt.

The amount for Bags should be added to remittance when ordering.

GRAND NEW POTATO.
DANIELS' SPECIAL.

Awarded a First Class Certificate by the Royal Horticultural Society, Chiswick, 25th September, 1894.

DANIELS' SPECIAL.

This new seedling has been selected for extraordinary cropping, combined with its superb cooking qualities. It is a handsome White Round maincrop variety, with eyes even with the surface, consequently there will be no waste in the peeling, and when cooked, like balls of flour. We have grown this sort at the rate of twelve tons per acre on medium soil, thus proving its great productiveness. As an exhibition variety it is one of the handsomest of the White Rounds. It was grown and tested at the Royal Horticultural Society's Gardens, Chiswick, during the past season, and in consideration of its productiveness and splendid cooking qualities was awarded a First Class Certificate.

Price, 14 lb. 2s. 6d., 56 lb. 8s. 6d., per cwt. 15s.

PRICE PER TON ON APPLICATION.

EVIDENCE OF QUALITY.

"I am glad to inform you that out of the 7 lbs. of Daniels' Special Potatoes I have raised 136 lbs."—**Mr. J. BURGE**, Carhampton.

"I was well pleased with the 7 lbs. of Daniels' Special Potatoes, from which I gathered 11¼ stones."—**Mr. J. SAYNER**, Grimsby.

"5½ lbs. Special Potatoes, set in a single row of 18 yards long, produced 17 sts. 10 lbs. of sound tubers."—**Mr. BUGBY**, Dunston.

"Your Seeds gave me the utmost satisfaction; last year I took several Prizes with them. Your Duke of York and Special Potatoes are wonderful croppers; although I had the Special cut down to the ground with frost last Spring, when I lifted them I found as many as twenty-two tubers at one root."—**Mr. F. J. ALLEN**, Nuneaton.

"I must say a word of praise about the Potatoes, Daniels' Special, that I had last year. They were the best crop of Potatoes I had in all my life."—**Mr. E. ROBERTS**, Clocwyn Brith.

SEED POTATOES.

FIRST EARLY VARIETIES.

DANIELS' EARLIEST WHITE KIDNEY.

Remarkable for its Earliness, Handsome Form, and Excellent Cooking Qualities.

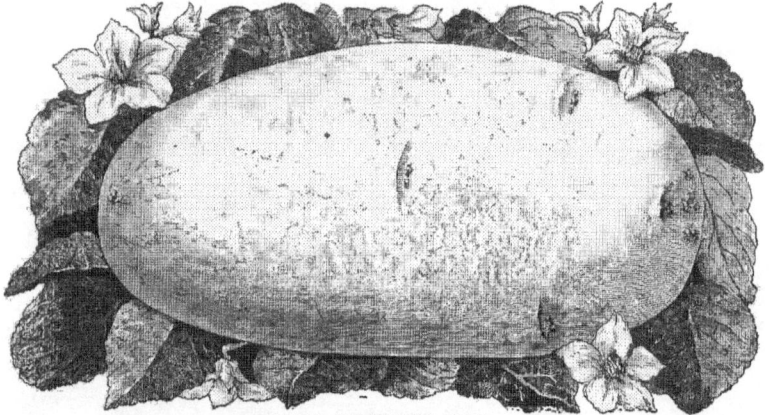

DANIELS' EARLIEST WHITE KIDNEY.

DANIELS' EARLIEST WHITE KIDNEY. This new seedling Potato is one of the earliest ever sent out, coming in a fortnight before the Ashleaf varieties. The tubers, which are kidney-shaped, are of medium size, eyes few and shallow, cooks well, and is a good cropper. We can recommend it to all requiring an early Potato, either for forcing or for the open ground.

Price, 14 lb. 4s., 56 lb. 14s.

		per 14 lb. s. d.	per 56 lb. s. d.
DANIELS' DEFIANCE ASHLEAF. The best and earliest kind, cooks well, and of fine flavour; very productive ... ... per cwt. 24s.		4 0	14 0
Daniels' Early Primrose. A first early Kidney, coming in at same time as Early Ashleaf, but is more prolific; the tubers are of the most excellent quality and flavour, and when cooked the flesh is beautifully mealy and of a delicate primrose colour, hence its name. From its handsome shape it is a most desirable exhibition kind		3 0	10 6
Early Ashleaf Kidney. Useful variety ... ... per cwt. 15s.		2 6	8 6
Kentish or **Mona's Pride Ashleaf.** Small foliage, heavy cropper ... per cwt. 15s.		2 6	8 6
Myatt's Ashleaf. A fine old variety ... ... per cwt. 15s.		2 6	8 6
Old Ashleaf (true). The finest-flavoured first early known (scarce)		4 0	14 0
Rivers' Royal Ashleaf. Very productive ... ... per cwt. 15s.		2 6	8 6
EARLY PURITAN. Awarded First Class Certificate, Royal Horticultural Society. An early variety of great excellence. A good cropper, and of first-class table quality. The tubers can be used when half grown, as even then they are wonderfully dry and of fine flavour. Its dwarf habit of growth, about fifteen inches high, renders it very suitable for all gardens, and on account of its fine cropping qualities it is now one of the chief market varieties.			
Price per Ton on application. per cwt. 14s.		2 6	8 6

EVIDENCE OF QUALITY.

NEW POTATO, DANIELS' EARLY QUEEN.

This splendid variety sent out by us last year has amply sustained the high recommendation we then gave it. It is a grand early variety of extra fine quality and enormous productiveness. It is kidney shaped, somewhat inclined to oblong; the eyes few and almost even with the surface. The skin is white, suffused with a delicate shading of pink. The flesh, which is very fine grained, is beautifully white and mealy when cooked, and of superior flavour.

The tubers are of handsome appearance, and very uniform in size, growing compactly round the haulm, which is only fifteen inches in height. It is a fine variety for exhibition, and has this season again yielded a heavy crop of fine tubers.

See also Coloured Plate.

DANIELS' EARLY QUEEN. Price, per lb. 6d., 7 lb. 2s. 6d., 14 lb. 4s. 6d., 56 lb. 16s.

EVIDENCE OF QUALITY.

"I feel I cannot refrain from testifying to the excellence of your Early Queen Potato, both as to quality and quantity as well as great richness of flavour. Out of the 1 lb. of Seed I had more than a Half Bushel of Potatoes, and this, considering the difficult season, proclaims it at once a most prolific cropper."—**Mr. H. GARD**, Wroxall.

"From the 7 lbs. of your Early Queen Potatoes I had from you last Spring I raised 156 lbs. of good Potatoes of very good quality."—**Mr. E. BASFORD**, Kingsbury.

FIRST EARLY VARIETIES *(continued)*.

	per 14 lb. s. d.	per 56 lb. s. d.
EARLY WHITE HEBRON. This grand Potato possesses all the well-known quality of the Beauty of Hebron, and has in addition a clear white skin, which renders it more valuable for market purposes. It is of excellent quality when cooked, and is enormously productive. We can thoroughly recommend this variety ... per cwt. 14s.	2 6	8 6
Daniels' "Harbinger." A first early White Round variety of great excellence; first-class for earliest crop, in frames or out of doors. Height one foot ... ... per cwt. 18s. 6d.	3 0	10 6
Daniels' First Early. A variety of the Early Rose type, but ripening ten days earlier than that well-known kind ... ... per cwt. 15s.	2 6	8 6
Daniels' Early Crimson Flourball. This is the earliest Red Round Potato yet introduced, and will be found most valuable for early exhibitions. The tubers are round in form, clustering compactly about the stems, which never grow more than a foot in height. The skin is of a beautiful rosy crimson colour, the eyes shallow, the flesh is beautifully white, dry, mealy, and fine-flavoured. At the Warminster trial Grounds of the Wiltshire County Council, this variety produced the exceptional crop of over sixteen tons per acre ... ... per cwt. 18s. 6d.	3 0	10 6
The Thorburn. A very early Coloured Kidney of the White Elephant type, and is said to be the best of all the early kinds, on account of its heavy cropping and good cooking qualities per cwt. 14s.	2 6	8 6
Beauty of Hebron. A well-known excellent variety ... ... per cwt. 14s.	2 0	7 6
Sharpe's Victor. Tubers round, somewhat inclined to oblong, very early and prolific, skin white; a most excellent variety ... ... per cwt. 15s.	2 6	8 6
Early White Beauty. Early White Kidney of handsome shape and clear white skin, is remarkably prolific, and of excellent table quality, resists the disease well. Its fine appearance makes it a most desirable exhibition variety ... ... per cwt. 15s.	2 6	8 6
Early Rose. A well-known variety. Fine for early use on light soils ... per cwt. 14s.	2 0	7 6
Mayflower. Early White Kidney, good quality; First Class Certificate, R.H.S. ...	3 0	10 6

EVIDENCE OF QUALITY.

"I am very pleased with the produce of your Seeds this year, especially Early Crimson Flourball and Princess May Potatoes."—Mr. J. H. POWELL, Carmarthen.

"The Duke of York Potatoes were very good, also Early Puritan. I got from one root nineteen sound Potatoes weighing 11 lbs.; and Table King turned out very good. All the Seeds were excellent."—Mr. G. H. NEWTON, Matlock.

SEED POTATOES.
DANIELS' TABLE KING.
AN EXCEEDINGLY FINE VARIETY OF EXTRAORDINARILY GOOD COOKING QUALITY.

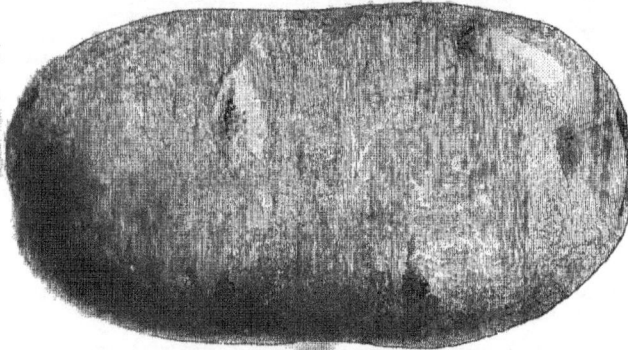

"I took First Prize at Diss, last week with your Table King Potato, four years I have taken First Prize with it."—Mr. R. DIXON, Wortham.

"Table King, I think, is rightly named, as it is just the sort to grow for table use. It produced a good crop of even-shaped tubers, and has successfully resisted disease."—Mr. H. JONES, The Gardens, Carrow House, Norwich.

DANIELS' TABLE KING.

DANIELS' TABLE KING. This remarkably handsome Potato has now been some time before the public. It is a second early, the tubers are somewhat kidney-shaped, but many are nearly round. They are mealy when cooked and of a most excellent flavour. The eyes are few and quite even with the surface. Its dwarf habit (one foot) renders it a most desirable sort for all gardens, and its handsome appearance, combined with its great productiveness, makes it a useful market variety. For exhibition it is first-class.   Price, 14 lbs. 2s. 6d., 56 lbs. 8s. 6d., cwt. 15s.

PRICE PER TON ON APPLICATION.

EVIDENCE OF QUALITY.

A Correspondent writes:—"**Daniels' Table King.** So far I must pronounce this variety the best of all. It is the most floury Potato I have seen in Ireland, and what is of equal importance it is of first-rate flavour, very prolific. In size and shape a gem for the exhibition table, whilst not a diseased tuber was found when lifting them.'—From *JOURNAL OF HORTICULTURE.*

SECOND EARLY AND MAINCROP.

	per 14 lb. s. d.	per 56 lb. s. d.
"THE DANIELS." This grand Potato is a cross between the Magnum Bonum and the White Elephant, combining the excellent qualities of both; but it more resembles the White Elephant in shape, size, and enormous productiveness, with the advantage of having a pure white skin. Its cooking qualities are all that can be desired, whilst the great demand for this variety shows that it is appreciated by the public ... ... per cwt. 14s.	2 6	8 6
DANIELS' REMARKABLE. This variety was raised by us some few years since, and after repeated trials has proved itself a first-class cropping variety, a good keeper, and of splendid table quality. The tubers are of an oblong round shape, white, large, and handsome; a fine exhibition variety ... ... per cwt. 15s.	2 6	8 6
Daniels' Reliable. This is a handsome White Kidney of extra cooking qualities and most excellent cropper; its eyes are few and quite even with the surface. It is a second early, and a fine exhibition kind ... per cwt. 15s.	2 6	8 6
Daniels' Red Robin Kidney. A very handsome exhibition Potato. The tubers are medium size, and of a rich crimson colour. The flesh is of a bright golden yellow; dry, mealy, and of excellent flavour when cooked. It is also a most abundant cropper, and a good disease-resister ... ... per 7 lb. 1s. 9d.	3 0	—
Daniels' Red Elephant. This is of the same robust constitution as the White Elephant, being of similar shape and habit, and an enormous cropper, like that variety; will be found invaluable for light sandy soil, producing an abundant crop of fine quality tubers where many other best kinds would fail ... ... per cwt. 15s.	2 6	8 6
Daniels' White Elephant. The original and true stock ... ... per cwt. 14s.	2 0	7 6
Adirondack. Abundant cropper, late keeper, and of finest quality; Red Round ... ... per cwt. 15s.	2 6	8 6
Late Rose. A well-known variety of fine quality and productiveness ... ... per cwt. 15s.	2 6	8 6
Cole's Favourite. White Kidney, good cropper, flesh white and floury when cooked, very handsome, clear skin; suitable for exhibition ... ... per cwt. 15s.	2 6	8 6
Crawley Prizetaker (new). A cross between International Kidney and Early Regent. It is a second early variety, of fine keeping qualities, a heavy cropper, and of good table quality. First Class Certificate, Royal Horticultural Society	3 0	—
President. A large, handsome White Kidney, heavy cropper, fine quality; useful for exhibition ... per cwt. 15s.	3 0	10 6
Windsor Castle. An excellent variety, tubers oblong or pebble-shaped, skin white, very heavy cropper, flesh firm, white, and of splendid quality. First Class Certificate, Royal Horticultural Society ... ... per cwt. 15s.	2 6	8 6
DANIELS' MARKET FAVOURITE. A fine new maincrop variety, in shape the tubers are somewhat oblong. The skin and flesh are white, the latter beautifully white and floury when cooked; it is a fairly vigorous grower, and an abundant cropper, the produce being very even in size with very few small ones	3 0	10 6

SEED POTATOES—MAIN AND LATE CROP.

DANIELS' UNIVERSAL.

The best cooking White Round Potato in cultivation.

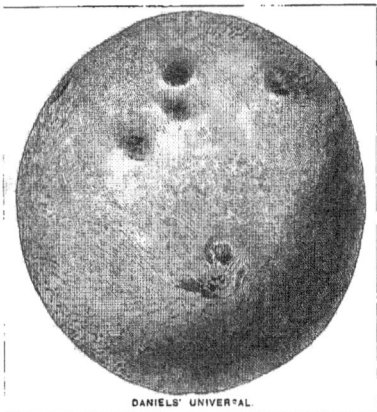

DANIELS' UNIVERSAL.

DANIELS' UNIVERSAL. A Round White variety, of the size and shape of a cricket ball; eyes few and shallow, skin slightly netted, flesh white and floury when cooked. A first-rate cropping variety, and an excellent keeper

per 14 lb. 2s, 6d., 56 lb. 8s. 6d., cwt. 15s.

Price per Ton on application.

DANIELS' FUTURE FAME. A grand Seedling of the Magnum Bonum type, and, like that variety, a disease-resister, but is at least a fortnight earlier, and a heavy cropper, and when cooked is white, dry, and mealy, and of faultless flavour. We can strongly recommend this variety to all growers for market   per 14 lb. 2s. 6d., 56 lb. 8s. 6d., cwt. 15s.

	per 14 lb.		per 56 lb.	
	s.	d.	s.	d.
SNOWDROP. Tubers well formed, eyes shallow, skin clear, and flesh beautifully white and mealy when cooked: an abundant cropper, and very distinct. First Class Certificate, R.H.S. per cwt. 14s.	2	6	8	6
Price per Ton on application.				
DANIELS' WHITE PERFECTION. This is one of the handsomest White Round Potatoes ever raised; the tubers are large, and the eyes few and shallow. Very productive, and of most excellent quality for table per cwt. 15s.	2	6	8	6
DANIELS' DREADNOUGHT. Disease-resisting, main-crop variety. This magnificent Potato somewhat resembles the Magnum Bonum, but far excels that variety in vigour of constitution and enormous productiveness; handsome, and of excellent table quality .. per cwt. 14s.	2	6	8	9
DANIELS' EMPEROR FREDERICK. A fine exhibition Potato. The tubers are large handsome kidney-shaped; skin a rich purple, mottled with crimson ... per 7 lb. 9d.	3	0		—
DANIELS' INDIAN PRINCE. This is a handsome Black Kidney, long, flat, and smooth. Although the colour is quite black, it is only skin deep, the tubers being beautifully white and floury when cooked ... per 7 lb. 2s.	3	6		—
DANIELS' NORFOLK BLACKBIRD. A great novelty. The tubers are long handsome kidney-shaped; the eyes few and quite even with the surface; the skin is smooth and glossy, and almost jet black. The flesh which partakes largely of the colour of the skin, is dry and mealy when cooked. Will be found invaluable to give variety to an exhibition collection ... per 1 lb. 6d., 7 lb. 2s. 6d.	4	6		—
DANIELS' KING KIDNEY. A remarkably robust White Kidney; producing a very heavy crop of handsome, marketable tubers, of superior cooking quality. It is the best disease-resister that we know of, and a first-class kind for poor soils; and fine for exhibition ... per cwt. 15s.	2	6	8	6
DANIELS' ROYAL NORFOLK RUSSET. Tubers medium size and roughly netted, eyes few and shallow, flesh white, fine grained, boils like a ball of flour, and of the finest flavour. Since sending this variety out we find it has been named by our Scotch friends "The Village Blacksmith" ...	3	0	10	6
DANIELS' PRINCESS MAY. Handsome Red Kidney, seedling from Edgcote Purple and Peerless Rose. The tubers are flat kidney shape, eyes shallow, the skin being of a bright glossy red ... per 7 lb. 2s.	3	6		—
Imperator. White Round. A most excellent variety, and is far superior to the Champion ... per cwt. 14s.	2	0	7	6
LILLIE LANGTRY (new). First Class Certificate, Royal Horticultural Society. A good variety of handsome appearance, in shape it is nearly round, but sometimes the tubers are oblong. The skin is white, and marked with pink about the eyes. It is a good cropper, and a useful sort for exhibition purposes ... per 7 lbs. 1s. 9d.	3	0		—
Magnum Bonum. A well-known White Kidney; first-class, main-crop variety ... per cwt. 14s.	2	0	7	6
Peerless Rose. A flat, smooth, very handsome kidney-shaped Potato; skin of a delicate pink colour, eyes even with the surface; fine quality, and excellent for exhibition ...	3	0	10	6
Pink Perfection. A handsome Round Potato, skin delicate pink, good quality; first-class for exhibition ...	3	0	10	6
Reading Giant. A late White Kidney of robust constitution, heavy cropper; fine table quality... per cwt. 14s.	2	6	8	6
Reading Russet. Red Round variety, good quality; fine for exhibition ...	3	0	10	6
Satisfaction. In shape it is almost round, or rather pebble-shaped, skin white, eyes upon the surface; a very heavy cropper, and of fine cooking quality ... per cwt. 15s.	2	6	8	6
Sirius (new). A White Round variety of enormous productiveness and good table quality ...	3	0	10	6
The Bruce. A Scotch variety; late White Kidney, robust grower, of good quality, and very prolific ... per cwt. 14s.	2	6	8	6
Vicar of Laleham. Skin of a rich dark purple, shape round, good cropper, cooks well, and fine for exhibition ...	3	0	10	6

EVIDENCE OF QUALITY.

"From the 7 lbs of **Dreadnought Potatoes** I had from you last year I lifted 214 lbs., and not one diseased amongst them."—Mr. T. HART, Townhope.

"I am very pleased to say that I have tested your **Future Fame** Potatoes, and was very much pleased with them. They are immense croppers, and of splendid table quality, and long keepers."—Mr. F. RIPLEY, Mirfield.

"I exhibited your **Universal Potato** at our Show, and out of twenty competitors was awarded First Prize. From 7 lbs. of this variety I raised 168 lbs., and from 7 lbs. of Early Puritan I raised 218 lbs."—Mr. J. F. GATE, Berkhampstead.

"I must say the **Universal** are all that can be desired, when cooked they are of a beautiful white floury nature."—Mr. A. BOOTY, Bottisham.

EFFICIENT, ODOURLESS, ECONOMICAL.

Sold in Packages, with complete Directions for Use, Postal Boxes, ¼-lb. 1s., 2½-lb. 2s. 3d., 6-lb. 4s. 6d., Post or Carriage Free, at prices quoted.

In Boxes, not Carriage Free, but can be enclosed in general order, without extra expense of carriage, 1-lb. 1s., 2-lb. 1s. 8d., 4-lb. 3s., 7-lb. 4s. 6d., 14-lb. 7s., 28-lb. 12s. 6d. Much cheaper by the cwt. Prices on application.

This preparation is purely and simply a Manure in a highly concentrated form, without any admixture of other ingredients to make up bulk, and will be found more CLEANLY, because it is entirely without smell, more EFFICACIOUS, because it is easily assimilated by all kinds of vegetable growths, and more ECONOMICAL, because it is cheaper in comparison with other Manures, where quantity is preferred to quality.

GARDEN STICKS AND LABELS.
FLOWER STICKS.

Unpainted Deal. In bundles. 1-ft., 9d. per 100; 1½-ft, 1s. 3d. per 100; 2-ft, 1s. 6d. per 100; 2½-ft., 2s. per 100; 3-ft., 2s. 6d. per 100; 3½-ft., 3s. per 100; 4-ft., 3s. 6d. per 100.

Bamboo Canes. 3-ft. 10-in., 2s. 6d., 3s., and 4s. per 100; 4½-ft. long, 8d. per doz.; 4s. 6d. per 100; 5-ft. long (medium), 1s. per doz., 7s. 6d. per 100; 5-ft. long (thick), 1s. 3d. per doz., 10s. per 100; 7-ft. long, 2s. per doz., 14s. per 100.

Bamboo Tips. 6 to 10 ft. long (suitable for forming arches, &c., the tips cut off making splendid supports for Carnations, &c.), 1s. per doz.

Dahlia Stakes (stout, square, painted green). 2-ft., 1s per doz.; 2½-ft., 1s. 3d. per doz.; 3-ft., 1s. 6d. per doz.; 3½-ft., 1s 9d. per doz.; 4-ft., 2s. per doz.; 4½-ft., 2s. 6d. per doz.; 5-ft., 2s. 9d. per doz.; 5½-ft., 3s. per doz.; 6-ft., 3s. 3d. per doz.

WOOD LABELS.

Best English Make, Painted. In bundles of 100, 4-in., 7d.; 5-in., 9d.; 6-in., 10d.; 7-in., 1s.; 8-in., 1s. 3d.; 9-in., 1s. 6d.

Plain. 4-in., 5d.; 5-in., 6d.; 6-in., 8d.; 7-in., 10d.; 8-in., 1s.; 9-in., 1s. 3d. 12-in., 2s. per 100.

TYING AND GRAFTING MATERIALS.

BOUQUET WIRE. In packets of 7-in. lengths, 1s. 3d. to 2s. per lb. Fine, for binding, ¼ lb. reels, 9d. each. For Camellias, in 7-in. lengths, 1s. 6d. per lb. Stout, for stems, in 7-in. lengths, 1s. to 1s. 6d. per lb.

FLORAL CEMENT OR GUM. For fixing the petals of Flowers. 1s. and 2s per bottle.

GRAFTING WAX. 1s. and 2s. per tin.

RAFFIA GRASS. The best material for Tying. 6d. per packet; 1s. 6d. per lb.

TAR TWINE. In balls, thick or thin. ½-lb. 9d., per lb. 1s. 3d.

Superior Milltrack Mushroom Spawn.

This illustration (from a photograph) represents a group of Mushrooms in all stages of growth (half natural size), placed upon a brick of the Spawn.

MUSHROOMS ALL THE YEAR ROUND

MAY BE HAD BY USING

DANIELS' MILLTRACK SPAWN.

COMPLETE INSTRUCTIONS FOR CULTIVATION WILL BE SENT WITH EVERY ORDER.

In Bricks, each 6d., 4 bricks 1s. 6d., 16 bricks or one bushel 5s.

EVIDENCE OF SUPERIOR QUALITY.

"The **Mushroom Spawn** I had from you a short time since has done remarkably well. I have a bed that is quite covered with Mushrooms from one end to the other; it is quite a sight worth seeing as far as a Mushroom bed is concerned."—**Mr. G. MARSHALL**, Ipswich.

"Mr. Beane begs to inform Messrs. Daniels Bros. that the **Mushroom Spawn** which he purchased of them in the Spring was in every way successful, producing a very large crop of good Mushrooms."—**L. BEANE, Esq.**, Nentishead.

"My **Mushrooms** from your Spawn last year have been and are quite a success."—**Sergt. A. KING**, Kingston-on-Thames.

FRENCH MUSHROOM SPAWN.

In Boxes, 2 lbs. 2s. 9d., 3 lbs. 4s., 4 lbs. 5s. 4d., 6 lbs. 8s. (if ordered to be sent per parcel post 3d. per lb. extra).

These Boxes are the sizes generally required by Mushroom growers, and can be sent out just as received, thus preserving the Spawn from breaking.

This Spawn is of very fine quality, and is in a more concentrated form than the English make.

SYRINGES.

SYRINGES. Bonton & Stone's best quality, fitted with Cooper's Patent Protector, and Stone's Patent Adjustable Plunger. No. 810G, 14 by 1, 5/-; No. 5, 14 by 1, 7/G; No. 5, 18 by 1¼, 10/G; No. 4, 16 by 1¼, 12/G; No. 3, 18 by 1¼ (Ball Valve), 18/G; No. 3, 20 by 1¼ (Ball Valve), 21/-.

RELIABLE
COMPOUND.

DANIELS' TOBACCO PAPER

Price in 2-lb. Packets, 3s.

Every packet is accompanied with full instructions for use.

RELIABLE
COMPOUND.

AFTER repeated trials at our Nurseries, and by some of the most eminent horticulturists, we have much pleasure in recommending this Tobacco Paper as the very best ever offered for fumigating purposes. This quality has been specially prepared for our retail trade, and will be found cheap, perfectly safe, and thoroughly effective. It is self-consuming, and will consequently be found of little trouble to use, and if kept in a cool, dry place, will retain its strength and soundness for years.

TOBACCO PAPER (for ordinary use), 1s. per lb.

SUNDRY GARDEN REQUISITES.

APHICIDES, or Spray Diffusers (Hughes'). A most useful and ingenious invention for distributing insecticides. Fitted with mouthpiece, and cork attached for mouth of bottle. Useful also as a means of sprinkling flowers when cut. 1s. 6d. each. Improved barrel-shaped. 1s. 3d. each.

APHIS BRUSHES. With Lacquered Brass Handles. 2s. each.

BASKETS (Truck). Made of strong wood, and are indispensable to every garden. No. 2, 11½-in. by 6-in., 1s.; No. 3, 13½-in. by 7½-in., 1s. 3d.; No. 4, 15-in. by 8½-in., 1s. 6d.; No. 5, 17¼-in. by 9¼-in., 1s. 9d.; No. 6, 20½-in. by 10½-in., 2s. 3d.; No. 7, 23-in. by 12-in., 2s. 6d.; No. 8, 26-in. by 14-in., 3s.; No. 9, 28-in. by 15-in., 3s. 6d.

BROOMS, BIRCH. 4d. each; 3s. 6d. per doz.

GARDENERS' APRONS. In Shaloon, best make. 4s. 6d., 4s. 9d., and 5s. each. Prices are governed by length and width.

GISHURSTINE. Is a perfect dubbing, invaluable as a means of rendering boots absolutely waterproof. 6d. and 1s. per tin.

LAYER PEGS (Zinc). In boxes of 100. 1s. each.

METALLIC GARDEN WIRE. For tying Roses and suspending labels, from No. 12 (thick) to No. 20 (thin). 1s. 6d. to 2s. per lb.

    ,,   **INK.** Produces indelible black writing. 6d. and 1s. per bottle.

    ,,   **LABELS.** Suitable for Gardens, Conservatories, Greenhouses, Forneries, Flower Pots, &c. From 2s. to 5s. per 100.

NAIL BAGS. Leather, best quality. 6s. each.

PENCILS, Wolff's Garden. 3d. each. New Economic ditto, 4d. each. Refills, 6d. per box.

STYPTIC. For preventing bleeding in Vines. 2s. 6d. per bottle.

TANNED NETTING (for protecting Fruit Trees, &c.). 1, 2, 3, and 4 yards wide. 1d. per square yard.

TOBACCO POWDER DISTRIBUTORS (India-rubber with brass nozzle), 2s. 6d. each; wood nozzle, 1s. 3d.

VERBENA PINS (Galvanized Wire). For pegging down Verbenas, &c. Per box of one gross (three inches long), 1s.

VIRGIN CORK. Quarter-cwt. 6s.; half-cwt. 11s.; per cwt. 20s. (Carriage Paid on 1-cwt. and upwards).

WALL NAILS. 3d. per lb.; 2s. 6d. per stone.

    ,,   New French, 4d. per lb.; 3s. per stone.

    ,,   **CHANDLER'S PATENT.** A useful invention; Shreds not required. Boxes of 100, 1¼ inch, 1s. 9d.

GARDENING GLOVES.

GENTLEMEN'S GARDENING GLOVES. Strong leather, for hedging. 1s. 6d. per pair.

  1st quality Leather. A very neat glove, and soft to the hand. 2s. 6d. per pair.

  Inseam Tan. Good cheap glove, soft and pliable. 1s. 3d. per pair.

  Oxford Tan. In several qualities; one of the strongest and most serviceable gloves made. 1s. 6d., 1s. 9d., 2s., and 2s. 3d. per pair.

  Drummond's. A one-button glove by one of the best makers, and in great demand. 1s. 6d., 1s. 9d., 2s., and 2s. 3d. per pair.

  Harvest Tan. Good strong make. 1s. 4d. per pair.

  Wash Leather. Suitable for light work generally, or for housemaids. 1s. and 1s. 6d. per pair.

LADIES' GARDENING GLOVES. Long Tan, best material, 1s. 4d. per pair.

  Leather Gauntlet. A really stylish and at the same time useful glove for more than one purpose. 2s. 6d. per pair.

THERMOMETERS AND BAROMETERS.

THERMOMETERS. Boxwood (Spirit or Mercury), 9d., 1s., 1s. 6d., and 2s. 6d. each.

  Boxwood, with storm glass, 2s. 6d. and 3s. 6d. each.

  Cast metal scales; for the garden, 3s. 6d. each. Ditto (cheaper make), plain zinc, 8-inch, 2s. each.

  Maximum and minimum registering; boxwood scales, tin japanned case. 4s. and 5s. 6d. each.

    ,, ,, ,, celluloid scales, tin japanned case (very durable, and easily kept clean). 6s. 6d. each.

    ,, ,, ,, (boxwood), without case. 3s. 6d. each.

  The same as the preceding, with bright zinc scales; in handsome case, japanned white. 5s. and 7s. 6d. each.

  Porcelain (Mercury), bevelled edge, first quality. 6s. 6d. and 6s. 6d. each.

  For hotbeds; box scales. 12 in., 5s. 6d.; 18 in., 10s.; 24 in., 12s. 6d. A few very handsome ones at 15s., 20s., and 25s. each.

BAROMETERS. Horticultural, very neat and accurate, clock face, 15s.

    ,, Very handsome, 17s. 6d.

JADOO FIBRE.
The new material for Plants, Bulbs, &c.

This new material is recommended very highly as a substitute for soil, especially where there is a difficulty in procuring the latter. It is suitable for Ferns, and all kinds of Stove and Greenhouse Plants, Fruits, &c.; and is especially good for filling vases and hanging baskets as it retains its moisture longer than ordinary soil, besides being much lighter.

Price—Peck bag, 1s.; bushel bag, 3s. 6d.; three bushel sack, 8s. Special rates for large quantities on application.

Saynor's Celebrated Pruning and Budding Knives, &c.

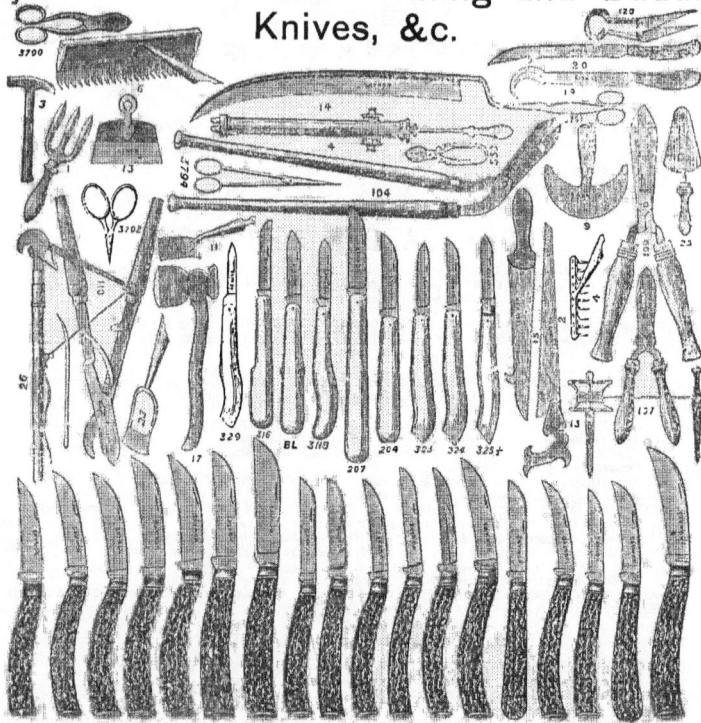

186	186½	187	188	189	191	191½	193	194	195	195½	196	197	200	312	312 SB	313	938
3/-	3/-	3/-	3/-	3/3	3/3	3/6	3/6	3/6	3/6	3/6	4/-	3/6	2/-	2/6	2/6	2/-	3/6

BUDDING KNIVES. No. 329, 3/6; 316, 3/-; BL, 3/-; 3NB, 3/-; 207, 3/6; 204, 3/-; 323, 2/6; 324, 3/-; 325½ 3/6.

„   „   No. 204B. " The Gardener's Favourite," brass bound, 3s. 6d. each.

ASPARAGUS „   3·6 each.

GARDEN FORKS AND SPADES.   3s. 6d. to 5s. 9d. each.

SCISSORS.   Flower-gathering—No. 3791, 6-in., 3/-; 8-in., 4/-.

„   Pruning—No. 3790, 6-in., 2/6; 7-in., 3/6; 8-in., 4/-.

„   „   With slide, 5/6, 6/6, and 7/6 per pair.

No. 26.   **Averruncators.** 4 to 12 ft. long, 7/6 to 12/6 per pair.
„   1.   **Ladies' Digging Forks.** 2/6 each.
„   3.   **Garden Hammers.** No. 2, 2/-; No. 3, 2/6.
„   23. **Dutch Hoes.** 5-in., 1/-; 6-in., 1/3; 7-in., 1/6.
„   13. **Draw Hoes.** 5-in., 10d.; 6-in., 1/-; 7-in., 1/2; 8-in., 1/4
„   17. **Gentlemen's Hatchets.** (Without claw head), 3/- ea.
„   4.   **Iron Rakes.** 8 teeth, 1/-; 10 tooth, 1/3; 12 teeth, 1/6
„   6.   **Daisy Rakes.** 6/6 each.
„   13. **Garden Reels.** 2/- each ; Lines (30 and 60 yds. long), 1/6 and 2/6 each.
„   110. **Sliding Pruning Shears.** 7/6, 8/6, and 9/6 each.
„   107. **Grass Shears.** 4/-. No. 100, 4/6 to 6/6 each.
„   104. **Edging Shears.** 7/6, 8/6, and 9/6 each.

SCISSORS.   Vine—No. 3794, 6-in., 2/6; 7-in., 3/6 per pair.
SECATEURS.   New, all bright, with improved spring, 7-in., 4/6; 8-in., 5/- per pair.
„   With spring, 6-in., 4/-; 7-in., 5/- per pair.
„   Patent spring, 2/6 per pair.

No. 120. **Sheep Shears.** 3/- each.
„   15.   **Pruning Saws, with Bill Hook.** 6/6 each.
„   2.   **Pruning Saws, cast Steel.** 3/- each.
„   9.   **Edging Irons, cast Steel.** 3/6 each ;
„   „   „   with handle, 4/6 each.
„   25.   **Bright Steel Trowels.** 6-in., 1/6; 7-in., 1/9; 8-in., 2/3 each.
„   19.   **Gooseberry Pruners, with hook.** 3/- each.
„   20.   **Gooseberry Pruners, straight.** 2/6 each.
„   14.   **Scythe Blades.** 36-in., 3/6 and 4/6.
„   11.   **Cast Steel Spuds.** 1/3 each.

Duns Switching and half-cut over Bills, best make, 4/- each.

NEW DECORATIVE DAHLIA,
GRAND DUKE ALEXIS.

GRAND DUKE ALEXIS. (Natural size.)

This has proved itself to be one of the most magnificent Dahlias sent out for some years, and a variety that will, undoubtedly, become highly popular. It is quite a new departure in the decorative section, each floret being rolled up at the edges, so that one side overlaps the other, giving the flower a most beautiful and attractive appearance. The blooms are often of immense size, of the most lovely pure white, and in a good light, show a glistening silk-like sheen; sometimes the centre and the back of the flower have a very faint tint of lilac, when the effect is extremely beautiful. The plant is a strong and vigorous grower, with handsome dark green foliage, and is very free-flowering. We can highly recommend this charming flower, which we offer at a price within the reach of all.

Strong Plants in May, 1s. each; or 3 for 2s. 6d.

DANIELS' SUPERB GODETIAS

DANIELS' SUPERB GODETIAS.

(See Coloured Plate.)

The Godetias form a magnificent class of free-flowering showy hardy annuals, and should be grown freely wherever a really beautiful display of annuals is desired. They are very effective for mixed beds or borders, and when grown in masses are extremely charming. Those of the Whitneyi type, and which include the fine varieties sent out by ourselves, produce immense flowers of the most brilliant and exquisite shades of crimson, carmine, rose and pink, to the purest satiny white; the plants being of a sturdy compact habit of growth, and literally covered for a long period with a profusion of lovely flowers. Grown in pots of five or six inches diameter they make beautiful subjects for the greenhouse, and the blooms if cut and placed in water will retain their beauty for a considerable time.

Cultivation.—For earliest blooming, sow the seeds in February or early in March in pots of firmly compressed light rich soil, and place in a gentle heat, prick out to strengthen, harden off and plant out in an open sunny position, in April or May, one foot or eighteen inches apart, or pot up for blooming under glass. For a general display and succession, sow thinly in the open ground at intervals from the early part of March to the end of April, and thin out or transplant if the plants come up too thickly. By sowing thinly in an open space in August or September, and transplanting to flowering quarters early in Spring, a grand display of charming flowers may be had early in Summer. All the Godetias are extremely hardy, and will thrive in any fairly good soil.

All the varieties marked by an asterisk (*) have been raised and sent out by DANIELS BROS.

		per pkt.—s.	d.
1	***MARCHIONESS OF SALISBURY** *(Plate, No. 3).* A quite new and charmingly effective variety, growing only about one foot in height, and bearing a profusion of very large beautiful flowers; colour, a bright carmine-crimson, the petals having broad, clearly-defined light margins, giving the plants, when in bloom, a fresh and lovely appearance. A variety of exceptional beauty. Award of Merit, Royal Horticultural Society, 9th July, 1895	2	6
2	**CARMINEA AUREA (Crimson and Gold)** *(Plate, No. 4).* A very distinct and beautiful variety, and quite a new break of colour amongst Godetias. The plants grow about one foot in height, and the numerous medium-sized flowers are of a bright deep rosy-crimson colour, the petals being beautifully edged with bright pale yellow, at times approaching a deeper or golden shade. Grown in a mass at our Seed Grounds during the past Summer, the effect was at once novel, rich, and pleasing	2	6
3	***DUKE OF YORK** *(Plate, No. 5).* This grand new scarlet variety surpasses all other Godetias in brilliancy and effectiveness. The plants are of the same dwarf sturdy habit of growth as *Duke of Fife*, with the same abundance of flowers, the individual blooms are of great size, and of the most intense satiny scarlet carmine colour, with lighter centres. Of splendid effect. One of the most beautiful of all hardy annuals	1	6
4	***DUCHESS OF FIFE** *(Plate, No. 2).* Height 1 foot. A most superb variety bearing large flowers. A lovely satiny white, each petal being distinctly marked by a brilliant carmine blotch. First Class Certificate, Royal Horticultural Society	1	0
5	,, ,, smaller pkt.	0	6
6	***DUKE OF FIFE.** Height 1 foot. Intensely rich satiny crimson blooms of fine form and substance, the individual blooms measuring 4 to 4½ inches across, with perfect habit of plant. Received an Award of Merit from the Royal Horticultural Society	1	0
7	,, ,, smaller pkt.	0	6
8	***DUCHESS OF ALBANY** *(Plate, No. 1).* Height 1 foot. The finest and most beautiful pure white Godetia ever raised. The flowers, which are very large and abundant, are of the loveliest pure satiny white. A variety of charming effect	1	0
9	,, ,, smaller pkt.	0	6
10	,, **New Dwarf.** Height ½ foot, pure white, a beautiful variety	0	6
11	***Bridesmaid.** Height 1 foot. Rose and white, charming variety ...	0	6
12	***Butterfly.** Height 1 foot. White, with crimson blotch on each petal, very showy ...	0	6
13	**"General Gordon.** Height 1 foot. Brilliant deep crimson ...	0	6
14	***Lady Albemarle.** Height 1 foot. Crimson scarlet; very showy ...	0	6
15	**A collection of six choice varieties, including Duke of York, Duchess of Albany, and Duchess of Fife**	1	6
16	**Daniels' Choicest Mixed,** from the above superb sorts ...	1	0
17	,, ,, ,, ,, smaller pkt.	0	6

OTHER VARIETIES.

		per pkt.—s.	d.
18	**Bijou.** Very dwarf and beautiful variety. Flowers pure white, marked with dark rose	0	6
19	**Pumila hybrida.** Dwarf, compact-growing varieties, fine mixed colours ...	0	6
20	**Reptans insignis.** Height 1 foot, trailing. White and crimson ...	0	3
21	**Rubicunda splendens, fl. pl.** A fine variety, growing about 2 feet high, with semi-double crimson flowers ...	0	3
22	**The Bride.** White, with crimson ring at base of petals. Height 2 feet ...	0	3

From the GARDENERS' MAGAZINE, *March 11th,* 1893.

"Turning to the quarters devoted to the annuals, we find the Godetias, of which several fine forms have been introduced by Messrs. Daniels, in strong force, painting the landscape with resplendent colouring. The newer varieties of these included Duke of Fife, which has rich crimson flowers, and Duchess of Fife, of which the flowers are satiny white, with carmine blotch on each petal. Older forms of special merit included Duchess of Albany, pure white; Bridesmaid, rose and white; Butterfly, white with crimson blotch on each petal; and General Gordon, brilliant crimson."

1. COMET. 2 & 3. DANIELS' DWARF PERFECTION. 4. IMPROVED PÆONY-FLOWERED.
5. DANIELS' PRIZE QUILLED.

Daniels' Superb Prize Asters.

We are justly celebrated for our magnificent strains of English, French, and German Asters, which form an important branch of our Flower Seed business, and would mention that our seeds of these having been grown especially for our retail trade may be relied on as the very finest procurable.

Cultivation of French and German Asters.

WHEN well grown nothing can exceed the chaste loveliness and exquisite colour-blendings of a nicely arranged bed of choice Asters, and certainly no plant can be more easily raised and grown to perfection. The principal types of form are represented in the Pæony-flowered, having noble blooms with long incurved petals; the Victorias, with their beautifully imbricated and perfect flowers; the tasseled, as shown in the Chrysanthemum-flowered; and the quilled, or Globe-flowered. As a rule Asters should not be sown before the first week in April, and to ensure a succession of fine bloom another sowing should be made in about a fortnight and a final sowing about the second week in May. These latter, although they will not probably produce such fine blooms as those sown earlier, will be found exceedingly useful for planting in any out-of-the-way place for furnishing a late supply of cut-flowers. Sow the seed in boxes or pans of light rich soil, covering very lightly, and after giving a gentle watering, place under glass where the young plants, when they come up, can have full benefit of sun and air. As soon as large enough to handle, the earlier sown plants should be pricked out in boxes or pans of good rich soil, and placed in a light and airy position under glass to strengthen. In about three weeks, if fairly attended to, these will be found to have made nice sturdy plants with good tufts of fibrous roots, and which, if carefully transplanted to their blooming quarters, will grow on without a check. Asters will thrive and flower well in almost any good garden soil, but if really fine blooms be required for exhibition, &c., it is advisable to have the ground well broken up, and a good quantity of thoroughly decayed manure worked in. The healthy growth of the plants, and the development of fine blooms, are greatly assisted by occasional applications of weak liquid manure up to the time of the plants showing the flower, when it should be discontinued, and the buds of those intended for exhibition thinned out to three or four on a plant, generally removing the centre bud; and neat stakes should be placed to the taller-growing varieties requiring support.

Daniels' Dwarf Perfection.

A quite new and superb strain of beautiful varieties that will become highly popular. The plants grow only about eight or ten inches high, with stiff, upright stems and branches, and form handsome circular bushes. The flowers are of immense size, perfectly double, beautifully imbricated, and of the most splendid form. This will be found a grand strain for bedding out, for ordinary garden decoration, or for exhibition.

				s.	d.					s.	d.
23	An assortment of 6 superb varieties		...	3	6	28	Pure white	...	... per pkt.	1	0
24	Crimson	...	... per pkt.	1	0	29	Brilliant carmine	...	...	1	0
25	Dark blue ...	...	...	1	0	30	Choicest mixed	...	...	2	6
26	Rose	...	...	1	0	31	,,	...	smaller pkt.	1	0
27	Light blue ...	...	...	1	0						

Daniels' Improved Pæony-flowered Perfection.

These Asters are of the greatest perfection, producing noble flowers of the most perfect Pæony form, and in a great variety of beautiful and brilliant colours. A decided improvement on the old form of Pæony-flowered Aster usually sent out, and are invaluable for exhibition. Have been awarded numerous First Prizes during the past season.

				s.	d.					s.	d.
32	An assortment of 16 splendid varieties	...		4	6	39	Dark scarlet and white	...	... per pkt.	1	0
33	,, ,, 12 ,,	...		3	6	40	Dark purple violet	...	... ,,	1	0
34	,, ,, 6 ,,	...		2	0	41	Pure white	...	... ,,	1	0
35	Brilliant crimson	...	... per pkt.	1	0	42	Dark blood red	...	... ,,	1	0
36	Sky blue ...	...	... ,,	1	0	43	Splendid mixed	...	... ,,	1	0
37	Delicate rose	...	... ,,	1	0	44	,,	...	smaller pkt.	0	6
38	Light blue and white	...	... ,,	1	0	45	,,	...	smallest pkt.	0	3

Daniels' Improved Victoria.

A truly magnificent class, growing to the height of about eighteen inches, and producing an abundance of perfectly double and beautifully imbricated flowers, which frequently measure four and a half to five inches across. The plants are of a handsome pyramidal form, and when grown for exhibition should be planted eighteen inches apart.

				s.	d.					s.	d.
46	An assortment of 16 beautiful varieties	...		4	6	51	Dark crimson and white	...	... per pkt.	1	0
47	,, ,, 12 ,,		...	3	6	52	Bright rose	...	... ,,	1	0
48	,, ,, 8 ,,		...	2	6	53	Rich purple	...	... ,,	1	0
49	Dark crimson	...	... per pkt.	1	0	54	Finest mixed	...	... ,,	1	0
50	Pure white	...	... ,,	1	0	55	,,	...	smaller pkt.	0	6

Daniels' Superb Prize Asters.

ASTER—NEW COMET. Showing habit of plant.

The New Japanese Chrysanthemum-flowered Aster "COMET."

New and extremely beautiful class of the same height and habit as the Dwarf Pæony Perfection Aster, forming fine, regular pyramids twelve to fifteen inches high, and covered profusely with large double flowers. The shape of the latter deviates from all classes of Asters in cultivation, and resembles very closely a large-flowered Japanese Chrysanthemum, the petals being long and somewhat twisted or wavy-like curled, are recurved from the centre of the flower to the outer petals in such a regular manner as to form a loose but still dense semi-globe. Well grown plants produce from twenty-five to thirty perfectly double flowers, measuring from 3½ to 4½ inches in diameter, and are very handsome in appearance.

		s.	d.
56	An assortment of six beautiful varieties ...	2	6
57	Pure white. Beautiful .. .. per pkt.	1	6
58	Rose and white, splendid variety ... „	1	0
59	Light blue and white, beautiful ... „	1	0
60	Choicest mixed ... ... „	1	0

Dwarf Chrysanthemum-flowered

This fine class is a decided acquisition. It commences blooming when other Asters are off, and is invaluable for a late display; its height is only nine inches, and in consequence of its fine dwarf habit of growth it is admirably suited for beds, edgings, pots, &c.

		s.	d.
61	An assortment of 12 fine varieties ...	3	0
62	„ 8 „ ...	2	0
63	Fiery scarlet ... ... per pkt.	1	0
64	Pure white ... ... „	1	0
65	Choicest mixed ... ... „	1	0
66	„ ... smaller pkt.	0	6

Daniels' Improved Prize Quilled.

A FINE strain of splendid varieties, producing beautifully formed, perfectly double flowers of the most charming colours. First-class for exhibition.

		s.	d.
67	An assortment of 12 choice varieties ...	2	6
68	„ 6 „ ...	1	6

		s.	d.
69	Choicest mixed ... ... per pkt.	1	0
70	„ ... smaller pkt.	0	6

IMBRICATED POMPONE. About nine inches high, bearing a profusion of brilliantly coloured, perfectly double flowers, with conspicuous white centres; very charming.

71	An assortment of 8 beautiful varieties	2s. 6d.
72	Choicest mixed ... ... per pkt. 1s. 0d.

VICTORIA NEEDLE. Very beautiful varieties of the most brilliant colours, all the blooms being handsomely quilled.

73	Six fine varieties	2s. 6d.
74	Choicest mixed ... ... per pkt. 1s. 0d.

WASHINGTON. Very large, splendid flowers, extra double, and exceedingly valuable for exhibition purposes.

75	Six choice varieties	2s. 6d.
76	Choicest mixed ... ... per pkt. 1s. 0d.

DWARF VICTORIA. Same form of flower and habit of plant as Victoria, but growing only ten inches in height.

77	An assortment of 6 beautiful varieties	2s. 6d.
78	Choicest mixed ... ... per pkt. 1s. 0d.

SNOWBALL or PRINCESS. An exquisitely beautiful variety, growing about one foot high, and producing quite a profusion of pure white, handsomely imbricated flowers.

79	Per packet ... ... 1s. 6d.

BALL OR JEWEL, ROSE AND WHITE. A very handsome variety, with large, densely double flowers, which are so symmetrically incurved as to form a perfect ball or globe. The flower is a lovely deep rose, the petals being edged with white.

80	Per packet ... ... 1s. 0d.

LADY IN WHITE. A charming new and quite distinct variety, with long narrow light green foliage, a remarkably free-branching habit of growth, and pure white double flowers; a novelty of the first rank, will prove a special value for cut flowers.

81	Per packet ... ... 1s. 6d.

NEW DWARF QUEEN. A novel and beautiful class not more than ten inches high, with large, double, imbricated flowers. Splendid.

82	Pure white ... ... per pkt. 1s. 0d.
83	Brilliant crimson ... ... 1s. 0d.

IMPROVED PYRAMIDAL BOUQUET. Only one foot high, and branches vigorously; one plant often produces one hundred blooms, all perfectly double.

84	An assortment of 8 choice varieties ... ... 1s. 6d.
85	Choicest mixed ... ... per pkt. 0s. 6d.

DWARF PÆONY-FLOWERED. A beautiful new class of Pæony-flowered Aster with the same form of incurved perfect flowers as the older varieties, but with a much more compact and handsome growth, the plants reaching only twelve inches in height.

86	An assortment of 8 choice varieties ... ... 2s. 0d.
87	Choicest mixed ... ... per pkt. 1s. 0d.

CROWN or COCARDEAU. A brilliant and showy class of beautiful varieties growing about fifteen inches high, the flowers all having conspicuous white centres.

88	An assortment of 6 choice varieties ... ... 1s. 6d.
89	Choice mixed ... ... per pkt. 0s. 6d.

"MIGNON," PURE WHITE. A very beautiful variety somewhat resembling the Victoria. The flowers are of the most refined form, and of the purest white; splendid for cutting.

90	Per packet ... ... 1s. 0d.

GIANT EMPEROR. Remarkably fine flowers, frequently measuring six inches across, perfectly double.

91	An assortment of 8 fine varieties ... ... 2s. 6d.
92	Choicest mixed ... ... per pkt. 1s. 0d.

Daniels' Superb Ten-week Stocks

DANIELS' LARGE-FLOWERED TEN-WEEK STOCKS.

Daniels' Superb Ten-week Stocks.

Cultivation of Stocks.

THE superb Large-flowered and other varieties of this beautiful class of annuals are all highly desirable, and we may say indispensable, for the Summer decoration of our gardens. Planted in groups or beds, such choice colours as scarlet, white, rose, purple, yellow, &c., are very telling in their effect with other plants, to say nothing of their delicious perfume; whilst large beds planted with some twelve or more distinct colours in carefully arranged lines, are very charming, and continue in their full beauty for a long period. The seed may be sown at any time from February to the end of April, but as a rule, the earlier the better. Sow in pans or boxes of light rich soil, scattering the seeds thinly and evenly (about four to the square inch is sufficiently thick), cover very lightly with fine soil, and give a gentle watering; after which place the boxes or pans under hand-lights, or in a frame close to the glass. Keep close and shaded for a few days, and when the young plants come up gradually admit air on fine warm days. Prick out to strengthen, as soon as the young plants can be handled, in pots, and place under hand-lights or in a frame close to the glass; shade from strong sun, and when established give plenty of air on fine days. Plant out about the end of April, or beginning of May, in good rich soil, nine inches or one foot apart in groups, beds, &c., as required. It is an excellent plan to pot up a score or so and grow on in small pots; these are very handy when coming into flower to replace any with single blooms which have shown on the borders and been removed. For succession sow in April and May under hand-lights, or in a sheltered place on a warm border, and plant out when ready. In planting out select, if possible, warm showery weather, and keep the plants well shaded and watered for a few days. A few sown in July and grown in pots will make nice plants for the greenhouse or conservatory in Winter. In planting out seedlings of Ten-week and other Stocks, it is customary with many to plant only the strongest and throw away the weaker as useless. This should never be done, as the weaker and smaller plants of a batch of seedlings almost invariably produce a large percentage of double flowers, and the "fine plants," which will be found to have coarse and forked roots, will be but too often found to produce but single flowers. If care be therefore taken to select in preference plants of a medium size, and having a nice tuft of fine fibrous roots, a much larger percentage of double flowers will be the result than if the plants are put out one and all indiscriminately, or the strongest only are selected.

Intermediate Stocks.—These are exceedingly useful for the greenhouse, or for window decoration in Winter and Spring. They do not require artificial heat, and are easily grown if protected from too severe frost. Sow the seeds in July or August, and prick the young plants into five inch pots, three in a pot, using a light rich soil, and place them in a cool frame or pit. Keep fairly moist and give plenty of air; liquid manure may be given with advantage at intervals, till the plants bloom.

Brompton Stocks.—The best time for sowing seeds of these is in May, and the most suitable place for planting out is where they receive some amount of shelter from severe frosts. Open spaces on shrubbery borders, or any similar position in the garden, will suit them well if they get a fair amount of warm sunshine, and the ground is tolerably rich. Sow the seeds thinly on beds of fine soil, and prick out six inches apart to strengthen, when the young plants have made three or four leaves. These will make nice sturdy plants for transferring to their blooming quarters in August or September; or the young plants may be taken from the seed bed, and planted out at once where intended to flower, if the ground is ready.

Daniels' Large-flowered Dwarf Ten-week.

(See Illustration.)

This is undoubtedly the finest strain of Ten-week Stocks ever raised, and, where space is limited, should always be grown in preference to others. It is the same in height as the old Ten-week, and with the same compact habit of growth; but its flowers when well grown are nearly double the size, of great substance and brilliancy, with the most delicious fragrance.

					s.	d.							s.	d.
93	24 Superb varieties	...	...	...	5	6	101	Canary yellow	...	...	... per pkt.	1	0
94	18 "	...	...	...	4	6	102	Light blue or mauve	...	...	"	1	0
95	12 "	...	...	...	3	0	103	Bright rose	...	...	"	1	0
96	6 "	...	...	...	1	6	104	Brilliant crimson rose	...	...	"	1	0
97	Deep scarlet	...	...	per pkt.	1	0	105	New dark blood red	...	...	"	1	0
98	Dark purple	...	...	"	1	0	106	Improved sulphur yellow	...	...	"	1	0
99	Pure white	...	...	"	1	0	107	Choicest mixed	...	...	"	1	0
100	Purple carmine	...	...	"	1	0	108	" "	...	...	smaller pkt.	0	6

Daniels' Giant Perfection Ten-week.

A GRAND class of tall-growing beautiful varieties. The plants attain a height of 2½ feet, are of a handsome pyramidal form, and throw up long central spikes of large, beautifully double flowers. This is an exceedingly fine strain that we can highly recommend.

				s.	d.						s.	d.
109	An assortment of 6 superb varieties	...		2	6	111	Pure white	...	...	per pkt.	1	0
110	Fiery crimson	...	...	per pkt.	1	0	112	Choicest mixed	...	per pkt. 6d. and	1	0

Dwarf German Ten-week.

A FINE and compact-growing class, with handsome double flowers of the most beautiful colours and delicious fragrance.

				s.	d.							s.	d.
113	An assortment of 12 choice varieties	...		2	6	115	Choicest mixed	...	...	... per pkt.	1	0
114	" " 6 " "	...		1	6	116	" "	...	...	smaller pkt.	0	6
						117	" "	...	...	smallest pkt.	0	3

From W. HUNTER, Esq., Glasgow.

July 26th.

"I am of the opinion that at present I have one of the grandest display of Stocks in the Country. I do not know if I ever saw anything to equal them."

From Mr. T. WALKER, Buckabridge.

July 11th.

"I have great pleasure in testifying to the quality of your Seeds. I have taken First Prize with your Stocks three years in succession at our Show."

Daniels' Superb Ten-week & other Stocks.

Dwarf Bouquet Ten-week—

118	An assortment of 8 distinct varieties	...	...	1s.	6d.
119	Finest mixed	...	... per pkt.	0s.	6d.

Large-flowered Wallflower-leaved Ten-week—

120	An assortment of 8 varieties	...	...	2s.	6d.
121	Choicest mixed	...	... per pkt.	1s.	0d.

Large-flowered Miniature Ten-week—

122	An assortment of 6 distinct varieties	...	...	1s.	6d.
123	Choicest mixed	...	... per pkt.	0s.	6d.

Large-flowered Globe Pyramidal Ten-week—

124	An assortment of 8 choice varieties	...	...	2s.	0d.
125	Mixed seed ..	...	... per pkt.	0s.	6d.

New Perpetual Ten-week.

A FINE new class, growing to the height of eighteen inches, and producing an abundance of bloom from July to November. First-class for cutting.

126	An assortment of 8 choice varieties	...	...	2s.	6d.
127	Choicest mixed	...	... per pkt.	1s.	0d.
128	**Mammoth White Column.** A grand variety of fine robust habit, growing to the height of about eighteen inches, but producing only one single long sturdy spike closely set with enormous double flowers of the purest white	... per pkt.		1s.	0d
129	**White Perfection.** This superb variety grows to a height of 1½ feet, is much branched, and almost a perpetual bloomer. If sown early in the Spring, it will flower with the beginning of June, continuing to bloom till destroyed by frost. In September and October, when other Stocks are off bloom, this is at its perfection, the mass of bloom is really remarkable per pkt.			1s.	0d.

Intermediate Stocks.

East Lothian Autumnal—
Splendid for late blooming on the open border or for Winter decoration in the greenhouse.

					s.	d.
130	**An assortment of 4 distinct varieties**	...			1	9
131	**Scarlet**	...	...	... per pkt.	1	0
132	**Crimson**	...	...	... ,,	1	0
133	**Purple**	...	...	... ,,	1	0
134	**White**	...	...	... ,,	1	0
135	**Choicest mixed**	...	...	...	1	0
136	,, ,,	...	...	smaller pkt.	0	6

Large-flowered Emperor—
Remarkable for their large flowers and vigorous habit. If sown in March will produce a magnificent effect in Autumn.

					s.	d.
137	An assortment of 10 splendid varieties	...	...		2s.	6d.
138	Finest mixed	...	... per pkt.		0s.	6d.

Autumn-flowering Intermediate—
A fine class for late flowering.

139	An assortment of 8 splendid varieties	...	...	2s.	6d.
140	Choicest mixed	...	... per pkt.	0s.	6d.

Brompton Stocks.

Giant or Brompton. Produce immense spikes of flowers and are very double. Sow in May or June, and plant out early in Autumn, for blooming the following Spring.

				s.	d.
141	An assortment of 12 choice varieties	...		3	0
142	,, 8 ,,			2	0
143	,, 6 ,,		...	1	6

				s.	d.
144	**Cottager's Scarlet.** Very fine and double per pkt.		1	0
145	**New Snow White.** Splendid double ,,		1	0
146	**Choicest mixed**	... per pkt. 6d. and	1	0

WALLFLOWERS.

THE Double German Wallflowers, with their grand spikes of beautifully-coloured flowers in April and May, are exceedingly fine, and, considering their easy culture, should be found in every garden. The Single-flowered varieties are also highly desirable for Spring gardening, producing a profusion of their finely-scented, handsome flowers almost throughout the Winter in a mild season.

DOUBLE GERMAN WALLFLOWER.

			per pkt.—s.	d.
147	**Double German,** an assortment of 12 choice vars.	...	3	6
148	,, ,, ,, 6 ,, ,,	...	2	0
149	,, **canary yellow**		1	0
150	,, **dark brown**		0	6
151	,, **creamy white** ⎫ extra fine		1	0
152	,, **blue** (violet) ⎬		1	0
153	,, **golden yellow** ⎭		1	0
154	,, **Daniels' Choicest mixed.** A splendid mixture, including all the most beautiful colours	...	1	0
155	,, ,, ,, smaller pkt.	...	0	6
156	**Single, Daniels' Early Queen.** Beautiful golden yellow flowers tinged with brown; remarkably early; sown in May will be in full bloom in October. Highly recommended		1	0
157	**Single, Eastern Queen.** Very pretty and distinct variety. The plants grow only about one foot in height, and the strong spikes of flowers are of a peculiar shade of chamois, changing to salmon rose, giving a most pleasing and striking effect in comparing with other Wallflowers, whilst it has the same agreeable scent as the old varieties	1	0
158	,, **Primrose Dame.** Clear primrose yellow; compact	...	0	6
159	,, **dwarf yellow.** Bedding ⎫ Very compact and useful	0	6
160	,, ,, **brown.** Bedding ⎬ for Spring bedding	0	6
161	,, **blood red.** Selected; splendid colour	...	0	3
162	,, **Harbinger.** Rich dark brown, early..	...	0	3
163	,, **Cloth of Gold.** Dwarf large-flowered	...	0	6
164	,, **blue or violet.** Beautiful colour, very distinct	...	0	6
165	,, **Daniels' Choicest mixed.** In beautiful variety	...	0	6
166	,, ,, ,, ,, ,, smaller pkt.		0	3

Daniels' Complete Collections of

Choice Flower Seeds for Amateurs.

Carefully arranged to ensure a fine display of flowers throughout the Summer and Autumn, and specially adapted to the requirements of the Cottage, Villa, or large Garden.

Collection A.—Price 5s. Post Free.

A choice assortment of thirty Hardy and Half-hardy Annuals, containing one full-sized packet of each of the following :—

Aster, Pæony-flowered	Convolvulus major	Lupinus nanus	Poppy, New Shirley
Briza maxima	Convolvulus minor	Marigold, dwarf French	Rhodanthe maculata
Candytuft, crimson	Godetia, choice mixed	Mathiola bicornis	Stock, Dwarf German
Candytuft, Empress	Helichrysum, mixed	Mignonette	Sweet Pea, mixed
Calliopsis Drummondi	Larkspur, dwarf Rocket	Nasturtium, climbing	Sweet Pea, scarlet
Calliopsis tinctoria	Leptosiphon albus	Nasturtium, Tom Thumb	Viscaria, scarlet
Clarkia integripetala	Linum grandiflorum	Nemophila insignis	Zinnia, fine double
Collinsia bicolor	rubrum	Phlox Drummondi	

Collection A A.—Price 7s. 6d. Post Free.

8 Choice vars. Victoria Aster	6 Half-hardy Annuals, including	1 Packet Zinnia, finest double
6 „ „ Dwarf Ten-week Stock, large-flowered	Phlox, Marigold, Portulaca, &c., &c.	1 „ Helichrysum, mixed
8 Choice Hardy Annuals	1 Packet Petunia, finest mixed	1 „ Rhodanthe maculata
1 Packet Balsam, choice double		1 „ Briza maxima
		1 Oz. Flower Seeds, dwf. mixed

Collection B.—Price 10s. 6d. Post Free.

6 Choice vars. Pæony Aster	12 Choice Hardy Annuals, the	1 Packet Camellia-flowered
6 „ „ Dwarf German Ten-week Stock, large-flowd.	most useful and showy kinds	Balsam
6 Varieties New Double Zinnia elegans	4 Choice varieties Everlasting Flowers	1 Packet Portulaca, fine double
6 Choice Half-hardy Annuals for bedding out	2 Choice Ornamental Grasses	1 „ Verbena, choice mixed
	1 Packet Petunia, choice mixed	1 Ounce Mignonette
		1 „ Mixed Flower Seeds

Collection C.—Price 15s. Post Free.

12 Choice vars. Pæony Aster	12 Choice Half-hardy Annuals	1 Packet Camellia-flowered
12 „ „ Dwarf German Ten-week Stock, large-flowd.	for bedding out	Balsam
6 Choice varieties New Double Zinnia elegans	6 Hardy Annuals, including Pansies, Hollyhock, &c.	1 Packet Portulaca, fine double
12 Choice Hardy Annuals, the most useful and showy kinds	4 Choice varieties Everlasting Flowers	1 „ Verbena, choice mixed
	2 Choice Ornamental Grasses	1 Ounce Nemophila insignis
	1 Packet Petunia, choice mixed	1 „ Mignonette
		2 Ounces Mixed Flower Seeds

Collection D.—Price 21s. Carriage Free.

12 Choice vars. Pæony Aster	12 Choice varieties Half-hardy Annuals, for bedding-out,	1 Packet Calceolaria, choicest mixed
12 „ „ Victoria Aster	pots, &c.	1 Packet Cineraria, choice mxd.
12 „ „ Ten-week Stock	6 Hrdy. Perennials & Biennials	1 „ Primula, choice frngd.
6 „ „ Double Zinnia	6 Choice varieties Everlasting	1 Ounce Nemophila insignis
12 „ „ Phlox Drumm.	Flowers	1 „ Sweet Peas, mixed
12 „ „ Showy Hardy Annuals	1 Packet Petunia, choice mixed	1 „ Mignonette
4 Choice Ornamental Grasses	1 „ Verbena, fine mixed	2 Ounces Mixed Flower Seeds

Daniels' Complete Collections of Flower Seeds for Amateurs *(continued).*

Collection D D.—Price 31s. 6d. Carriage Free.

12 Vars. Improved Pæony Aster	12 Vars. Half-hardy Annuals for	8 Choice varieties Everlasting
12 „ „ Victoria Aster	bedding out, &c.	Flowers
12 „ Dwarf Ten-week Stock	12 Hrdy. Perennials & Biennials	6 Ornamental Grasses
6 „ Giant Ten-week Stock	including Dianthus, Del-	1½ Ounce Mignonette
12 „ Phlox Drummondi	phiniums, &c.	1 „ Nemophila insignis
6 „ Double Zinnia	6 Vars. of Seeds for the Green-	2 Ounces Sweet Peas
6 „ Camellia-flowd. Balsam	house, including Calceolaria	2 „ Mixed Flower Seeds
18 „ Showy Hardy Annuals	Cineraria, Primula, &c.	

Collection E.—Price 42s. Carriage Free.

16 Vars. Improved Pæony Aster	4 Vars. Brompton Stock	12 Hrdy. Perennials & Biennials
12 „ „ Victoria Aster	6 „ Double German Wall-	including Dianthus, Pansy,
6 „ Prize Quilled Aster	flower	Polyanthus, Hollyhock, &c.
18 „ Dwarf German Ten-	12 Vars. Everlasting Flowers	6 Greenhouse Perennials and
week Stock, Large-flowered	6 Ornamental Grasses	Biennials
6 Vars. Giant or Tree Ten-week	18 Hardy Annuals, the most	6 New or very choice Annuals
Stock	useful and showy sorts	1 Ounce Nemophila insignis
12 Vars. Phlox Drummondi	8 Choice Half-hardy Annuals	2 Ounces Mignonette
6 „ New Double Zinnia	for bedding out, &c.	4 „ Sweet Peas, mixed
6 „ Camellia Balsam		3 „ Mixed Flower Seeds

Collection F.—Price 63s. Carriage Free.

16 Vars. Improved Pæony Aster	8 Vars. Portulaca	12 Choice varieties Everlasting
16 „ „ Victoria Aster	6 „ Wallflower, Double	Flowers
12 „ Dwrf. Chrysanthemum	6 „ Hollyhock, Chater's	6 Choice Ornamental Grasses
Aster	30 „ Showy Hardy Annuals	6 Choice vars. Hardy Climbers
12 Vars. Prize Quilled Aster	18 Choice varieties Half-hardy	6 Vars. ornamental-foliaged
18 „ Ten-week Stock, Dwf.	Annuals for bedding out,	plants for sub-tropical gar-
6 „ Giant Ten-week Stock	pots, &c.	dening
6 „ Giant Brompton Stock	12 Choice varieties Hardy Per-	1 Ounce Nemophila insignis
6 „ Camellia Balsam	ennials and Biennials	8 Ounces Sweet Peas, mixed
12 „ Phlox Drummondi	12 Choice varieties of Seeds of	4 „ Mignonette
12 „ Double Zinnia	Greenhouse Plants	4 „ Mixed Flower Seeds

The Amateur's Packet of Choice Flower Seeds.

(Entered at Stationers' Hall.)

Price 2s. 6d. post free.

Contains the following Choice Assortment in full-sized packets, with cultural directions. This is a very cheap and splendid collection, which we can highly recommend.

Aster, choicest Pæony-flowered	Helichrysum, choice mixed	Poppy, New Shirley
Calliopsis Drummondi	Leptosiphon densiflorus albus	Scarlet Linum
Candytuft, Empress	Mignonette, Victoria Giant	Stock, Ten-week, finest double
Collinsia bicolor	Nasturtium, Empress of India	Sweet Peas, mixed
Clarkia integripetala rosea	Night-scented Stock	Viscaria oculata rosea
Godetia, splendid mixed	Phlox Drummondi grandiflora	Zinnia, finest double, mixed

OPINIONS FROM THE PRESS.

"Messrs. DANIELS BROTHERS, of Norwich, have sent one of their Amateur's Packets of Choice Flower Seeds as a specimen. It is remarkably cheap, and the varieties are well selected."—*Morning Post.*

"We have received from Messrs. DANIELS one of their half-crown packets of Flower Seeds. We caused one of these packets to be tried last year and the results were most satisfactory."—*Illustrated Sporting News.*

"We have great pleasure in acknowledging an Amateur's Packet of Flower Seeds sent us by Messrs. DANIELS, the well-known seedsmen of Norwich. Last year we were favoured in a similar manner, and from our experience of results obtained, we predict that this collection will become one of the most popular with amateur gardeners. The Asters and Stocks are from a very choice strain."—*Lady's Pictorial.*

English and Foreign Flower Seeds in Collections.

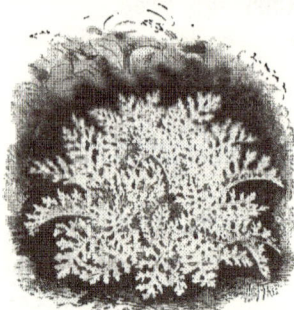

CINERARIA CANDIDISSIMA.
Per packet 1s.

PERILLA NANKINENSIS.
Per packet 3d.

PYRETHRUM SELAGINOIDES
Per packet 6d.

HARDY ANNUALS—
167   One hundred showy and useful varieties, including Godetia, Nemophila, Viscaria, Clarkia, Collinsia, Convolvulus, Sweet Pea, &c.   ... 16s. 0d.
168   Fifty ditto   ...   . 8s. 6d.
169   Twenty-five ditto   ...   . 5s. 0d.
170   Twelve ditto   ...   . 2s. 6d.

HARDY AND HALF-HARDY ANNUALS—
171   One hundred choice varieties, including Aster, Stock, Nemophila, Marigold, Phlox, Sweet Pea, &c.   ...   ... 21s. 0d.
172   Fifty ditto   ...   . 11s. 6d.
173   Twenty-five ditto   ...   . 6s. 0d.
174   Twelve ditto   ...   . 3s. 6d.

HARDY PERENNIALS AND BIENNIALS—
175   Twenty-five choice varieties, including Pansy, Carnation, Hollyhock, Polyanthus, Auricula, &c.   ...   . 10s. 6d.
176   Twelve ditto   ...   . 6s. 6d.

STOVE & GREENHOUSE PERENNIALS & BIENNIALS—
177   Twenty-five choice varieties, including Calceolaria, Cineraria, Primula, Gloxinia, Begonia, &c.   ...   . 18s. 6d.
178   Twelve ditto   ...   . 10s. 6d.

PLANTS FOR THE SUB-TROPICAL GARDEN—
179   Twelve superb varieties   ...   . 4s. 6d.
180   Six ditto   ...   . 2s. 6d.

EVERLASTING FLOWERS—
181   Twenty-four choice varieties   ...   . 5s. 0d.
182   Twelve ditto   ...   . 2s. 6d.

ORNAMENTAL GRASSES—
183   Twelve varieties   ...   . 2s. 6d.

CLIMBING PLANTS, Hardy and Half-Hardy Annuals—
184   Twelve choice varieties   ...   . 3s. 6d.
185   Six ditto   ...   . 1s. 6d.

CONVOLVULUS MAJOR—
186   An assortment of 12 beautiful colours   ...   ... 2s. 0d.

GODETIAS—
187   Six new and beautiful sorts   ...   . 1s. 6d.

ORNAMENTAL GOURDS—
188   Twelve beautiful miniature varieties   ...   ... 2s. 6d.

LARKSPUR, Giant Rocket, Hyacinth-flowered—
189   Six fine and distinct sorts   ...   . 1s. 6d.

LARKSPUR, Double Dwarf Rocket, Hyacinth-flowered—
190   Twelve extra choice varieties   ...   . 2s. 0d.

MARIGOLDS, African—
191   An assortment of 6 choice varieties   ...   ... 1s. 6d.

MARIGOLDS, French—
192   Six varieties   ...   . 1s. 6d.

MIGNONETTE—
193   Six choicest varieties   ...   . 1s. 6d.

DWARF PLANTS FOR ROCKWORK—
194   Twelve fine sorts, annual and perennial   ...   ... 3s. 0d.

NASTURTIUM, TOM THUMB, Dwarf—
195   Eight brilliant varieties   ...   . 1s. 6d.

NEMOPHILAS—
196   Ten beautiful sorts   ...   . 2s. 0d.

POPPIES, Double Dwarf Ranunculus-flowered—
197   Six brilliant varieties   ...   . 1s. 6d.

POPPIES, Double, Carnation-flowered—
198   Twelve fine varieties   ...   . 2s. 0d.

SCABIOUS, Large-flowered double German—
199   Eight fine varieties   ...   . 1s. 6d.

TROPÆOLUM LOBBIANUM, AND HYBRIDS—
200   Twelve splendid varieties   ...   . 2s. 6d.

SWEET-SCENTED ANNUALS—
201   Twelve fine varieties   ...   . 2s. 6d.

SALPIGLOSSIS GRANDIFLORA—
202   Six beautiful varieties   ...   . 1s. 6d.

SWEET PEAS, Eckford's Superb New Varieties—
203   An assortment of 12 choice sorts   ...   ... 3s. 0d.
204   Six ditto   ...   . 1s. 6d.

SWEET PEAS, ordinary class—
205   Twelve choice varieties   ...   . 2s. 0d.

PLANTS FOR BEES (Annuals)—
206   The Apiarian's Packet, containing 14 selected varieties, in full-sized packets   ...   . 2s. 6d.
207   An assortment of 8 choice varieties   ...   ... 1s. 6d.

Daniels' Choice Florists' Flower Seeds.

In the rearing of Florists' Flowers from seed the first essential point is to secure carefully hybridised seed saved from the finest flowers of the finest kinds, the chances of success in raising some really good varieties being vastly greater from a few plants from seed of the choicest quality than from a large number raised from seed of an inferior description.

PRIZE AURICULA.

Auriculas.

per pkt.—s. d.

208	**DANIELS' PRIZE MIXED.** From a fine collection of choice named flowers, including the green-edged and grey-edged sorts, highly recommended			...	5	0
209	,, ,, smaller pkt.				2	6
210	**ALPINE.** From a superb collection, including all the most beautiful shades of colour; a very hardy and desirable class				1	0
211	,, ,, ,, smaller pkt.				0	6

From Mr. B. WATERS, Ditchingham.

May 15th.
" I am pleased to state I have had a splendid show of Auriculas this Spring from your Seeds."

Antirrhinums.

THESE brilliant and free-flowering hardy border plants have been highly improved during the past few years, and should be found in every garden. Treated as half-hardy annuals they bloom freely the first year from seed, and afford a valuable display during the Summer and Autumn months. Many of the varieties are very beautiful. The colours vary from intense crimson to carmine, rose, primrose, yellow, pure white, &c. Some of the kinds have conspicuous white-throated flowers, which make them very attractive, whilst the flowers of some are handsomely striped. The Tom Thumb varieties are only about six inches in height when fully grown, and are very pretty for dry rockeries, &c. Sow in March in light rich soil, and place in a gentle heat; or sow in April under a hand-light, prick out to strengthen, and plant out soon as large enough. These will flower the first year from seed, and furnish a fine display of bloom during Summer and Autumn.

per pkt.—s. d.

212	**An assortment of 12 brilliant tall vars.,** with names				2	6
213	,, 6 ,, ,,				1	6
214	**Tall varieties,** choice mixed				0	6
215	,, ,, smaller pkt.				0	3
216	**TOM THUMB, 6** brilliant varieties with names				1	6
217	,, ,, Choicest mixed				0	6

Balsams,
Daniels' Camellia-flowered.

We have much pleasure in again offering our magnificent strain of these superb Balsams, the seed of which has been carefully grown and selected under glass during the past season, and which we have no hesitation in saying, will be found of an unsurpassably fine quality, our Balsams being noted for their large size, perfect doubleness and symmetry of form, with the most brilliantly striking and exquisitely delicate and beautiful colouring. Have been awarded numerous First Prizes.

per pkt.—s. d.

218	**An assortment of 6 splendid vars.,** 25 seeds each				2	6
219	**Pure scarlet**				1	0
220	**Pure white**				1	0
221	**Delicate rose**				1	0
222	**Crimson**				1	0
223	**Violet spotted**				1	0
224	**Choicest mixed**				2	6
225	,, ,, ... smaller pkt.				1	6
226	Camellia-flowered German. Double; fine mixed	6d. and				1	0
227	Rose-flowered. Double; fine mixed	6d. and				1	0

From Mr. S. W. VICKERY, Uffculme.

Aug. 16th.
" I am pleased to be able to inform you that I took First Prize in the open class for Three Balsams grown from your Seed I had from you; they were a splendid strain both as regards the size and quality of bloom."

DANIELS' CAMELLIA-FLOWERED BALSAM.

From Mr. J. ROBSON, Adon, Cockington.
Oct. 29th.
" The Begonia Seed I had from you in the spring proved very good."

Daniels' Choice Florists' Flower Seeds.

Begonias—Tuberous-rooted Hybrids.

This magnificent class of handsome flowering plants has been highly improved of late years, and being so admirably suited for greenhouse or conservatory decoration, and for bedding out, should be grown by every one having accommodation for them.

DOUBLE-FLOWERED BEGONIA.

Sow the seeds in February or March on the surface of well-drained pots or pans of rich sandy loam and finely sifted leaf-mould, and place in a heat of about sixty-five degrees. When sowing make the soil tolerably firm, level and sprinkle the surface with tepid water, after which sow the seeds; no covering of soil is necessary, a piece of glass placed over the pot to retain the surface moisture being all that is required. As the seed of Begonias does not germinate very quickly or evenly, and a long interval will often occur between the first and last plants coming up, the young seedlings should be carefully lifted as soon as large enough to handle, and pricked into pots or pans to grow on, and this will make room for the succeeding young plants.

Those sown in February or March if grown on freely will commence blooming in June, and will make really fine plants for the succeeding year. Seeds may also be sown in June or July, the plants of which will form nice healthy roots before Winter. The roots may be stored during Winter in a similar way to Dahlias, and should be kept dry; but they should not be subjected to a lower temperature than forty-five or fifty degrees. The tuberous-rooted Begonias are all charmingly suited for the decoration of the greenhouse, conservatory, or window, and planted out of doors in fairly sheltered positions make fine showy beds, and are much superior to Geraniums.

		per pkt.—s. d.
228	**DANIELS' PRIZE SINGLE.** Carefully saved from a grand collection of the choicest English varieties, will produce some splendid flowers ...	2 6
229	,, ,, smaller pkt.	1 6
230	**DANIELS' PRIZE DOUBLE.** A superb strain, carefully hybridised, saved from finest varieties	2 6
231	,, ,, smaller pkt.	1 6

Fibrous-rooted Begonias.

		per pkt.—s. d.
232	**Semperflorens alba** } Useful varieties for bedding out or { 1 0	
233	,, **rosea** } edging. Highly recommended { 1 0	
234	**Schmidti.** White, shaded with rose. Very free bloomer. Sown in heat in February may be had in bloom throughout the Summer and Autumn ..	1 6
235	**Rex, Varieties.** Beautiful plants for the stove or greenhouse. Saved from choicest sorts	1 6

Cyclamen Persicum.

The best time for sowing the seeds is in October or November, and again in January, February, or March, for a succession. When sowing, use a light rich soil, press down firmly into the seed pots or pans, placing the seeds about half an inch apart on the surface, and covering them about a quarter of an inch deep with soil; water carefully and place in a gentle heat. As the young plants become large enough to handle they should be carefully lifted and potted off singly into small pots, shifting them into larger as these fill with roots, and finishing with the forty-eight size, which will be large enough for blooming. The best soil to use for potting Cyclamens is composed of about equal parts of fibrous loam and leaf-mould, with a portion of well-decayed cow-dung and sufficient silver sand to keep the soil porous. The essential conditions of successful cultivation of Cyclamens are a moist and even temperature—sudden changes are especially to be avoided—a free circulation of air, an abundance of light and water, and the plants should be kept free of insects.

		per pkt.—s. d.
236	**DANIELS' GIANT PRIZE MIXED.** A magnificent strain of a highly improved type, having large, beautifully mottled coriaceous leaves and stout flower stalks. The blooms, which are carried well above the foliage, are of splendid size, each flower frequently measuring from two and a half to three inches in length ...	2 6
237	,, ,, ,, smaller pkt.	1 6
238	**Wiggins' Covent Garden.** A fine large-flowered strain of beautiful varieties ...	1 6
239	**Persicum,** choice mixed. In fine variety ...	1 0

Cockscombs.

Sow the seeds in February or March in pots or pans of light rich soil and plunge in a good heat. The object being to keep the plants in free growth without a check, the young plants should be carefully pricked out into small pots as soon as they can be handled, and as these fill with roots they should be shifted into larger pots. Those of eight inches diameter are large enough to finish with, but the plants must be kept in heat till the combs are formed, which will take place when the plants become pot-bound. Should some of the plants be too tall when grown but have fine combs, the defect of height may be easily remedied by cutting off the combs with a sufficient length of stem, potting them firmly into five or six inch pots, and plunging them for a few days in a good hot-bed. These will strike readily, and fine combs on dwarf handsome plants will be the result. A light rich friable soil is the best, and the plants when in full growth will be much improved by an occasional dose of weak liquid manure.

		per pkt.—s. d.
240	**Daniels' Giant Prize.** A magnificent strain, saved from combs measuring thirty-six inches by twelve inches, of the richest deep crimson colour; when well grown are unrivalled for exhibition .. ... 1s. 6d. and	2 6
241	**Dwarf crimson.** Rich crimson	0 6
242	**Crimson-feathered** } Long handsome plumes,	0 6
243	**Golden-feathered** } splendid for conservatory	0 6
244	**New dwarf feathered.** Splendid mixed ...	0 6
245	**An assortment of 6 fine dwarf vars.** ...	1 6
246	**Choicest mixed.** Dwarf	0 6

Daniels' Choice Florists' Flower Seeds.

Daniels' Superb Calceolarias.

We have much pleasure in offering our splendid strain of Calceolaria hybrida, which has been carefully saved from a magnificent collection during the past season, and which has been awarded many First Prizes. The flowers will be found of large size, beautiful form, and tigred and spotted with the most exquisite and brilliant markings.

Sow the seeds of these in May, June, or July, in well-drained pots or seed-pans; cover the drainage with rough fibrous loam, and fill up the surface with fine light sifted mould and silver sand ; water with a fine rose water-pot, after which sow the seed, placing a piece of glass over the pot to retain the moisture, no covering of soil being required. Place the pots in a cool frame or under a hand-light, taking care to shade from the sun. Remove the piece of glass as soon as the plants are up, and when large enough to handle, prick off one inch apart into pots or pans made up as before, placing in a somewhat close situation, and when of sufficient size pot off singly, and treat in a similar manner to that recommended for tender annuals. Calceolarias should however be always kept in a cool, moist position, a dry heated atmosphere being very prejudicial to their growth, and should be kept well supplied with fresh air.

				per pkt.—s.	d.
247	**DANIELS' CHOICEST MIXED**		... ...	5	0
248	,,	,,	,, smaller pkt.	2	6
249	,,	,,	,, smallest pkt.	1	6
250	**NEW DWARF.** A beautiful strain of handsome varieties growing only about ten inches high, and bearing a profusion of large brilliantly marked and spotted flowers		...	2	6
251	,,	,,	,, smaller pkt.	1	6

DANIELS' PRIZE CALCEOLARIAS.

Carnations and Picotees.

Sow in March or April in pans of rich soil, scattering the seeds thinly, and covering to the depth of about a quarter of an inch, and after watering place under glass. Prick out on well-prepared nursery beds to strengthen when the young plants have made four or five leaves, and plant out in September where intended to bloom, or pot up for the greenhouse. Those remaining in the open ground should have the benefit of a slight protection in severe weather, and be planted in a warm and dry position. A first-class strain of seed will produce at least eighty per cent. of fine double flowers, and the choicer varieties should be set aside for propagation by layering or cuttings.

				s.	d
252	**CARNATIONS.** An assortment of 50 choice varieties, including the finest of the self, flake, yellow, fancy, bizarre, and perpetual-flowering varieties...		..	10	6
253	,,	**25 varieties**	... ...	6	0
254	,,	12 choicest self varieties	...	4	6
255	,,	12 ,, flake varieties	...	4	6
256	,,	12 ,, bizarre varieties ...	...	4	6
257	,,	12 ,, yellow flake varieties	...	5	0
258	,,	12 ,, fancy varieties	..	4	6
259	,,	12 ,, yellow fancy varieties	..	5	0
260	,,	**DANIELS' CHOICEST MXD.** per pkt.		5	0
261	,,	,, ,, ,, smaller pkt.		2	6
262	,,	,, ,, ,, smallest pkt.		1	6
263	,,	choicest yellow	...	3	6
264	,,	pure white. Very choice	..	3	6
265	,,	**NEW DWARF.** Very fine and compact	.	2	6
266	,,	**GRENADIN.** Brilliant scarlet	...	1	6
267	,,	Pure white	...	1	6
268	,,	**DANIELS' PERPETUAL or TREE.** Very choice ; magnificent for pot culture		5	0
269	,,	,, ,, ,, smaller pkt.		2	6
270	,,	**MARGARET.** Pretty double, fringed flowers, deliciously scented. Sown early will bloom freely the first year from seed : splendid for pots		1	0
271	**PICOTEES.** An assortment of 50 choice varieties, including the finest white-ground, yellow-ground, and perpetual-flowering varieties		...	10	6
272	,,	**25 varieties**	... ...	6	0
273	,,	12 choicest white-ground varieties...		4	0
274	,,	12 ,, yellow-ground varieties ...		5	0
275	,,	**DANIELS' CHOICEST MIXED**		5	0
276	,,	,, ,, ,, smaller pkt.		2	6
277	,,	,, ,, ,, smallest pkt.		1	6
278	**GARDEN PINK.** Very choice double, mixed 1s. 6d. and			2	6

CARNATIONS AND PICOTEES.

From **Mr. T. HOSSACK**, Seaford.
July 29th
"The **Carnation** Seed which I had from you last year has turned out splendid ; they were greatly admired by all who saw them."

Daniels' Choice Florists' Flower Seeds.

DANIELS' SUPERB CINERARIAS.

Daniels' Superb Cinerarias.

Our grand strain of Cineraria hybrida, as figured, has been carefully saved from our fine collection of named and choicest seedling flowers, and which we have every confidence in recommending as unsurpassable. The colours will be found varied and brilliant, combined with a faultless habit of plant and form of flower.

WHEN required for a general display in early Spring, the seeds should be sown in July or early in August, and when for Winter blooming, a few should be sown in March or April. Where the quantity of glass available is somewhat limited, the July sown will, however, be found the most useful. Sow in well-drained pots or pans of light rich soil, giving the seeds but a very slight covering, and place in a cool frame or under a hand-light in a shady spot, pot off singly into small pots as soon as the young plants are large enough, and shift as required. Good Cinerarias may also be easily raised by sowing in July or August in a moist shady situation in the open air, taking care to pot up in September. Cinerarias will bear a great amount of cold, but should never be exposed to frost. Green fly, damp, excessive waterings, and extreme dryness should also be carefully guarded against.

		per pkt.—s. d.
279	**DANIELS' CHOICEST MIXED** 1s 6d., 2s. 6d., and	5 0
280	**PURE WHITE.** Very useful ...	1 6
281	**BLUE.** Fine dark colour ...	1 6
282	**NEW DWARF.** A fine compact-growing class with large handsome flowers, height from four to six inches, exceedingly floriferous. Choicest mixed ...	2 6
283	**DOUBLE-FLOWERED.** Very fine, will produce a large percentage of handsome double flowers ... 2s. 6d. and	5 0

Annual Chrysanthemums.

AN exceedingly showy family of hardy annuals, for mixed beds or borders, growing from eighteen inches to two feet high. Our illustration conveys a very fair idea of the beauty of the C. carinatum section. C. Burridgeanum, and the new double-flowered hybrids are very handsome, the latter producing very beautiful and rich colours; all the varieties are easy of cultivation. Very floriferous and useful for cutting.

		per pkt.—s. d.
284	**Carinatum Burridgeanum.** Crimson, white, and yellow ...	0 3
285	„ **hybridum, fl. pl.** A beautiful strain, producing finely-formed double flowers in great variety of colour ...	1 0
286	„ **Tricolor, Eclipse.** This type is well shown by our illustration; very useful for cutting	0 6
287	„ **atrococcineum.** Deep crimson ...	0 3
288	„ **aureum.** Bright yellow ...	0 3
289	„ **Dunnetti, double white** ...	0 3
290	„ „ **double yellow** ...	0 3
291	**Coronarium, double yellow** } Fine border	0 3
292	„ „ **white** } plants	0 3
293	**Segetum grandiflorum.** Large golden yellow; very useful for cutting	0 3
294	**Frutescens** (*White Marguerite*, or *Parisian Daisies*) ...	0 6
295	„ **Etoile d'Or.** A golden yellow form of the preceding ...	0 6

FLORISTS' CHRYSANTHEMUMS, see page 67.

CHRYSANTHEMUM CARINATUM TRICOLOR, ECLIPSE.

From C. H. THORP, Esq., Hagnalstown
April 6th.
" I think it right to say that the **Cinerarias** I had from you were exceptionally good."

From H. WADDLE, Esq., Llanelly.
" I must add a word in praise of your **Primulas** and **Cinerarias**; the strains are perfection."

Daniels' Choice Florists' Flower Seeds.

Dahlias—Single and Double.

Sow in February or March in light rich soil, and place in a gentle heat; when the young plants are about two inches high, pot off singly into small pots, place in a frame or greenhouse where a gentle heat is maintained, gradually hardening them off preparatory to planting out towards the end of May. After they are transferred to the open air, give them a slight protection for a few nights if the weather be cold. A liberal application of weak liquid manure in dry weather will greatly assist in the development of fine flowers.

The single-flowered varieties are especially valuable for cultivation in this way. They commence blooming in July or August, and continue with a profusion of lovely flowers till killed by the frost; are exceedingly useful for cut flowers, and should be grown freely in every garden.

		per pkt.—s. d.
296	**SINGLE-FLOWERED HYBRIDS.** Carefully saved from our grand collection of choice named flowers, and may be expected to produce some fine novelties	1 0
297	,, ,, ,, ,, smaller pkt.	0 6
298	**LARGE-FLOWERED DOUBLE.** Carefully saved from our superb collection of upwards of 250 choicest show and fancy varieties. Will produce a large percentage of fine double flowers	1 6
299	**POMPONE or BOUQUET.** Beautiful miniature varieties with handsome double flowers	1 6
300	**CACTUS-FLOWERED.** From finest varieties	1 6

Delphiniums.

BEAUTIFUL hardy border perennials, with noble spikes of handsome flowers, varying in colour from pure white to the richest blues and purples; exceedingly useful for cut flowers, &c.

		per pkt.—s. d.				per pkt.—s. d.
301	**Barlowi.** Dark blue, shaded red ...	1 0	308	**Formosum cœlestinum.** Beautiful light blue	0 6
302	**Cardinale.** Scarlet, fine ...	1 6	309	**Hermann Stenger.** Violet mauve, double	1 0
303	**Cashmerianum.** Very fine dark blue ...	0 6	310	**Zalil (Sulphureum).** With long spikes of	
304	**Chinense pumila alba.** White, dwarf ...	0 6		beautiful yellow flowers	1 0
305	,, ,, **cœrulea.** Light blue, dwarf...	0 6	311	**Nudicaule.** Orange scarlet, very distinct, fine ...	0 6
306	**Elatum "Le Mastodonte."** Bright blue with		312	**Choicest mixed single.** In beautiful variety...	0 6
	white centre	0 6	313	**Double-flowered, choicest mixed.** Fine	
307	**Formosum.** Rich dark blue, beautiful ...	0 4		new varieties	1 0

Dianthuses.

DIANTHUS DIADEMATUS FL. PL.

THE Chinese or Indian Pinks constitute one of the most brilliant and splendid groups of hardy biennials in cultivation. All the varieties are easily raised from seed; and sown early in Spring under glass and transplanted, they make charming beds during the Summer and Autumn. The Heddewigi section produce the largest flowers, and are perhaps the most beautiful; but all are richly deserving of extensive cultivation, and no garden should be found without some of the varieties.

		per pkt.—s. d.
314	**Heddewigi, Crimson Gem.** Splendid dark crimson; single ...	0 6
315	,, ,, **diadematus fl. pl.** *(The Diadem Pink).* Fine double flowers	0 6
316	,, ,, **The Bride** (new). White, with purple centre ...	1 0
317	,, ,, **atropurpureus fl. pl.** Large dark blood red; splendid	0 6
318	,, ,, **Choicest mixed single**	1 0
319	,, ,, ,, ,, smaller pkt.	0 6
320	,, ,, **laciniatus sanguineus.** Brilliant scarlet ...	0 6
321	,, ,, ,, **Snowflake,** beautiful pure white ...	0 6
322	,, ,, ,, Choicest double-flowered, mixed ...	0 6
323	,, ,, ,, Single-flowered, choice mixed ...	0 6
324	,, ,, **Salmon Queen.** The flowers are nicely fringed and well-formed, the colour being a most brilliant salmon, a quite distinct and perfectly new tint ...	1 6
325	**Chinensis** *(Indian Pink).* An assortment of 12 choice double-flowered varieties	2 6
326	,, **Finest double, mixed**	0 6
327	,, **alba fl. pl.** White, double	0 6

Fuchsias.

Sow in February or March in a gentle heat, and treat as recommended for tender annuals. These beautiful free-flowering plants will bloom well the first year from seed, and plants raised from a first-class strain will produce the most satisfactory results. The single varieties are all handsome in flower and elegant in growth of plant; and the double-flowered, with white or purple corollas, are very fine and desirable.

From a fine collection, including all the newest and best white corolla and other varieties.

		per pkt.—s. d.
328	**Choicest mixed.** Single	2 6
329	,, ,, Double	2 6
330	**Boliviana.** A fine species, with long racemes of splendid scarlet flowers	2 6

Daniels' Choice Florists' Flower Seeds.

GAILLARDIA HYBRIDA GRANDIFLORA.

DOUBLE HOLLYHOCK.

Gaillardia hybrida grandiflora.

SPLENDID hardy perennials, blooming the first year from seed sown in March or April in a cool frame. The very large and beautiful flowers are almost unique in their charming blendings of the many rich shades of brown, maroon, and golden yellow, and being of good substance are first-class to cut for indoor decoration. The seed we offer has been carefully saved at our Nurseries during the past season, from a choice collection of the finest named and seedling varieties.

			s.	d.
331	Choicest mixed seed, saved from a charming collection of named flowers ... per pkt. 6d. and		1	0

Gloxinias.

THESE, the most exquisitely beautiful of all greenhouse plants, bloom freely the first year from seed, and should be grown largely by every one having accommodation for them. Sow in February or March on a good moist heat, in the way recommended for Calceolarias. Pot off singly into small pots as soon as the young plants can be handled, and shift into larger as required, keeping the plants going with a good liberal warmth, and finally potting off into pots of about six inches diameter, using a light and rich soil, and continuing with a moderate heat and giving air on warm days. Treated in this way, a charming display of bloom may be had during July and August, and from a good strain of seed some really grand flowers will be the result.

Gloxinia hybrida grandiflora erecta.

We have much pleasure in offering our fine strain of seed, which has been grown expressly for our retail trade. The blooms will be found of immense size, and of the most brilliant, varied, and beautiful colours and markings. The leaves, which are large, and of great substance, have a rich velvety appearance, and being finely reflexed, the plants are exceedingly handsome.

					per pkt.—s.	d.
332	Corona. Enormous blooms. 3 to 4½ inches across, with six, and often seven, divisions or lobes, and a large richly-veined throat of deep violet red, passing into a beautiful indigo towards the orifice; the pure white outer ground is marked with innumerable dark blue dots				1	6
333	Cœlestina. Azure blue with white throat; splendid				1	6
334	Defiance. A grand variety, bearing large upright flowers of the most intense scarlet-crimson colour; comes quite true from seed				1	6
335	Fire King. A magnificent variety, bearing large, erect, well-formed flowers, of an intense glowing dark scarlet colour, with stout, handsome, rich green foliage ...				1	6
336	Striped and spotted varieties. Very choice ...				2	6
337	Splendid varieties, mixed ...	...	...	...	5	0
338	,,	,,	,,	... smaller pkt.	2	6
339	,,	,,	,,	... ,,	1	6

Hollyhock—Daniels' Prize.

THESE magnificent flowers, with their stately spikes of handsome bloom, form grand and conspicuous objects in the flower garden during Summer and Autumn, and should always be grown where convenient They are easily raised from seed, and sown in January or February in a good heat under glass will bloom splendidly the same year. When grown in this way a light rich soil should be used; the plants should be potted singly into small pots as soon as large enough to handle, shifting into larger as those fill with roots, gradually hardening off, and finally planting out early in May. The seed we offer has been grown especially for our retail trade, and may be relied on to produce some grand double blooms in the most beautiful variety of colours.

			s.	d.
340	Daniels' choicest double, mixed ... per pkt.		2	6
341	,, ,, ,, smaller pkt.		1	6
342	Twelve superb double-flowered varieties, separate		5	0
343	Six ,, ,, ,, ,,		2	6

Daniels' Choice Florists' Flower Seeds.

DANIELS' STRIPED FRENCH MARIGOLDS.

Daniels' Superb Marigolds.

We give special attention to the growth and selection of our choice strains of Marigolds, and can highly recommend our Orange and Lemon African and Striped French as being the finest procurable.

		per pkt.—s. d.	
344	**ORANGE AFRICAN.** A magnificent selection from a prize strain, bearing immense brilliant, orange-coloured, perfectly double flowers, often seven to eight inches across	1	0
345	,, smaller pkt.	0	6
346	**LEMON AFRICAN.** The same as preceding in size and form of flower, and habit of plant, but varying in colour	1	0
347	,, smaller pkt.	0	6
348	**DANIELS' STRIPED FRENCH (Scotch Prize).** A fine strain of beautifully striped flowers of the most perfect form and doubleness. Grown expressly for our retail trade by one of the best growers in Scotland	2	6
349	,, smaller pkt.	1	6
350	**DANIELS' TALL FRENCH** (English saved). A very showy strain. Flowers large, perfectly double and beautifully striped and marked with golden yellow and rich brown ... ... 6d. &	1	0
351	**Dwarf, striped.** Ordinary class ... 3d. &	0	6
352	**Aurea floribunda.** Dwarf golden yellow ...	0	6
353	**Pulchra nana.** Golden yellow, dark centre, very dwarf	0	6
354	**Dwarf Brown French**	0	3
355	**Signata pumila.** Excellent for bedding	0	3
356	**Legion of Honour.** Single, golden yellow with crimson blotch, very pretty	0	6

Pentstemons.

THIS beautiful class of showy hardy free-flowering perennials has been much improved of late years. The plants are easily raised from seed sown in Spring on a gentle heat, and will afford a splendid show throughout the Autumn months. Some of the varieties with white throats are extremely handsome.

		per pkt.—s. d.	
357	**Gentianoides.** Very fine, various beautiful colours	0	9
358	**Lobbi.** Splendid yellow	1	0
359	**Murrayanus.** Brilliant scarlet	1	0
360	**Palmeri.** Peach-coloured, fine	1	0
361	**Wrighti.** Fine scarlet	0	6
362	**Choicest mixed hybrids.** From named flowers	1	0

Pelargoniums—Geraniums.

Sow in February or March in pots or pans of light rich soil, covering the seeds to the depth of about one-eighth of an inch, and place in a heat of about sixty-five or seventy degrees. Pot off the young plants singly into small pots, and shift into larger as these fill with roots. With liberal treatment these will bloom the first year, and, although many will not be up to the standard of first-class florists' flowers, some really beautiful varieties may be expected from a good strain of seed, and all will be found well worth the small amount of time and trouble expended. Seeds may also be sown in July and August for blooming the following Spring.

		per pkt.—s. d.	
363	**Large-flowered Show.** Very choice mixed ...	1	6
364	**French Blotched or Spotted.** Magnificent ...	2	6
365	**Fancy.** Choicest mixed	1	6
366	**Impregnated Tricolor and Bronze Leaved**	2	6
367	,, ,, ,, smaller pkt.	1	6
368	**Zonal and Nosegay.** From the newest varieties ...	2	6
369	,, ,, ,, smaller pkt.	1	6

DANIELS' SUPERB PRIZE PANSIES.

From **Mr. J. LOCKE**, Plympton St. Mary.

July 25th.

"I am pleased to inform you that the 1s. 6d. packet of **Pansy** Seed I had of you for a friend has given great satisfaction; taking First Prize against all comers at the Plympton Cottage Garden Show, and were the best Pansies in the Show."

From **Mr. C. ASHMAN**, Coleford.

March 15th.

"The **Pansy** Seed that I received from you proved to bring forth a most splendid show of Pansies; they were admired by all who passed by."

From **Mr. R. DAVIES**, Corris.

June 18th.

"I am glad to inform you that I took First Prize with **Pansies** at Corris Show last August; also First at Machynlleth."

From **Mr. J. MAYDEW**, Market Drayton.

"The **Primulas** I had of you last year were really splendid."

From **Mr. W. BREEDON**, Chirbury.

Aug. 5th.

"The last **Primulas** I had of you were the finest I ever grew; they continued in blossom upwards of twelve months."

Daniels' Choice Florists' Flower Seeds.

Daniels' Superb Prize Pansies.

Our Strains of Pansy are very fine.

THESE beautiful free-flowering hardy plants are easily raised from seed, and will richly repay the small cost and trouble required to grow them to perfection. For blooming in Summer and Autumn, sow in February, March, and April, in pans or boxes of light rich soil placed in a gentle heat, and as soon as the young plants are large enough, prick out about two inches apart on rich soil to strengthen, and finally plant out six or eight inches apart, in ground into which a good quantity of well-decayed manure has been worked. Pansies delight in a somewhat shady position, and plenty of moisture in dry weather. The finest blooms are produced the second year, but grand flowers may be had by sowing in July or August in the open ground, and planting out in the following Spring into good rich soil.

		per pkt.—s.	d.
370	**DANIELS' PRIZE BLOTCHED.** A magnificent strain of fine varieties, producing large, handsome flowers of great substance and variety of colouring, the petals of which are beautifully blotched or stained. Splendid varieties mixed	2	6
371	smaller pkt.	1	6
372	**ENGLISH SHOW AND FANCY.** Carefully saved from a fine collection of choice English Show and Fancy varieties	1	6
373	**IMPROVED STRIPED.** A fine class producing large, beautifully formed flowers of the most brilliant and exquisite tints in colouring, the blooms being handsomely striped. A great improvement on the striped Belgian varieties	0	6
374	**PEACOCK.** This charming variety is exceedingly attractive, its beautiful combination of colours amply justifying its name. On each of the upper petals is a large blotch of peacock blue on a maroon ground surrounded with crimson, and margined with a narrow edging of white. The remaining petals are crimson heavily shaded with rich maroon, the lower one being ornamented with a spot of peacock blue, all edged with white, in the same manner as the upper petals	1	0
375	**Giant Emperor William.** A superb new variety, with very large deep ultramarine blue flowers	1	6
376	**Giant King of the Blacks.** Fine large flowers of an intense dark colour, almost as black as jet	1	6
377	**Giant Golden Queen.** A superb Pansy, bearing immense bright golden-yellow flowers, marked in the centre with a few small dark stripes. Highly recommended as a really first-class bedder	1	6

		per pkt.—s.	d.
378	**Yellow Giant.** Pure yellow, with large black centre; fine	1	0
379	**Giant Lord Beaconsfield.** Beautiful variety of a rich deep purple violet colour, shading off in the top petals to white; a very effective bedder	1	6
380	**White Giant.** Pure white, with purple eye; beautiful	1	0
381	**Giant Striped.** The perfection of striped Pansies. The plants are of sturdy, compact habit of growth, and the very large flowers are elegantly striped with the most brilliant and charming colours	1	0
382	**TRIMARDEAU or GIANT.** An entirely distinct and splendid class of vigorous compact growth, producing immense flowers of good form and colour	1	0
383	**Candidissima** (Snow Queen.) Delicate satiny white, very pretty	0	6
384	**Emperor William.** An exceedingly fine variety for bedding out, &c.; colour a rich ultramarine blue; distinct and beautiful	0	6
385	**Quadricolor.** Very beautiful and distinct	0	6
386	**Blue King.** Bright deep blue; fine for bedding	1	0
387	**Cliveden Yellow.** Fine golden yellow	0	6
388	**,, Purple.** Purplish maroon	0	6
389	**,, White**	0	6
390	**Light blue.** Beautiful colour	1	0
391	**Pure white.** Very beautiful	1	0
392	**Pure yellow.** Bright golden yellow	1	0
393	**Rich purple.** Lovely dark colour	1	0
394	**King of the Blacks.** Black as jet	1	0
395	**Mixed.** Ordinary class, good showy vars. 3d. and	0	6
396	**An assortment of 12 beautiful vars.** (German)	2	6
397	,, ,, 6 ,, ,,	1	6

(The column of text between items 388–394 reads vertically: "Exceedingly valuable and beautiful varieties for Spring bedding; very floriferous and constant bloomers.")

Chrysanthemums.

THESE superb Autumn-blooming hardy perennials will bloom finely the first year from seed sown in Spring on a gentle heat, and the plants grown on freely. The seed we offer has been carefully saved from a fine collection of choice named varieties, and may be expected to produce some grand flowers.

			per pkt.—s.	d.
398	**Large-flowered,** incurved, &c., choicest mixed		1	6
399	**Japanese.** Fine new		1	6
400	**Pompone.** Miniature vars.		1	6

Coleus, Choicest Mixed.

CAREFULLY saved from the newest and finest varieties. These beautiful ornamental-foliaged plants are easily raised in the way recommended for tuberous-rooted Begonias, and being of rapid growth, soon form nice plants for the greenhouse or drawing-room, their exquisite and varied markings and variegations making them highly interesting.

			per pkt.—s.	d.
401	**NEW LARGE-LEAVED HYBRIDS.** This is a grand strain of large-leaved and brilliantly coloured varieties, invaluable for the decoration of the greenhouse or conservatory. The seed offered has been carefully hybridised, and will produce a splendid variety of beautiful foliage		2	6
402	**An assortment of 12 choice sorts,** 10 seeds each		3	0
403	**Choicest mixed**		1	6

From F. **FOWELL**, Esq., Hopton.

June 18th.
"I have had a splendid show of **Blotched Pansies** this year from your Seed, and they still look rich and have been much admired."

From Mr. H. **FOSTER**, Ipswich.

Feb. 19th.
"I have some of your **Primulas** in bloom now, the equal of which I have never seen before; they are simply perfection."

Daniels' Choice Florists' Flower Seeds.

DANIELS' SUPERB MIMULUS.

From **Mr. T. PORLEY,** Ipswich.

Aug. 18th.
" Respecting the Carnation Seed I had from you last year, I wish to inform you it turned out a most splendid lot of double flowers all shades and colours. '

Mimulus.

Sow the seeds in March or April on the surface of pots or pans of firmly pressed light rich soil, cover very slightly with fine soil and sand, sprinkle gently with a fine rose water-pot, and place in a gentle heat of about sixty degrees, not more. A piece of glass laid over the pot or pan will assist germination by ensuring an even moisture. When the young plants come up, keep near the glass and give plenty of air, and soon as they can be handled pot off singly into small pots, or prick out five or six in a five-inch pot to strengthen, give plenty of air and moisture, and plant out in May, or shift into larger pots for continuing under glass. A somewhat shady position is the most favourable for blooming, and, when planted out, a north or north-westerly aspect will be best, and the plants should have an abundance of water in dry weather.

		per pkt.—s.	d.
404	**DANIELS' LARGE-FLOWERED.** A magnificent break, remarkable for the great size and rich colouring of the flowers and the vigorous habit of the plants. First-class for pot culture in the greenhouse, conservatory, or window Choicest mixed	1	0
405	„ ,, smaller pkt.	0	6
406	**Giant Emperor, Duplex.** A superb large-flowered variety of the hose-in-hose type. The calyx is of large size, and of the same rich and beautiful colouring as the flower itself. A charming plant for pot culture or the gardou ...	1	0
407	**Cupreus Brilliant.** Orange scarlet ...	0	4
408	**White-ground varieties.** Choice mixed ...	0	6
409	**Hose-in-Hose varieties.** Mixed ...	0	6
410	**Choice mixed.** Good varieties ...	0	3
411	**Moschatus** (*Musk plant*). Well known ...	0	4
412	„ **compactus.** A new and excellent variety of the preceding, very dwarf and compact	0	6

Lobelias.

To secure fine plants of the *erinus* or *speciosa* varieties of these for bedding out the following May, some prefer to sow the seed in Autumn, but February or March is good time for sowing if the plants have careful attention and are grown on freely. Sow the seeds thinly in pans or pots of sandy loam, cover very lightly, and place in a gentle heat of about sixty degrees, keep moist, and soon as the young plants can be handled, pot off singly into small pots of light rich soil, keep near the glass in a gentle heat, and give plenty of air on fine days. Carefully picking off all the flower buds will greatly assist their growth, and they should on no account be allowed to suffer from want of moisture. Other excellent methods are to prick the young plants five or six in a five-inch pot, or better still, to plant them thinly in shallow trays of rich soil, keeping in gentle heat, giving air, &c., as recommended. These will generally form compactly-grown sturdy plants, that will quickly produce a beautiful effect when planted out. Lobelias intended for pots or window boxes succeed best when planted out thinly in good soil in an open situation, and carefully lifted when they have formed nice tufty plants: these will at once commence blooming, and produce an effect that could not be otherwise obtained.

The beautiful perennial *L. fulgens Victoria*, growing about two feet high, with its rich metallic foliage and brilliant scarlet flowers, comes quite true from seed, and sown in February or March on a gentle heat will make nice plants for bedding-out in May or June for blooming the following Autumn. The roots of these should be protected in severe weather by a covering of cocoa-nut refuse, ashes, or any light similar material, or they may be lifted after flowering, and stored in a cool pit or frame for the Winter, and planted out again the following April or May,

		per pkt.—s.	d.
413	**BARNARD'S PERPETUAL** (new). This splendid novelty is without doubt the finest Lobelia yet raised. The flowers are of the most brilliant ultramarine blue, strikingly ornamented with a pure white marking at the base of each of the two lower petals. It is of compact habit, and alike useful for bedding or growing in pots, while the bright and effective colouring of its flowers, combined with its perpetual blooming character, ensures it the premier position in parterres and ribbon borders. It was awarded a Certificate of Merit by the Royal Horticultural Society, when exhibited in May, 1882, at the Temple Show	1	0
414	**Speciosa** (true). Fine dark blue ...	0	6
415	„ **superba.** Dark blue with large white eye	0	6
416	„ **White Perfection.** Very fine white	0	6

		per pkt.—s.	d.
417	**Paxtoniana.** Blue and white, pretty ...	0	3
418	**Erinus compacta.** Bright blue ...	0	6
419	„ „ **alba** (White Gem). Fine ...	0	6
420	„ „ **Distinction.** Bright rose...	0	6
421	„ „ **Emperor William.** Rich dark blue...	0	6
422	„ „ **Cobalt blue.** Very fine dark blue ...	0	6
423	„ **Royal Purple** (new). Rich violet purple, with large white eye, very distinct ...	1	0
424	**Gracilis.** Blue ...	0	3
425	„ **alba.** White	0	3
426	**Pumila magnifica.** Splendid dwarf compact variety, with large dark blue flowers ...	1	0
426	**Ramosa.** Dark blue... ...	0	3
427	„ **alba.** White	0	3
428	**Fulgens, Queen Victoria.** Brilliant scarlet...	1	0

SWEET PEAS—(Lathyrus odoratus).

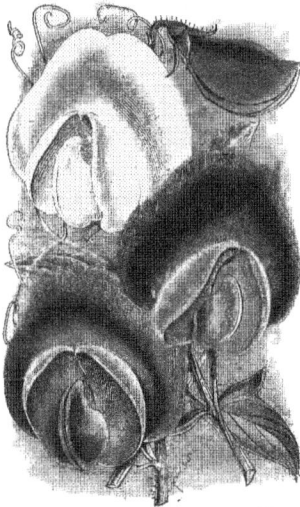

These well-known beautiful hardy annual climbers may be reckoned amongst the most delightful of our garden flowers, they are exceedingly useful for covering wire fences or trellises, and when in full bloom produce the most lovely effect. The brilliantly coloured and charmingly tinted flowers are deliciously fragrant, and when cut and placed in water will retain their beauty for several days. The cut blooms are admirably suited for mixed bouquets, and for specimen-glasses; a few choice blooms with a spray of Maiden-hair Fern have a very refined and pleasing appearance, whilst for button-holes, a combination spray of such fine sorts as Countess of Radnor and Primrose, is almost equal to a spray of choice Orchids.

SUPERB NEW VARIETIES OF 1895.

per pkt.—s. d.

429 **BLANCHE BURPEE—New Giant White.** A pure white, of exquisite form and immense size, having a bold rigid upright, shell-shaped standard, of great substance ... 6d. and 1 0

430 **DUCHESS OF YORK.** White, deeply striped and barred with delicate pinkish purple; a very pleasing shade of colour, and a large flower of perfect form ... 2 6

431 **DUKE OF YORK.** The standard is bright rosy pink with a primrose tint in it; the wings are primrose tinted white, and it is a distinct fine variety ... 2 6

432 **ELIZA ECKFORD.** Award of Merit, Royal Horticultural Society. Standards a pretty line of rose, the back of the standards having each a flake of deep rose and tinted with the same; the wings delicately striped with rose ... 2 6

433 **METEOR.** The standards very bright orange salmon; the wings delicate pink with slight veins of purple, a flower possessing rare novelty; very rich ... 2 6

434 **MRS. JOSEPH CHAMBERLAIN.** White, striped and flaked heavily with bright rose, a charming flower, fine form; very striking and pretty ... 2 6

435 **NOVELTY.** Orange rose standards; the wings delicate mauve, lightly margined with rose; very bright ... 1 6

NEW VARIETIES (Eckford, &c.).

per pkt.—s. d.

436 **Apple-blossom.** Rose and white, pretty ... 0 6
437 **Boreatton.** Fine deep maroon self ... 0 6
438 **Captain of the Blues.** Bright purple blue with pale blue wings; a very striking variety ... 0 6
439 **Cardinal.** Shining crimson scarlet ... 0 6
440 **Countess of Radnor.** Pale mauve standards with a deeper shading of mauve, wings pale lilac or delicate mauve, most chaste and lovely variety 0 6
441 **Dorothy Tennant.** Pucy violet or rose mauve self, very distinct and beautiful. F.C.C. ... 0 6
442 **Emily Eckford.** A superb flower of a well-marked cerulean tint, the standards suffused with reddish mauve, closely approaches a true blue ... 1 6
443 **Firefly.** A self-coloured, intense, glowing crimson, good size and substance, a very free bloomer ... 1 0
444 **Her Majesty.** A beautiful soft rosy pink ... 0 6
445 **Imperial Blue.** Blue shaded mauve, very distinct 0 6
446 **Isa Eckford.** Creamy white, suffused with rosy pink. First Class Certificate, R.H.S. ... 0 6
447 **Lady Beaconsfield.** Salmon standards tinted with rose, the wings pale yellow; very distinct and beautiful ... 2 0
448 **Lady Penzance.** Pale but very bright rose, very striking and distinct, a most chaste and lovely flower ... 2 0
449 **Lemon Queen.** Delicate pink standards, tinted with lemon, with blush almost white wings ... 0 6
450 **Miss Blanche Ferry.** Bright rosy crimson standards, with creamy white wings; very pretty 0 6
451 **Miss Hunt.** Pale carmine salmon standards, with soft pink wings; very pretty indeed ... 0 6
452 **Mrs. Eckford.** Delicate, shaded primrose, a most exquisite variety. First Class Certificate, R.H.S. 1 0

453 **Mrs. Gladstone.** Delicate pink standards, the wings blush edged with delicate pink. F.C.C. 0 6
454 **Mrs. Sankey.** Pure white, a large, bold flower; a fine improvement on all other whites ... 0 6
455 **Orange Prince.** Bright orange pink, flushed with scarlet. First Class Certificate, R.H.S. ... 0 6
456 **Ovid.** The standards and wings bright rose pink margined with rose, a very pleasing flower; a great gem ... 2 0
457 **Peach Blossom.** Salmon pink standards, the wings soft pink, very pleasing indeed ... 2 0
458 **Primrose.** A near approach to a yellow Sweet Pea. The standards and wings pale primrose yellow, quite novel and distinct in colour. F.C.C. ... 0 6
459 **Purple Prince.** Maroon standards, shaded with bronze and purple-blue wings; very fine & distinct 0 6
460 **Royal Robe.** Delicate pink standards, wings soft blush pink, a lovely flower; an exquisite variety 2 0
461 **Senator.** Creamy ground, shaded and striped with chocolate; a lovely variety. F.C.C. ... 0 6
462 **Splendour.** Rich, bright, pinkish rose, shaded with crimson. Flowers large and of the finest form: a most superb and distinct variety ... 0 6
463 **Stanley.** Deep maroon self, large, very handsome, distinct, beautiful flower, of the finest form and substance; a great advance ... 2 0
464 **The Queen.** Rosy pink, shaded with mauve ... 0 6
465 **Venus.** Salmon buff, the standards delicately shaded rosy pink, very distinct; a most charming flower. Award of Merit, Royal Horticultural Society ... 1 0
466 **Waverley.** Rosy claret shaded standards, pale blue wings shaded with rose; very distinct ... 1 0
467 **Eckford's varieties.** Choicest mixed 6d. and 1 0

SWEET PEAS.

ECKFORD'S VARIETIES IN COLLECTIONS.

The sorts given in these collections are carefully selected to ensure the best possible variety. Grown separately in this way, Sweet Peas are highly interesting.

				s. d.
468	18 Choice Varieties, 25 seeds each			4s. 6d.
469	12 ,, ,, 25 ,, ...			3s. 0d.
470	6 ,, ,, 25 ,, ...			1s. 6d.

SWEET PEAS—Ordinary Class.

per pkt.—s. d.

471 **An assortment of 12 Choice Varieties** ... 2 0
472 **Invincible Scarlet.** Brilliant scarlet ... 0 3
473 **White.** Very useful ... 0 3
474 **Painted Lady.** Rose and white ... 0 3
475 **Black or Purple.** Dark purple ... 0 3
476 **Striped.** Scarlet striped ... 0 3
477 **Mixed.** In beautiful variety ... per pint 3s. 0 3

Daniels' Choice Florists' Flower Seeds.

PETUNIA, DOUBLE, FRINGED.

Petunias—Daniels' Superb Fringed.

A NEW and splendid class, producing large and strikingly beautiful flowers, the edges of the petals being elegantly laciniated or fringed.

				s.	d.
478	Single, very choice, mixed	... per pkt.	2	0
479	,, ,, ,,	smaller pkt.	1	0
480	Double, an assortment of 6 superb vars.	3	6
481	,, Choicest mixed ...	...	2	0
482	,, ,, ,,	... smaller pkt.	1	0
483	,, Brilliant Rose. Beautiful bright rose; most charming variety	...	2	0
484	Lady of the Lake. Beautiful large fringed, pure white, double flowers, superb	...	2	0

Petunia—Ordinary Class.

485	Choicest mixed. Beautiful showy varieties for beds or borders ...	...	1	0
486	,, ,, ... smaller pkts. 3d. &	0	6
487	Large-flowered Striped. Very choice	...	1	0
488	New Dwarf Striped. A fine new compact and distinct variety, growing about eight inches high; bearing a profusion of pretty striped flowers	1	0

From **Miss MARTIN**, Newmarket.

March 19th.

"Miss Martin purchased in 1894, of Messrs. Daniels, a packet of mixed **Fern-leaved Primula**, and they have come up most beautiful plants with fine foliage and lovely colours."

Daniels' Superb Petunias.

PETUNIAS in their many beautiful varieties form a highly interesting and desirable class of free-flowering plants for pot or garden culture; those of the *grandiflora* section, both single and double-flowered, being especially valuable. The blooms of these are of immense size, beautifully formed, and of the most charming and delicate colours; some of the flowers are exquisitely veined or pencilled, others blotched or striped. The new "Fringed" varieties, both double and single, produce some charming flowers, the edges of the petals being elegantly cut or fringed, whilst the colours are most varied and beautiful. The seed we offer has been carefully saved from fecundated flowers of the finest varieties; but as Petunias raised from seed have a tendency to "sport," we cannot guarantee more than sixty or seventy per cent. of flowers true to description. All will, however, be found well worth growing, and occasionally some fine novelties may be secured. Petunias for indoor cultivation may be sown in January or early in February, but those intended for bedding out do not require to be sown before March. A soil composed of two parts leaf-mould and one part loam, with the addition of a little sharp sand, forms an excellent compost for these, but the seeds being very small require special care in sowing. Fill your pots or seed pans to near the rim and press the soil down firmly and evenly, sow thinly, and cover the seeds very slightly with fine soil, sprinkle gently with a fine rose water-pot, and place in a gentle heat of sixty or sixty-five degrees, not higher, and keep nicely moist. As soon as the young plants can be handled, prick them out about one inch apart in pots to strengthen, and when sufficiently advanced in growth pot off singly into small pots, gradually harden off when established, and plant out about the middle of May, or shift into large pots as required. In planting Petunias out of doors, ground should be selected that has not been freshly manured, otherwise a superabundant foliage will retard the flowering.

Petunia hybrida grandiflora.

A FINE and distinct class of beautiful, large-flowering varieties, producing blooms of immense size, and of the most charming colours; much superior to the old varieties of *Petunia hybrida*. The plants are robust in habit of growth, and admirably suited as pot-plants for the greenhouse or conservatory.

		per pkt.—s.	d.
489	An assortment of 12 choice varieties	...	3	6
490	,, 6 ,,	...	2	0
491	Alba. White, beautiful	...	1	0
492	Atrosanguinea. Very bright and effective. The blooms are of great size, and of a brilliant dark blood-crimson colour, the throat is well-opened and of a beautiful pure white, forming a most brilliant contrast with the outer parts of the flower ...	1	6
493	Kermesina. Fine, bright crimson	...	1	0
494	Maculata. Blotched, very handsome ...	...	1	0
495	Marginata. Fine large-flowered, bordered and veined with green	...	1	0
496	Prince of Wurtemberg. Beautiful rose, very large, extra fine	...	1	0
497	Purpurea. Fine dark, splendid	...	1	0
498	Rosea. White-throated, rose and white, very lovely	...	1	0
499	Superbissima. Magnificent variety, enormous flowers, fine robust plants	...	1	6
500	Venosa. Veined varieties	...	1	0
501	Violacea. Splendid bright deep violet ...	...	1	0
502	Choicest mixed	...	2	6
503	,, ,, ...	smaller pkt.	1	6

Petunia—Double-flowered.

SAVED from carefully hybridised flowers, will produce a good percentage of large, handsome, double flowers.

			s.	d.
504	Very choice, mixed	... per pkt.	2	6
505	,, ,,	smaller pkt.	1	6
506	An assortment of 6 choice sorts	...	2	6
507	Green-edged double varieties. Very choice, mixed	...	...	2	6

POPPY, NEW SHIRLEY.

MIGNONETTE DANIELS GIANT RED.

POPPIES—(Papaver).

A brilliant and charmingly effective group of plants, all annuals with the exception of the Nudicaule varieties and P. orientale; splendid for garden or shrubbery decoration during Summer and Autumn. The Shirley and Nudicaule varieties are especially valuable as cut flowers, and if cut and placed in water as the flowers are just opening, they will remain in full beauty for a long time.

		per pkt.—s.	d.
508	**POPPY—NEW SHIRLEY** (*see illustration*). Beautiful strain of Hardy Annual Poppy. The flowers are large, exceedingly graceful and elegant; the colours are pure, soft, and varied, and range from blush-white, rose, delicate pink, and carmine through innumerable tints to bright sparkling crimson; the petals have a glossy, satin-like, wavy surface of exquisite softness, which makes the flowers literally ripple with colour under the slightest movement ...	1	0
509	,, ,, ,, smaller pkt.	0	6
510	**SNOWDRIFT.** Beautiful pure white delicately fringed flowers, dwarf: charming variety ...	0	6
511	**THE TULIP POPPY** (*P. glaucum*). Splendid variety from Armenia, flowers large, vivid scarlet	1	0
512	**CARDINAL POPPY.** Very large double flowers, glowing scarlet on a white ground ...	0	6
513	**Pæony-flowered, double. Scarlet**	0	3
514	,, ,, ,, Pure white	0	3
515	,, ,, ,, Choicest mixed	0	3
516	**Carnation-flowered, double.** Choicest mixed ...	0	3
517	**Dwarf Ranunculus-flowered, double.** Choicest mixed ...	0	3
518	**Danebrog.** Brilliant scarlet blotched with silvery white ...	0	6
519	**Lœvigatum.** Brilliant dark scarlet, with black spots; very effective ...	0	6
520	**Pavonium** (*The Peacock Poppy*). Scarlet and black; very showy ...	0	6
521	**Umbrosum.** Height 18 inches; glowing vermilion with black spots ...	0	6
522	**Bracteatum nanum splendens.** Brilliant scarlet; dwarf Perennial Poppy ...	0	6
523	**Nudicaule.** Bright yellow	0	6
524	,, **album.** White	0	6
525	,, **miniatum.** Bright orange	0	6
526	,, **coccineum fl. pl.** Double flowering, bright orange scarlet variety ...	1	0
527	,, **Choicest mixed**	0	6
528	**Orientale.** Rich scarlet; a fine hardy perennial; two feet ...	0	6

(523–527) Iceland Poppies, charming hardy perennials, growing about one foot high.

Mignonette.

WELL-KNOWN deliciously fragrant hardy annuals. The following list includes the finest varieties for pot and garden culture.

		per pkt.—s.	d.
529	**DANIELS' GIANT RED.** A grand variety, growing two feet high, and throwing up very large spikes of red, highly-scented flowers ... 6d. and	1	0
530	**Golden Queen.** Flowers of a golden hue, dwarf and compact ...	0	6
531	**Machet.** A fine, sturdy, compact growing variety; one of the best for pots ...	0	6
532	**Crimson Queen.** A fine robust variety, excellent for pots ...	0	6
533	**Giant Pyramidal.** Reddish buff flowers; a fine tall variety ...	0	6
534	**Parsons' White.** A fine tall growing sort, with whitish spikes of fragrant bloom ...	0	6
535	**Pumila erecta.** A beautiful dwarf growing sort; excellent for pots ...	1	0
536	**A collection of six choice varieties** ...	1	6
537	**Large-flowered** ... per lb. 6s.; per oz. 6d.	0	3

Daniels' Choice Florists' Flower Seeds.

PHLOX DRUMMONDI GRANDIFLORA.

Phlox Drummondi.

ALL the varieties of this beautiful class of annuals are worthy of extensive cultivation, especially those of the *grandiflora* class, which produce such a charming profusion and diversity of their large beautifully formed and brilliantly coloured flowers. Those of the *compacta* section growing only about four to six inches in height are also highly desirable, being splendid for massing or beds, or for edgings, producing an effect that can probably be obtained by no other plant. All the sorts continue in bloom for a long season, and apart from their great usefulness for bedding are valuable for pot culture in the greenhouse, where they will give a beautiful display. Sow the seeds in February, March, or early in April, in pans or boxes of light rich soil; sow thinly, press down firmly, cover lightly, water, and place in a gentle heat. The young plants will be up in a few days, and soon as they can be fairly handled they should be pricked out about two inches apart in pans or boxes to strengthen, or potted singly into small pots, keep close for a few days, and when they are established give abundance of air, keeping close to the glass to induce a sturdy growth. May is soon enough for planting out, and a rather dry and sunny position is to be preferred. The dwarf kinds should be planted about eight inches or one foot apart; the others, which grow from nine inches to one foot in height, with a spreading habit, may be planted eighteen inches or two feet apart.

Phlox Drummondi nana compacta.

A BEAUTIFUL compact-growing class, many of the varieties only four or six inches high. Splendid for bedding, and first-class for pots or edgings of flower beds.

					per pkt.—s.	d.
538	**Six choice varieties**	...	...	...	2	6
539	**Atropurpurea.** Dark purple	...	...	...	0	6
540	**Carminea.** Bright carmine red	...	...	0	6
541	**Rosea.** Rose	...	...	...	0	6
542	**Snowball.** Pure white, very fine	...	...	0	6
543	**Fireball.** Brilliant scarlet	...	...	0	6
544	**Splendens.** Crimson, with white eye; splendid		1	0
545	**Victoria.** Deep scarlet, splendid	...		0	6
546	**Choicest mixed** ...	...	...	...	1	0
547	,, ,,	...	...	smaller pkt.	0	6

Phlox Drummondi grandiflora.

THE *Grandiflora* varieties form a magnificent class; the plants are robust in habit, and the flowers, which are of various rich and beautiful colours, have in many of the varieties large conspicuous white eyes; the individual blooms are of fine substance and scarcely inferior in size to the perennial sorts, and are a decided improvement on the old varieties of *P. Drummondi.*

					per pkt.—s.	d.
548	**An assortment of 12 splendid varieties**	...	3	6
549	,, 8 ,, ,,		2	6
550	**Alba.** Pure white	...	...	...	0	6
551	**Atropurpurea.** Dark purple	...	...	0	6
552	**Carminea.** Beautiful carmine, white eye	...	0	6
553	**Coccinea.** Brilliant scarlet	...	...	0	6
554	**Coccinea striata.** Beautiful scarlet-striped	...	0	6
555	**Rosea.** Delicate rose, white eye	...	...	0	6
556	**Stellata atropurpurea.** Purple, white eye	...	0	6
557	**Violacea.** Violet blue, white eye	...	...	0	6
558	**Splendens.** Fine vivid crimson, white eye	...	0	6
559	**Stellata splendens.** Brilliant crimson, with white eye, fine	...	...	...	1	0
560	**Choicest mixed.** In beautiful variety	...	1	0
561	,, ,,	...	smaller pkt.	0	6

From Mr. JOHN KENDALL.
Gardener to H. Waddle, Esq., Llanelly.

"The Begonias we had of you are now at this date beautiful, notwithstanding the wet weather only in August; I have also a fine lot of Gloxinias from your Seed."

Sept. 2nd.

From Mr. E. WHITE, Chapmanslade.

"The Seeds supplied by you have turned out remarkably well. The Asters and Stocks are something splendid, I took First Prize with Asters this year."

Phlox Drummondi cuspidata.
THE NEW STAR PHLOXES.

A VERY pretty class, with neat stellate flowers, of the most beautiful colours.

					per pkt.—s.	d.
562	**Choicest mixed.** In beautiful variety	...	1	0
563	,, ,,	...	...	smaller pkt.	0	6

Phlox Drummondi—Original Class.
VERY SHOWY and FREE-FLOWERING.

					per pkt.—s.	d.
564	**An assortment of 12 brilliant varieties**	...	2	6
565	,, ,, 6 ,, ,,		1	6
566	**Choicest mixed.** In beautiful variety	...	0	6
567	,, ,,	...	...	smaller pkt.	0	3

Perennial Phloxes.

THE many beautiful varieties of this splendid class of hardy perennials are too well known to need any description of ours. The seed we offer has been carefully saved from our fine collection of choice named flowers, and may be expected to produce some really fine varieties.

					per pkt.—s.	d.
568	**Tall varieties.** Splendid mixed	...	...	1	0
569	**Dwarf** ,, ,,	...	...	1	6

From Mr. G. BOLAND, Trimdon.

Feb. 22nd.

"The Stock Seed you have supplied me with for the last two years has given great satisfaction, having shown and taken First Prize for both years."

Daniels' Choice Florists' Flower Seeds.
Daniels' Superb Fringed Primulas.

It is with very much pleasure that we offer the grand strains of Primulas named below, all of which have been specially grown for our retail trade, and which cannot fail to give the highest satisfaction. The flowers will be found of great size and perfect form, combined with the most brilliant and charming colours, and a habit of plant which leaves nothing to be desired.

DANIELS' SUPERB FRINGED PRIMULAS.

The beautiful varieties of *Primula sinensis* may be sown in March, April, May, and June. The earlier sown are, however, to be preferred for making fine strong plants with an abundance of bloom. Great care must be taken to have a well-drained pot or seed-pan filled to within half an inch of the top with sifted leaf-mould; leave the surface rather rough, and sprinkle the seeds thinly upon it. The most successful raisers do not cover with soil, but after sowing the seed press down the surface tolerably firm, and place a square of glass over the pot. Place in a good strong heat, shaded from strong light, and water very gently when the soil becomes dry. The seeds will germinate in two or three weeks, after which remove the glass and keep in a shady position. Pot off into small pots when the young plants are about half an inch above ground, and place near the glass in the frame or greenhouse. In their after culture Primulas should be kept as near as convenient to the glass, have plenty of fresh air, and never be kept for a long period in a high temperature, or in a dry heated atmosphere.

		per pkt.—s.	d.
570	**DANIELS' CRIMSON KING.** One of the most splendid of the high-coloured varieties, flowers of great size and substance, and of the most brilliant and intense deep crimson-scarlet colour ... ... 2s. 6d. and	5	0
571	**DANIELS' QUEEN OF ROSES.** Beautiful soft rosy pink, a flower of great size and substance ... ... 2s. 6d. and	5	0
572	**DANIELS' WHITE PERFECTION.** A beautiful pure white of the fern-leaved type, of splendid habit ... ... 2s. 6d. and	5	0
573	**DANIELS' SUPERB BLUE.** Carefully saved from beautifully fringed flowers of perfect form and of the deepest shade of blue; splendid colour ... ... 2s. 6d. and	5	0
574	**DANIELS' EMPRESS GIANT WHITE.** Immense white flowers, borne on strong stems, with very robust foliage; a grand variety ...	3	6
575	**DANIELS' CRIMSON SCARLET.** Very brilliant and most charming variety	3	6

		per pkt.—s.
576	**PURITY.** Snow white; a splendid flower of great size and substance	2 6
577	**RUBY QUEEN.** Rich ruby red, a distinct and beautiful flower	3 6
578	**ALBA MAGNIFICA.** Beautifully fringed, pure white flowers, with citron-yellow eye ...	2 6
579	**CARMINEA ALBA PUNCTATA.** Beautiful carmine, spotted with white	1 6
580	**CHISWICK RED.** Brilliant crimson-scarlet, very robust in habit, finely-cut foliage ...	1 6
581	**Coccinea magnifica.** Brilliant scarlet, with clear sulphur yellow eye, exquisitely fringed, large flowers	2 6
582	**Florence.** Scarlet, shaded madder red	1 6

		per pkt.—s.
583	**Magenta Queen.** New, brilliant and charming variety	1 6
584	**Marginata.** Lilac, with white border, distinct and beautiful	1 6
585	**Purpurea magnifica.** Rich crimson purple, splendid	1 6
586	**Village Maid.** White, striped with carmine, beautiful	1 6
587	**DANIELS' CHOICEST RED VARIETIES, MIXED** .. 1s. 6d. and	2 6
588	**DANIELS' CHOICEST WHITE VARIETIES, MIXED** ... 1s. 6d. and	2 6
589	**DANIELS' CHOICEST MIXED.** In beautiful variety. Including some of the finest of our choice Single Primulas 1s. 6d., 2s. 6d., and	5 0

DOUBLE-FLOWERED FRINGED VARIETIES.

Exceedingly useful for flowering in the greenhouse during Winter, to cut for bouquets, &c.

		per pkt.—s.	d.
590	**DOUBLE PURE WHITE,** Fringed. Very useful for cutting	2	6
591	,, **BRIGHT CRIMSON,** Fringed. Splendid colour	2	6
592	,, **CARNATION-FLAKED,** Fringed. White flake with rose, very pretty	2	6

		per pkt.—s.	d.
593	**DOUBLE MAGENTA RED, FRINGED.** Very brilliant	1	6
594	,, **MARGINATA.** Lilac, edged with white	2	6
595	,, **PRINCE OF WALES,** Fern-leaved. Rich glowing scarlet, splendid	2	6
596	,, **CHOICEST MIXED.** Including the most beautiful sorts 1s. 6d., 2s. 6d., and	5	0

From Mrs. NEWBURY, Wotton Bridge.

Aug. 22nd.
"I have most lovely plants of Blue Primulas from the Seed I had of you last year, they have been greatly admired by every one."

From Mrs. HUNTER, Dainsforth, Bridgnorth.

May 9th.
"Mrs. Hunter had some Primula Seed from Messrs. Daniels last year which pleased her very much."

Daniels' Choice Florists' Flower Seeds.

Polyanthuses.

THE fine old hardy Gold-laced Polyanthus, which blooms about the same time as the Primrose, is a great favourite in most gardens, and too well known to need any description. The new varieties of *Giant* and *Magenta King* are very fine, and should be grown by all who are not already familiar with them.

			per pkt.—s.	d.
597	**Gold-laced.** Fine dark varieties, from a choice collection,			
	beautifully laced		2	6
598	" " smaller pkt.		1	6
599	**Cloth of Gold.** Fine yellow	...	1	6
800	**Hose-in-hose varieties.** Choice mixed	...	1	0
601	**Magenta King.** Very fine, crimson, yellow eye	...	1	6
602	**New Giant.** Crimson } Fine showy varieties for bedding		1	0
603	" " White }		1	0
604	" " Yellow } out, &c.		1	0
605	**Choice mixed.** Good showy sorts	...	1	0
606	" "	smaller pkt.	0	6

POLYANTHUS, GOLD-LACED.

From the Rev. R. HAY HILL, Braintree.
April 27th.
"The Rev. R. Hay Hill is much pleased with the Hollyhocks and **Polyanthus.**"

Hardy Primroses.

A BEAUTIFUL free-flowering class of hardy plants, which has been highly improved of late years, invaluable for Spring gardening. The hybrid varieties vary in colour from the palest and most delicate sulphur-yellow, through all the soft shades of rose and purple to the most intense and brilliant crimson. In a mild season many of the varieties will commence blooming in the Autumn and continue through the Winter, but from the beginning of April to the middle of May they are generally in full bloom, and present a most lovely appearance. A partially shaded border, with a westerly aspect, will grow them to perfection in almost any moderately rich soil.

			per pkt.—s.	d.
607	**Large-flowered Hybrids.** A grand strain of beautiful			
	high-coloured flowers, all of the true Primrose type, with			
	the flowers large and brilliant; very fine	...	2	6
608	" " smaller pkt.		1	6
609	**Very choice mixed.** From a good collection ...	...	2	6
610	**Crimson Beauty.** Rich crimson, splendid	...	2	6
611	**White Queen.** Pure white, beautiful	...	2	6
612	**Common Yellow**	...	0	6

Sweet William, Daniels' Prize.

WE have given great attention for several years past to our splendid strain of these, which we have much pleasure in offering. The sorts embrace a great variety of the choicest auricula-eyed, margined, selfs, &c., of the most brilliant types. The flowers are beautifully formed, of good substance, and are almost invariably awarded First Prize wherever exhibited.

		per pkt.	s.	d.
613	**DANIELS' PRIZE MIXED.** In beautiful variety ...		1	0
614	" " smaller pkt.		0	6
615	**Dark crimson.** Splendid colour	...	0	4
616	**Double Pure White.** A fine variety	...	0	6

SWEET WILLIAM, DANIELS' PRIZE.

From Mr. S. GAPPER, Axminster.
April 11th.
"The **Sweet William** you sent us were a perfect picture and much admired."

Violas—Bedding.

A PROFUSE-FLOWERING and invaluable class of hardy perennial bedding plants, continuing in bloom from early Spring till late in the Autumn months. Highly desirable for Spring gardening, and afford some charming effects in association with Spring-flowering Bulbs, &c. The following list includes the finest varieties in cultivation, and which we highly recommend.

			per pkt.—s.	d.
617	**An assortment of 6 splendid varieties** ...	...	3	6
618	**Admiration.** Splendid dark violet, yellow eye ...	...	1	0
619	**Blue Perfection.** Dark bluish purple	...	1	0
620	**White Perfection.** Splendid pure white	...	1	0
621	**Sensation.** Very fine purple	...	1	0
622	**Magnificent.** Deep rich purple, large flowers, very fine ...		1	0
623	**Mauve Queen.** Light mauve, fine	...	...	0	6
624	**Golden Gem.** Rich golden yellow	...	...	1	0
625	**Snowflake.** Splendid pure white	...	...	0	6
626	**Scotch Prize.** Extra choice mixed	...	...	1	6
627	**Sweet Scented.** Beautiful large-flowered varieties, deliciously scented	... ...	2	6
628	**Choicest mixed**	...	1	0
629	" "	smaller pkt.	0	6

Daniels' Choice Florists' Flower Seeds.

ZINNIA ELEGANS, NEW GIANT DOUBLE.

From **Mr. W. KAYS**, Little Stanbridge.

Nov. 9th.
"The Stocks, Asters, and Zinnias that I had from you have done very well."

Zinnia elegans fl. pl.

THERE is no class of annual flowers which has been so highly improved of late years as the double-flowered Zinnias, which may now be pronounced almost perfection. The flowers, which are large and perfectly double, range in colour from white to the most intense scarlet, orange, rose, salmon, purple, &c., and, considering their easy cultivation, should be grown freely in every garden.

		per pkt.—s.	d.
630	An assortment of 12 splendid varieties	2	6
631	" 6 "	1	6
632	Sulphur yellow. Finest double	0	4
633	Scarlet "	0	4
634	Salmon Red "	0	4
635	Purple "	0	4
636	White "	0	4
637	Golden Yellow "	0	4
638	Rose "	0	4
639	Striped and Flaked "	0	6
640	Choicest mixed "	1	0
641	" " smaller pkt.	0	6
642	New dwarf, double. Splendid mixed ...	1	0
643	Pompon. fl. pl. A charming new class, with small but very regularly-formed double flowers in all the most brilliant and beautiful colours ..	1	0
644	Darwini fl. pl. Beautifully imbricated double flowers	1	0
645	Haageana fl. pl. Distinct, small, double-flowered variety, orange, height one foot, trailing ...	0	6
646	New Giant Double. A very fine new class of a robust habit of growth, and producing perfectly double flowers of an immense size, and of the most brilliant and beautiful colours; splendid for exhibition.		
	" An assortment of 8 beautiful vars.	2	6
647	" Choicest mixed	1	0

Verbena hybrida.

Sow in February or March in pans or trays of light rich mould, and place in a gentle heat. As soon as the young plants have made three or four leaves pot them off singly into small pots, keep close till established, when they should be placed near the glass and have plenty of air, gradually harden off and plant out in May where intended to flower. Seedling Verbenas are almost invariably very vigorous in growth, and if raised from a good strain of seed will produce some charming flowers.

		per pkt.—s.	d.
648	Candidissima. Fine pure white	1	0
649	Dark blue, white eye. Very fine	1	0
650	Auriculæflora. Beautiful large-flowered varieties with conspicuous white eyes	1	0
651	Defiance. Scarlet, fine	1	0
652	" compacta. New. Rich scarlet, very dwarf	1	0
653	Carnation-striped. From a fine collection ...	1	0
654	New Fordhook Mammoth. A grand new strain of Giant Verbenas from the United States, that produces uniformly flowers and trusses of an immense size, and in the most beautiful variety of colours	1	0
655	Choicest mixed, in beautiful variety ...	1	0
656	" " " " smaller pkt.	0	6

From **Miss DEANE**, Box.

July 2nd.
"Miss Deane wishes to say that she never had better Stocks and Asters than those raised from the last Seeds sent by Messrs. Daniels."

From **Mr. J. W. HARRISON**,
Gardener to the Right Hon. Lady Arundel, Wardour Castle.

Sept 9th
"The Gloxinia Seed supplied by you this year has produced some magnificent flowers; they are now in full bloom and are greatly admired by all who see them."

DANIELS' GENERAL LIST OF FLOWER SEEDS.

For Cultural Instructions see page 86.

ABBREVIATIONS.

hA   Hardy annual.

hhA Half-hardy annual.

tA   Tender annual.

hB   Hardy biennial.

hhB Half-hardy biennial.

tB   Tender biennial.

hP   Hardy perennial.

hhP Half-hardy perennial.

Those Perennials and Biennials marked with an asterisk (*) will bloom the first year from seed.

ABBREVIATIONS.

tP   Tender perennial.

spr Spreading or trailing.

cl   Climbing.

gs   Greenhouse shrub.

h   Plants of a shrubby habit of growth.

st   Stove plants.

bb   Having bulbous or tuberous roots.

N.B.—In ordering, the numbers only will suffice, but as the numbers are altered every year, the date of Catalogue should also be given.

NEW DWARF SWEET PEA,
"CUPID."
See List of Novelties.

No.	Name.	Hard Dur.	Ht in feet.	Colour.	Months of Flowering	Per Pkt.	Observations.
						s. d.	
657	Abronia umbellata	hhA	spr.	pink	Ju to Sp	3	} Pretty Verbena-like annuals, excellent for rockwork, &c.
658	„ arenaria	„	„	yellow	„	4	
659	Abutilon, choice mixed hybrids	gs	6–8	various	My to Au	1 0	Handsome greenhouse plants.
660	Acacia lophantha	hhP	3–5	yellow	„	6	Beautiful plant for pot culture
661	Acanthus mollis	hP	3	pink & white	Ju to Sp	6	Fine herbaceous plant.
	Acroclinium, *see page* 85.						
662	Æthionema grandiflora ...	„	1	rose	My & Ju	6	Beautiful hardy border plant.
663	Ageratum, Imperial dwarf blue	hhA	½	blue	Ju to Oc	4	} Valuable bedding plants of dwarf habit, exceedingly floriferous, and very useful for edgings.
664	„ „ „ white	„	„	white	„	4	
665	„ Ada Bowman	„	„	delicate blue	„	6	
666	Agrostemma coronaria atrosanguinea	hP	2	dark crimson	Jy to Sp	3	Fine showy perennial.
667	Agrostis pulchella	hA	¾	—	„	3	} Elegant ornamental grasses.
668	„ minutiflora	„	1	—	„	6	
669	*Alonsoa linifolia	hhB	1¼	orange scarlet	Jy to Oc	6	} Excellent for mixed borders or as pot-plants, showy and pretty. A. myrtifolia is a fine new species, having large handsome flowers.
670	„ „ gracilis ...	„	„	„	„	6	
671	* „ myrtifolia	„	„	scarlet	„	6	
672	Alstrœmeria, choice mixed ...	hhB	2	various	Ju to Au	4	Fine new varieties.
673	Alyssum maritimum	hA	¾	white	Ju to Oc	3	Useful for edgings, borders, &c.
674	„ saxatile compactum ...	hP	„	yellow	Ap & My	4	Fine for rockwork or borders.
675	Amaranthus, Hender's Hybrids	hhA	1½	various	Ju to Sp	1 6	} A brilliant class of plants for decorative purposes; very useful for conservatory
676	„ melancholicus ruber ...	„	1–1½	blood red fol.	„	4	
677	„ tricolor splendens ...	„	1	var. col. leaf	„	6	
678	Anagallis grandiflora coccinea	„	¼	scarlet	Jn to Oc	6	} Very pretty free-flowering annuals for beds, rock-work, &c. A. grandiflora coccinea is very fine.
679	„ Indica	„	„	blue	„	3	
680	„ fine varieties, mixed ...	„	„	various	„	4	
681	Anchusa angustifolia	hP	2	azure blue	„	6	Beautiful Forget-me-not-like flowers.
682	*Anemone coronaria, finest mixed	„	1	various	Fo to Au	3	Beautiful early flowering vars.
683	* „ fulgens	„	„	brill. scarlet	Ap to Ju	6	Very showy.
	Antirrhinum, *see page* 59.						
684	Aquilegia alpina superba ...	„	1½	blue & white	My to Jy	6	} *Columbines.* This class of hardy perennials will thrive in almost any soil or position, and are admirably suited for shrubbery borders, large rockeries, or permanent beds where not often disturbed, and where they form beautiful objects. They vary in height from two to three feet. A. glandulosa vera, cærulea hybrida, and Stuarti are especially worthy of notice.
685	„ Californica hybrida ...	„	2	orange yellow	„	6	
686	„ chrysantha	„	2½	pale yellow	„	6	
687	„ „ grandiflora alba	„	„	white	„	1 0	
688	„ cærulea	„	„	sky blue	„	6	
689	„ „ hybrida ...	„	„	blue & yellow	„	6	
690	„ glandulosa vera ...	„	1½	dk. blue & wh.	„	1 0	
691	„ Skinneri	„	„	scarlet & yell.	„	6	
692	„ Stuarti	„	2	blue & white	„	1 0	
693	„ caryophylloides fl. pl. ...	„	„	striped	„	6	
694	„ mixed, single and double ...	„	„	various	„	3	
695	„ double, white	„	„	white	„	3	

Flower Seeds, General List *(continued)*.

No.	Name.	Hard Dur.	Ht in feet.	Colour.	Months of Flowering	Per Pkt.	Observations.
						s. d.	
696	**Arabis alpina**	hp	½	white	Mr to My	3	Early flowering rock or border plant.
697	**Asperula azurea setosa**	hA	1	blue	My to Au	3	Pretty sweet-scented annual
698	**Aster tenella**	„	½	mauve	Au & Sp	3	Dwarf annual *Michaelmas Daisy*.
	Asters, French and German, *see pages* 51, 52.						
699	**Aubrietia Leichtlini**	hp	„	carmine rose	Mr to Ju	1 0	Charming dwarf-growing plants of spreading habit. First-class for rockwork or dry borders.
700	„ **græca**	„	„	blue	„	6	
701	„ **violacea**	„	„	bright violet	„	6	
	Auricula, *see page* 59.						
702	**Avena sterilis**	hA	3	—	Jy & Au	3	*Animated Oats.* Curious.
	Balsam, *see page* 59.						
703	**Bartonia aurea**	„	1½	golden yellow	„	3	Showy hardy annual.
704	**Beet, dwarf dark-leaved** ...	hB	1	dk. pur. fol.	Ju to No	6	Fine varieties for bedding.
705	„ **Dracæna-leaved** ...	„	„	„	„	6	
706	„ **Chilian**	„	2	variegated fol.	„	6	Brilliant and handsomely marked foliage. Splendid in Autumn.
	Begonia, tuberous-rooted, *see page* 60.						
707	**Borecole, variegated**	„	„	„	Oc to Mr	6	Very handsomely variegated.
708	**Brachycome iberidifolia** ...	hhA	1	blue	Jy & Au	3	*Swan River Daisy.* Very pretty.
709	**Briza maxima**	hA	„	—	„	3	*Giant Maiden Hair Grass.*
710	**Bromus brizæformis** ...	„	2	—	„	3	Fine ornamental grass.
711	**Browallia elata grandiflora** ...	hhA	1½	blue	Ju to Oc	6	Beautiful plants for pots in the greenhouse or conservatory.
712	„ **Roezli**	„	„	white & blue	„	6	
713	**Cacalia aurea**	hA	1	orange	Ju to Au	3	Useful hardy annuals, for bouquets, &c.
714	„ **coccinea**	„	„	scarlet	„	3	
715	**Calandrinia speciosa**	„	spr.	bright purple	Ju & Jy	3	Showy annuals for borders, rockwork, or any warm situation.
716	„ „ **alba**	„	„	pure white	„	3	
717	„ **umbellata**	hp	½	brill.mag.pur.	Ju to Au	6	Remarkably brilliant perennial.
718	**Calceolaria, shrubby, mixed** ...	hhp	1	various	My to Oc	1 6	Useful bedding-out varieties
	„ hybrida, *see page* 61.						
719	**Calendula officinalis Meteor** ...	hA	1½	orange & yel.	„	3	Double-flowered *Pot Marigolds*, in bloom till late in the Autumn.
720	„ „ **sulphurea fl. pl.**	„	„	pale yellow	„	6	
721	„ **Prince of Orange**	„	„	orange	„	3	
722	**Callirhoe pedata nana compacta** ...	hhA	1	crimson	Ju to Oc	3	Brilliant annual.
723	**Calliopsis atrosanguinea**	hA	2	dark brown	Jy to Sp	3	Well-known brilliant and useful annuals, remaining in bloom for a long time. Well adapted for growing in and near large towns, and exceedingly useful for cutting.
724	„ **Burridgii**	„	„	yel. & brown	„	3	
725	„ **Drummondi**	„	1½	golden yellow	„	3	
726	„ **cardaminifolia nana atrosang.**	„	2	dark crimson	„	3	
727	„ **tinctoria**	„	„	yel. & brown	„	3	
728	„ **nana, dwarf vars. mixed**	„	½	various	„	6	
729	**Campanula medium, Dean's hybrid** ...	hB	2½	„	Ju to Au	6	*Canterbury Bells.* These are a highly interesting and desirable class of handsome flowering plants for the decoration of the garden. The large bells of the pure white varieties are especially handsome, and should be freely grown for the contrast they afford with most other flowers. The double-flowered vars. are very fine.
730	„ „ **single blue** ...	„	„	dark blue	„	3	
731	„ „ „ **white** ...	„	„	pure white	„	3	
732	„ „ „ **rose** ...	„	„	rose	„	4	
733	„ „ „ **mixed** ...	„	„	various	„	4	
734	„ „ **double mixed** ...	„	„	„	„	3	
735	„ „ **calycanthema, blue**	„	„	blue	„	6	
736	„ „ „ **alba** ...	„	„	white	„	6	
737	„ „ „ **rosea** ...	„	„	rose	„	6	
738	„ **Loreyi**	hA	1	blue	„	3	C. pyramidalis and alba form very useful and handsome pot plants, whilst C. turbinata is a splendid dwarf growing sort for the garden, rockeries, &c.
739	„ **pentagonia**	„	„	purple	„	3	
740	„ **pyramidalis**	hp	3	blue	„	3	
741	„ „ **alba**	„	„	white	„	3	
742	„ **turbinata**	„	1	blue	„	4	
743	**Candytuft, New carmine**	hA	„	carmine	My to Au	6	Useful and exceedingly showy annuals for beds, rockwork, borders, &c., and afford a brilliant display of colour for a long period. The new carmine, creamy white, dark crimson, and Dobbie's New Spiral, are very beautiful varieties, and should be grown in every garden.
744	„ „ **creamy white** ...	„	„	creamy white	„	3	
745	„ **extra dark crimson** ...	„	„	crim. purple	„	3	
746	„ **Dobbie's White Spiral** ...	„	„	pure white	„	4	
747	„ **purple**	„	„	purple	„	3	
748	„ **white rocket** ...	„	„	white	„	3	
749	„ **mixed**	„	„	various	„	3	
750	„ **Empress**	„	„	pure white	„	6	
751	„ **New dwarf crimson** ...	„	½	crim. purple	„	4	A beautiful new class, of a dwarf habit of growth, exceedingly fine for edgings, rockwork, &c.
752	„ „ **Rose** ...	„	„	rose	„	6	
753	„ „ **mixed** ...	„	„	various	„	4	
754	„ **Tom Thumb**	„	„	pure white	„	3	
755	***Canna, Crozy's New Hybrids...**	hhp	3	„	Jy to Sp	1 0	Fine dwarf habit of growth, and flowers of great size and beauty.
756	* „ **Queen Charlotte** (new) ...	„	2-3	scarlet & yel.	Ju to Oc	1 6	Handsome-foliaged plants, excellent for the sub-tropical garden or the greenhouse.
757	* „ **fine dark-leaved varieties**	„	3-6	various	Jy to Sp	6	
758	**Cannabis giganteus**	hhA	6-8	orn. fol.	Ju to Oc	4	*Giant Hemp.* For sub-tropical garden.
759	**Capsicum, Prince of Wales** ...	„	1½	yel. fruit	„	6	Fine ornamental pot-plants, bearing a profusion of handsome fruits.
760	„ **Tom Thumb**	„	¾	scarlet fruit	„	6	
	Carnation, *see page* 61.						
761	**Castilleja indivisa**		½	brilliant crim.	Jy to Sp	6	Very brilliant and beautiful.
762	**Centaurea candidissima (ragusina)** ...	hhp	1	white foliage	„	1 0	Handsome silvery-foliaged plants for bedding out or the greenhouse.
763	„ **Clementei**	„	„	„	„	1 0	
764	**Centaurea cyanus minor, dark blue** ...	hA	2	dark blue	„	3	*Cornflowers.* Showy hardy annuals. Useful for bouquets.
765	„ „ „ **mixed**...	„	„	various	„	3	

Flower Seeds, General List (*continued*).

No.	Name.	Hard Ht in Dur. feet.	Colour.	Months of Flowering	Per Pkt.	Observations.
					s. d.	
766	Centaurea cyanus, new dwarf vars.	hA	⅔ various	Jy to Sp	1 0	
767	„ depressa	„	1½ bluo	Jy & An	3	⎱ Very useful for bouquets.
768	„ „ rosea	„	„ rose	„	3	⎰
769	Centranthus macrosiphon	„	1 red	Jy to Sp	3	Showy border annual.
770	Cerastium Biebersteini	hP	„ white	„	6	⎱ Useful white-foliaged bedding plants.
771	„ tomentosum	„	„ „	„	3	⎰
772	Chamærops humilis	gs	6 orn. foliage	Fo to Ap	6	*Dwarf Fan Palm.* Very ornamental.
773	Chamæpeuce casabonæ	hhn	1 lilao	Ju to Au	6	*Fishbone Thistle.* Curious.
774	Chelone barbata coccinea	hP	3 scarlet	Jy & Au	3	Pretty Pentstemon-like flowers.
	Chrysanthemum Annual, *see page* 62.					
	„ Indicum „ 67.					
775	Cineraria candidissima	hhP	1½ yellow	Ju to Au	6	Silvery-foliaged bedding plant.
	„ hybrida, *see page* 62.					
776	Cistus, Rock, finest mixed	„	1 various	„	3	*Rock Rose.* Very handsome.
777	Clarkia elegans, double white	hA	2 white	Jy to Sp	4	
778	„ „ Purple King	„	„ purple	„	4	⎫ An exceedingly useful class of hardy
779	„ „ Salmon Queen	„	„ salmon	„	4	⎪ annuals, admirably suited for sowing
780	„ „ integripetala, double rose	„	1 rosy pink	Ju to Oc	3	⎪ in patches, &c., in mixed border,
781	„ „ „ alba, double white	„	1 pure white	„	3	⎪ and are very easy of cultivation.
782	„ „ „ limbata	„	„ pink & white	„	3	⎬ The integripetala varieties, pulchella
783	„ „ „ Tom Thumb	„	½ rosy pink	„	3	⎪ marginata, and the dwarf double-
784	„ „ pulchella	„	1 „	„	3	⎪ flowered Tom Thumb are very hand-
785	„ „ „ alba	„	„ pure white	„	3	⎪ some. The new varieties of elegans
786	„ „ „ marginata fl. pl.	„	½ pink & white	„	3	⎪ are also very fine and desirable.
787	„ „ „ Tom Thumb, double	„	½ dark crimson	„	6	⎪
788	„ mixed	„	1 various	„	3	⎭
789	Clematis hybrida, choice mixed	hP cl.	„	My to Oc	1 0	Valuable hardy climbers.
790	Clianthus Dampieri	gs	4 scarlet & blk.	Ap to Jy	1 0	*Parrot-beak plant.* Magnificent.
791	Clintonia pulchella	hhA	½ blue & white	Ju to Sp	6	Beautiful for pots, borders, rockwork, &c.
792	Cobœa scandens	hhP cl.	purple	My to Oc	6	⎱ Well-known useful climbers.
793	„ alba	„ „	white	„	6	⎰
	Cockscombs, *see page* 60.					
794	Coix lachryma	hhA	1 —	Jy & Aug	3	*Job's Tears.* Ornamental grass.
	Coleus, *see page* 67.					
795	Collinsia bicolor	hA	lilac & white	My to Au	3	⎫
796	„ candidissima	„	white	„	3	⎬ Much admired and useful annuals.
797	„ multicolor	„	var. coloured	„	3	⎭
798	Collomia coccinea	„	1½ scarlet	Jy to Oc	3	Useful for bees, pretty.
	Columbine (*see Aquilegia*).					
799	Commelina cœlestis	hhP	sky blue	Ju to Au	3	Attractive plant with fine glossy foliage.
800	Convolvulus major, crimson	hhA cl.	crimson	Jy to Oc	3	⎫
801	„ „ white	„ „	white	„	3	⎪ A fine class of hardy annual climbers
802	„ „ purple	„ „	purple	„	3	⎪ suitable for covering walls, trellis,
803	„ „ rose	„ „	rose	„	3	⎬ wire-fencing, arbours, &c., &c. Very
804	„ „ striped	„ „	various	„	3	⎪ pretty in association with Tropæolum
805	„ „ mixed	„ „	„	„	3	⎪ canariense.
806	„ „ new double	„ „	white	„	1 0	⎭
807	„ minor, dark purple	hA	1 dark purple	„	3	⎱ The true dark purple variety, ex-
808	„ „ crimson violet	„	„ crim. violet	„	6	⎰ ceedingly rich-coloured.
809	„ Mauritanicus	hhP trl.	lavender	Jy to Sp	3	⎱ Splendid variety. Useful variety for hanging-baskets,
810	Convallaria majalis	hP	1 white	Ap to Ju	6	*Lily of the Valley.*
811	Cosmos bipinnatus grandiflorus albus	hhA	3-4 „	Jy to Oc	6	Very useful for cut flowers.
812	Cowslip, common field	hP	⅔ yellow	My & Ju	4	⎱ *Primula elatior, vars.* Very pretty for
813	„ Crimson Giant	„	1 crimson	„	1 0	⎰ shady banks, &c.
	American (*see Dodecatheon meadia*).					
814	Cuphea platycentra	hhP	scarlet	Jy to Oc	6	Useful bedding plant.
	Cyclamen, *see page* 60.					
	Dahlia, *see page* 63.					
815	Daisy, double, red or crimson	hP	½ dark red	Ap to Jy	1 0	⎫ *Bellis perennis*—well known useful
816	„ „ pure white	„	„ white	„	1 0	⎬ plants for Spring gardening, edg-
817	„ „ mixed	„	„ various	„	1 0	⎭ ings, &c.
818	Datura atropurpurea plenissima	hhA	½ dark purple	Jy to Sp	6	Splendid large-flowered varieties. Very
819	„ Huberiana fl. pl.	„	1 white	„	4	⎰ handsome for mixed borders.
820	„ chlorantha fl. pl.	„	2 yellow	„	3	Very sweet scented.
821	„ coccinea	„	1½ bright rose	„	1 6	Splendid variety
	Delphinium, *see page* 63.					
	Dianthus, *see page* 63.					
822	Digitalis, maculata superba	hP	3 sptd. vars.	Jy & Au	6	⎫ *Foxgloves.* A showy class of hardy
823	„ monstrosa alba	„	4 white	„	4	⎪ perennials admirably suited for
824	„ very choice mixed	„	3 various	„	3	⎬ shrubbery borders, &c. D. maculata
825	„ Ivory's superb strain	„	3 „	„	6	⎪ superba is very fine.
826	Dodecatheon meadia	„	1 purple	Ap to Ju	1 0	⎱ *American Cowslip.* Valuable hardy perennial.
827	Eccremocarpus scaber	hhP cl.	orange	Jy to Sp	6	Handsome climber of quick growth.
828	Echeveria secunda glauca	gP	½ yellow	„	1 6	Useful succulent bedding plant.
829	Echinops ritro	hP	3-4 azure blue	Ju to No	6	Singular and handsome border plant.
	Edelweis, see page 85.					

Flower Seeds, General List *(continued)*.

No.	Name.	Hard Dur.	Ht in feet.	Colour.	Months of Flowering	Per Pkt.	Observations.
						s. d.	
	Egg Plant (*see Solanum*).						
830	**Elymus caput Medusæ**	hP	1½	—	Jy & Au	3	Fine ornamental grass.
831	**Eragrotis elegans**	hA	„	—	Au & Sp	3	*Love-grass.* Elegant.
832	**Erinus alpinus**	hP	3-4	rosy purple	Ap to Ju	6	Beautiful little alpine plant.
833	***Erysimum Peroffskianum**	hA	1½	orange	Jy to Sp	3	Showy hardy annual.
834	**Erythræa Muhlenbergia**	„	„	rose & white	„	6	Beautiful hardy annual.
835	**Erythrina crista galli**	gs	15	scarlet	My to Jy	6	*Coral Tree.* Greenhouse shrub.
836	**Erythrolæna conspicua**	hhB	4	or. carmine	Jy & Au	1 0	Thistle-like plant from Mexico.
837	***Eschscholtzia crocea fl. pl.**	hB	1	orange	Jy to Sp	6	Brilliant and exceedingly showy plants. E. grandiflora rosea, Mandarin, and the double-flowered varieties are very fine.
838	* „ „ **alba fl. pl.**	„	„	white	„	6	
839	* „ **grandiflora carminea**	„	„	carmine	„	6	
840	* „ **Mandarin**	„	„	scarlet	„	4	
841	* „ **Californica alba**	„	„	white	„	3	
842	* „ **crocea**	„	„	orange	„	3	
843	**Eucharidium Breweri**	hA	„	rosy lilac	My to Au	1 0	Free-blooming, pretty annuals, somewhat resembling the Clarkias, but more compact in habit. E. Breweri is very fine.
844	„ **grandiflorum album**	„	„	white	„	3	
845	„ „ **roseum**	„	„	rose	„	3	
846	**Eutoca viscida**	„	„	deep blue	My & Ju	3	Pretty annual with sky-blue flowers.
	Evening Primrose (*see Œnothera*).						
847	**Flos Adonis**	„	1½	scarlet	Jy & Au	3	*Pheasant's-eye.* Showy annual.
	Foxglove (*see Digitalis*).						
	Fuchsia, *see page* 63.						
848	***Gaillardia hybrida grandiflora**	hP	2	various	Jy to Oc	0 6	Saved from choice named flowers.
849	„ **amblyodon**	hhA	„	deep red	Jy to Sp	3	Splendid plants for beds or borders. Very showy.
850	* „ **picta fistulosa**	hhP	„	crim. yellow	„	3	
851	„ „ **Lorenziana**	hhA	1	red and yellow	„	6	New and beautiful variety.
852	**Gentiana acaulis**	hP	½	dark blue	Ap to Jy	1 0	Beautiful early flowering border plant.
	Geranium, *see* Pelargonium *page* 65.						
853	**Geum coccineum fl. pl.**	„	2	scarlet	Ju to Oc	3	Double Ranunculus-like flowers.
854	**Gilia achillæfolia alba**	hA	1½	white	Jy to Sp	3	Very pretty free-flowering annuals, suitable for patches on mixed beds or borders, or for rockwork.
855	„ „ **major**	„	„	blue	„	3	
856	„ **nivalis**	„	„	white	„	3	
857	„ **tricolor**	„	„	various	„	3	
858	**Gladiolus gandavensis, mixed**	hhP	3-4	„	Jy to Oc	1 0	Saved from choicest sorts.
859	**Glaucium luteum**	hA	2	yellow	Jy & Au	3	*Horned Poppy.* Curious.
	Gloxinia, *see page* 64.						
	Golden Feather (*see Pyrethrum aureum*).						
860	**Gourd, small ornamental varieties**	hhA	cl.	„	Jy to Oc	6	Pretty climbers with ornamental fruit
861	**Grammanthes gentianoides**	„	½	scarlet	Ju to Oc	6	Excellent for hanging-baskets, pots, &c.
862	**Grevillea robusta**	gs	—	—	—	6	Beautiful greenhouse shrub
863	**Gynerium argenteum**	hP	8-10	—	Sp & Oc	6	*Pampas Grass* of S. America.
864	**Gypsophila elegans**	hA	1½	pink	Jy to Sp	3	A fine annual from the Crimea.
865	„ **paniculata**	hP	„	white	„	4	Useful for bouquets
866	**Hawkweed, red**	hA	2	red	„	3	Useful and showy annuals.
867	„ **white**	„	1½	white	„	3	
868	„ **yellow**	„	„	yellow	„	3	
869	**Heuchera sanguinea**	hP	„	coral red	„	1 6	Charming hardy perennial, excellent for cutting.
	Helianthus (*see Sunflower*).						
	Helichrysums (*see Everlasting Flowers*).						
870	**Heliotrope, splendid mixed**	hhP	1	greyish blue	My to Oc	6	Deliciously fragrant bedding plants.
871	**Heracleum giganteum**	„	6-8	„	Ju to Oc	3	*Giant Cow Parsnip.* Fine plant for shrubberies and waste places.
872	**Hibiscus Africanus major**	hA	2	lemon, dk. eye	Jy to Oc	3	Handsome annual.
	Hollyhock, *see page* 64.						
873	***Honesty, purple or lilac**	hB	„	lilac	Ju & Jy	3	*Lunaria biennis* varieties. Fine for shrubbery borders, &c.
874	* „ **white**	„	„	white	„	4	
875	„ **New crimson**	„	„	crimson	„	6	
876	**Honeysuckle, French, red**	hP	„	red	„	3	Showy perennials, excellent for growing under trees, on mixed borders, &c.
877	„ „ **white**	„	„	white	„	3	
878	**Hordeum jubatum**	hA	1	—	Jy to Sp	3	Handsome ornamental grass.
879	**Humulus Japonicus**	hhA	cl.	—	—	3	*Japanese Hop.* Rapid and useful climber for trellises, &c. The variegated variety is very handsome.
880	„ „ **variegatus**	„	„	—	—	6	
881	**Iberis Gibraltarica**	hP	¾	pink & white	Ap & My	4	Fine hardy perennials for rockwork or borders.
882	„ **sempervirens**	„	„	white	„	3	
883	**Ice Plant**	hhA	spr.	„	Jy & Au	3	Useful for garnishing.
884	**Impatiens Sultani**	gP	1	magen. crim.	Ja to Dec	1 0	Splendid pot plant for the greenhouse.
885	**Ionopsidium acaule**	hA	½	violet	Ap to Oc	3	Charming little plant for rockwork.
886	**Ipomœa coccinea**	hhP	cl.	scarlet	Jy & Au	3	Beautiful climbers for the greenhouse, verandahs, trellises, &c.
887	„ **hederacea superba**	hhA	„	blue & white	Jy to Oc	4	
888	„ **Leari**	gP	„	violet & white	Ju to Sp	6	
889	„ **rubro-cærulea**	„	„	blue and red	Au to Oc	6	
890	**Ipomopsis elegans**	hhP	5	scarlet	Au & Sp	3	Splendid for beds or borders.
891	**Isolepis tenella**	„	½	—	Jy to Sp	6	Pretty grass for pot culture.
892	**Isotoma axilaris**	„	1	blue	„	3	Handsome long-blooming plant.
893	**Jacobæa, double, crimson**	hhA	„	crimson	„	3	Useful varieties for bedding out, to cut for bouquets, &c.
894	„ „ **white**	„	„	white	„	3	

JACOBÆA, DOUBLE, CRIMSON. See page 79.

GRAMMANTHES GENTIANOIDES. See page 70.

GODETIA, REPTANS INSIGNIS. See page 49.

MYOSOTIS ALPESTRIS GRANDIFLORA. See page 81.

MARIGOLD, LEGION OF HONOUR. See page 65.

MARIGOLD, PULCHRA NANA. See page 65.

Flower Seeds, General List (*continued*).

No.	Name.	Hard Dur.	Ht in feet.	Colour.	Months of Flowering	Per Pkt.	Observations.
						s. d.	
895	**Kalanchoe carnea**	gP	2	pink	Ju to Mr	1 6	Charming greenhouse plant.
896	**Kaulfussia amelloides**	hA	¼	light blue	Jy & Au	3	Pretty little Aster-like plants of dwarf habit.
897	„ „ **rosea**	„	„	rose	„	3	
898	„ **atroviolacea**	„	„	dark purple	„	3	
899	„ **kermesina**	„	„	crimson	„	6	
900	**Lagurus ovatus**	„	1½	—	„	3	*Hare's-tail Grass*
901	***Lantana, choice mixed**	hhP	1	various	My to Oc	6	Choice bedding or pot plants.
902	**Larkspur, dwarf rocket, double** ...	hA	„	„	Jy & Au	3	Fine double-flowered varieties of various beautiful colours.
903	„ **candelabra-formed**	„	„	„	„	4	
904	„ **Emperor, choice mixed double**	„	1½	„	„	6	
905	„ **Stock-flowered**	„	„	rosy scarlet	„	6	
906	„ **Tall branching**...	„	3	various	„	3	
907	**Lapageria rosea**	gP	cl.	rose	Ju to Oc	2 6	Beautiful stove or greenhouse climber.
908	**Lavatera arborea variegata**	hhP	6-8	purple	Jy to Sp	1 0	Beautifully variegated foliage.
909	„ **red**	hA	3	red	Jy & Au	3	Showy hardy annuals.
910	„ **white**	„	„	white	„	3	
911	**Lavender, common garden**	hP	„	lavender	„	3	*Lavendula spica.* Well known.
912	**Layia elegans**	hA	1	yell. & white	„	6	Pretty yellow flowers edged with white.
913	**Leptosiphon aureus**	„	½	golden yellow	Jy to Oc	3	Handsome showy annuals. L. densiflorus albus is one of the purest white flowers in cultivation. L. roseus and carmineus are lovely little compact-growing varieties of beautiful colours.
914	„ **carmineus**	„	„	carmine	„	6	
915	„ **densiflorus**	„	1	lilac & white	„	3	
916	„ „ **albus**	„	„	pure white	„	3	
917	„ **roseus**	„	½	rose	„	4	
918	„ **French hybrids, mixed** ...	„	„	various	„	3	
919	**Leptosyne maritima**	„	3	yellow	Jy to Sp	6	Very useful for cutting
	Lily of the Valley (*see Convallaria*).						
920	**Limnanthes Douglasi** ...	„	½	white & yel.	My to Sp	3	Pretty dwarf annual.
921	**Linaria reticulata aurea purpurea** ...	„	½	yel. & maroon	Jy to Sp	6	Pretty hardy annual.
922	**Linum grandiflorum rubrum** ...	hhA	1	crim. scarlet	Ju to Oc	3	Very brilliant and showy.
923	„ **flavum** ...	hP	„	yellow	„	4	Useful perennial for borders or pots.
924	**Lisianthus Russellianus** ...	gA		blue	Ju to Au	1 0	Beautiful greenhouse annual
	Lobelias, *see page* 68.						
925	**Lophospermum scandens**	hhP	cl.	blush	„	4	Very useful climber.
926	**Love-lies-bleeding, red**	hA	2	crimson	Jy & Au	3	Showy border annuals.
927	„ „ **white**	„	„	pale yellow	„	3	
928	**Lupinus albo-coccineus**	„	„	scar. & white	Ju to Oc	3	These handsome and easily cultivated annuals certainly deserve their high popularity. L. subcarnosus is a strikingly handsome variety that continues in bloom for a long time. L. sulphureus superbus and albococcineus are beautiful.
929	„ **Cruikshanki**	„	3-5	bl. wh. & yell.	„	3	
930	„ **hybridus superbus**	„	2	pur. ro. & wh.	„	3	
931	„ **subcarnosus**	„	1	dk. bl. & wh.	„	3	
932	„ **sulphureus superbus**	„	1½	sul. yellow	Ju to Sp	3	
933	„ **nanus**	„	1	blue & white	„	3	
934	„ „ **albus**	„	„	white	„	3	
935	„ **polyphyllus**	hP	4	blue	Ju to Au	3	Useful perennials for shrubbery borders, &c.
936	„ „ **albus**	„	„	white	„	3	
937	**Lupins, large blue**	hA	2	blue	Jy to Sp	3	Suitable for mixed borders in front of shrubs, &c.
938	„ „ **yellow**	„	1½	yellow	„	3	
939	„ „ **rose**	„	2	rose	„	3	
940	„ „ **white**	„	„	white	„	3	
941	„ „ **mixed**	„	„	various	„	3	
942	**Lychnis Haageana**	hP	1	„	Ju & Jy	3	Showy herbaceous perennials, with brilliant flowers.
943	„ **fulgens**	„	„	brill. scarlet	„	3	
944	**Maize, striped-leaved Japanese** ...	hhA	3-5	—	Jy to Sp	3	Fine ornamental plants for the subtropical garden.
945	„ **Giant**	„	6-8	—	„	3	
946	**Malva moschata alba**	hP	1	white	„	6	Fine showy hardy perennial.
947	**Malope grandiflora**	hA	3	crimson	„	3	Brilliant and showy annuals of easy cultivation.
948	„ „ **alba**	„	„	white	„	3	
949	„ „ **rosea**	„	„	rose	„	3	
	Marigolds, *see page* 65.						
950	***Marvel of Peru. Choicest mixed** ...	hhP	2-3	various	Ju to Au	3	Well-known useful perennials.
951	**Martynia fragrans**	hhA	2	str. crimson	„	3	Large-flowered handsome annual.
952	**Mathiola bicornis**	„	1	lilac	Ju to Sp	4	*Night-scented Stock.* Fragrant.
953	**Matricaria eximia crispa fl. pl.** ...	hP	2	white	Jy to Oc	6	*Double-flowered Feverfew.* Pretty.
954	**Maurandya Barclayana grandiflora** ...	hhA	cl.	blue	My to Sp	6	Fine and useful climbers.
955	„ „ **alba**	„	„	white	„	6	
956	**Mesembryanthemum tricolor** ...	„	½	or. wh. & pur.	Ju to Sp	3	Excellent for sunny rockwork, pretty Daisy-like flowers.
957	„ **cordifolium variegatum** ...	hhP	„	rosy purple	„	1 0	Useful for carpet bedding, &c.
	Mimulus, *see page* 68.						
	Mignonette, *see page* 71.						
958	**Mina lobata**	hhA	12	orange scarlet	Jy to Oc	1 6	Splendid climber for trellises, &c.
959	**Musk Plant**	hP	¼	yellow	Ju to Sp	4	*Mimulus moschatus.*
960	**Myosotis alpestris grandiflora** ...	„	½	sky bl. yel. eye	„	6	*Forget-me-nots.* Well-known beautiful little plants, invaluable for Spring gardening, &c. *M. disitiflora* is the best variety for Spring gardening. A partially shaded and rather moist position is most favourable.
961	„ **azorica**	„	1	dark blue	„	6	
962	„ „ **alba**	„	„	white	„	6	
963	„ **disitiflora**	„	½	sky blue	Mr to Ju	1 0	
964	„ „ **alba**	„	„	white	„	1 0	
965	„ **palustris** (the true *Forget-me-not*) ..	„	1	blue	Ju to Sp	6	

Flower Seeds, General List *(continued)*.

No.	Name.	Hard Dur.	Ht in feet.	Colour.	Months of Flowering	Per Pkt. s. d.	Observations.
966	**Nasturtium, Tom Thumb, King** ...	hA	¾	rich scarlet	Jy to Sp	4	A brilliant and invaluable class of annuals very easy of cultivation. King of Tom Thumbs and Empress of India are the most brilliant of all. Among the others we may mention Golden King, cærulea rosea, and Ruby King as being partionlarly fine. Will thrive in almost any soil, but should have a sunny, rather dry situation, to bloom them to perfection.
967	„ „ Empress of India ...	„	„	deep scarlet	„	6	
968	„ „ dark crimson ...	„	„	dark crimson	„	3	
969	„ „ scarlet ...	„	„	scarlet	„	3	
970	„ „ Lady-bird ...	„	„	sptd. yel. & rd.	„	6	
971	„ „ cærulea rosea ...	„	„	bluish rose	„	3	
972	„ „ Golden King	„	„	golden yellow	„	6	
973	„ „ King Theodore ...	„	„	maroon	„	3	
974	„ „ Ruby King	„	„	purplish red	„	6	
975	„ „ Crystal Palace Gem ...	„	„	sulph. & mar.	„	3	
976	„ „ Pearl	„	„	cr. white	„	3	
977	„ „ yellow	„	„	yellow	„	3	
978	„ „ mixed	„	„	various	„	3	
	„ climbing (*see Tropæolum*).						
979	**Nemesia strumosa**	hhA	1½	various	Jy & Au	1 6	Brilliant annuals
980	„ versicolor	hA	¼	blue & white	Ju to Au	3	Useful for rockwork, pots, &c.
981	**Nemophila atomaria atro-cærulea** ...	„	spr.	deep blue	My to Sp	6	Extremely pretty early flowering annuals, useful for beds or borders, pots in the greenhouse, &c. N. insignis is fine for Spring gardening.
982	„ insignis	„	„	blue & white	„	3	
983	„ „ **alba**	„	„	white	„	3	
984	„ **maculata grandiflora**	„	„	white & violet	„	3	
985	**Nerium Oleander**	gs	6	rose	Ju to Sp	6	Valuable greenhouse shrub.
986	**Nertera depressa**	hP	½	white	Ju to Au	1 0	Bears bright coral red berries.
987	**Nicotiana affinis**	hhP	3	white	My to Sp	6	Fiue for the sub-tropical garden. N. affinis has long white tubular flowers, deliciously scented.
988	„ colossea	„	8	pink	„	1 0	
989	„ **macrophylla gigantea** ...	hhA	6-8	„	„	4	
990	„ **Virginica**	„	5-6	„	„	3	
991	**Nierembergia gracilis**	hhP	½	white & lilac	Ju to Sp	6	Useful for clumps, edgings, &c.
992	**Nigella damascena**	hA	1	pale blue	„	3	*Love-in-a-mist.* Curious.
993	**Nolana atriplicifolia**	„	spr.	blue & white	Jy to Sp	3	Pretty trailers, similar to Convolvulus minor
994	„ „ **alba**	„	„	white	„	3	
995	**Nyctarine selaginoides**	hhA	„	white & pink	„	3	Excellent for rockeries, &c.
996	***Obeliscaria pulcherrima**	hP	2	crim. & yellow	Jy to Oc	3	Curious hardy perennial.
997	**Œnothera acaulis (taraxacifolia)** ...	„	½	white	Ju to Au	6	A free-flowering class of plants useful for mixed beds, borders, &c. Œ. Lamarckiana is more suitable for shrubbery borders.
998	„ bistorta Veitchii	hA	1	yel. crim. spot	Jy to Sp	3	
999	„ Lamarckiana	hP	3	yellow	Ju to Au	3	
1000	„ **macrocarpa** (Missouriensis) ...	„	spr.	„	Ju & Jy	4	
1001	**Oxalis rosea**	hhA	½	rose	Ap to Jy	6	Useful plants for rockwork, edgings, hanging-baskets, pots, &c.
1002	„ „ **alba** ...	„	„	white	„	6	
1003	„ **Valdiviana**	hP	⅓	yellow	Ju to Oc	6	
1004	„ tropæoloides	gPb	„	„	„	6	
1005	**Oxyura chrysanthemoides** ...	hA	1	yel. & white	Ju to Au	3	Showy hardy annual.
1006	**Pæony, Herbaceous, choicest double**	hP	2	various	Ju & Jy	1 0	Showy herbaceous plants.
1007	**Panicum sulcatum** ...	hhP	1½	—	Jy & Au	3	*Prairie Grass.*
	Pansy, *see page* 67.						
1008	**Passiflora cærulea** ...	hP	cl.	blue	Ju to Oc	6	Valuable hardy climber for walls, &c.
1009	**Peas, Everlasting, rose** ...	„	6-8	rose	Ju to Au	4	Very useful hardy climbers, for walls, trellises, &c.
1010	„ „ white ...	„	„	white	„	6	
	Peas, Sweet, *see page* 69.						
	Pelargonium, *see page* 65.						
	Peutstemon, *see page* 65.						
1011	**Pennisetum longistylum**	hA	2	—	Jy & Au	3	Oruamcutal grass.
1012	**Perilla Nankinensis**	hhA	1¼	dark purple	Ju to Au	3	Valuable dark-foliaged bedding plant.
	Petunias, *see page* 70.						
1013	**Phacelia campanularia**	hA	1	rich blue	Jy & Au	6	Superb new annual from California.
	Phloxes, *see page* 72.						
	Pink, *see pages* 61, 63.						
	Polyanthuses, *see page* 74.						
1014	**Portulaca grandiflora alba fl. pl.** ...	hhA	½	pure white	Ju to Sp	6	These constitute the most brilliant class of half-hardy annuals in cultivation. The plants are of a spreading habit of growth, only reach a height of from four to six inches, and are splendid for sunny rockwork, warm dry borders, pots in the greenhouse, &c. The seed has been carefully saved, and will produce a large percentage of strikingly handsome flowers.
1015	„ „ **aurea fl. pl.**	„	„	golden yellow	„	6	
1016	„ „ **rosea fl. pl.**	„	„	bright rose	„	6	
1017	„ „ **splendens fl. pl.** ...	„	„	crimson	„	6	
1018	„ „ **Thellusoni fl. pl.** ...	„	„	scarlet	„	6	
1019	„ „ **choicest mixed double**	„	„	various	„	1 0	
1020	„ „ „ smaller pkt.	„	„	„	„	6	
1021	„ „ **an assortment of 8 beautiful vars.,** one packet of each ...	„	„	„	„	1 6	
1022	„ „ **single-flowered** ...	„	„	„	„	6	
1023	**Potentilla, choice mixed, double** ...	hP	2	„	Ju to Au	6	Showy herbaceous perennials.
1024	**Primula japonica**	„	1¼	„	Jy to Sp	6	Charmingly beautiful varieties.
1025	„ **obconica**	hhP	1	pale lilac	Oc to Jy	1 0	Beautiful for the cool greenhouse.
1026	„ **rosea**	hP	1½	rosy crimson	Jy to Sp	1 6	
1027	„ **cortusoides**	„	¾	rose	Mr to Ju	6	
1028	„ **denticulata**	„	¾	bluish lilac	Jy to Sp	1 0	
1029	**Prince's Feather, giant**	hA	3	crimson	Jy & Au	3	Useful for large borders, &c.
1030	**Pyrethrum parthenifol. aureum** ...	hP	¼	wh., yel. fol.	Jy to Sp	4	*Golden Feather.* Valuable bedding plant
1031	„ „ **laciniatum**	„	„	„	„	6	A fine variety of compact growth.
1032	„ „ **selaginoides**	„	„	„	„	6	A fine acquisition.
1033	„ „ **aureum cristatum** ...	„	„	„	„	1 0	Dense, compact growth.
1034	„ **hybridum fl. pl., mixed** ...	„	2	various	„	1 0	New and highly improved class.

No.	Name.	Hard Dur.	Ht in feet.	Colour.	Months of Flowering	Per Pkt. s. d.	Observations.
	Primrose, *see page* 74.						
	Primulas, *see page* 73.						
	Rhodanthe, *see page* 85.						
1035	**Ricinus Borboniensis arboreus** ...	hhA	12	green fol.	Ju to Sp	4	Stately plants with large handsome foliage, excellent for sub-tropical gardening. R. Borboniensis arboreus attains gigantic dimensions.
1036	„ **major sanguineus**	„	6-8	pale red fol.	„	3	
1037	„ **communis major**	„	„	green fol.	„	3	
1038	„ **Gibsoni**	„	„	red fol.	„	6	
1039	„ **Zanzibariensis** (new)	„	„	various	„	1 0	
1040	**Rocket, Sweet, purple**	hP	1½	purple	Ju to Au	3	Useful herbaceous perennials, very fragrant.
1041	„ „ **white**	„	„	white	„	3	
1042	**Rivinia humilis**	gP	2	„	„	6	Handsome plant for the greenhouse.
1043	**Salpiglossis grandiflora, coccinea** ...	hhA	„	crimson	Jy to Sp	6	Beautiful large-flowered annuals, with richly-coloured handsome blooms.
1044	„ „ **sulphurea**	„	„	yellow	„	6	
1045	„ „ **purpurea** ...	„	„	purple	„	6	
1046	„ „ **choice mixed**	„	„	various	„	6	
1047	**Salvia splendens**	hhP	3	scarlet	Ju to Oc	6	Free-flowering handsome perennials for borders, &c. S. argentea has beautiful silvery foliage, quite covering the ground.
1048	„ **patens**	„	2	rich blue	„	1 0	
1049	„ **coccinea**	„	„	scarlet	Jy to Sp	4	
1050	„ **argentea**	„	½	silver fol.	„	4	
1051	**Saintpaulia Ionantha**	gP	¼	blue	Oc to My	1 0	The *Zanzibar Violet*, very pretty.
1052	**Sanvitalia procumbens fl. pl.**	hA	spr.	yellow	Jy & Au	3	Useful hardy annual.
1053	**Saponaria Calabrica rosea**	„	¾	bright rose	Ju to Oc	3	Pretty and useful annuals for beds or borders. S. multiflora compacta and alba are charming new varieties of a fine dwarf habit of growth.
1054	„ „ **alba**	„	„	white	„	3	
1055	„ „ **Scarlet Queen** ...	„	„	scarlet	„	4	
1056	„ **multiflora compacta**	„	½	pink	„	4	
1057	„ „ „ **alba** ...	„	„	white	„	4	
1058	„ **ocymoides**	hP	spr.	pink	Jy & Au	3	Showy hardy perennial.
1059	**Scabiosa grandiflora fl. pl. Fireball**	hB	3	fiery scarlet	„	1 6	*Double German Scabious.* A beautiful and exceedingly useful class of hardy biennials or perennials. Treated as annuals will bloom freely the first year from seed, and yield an abundance of richly coloured fragrant flowers.
1060	„ „ „ **Snowball**	„	3	white	Ju to Sp	6	
1061	„ „ „ **New Golden** ..	„	2	golden yellow	„	6	
1062	„ „ „ **rosea alba** ...	„	2	rose & white	„	6	
1063	„ „ „ **atropurpurea**	„	3	purplish	„	3	
1064	„ „ „ **choicest mxd.**	„	3	various	„	3	
1065	„ **caucasica**	hP	3	lilac blue	Jy to Oc	1 0	Superb hardy perennial.
1066	**Schizanthus pinnatus**	hA	1½	pk. wh. & blk.	Ju to Au	3	Elegant-growing half-hardy annuals, excellent for mixed beds or borders or for pots in the greenhouse in Spring.
1067	„ **papilionaceus**	hhA	„	crim.&yel.spt	„	3	
1068	„ **retusus**	„	2	crim. yellow	„	3	
1069	„ „ **albus**	„	„	white	„	3	
1070	**Schizopetalon Walkeri**	„	1	„	My to Au	4	Beautifully fragrant annual.
1071	**Scyphanthus elegans**	„	6	yellow	Jy & Au	4	Useful half-hardy plant.
1072	**Sedum azureum**	hA	½	sky blue	„	3	*Stone-crop.* Elegant little plant.
1073	**Sensitive Plant**	tA	2	pale pink	Jy to Sp	6	*Mimosa pudica.* Ornamental for pots.
1074	**Silene armeria rubra**	hA	1½	bright red	Jn to Sp	3	Bright profuse-flowering annuals. S. pendula and varieties are admirably suited for Spring gardening, and form a charming contrast with blue Nemophila, &c.
1075	„ „ **alba**	„	„	white	„	3	
1076	„ **pendula ruberrima** ...	„	1	rosy carmine	My to Sp	3	
1077	„ „ **Snow King** ...	„	½	white	„	4	
1078	„ „ **compacta** ...	„	„	rosy carmine	„	3	
1079	„ „ **new double** ...	„	1	rosy pink	„	4	
1080	**Solanum melongena purpurea** ...	tA	1½	purple-fruited	Ju to Sp	4	*Egg Plants.* Excellent for garnishing purposes.
1081	„ „ **alba**	„	„	white-fruited	„	4	
1082	„ **finest hybrids, mixed**	hhP	„	orn. fruit	Jy to No	6	Fine decorative plants for Winter.
1083	„ **hæmatocarpum**	hhA	3	ornament. fol.	Jy & Au	6	Magnificent ornamental-foliaged plants for sub-tropical gardening
1084	„ **Warscewiczii**	„	6	„	„	6	
1085	**Sphœnogyne speciosa aurea**	hA	1	golden yellow	Jy to Sp	3	Showy hardy annual.
1086	**Spraguea umbellata**	hhA	½	flesh	Jy to Oc	6	Fine for greenhouse or warm border.
	Statice (*see Everlasting Flowers*).						
1087	**Stellaria graminea aurea**	„	spr.	white	My to Oc	1 0	*Golden Chickweed.* Bright yellow foliage, useful for carpet bedding.
1088	**Stipa pennata**	hP	2	—	Jy to Oc	3	*Feather Grass.* Very graceful.
	Stocks, *see pages* 53—55.						
	Stock, Night-scented (*see Mathiola*)						
1089	**Streptocarpus, new hybrids**	gP	½	various	„	1 6	Pretty pot plants.
1090	**Sultan, Sweet, purple**	hA	1	purple	Jy & Au	3	Useful sweet-scented border annuals.
1091	„ „ **white**	„	„	white	„	3	
1092	„ „ **yellow**	„	1½	yellow	„	3	
1093	**Sunflower, large double**	„	5-6	rich orange	Jy to Oc	4	Fine decorative plants for the garden. The large double has immense double blooms of a rich orange yellow. Primrose Dame is a single-flowered variety with delicate primrose flowers, and is very distinct. The Miniature is a charming small-flowered single, useful for cutting.
1094	„ „ **single**	„	„	golden yellow	„	3	
1095	„ **Miniature**	„	3-4	deep yellow	„	6	
1096	„ **Primrose Dame**	„	5-6	delicate prmrs	„	6	
1097	„ **Giant Yellow, single** ...	„	6-8	rich yellow	„	3	
1098	„ **Dwarf, double**	„	3-4	deep yellow	„	4	
1099	„ **Thousand-flowered** ...	„	8-10	yellow	„	1 0	
	Sweet William, *see page* 74.						
1100	**Tacsonia insignis**	gP	cl.	bril. crimson	Au to Oc	1 0	Superb greenhouse evergreen climbers, very brilliant.
1101	„ **Van Volxemi**	„	„	dark crimson	„	1 0	
1102	**Thunbergia, finest mixed**	gA	„	various	Jn to Sp	4	Beautiful little plants for pots, &c.
	Tobacco (*see Nicotiana*).						
1103	**Torenia Fournieri**	„	1	pur. & yellow	My to Oc	6	Pretty pot-plant for the greenhouse.
1104	**Tritoma uvaria grandiflora** ...	hP	4	scar. & orange	Au to Oc	4	Handsome for large borders, &c.

Flower Seeds, General List (continued).

No.	Name.	Hard Ht in Dur. feet.		Colour.	Months of Flowering	Per Pkt.	Observations.
						s. d.	
1105	Tropæolum canariense ...	hhA	cl.	yellow	Jy to Oc	4	Canary-creeper. Well known.
1106	„ Lobbianum, brilliant ...	„	„	bril. scarlet	„	4	Splendid and brilliant climbers or
1107	„ „ Lucifer ...	„	„	intense scarlet	„	6	trailers for trellises, rockeries, large
1108	„ „ Queen Victoria	„	„	striped	„	6	hanging-baskets, vases, &c. Should
1109	„ majus atrosanguineum	hA	„	dark red	„	3	be grown in rather poor soil to
1110	„ „ Scheuermanni	„	„	yellow & red	„	3	induce the fullest development of
1111	„ „ aurantiacum ...	„	„	orange	„	3	bloom. The Lobbianum varieties
1112	„ „ Schultzi	„	„	rich scarlet	„	4	are very handsome.
1113	„ „ mixed ..	„	„	various	„	3	Common climbing Nasturtium.
1114	Venus' Looking-glass, blue ...	„	1	blue	Jy & Au	3	Useful hardy annuals for beds, borders,
1115	„ „ white ...	„	„	white	„	3	rockwork, &c.
1116	„ „ Navelwort ...	„	„	rose	„	3	
1117	Verbena, lemon-scented ...	gP	3-5	blush	Ju to Sp	1 0	Aloysia citriodora. Beautifully fragrant plant for greenhouse or window.
1118	„ venosa... ...	hP	spr.	purple	My to Sp	6	Valuable border-plant.
	„ hybrida, see page 75.						
1119	*Veronica spicata	„	1½	blue	Jy to Sp	3	Elegant herbaceous plant.
1120	Violet, Sweet-scented, The Czar	„	½	purple	Oc to Ap	6	Viola odorata. Well-known and
1121	„ „ large white	„	„	white	„	6	popular favorites.
1122	„ „ common ...	„	„	blue	„	4	
1123	Vinca rosea	gs	3-4	rose	Ju to Sp	6	Useful plants for the greenhouse.
1124	„ „ alba	„	„	white	„	6	
	Violas, see page 74.						
1125	Viscaria cardinalis	hA	1	bril. crimson	Au to Oc	3	Brilliant, profuse-flowering annuals,
1126	„ elegans picta ...	„	„	rose & crimson	„	3	very easy of cultivation, and should
1127	„ alba pura	„	„	pure white	„	4	be in every garden.
1128	„ Dwarf, blue	„	¼	blue	Jy to Oc	6	
1129	„ „ bright rose	„	„	rose	„	6	Splendidly effective and charming
1130	„ „ pure white	„	„	white	„	6	varieties.
1131	Virginian Stock, red	„	1	red	My to Au	3	Early flowering annuals, useful for
1132	„ „ white ...	„	„	white	„	3	beds or borders; if neatly clipped
1133	„ „ yellow ...	„	„	pale yellow	„	3	will form a pretty and compact
1134	„ „ Crimson King	„	„	crimson	„	4	edging. The new Crimson King
1135	„ „ mixed ...	„	„	various	„	3	is very fine.
	Wallflowers, see page 55.						
1136	Whitlavia grandiflora ...	hhA	1½	dark blue	Ju to Sp	3	Pretty border annual.
1137	Wigandia caracasana... ...	hhs	10	lilac	Jy to Sp	6	Splendid for sub-tropical garden.
1138	Winter Cherry	hP	2	red fruit	—	3	Physalis alkekengi. Very useful for Winter decoration.
	Xeranthemum (see Everlasting Flowers).						
	Zinnia, see page 75.						

THE COTTAGER'S PACKET OF CHOICE FLOWER SEEDS.

(Registered.)

Containing Twelve selected varieties, including Aster, Stock, Mignonette, Scarlet Linum, &c.

Post Free, 1s. 2d.; two packets, 2s. 2d.; twelve packets, 10s. 6d.

FLOWER SEEDS IN PENNY PACKETS.

WE supply all the most popular sorts of Flower Seeds in Penny Packets, our own selection, at the following rates Post Free. 100 packets in 100 choice varieties, 8s.; 50 packets in 50 choice varieties, 4s. 2d.; 25 packets in 25 choice varieties, 2s. 2d.

STIPA PENNATA

ORNAMENTAL GRASSES.

Graceful and elegant occupants of the Flower Garden.

Very useful for cutting for home decoration in Winter.

A collection of twelve varieties, one packet of each, 2s. 6d.

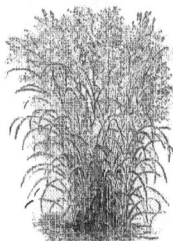

PANICUM SULCATUM.

EVERLASTING FLOWERS FOR WINTER BOUQUETS

The popularity of Everlasting Flowers has been wonderfully on the increase during the past few years, and not without reason, for their culture is very easy and simple, and their flowers, if carefully gathered, dried, and preserved, will retain their beauty for years. Their bright and pleasing colours will be found of great service in the decoration of the Church or the home, in Winter, when other flowers are scarce. Many of the light varieties may be dyed of various brilliant colours; and, made up into bouquets with some of the Ornamental Grasses, are truly charming. Everlasting Flowers for preserving should be cut just as the blossoms are beginning to expand, or when they are not more than half open, and tied in bunches and hung up in a cool place to dry, with the flowers downwards. Small bunches are preferable for drying, as large bunches are apt to mould and spoil.

The Helichrysums are perhaps the most useful, and produce a great variety of brilliant and beautiful colours. *Rhodanthe maculata* and *Rhodanthe maculata alba* are two charming and elegant varieties of fine double habit. *Rhodanthe maculata fl. pl.* is a fine new double-flowered variety of great merit. The Acrocliniums and Xeranthemums are also exceedingly useful, both for garden decoration or dried flowers.

GROUP OF HELICHRYSUMS.

From Mr. W. D. NEAVE,
Lewisham, New South Wales.
Nov. 19th.
"Your Seeds, as usual, have turned out first-rate. The Blotched Pansies took First Prize, 24 varieties, and Second Prize, 12 varieties, at The Liberty Plains H. S. Show on the 7th and 8th November. The Carnations are just beginning to flower; there are some splendid ones out now."

From ALEX. PURVIS, Esq.,
South Shields.
March 9th.
"In the last three years I have gained twenty-seven Prizes of our Chrysanthemum Show, and have competed against professionals. I am an ardent amateur, and have come to the conclusion that your Seeds are the best and most reliable from personal experience."

No.	Name.	Hard'y Dur.	Ht in feet.	Colour.	Months of Flowering	Per Pkt. s. d.	Observations.
1139	Acroclinium roseum	hhA	2	rose	Jy to Sp	3	
1140	„ roseum, double ...	„	„	„	„	6	} Very useful and free flowering.
1141	„ album	„	„	white	„	3	
1142	*Ammobium alatum grandiflorum	hP	„	„	My to Au	3	*Winged Sandflower.* Pretty.
1143	*Catananche bicolor	„	„	white & blue	Jy to Oc	6	
1144	* „ cœrulea	„	„	blue	„	3	
1145	Gnaphalium fœtidum ...	hA	1½	yellow	Jy to Sp	3	} Useful *Everlastings*. G. leontopodium is a beautiful silvery white alpine variety of dwarf growth.
1146	„ leontopodium (*Edelweis*)	hP	½	white	„	6	
1147	„ orientale fl. pl.	„	1½	yellow	„	6	
1148	Gomphrena globosa nana compacta ...	tA	1	violet red	Ju to Sp	6	} *Globe Amaranth.* Very pretty for the greenhouse during the Summer and Autumn.
1149	„ „ alba	„	„	white	„	6	
1150	„ „ choice mixed ...	„	2	various	„	6	
1151	Helichrysum, an assortment of 12 beautiful vars. 2s. 6d. ...	hA	2½	scarlet	Jy to Oc		
1152	„ scarlet	hA	2½	scarlet	Jy to Oc	3	} A brilliant and splendid class of showy annuals that remain in bloom for a long period. Exceedingly useful to gather for vases, &c., for Winter decoration. The colours vary from dark crimson or purple to orange-scarlet and yellow, to pure white, and delicate rose, and are all very handsome (*see illustration*).
1153	„ yellow	„	„	yellow	„	3	
1154	„ purple ...	„	„	purple	„	3	
1155	„ rose ...	„	„	rose	„	3	
1156	„ white ...	„	„	white	„	3	
1157	„ finest mixed ...	„	„	various	„	3	
1158	„ minimum album ...	„	1½	white	„	4	
1159	„ „ luteum	„	„	yellow	„	4	
1160	„ „ roseum	„	„	rose	„	4	
1161	„ „ rubrum	„	„	dark red	„	4	
1162	„ „ mixed	„	„	various	„	6	
1163	Helipterum anthemoides ...	hhA	1	yellow	„	3	} Beautiful dwarf-growing varieties.
1164	„ corymbiflora ...	„	„	white	„	3	
1165	„ Sandfordi ...	„	„	yellow	„	3	
1166	Rhodanthe atrosanguinea ...	„	„	dark red	„	6	} A charming group. R. maculata fl. pl. is a fine new variety, with handsome rose-coloured double flowers, whilst R. maculata alba is probably the most beautiful of all white overlastings.
1167	„ maculata ...	„	„	rose & crim.	„	4	
1168	„ „ alba ...	„	„	silvery white	„	6	
1169	„ „ fl. pl. ...	„	„	rose	„	6	
1170	„ „ mixed ...	„	„	various	„	4	
1171	„ Manglesi fl. pl. ...	„	1½	rose	„	1 0	
1172	Statice Bonduelli	hA	1½	yellow	„	6	} Very useful and showy varieties.
1173	„ spicata	„	1	pink	„	6	
1174	„ candidissima ...	„	1½	white	„	6	
1175	„ Suworowi ...	„	2	rose	„	6	
1176	Waitzia aurea grandiflora ...	hhA	1	orange	„	6	Compact-growing, pretty annual.
1177	Xeranthemum annuum superbissimum fl. pl. ...	hA	„	purple	„	6	} Very handsome and free-flowering everlastings. Excellent for garden decoration.
1178	„ „ „ album fl. pl. ...	„	„	white	„	6	
1179	„ annuum purpureum „	„	„	purple	„	3	
1180	„ „ album „	„	„	white	„	3	
1181	„ „ roseum „	„	„	rose	„	3	

Thirty-six varieties, one packet of each, post free, 6s. 6d.; 24 ditto, 5s.; 12 ditto, 2s. 6d.

On the Rearing of Flowers from Seed.

Hardy Annuals.

THE many beautiful varieties of hardy annuals available for the Summer decoration of our gardens are worthy of a much more extensive growth, and a better cultural treatment than they usually receive, and, well-grown, will produce flowers of a size and brilliancy that will surprise many who are only accustomed to the weedy, starved representatives so often seen of this fine class. Although hardy annuals will thrive fairly in almost any soil or situation, some little preparation of the ground before sowing is necessary to grow them to perfection; and the first consideration is to reduce the surface to a fine and even tilth, carefully removing all large stones and clods, and if the soil be poor, working in a liberal quantity of well-decayed manure.

For a general display, perhaps the best time for sowing is about the middle of March, and for a later succession, April; but we have seen annuals sown in May, and even the early part of June, that have bloomed splendidly in the Autumn months. After sowing, the cultivation of hardy annuals is extremely simple, early and vigorous thinning out of the clumps or patches being nearly all that is necessary to ensure an abundance of fine plants, with a profusion of handsome flowers. Various methods are adopted in sowing; but perhaps the simplest and best plan for garden decoration is to sow in shallow furrows, in circles of from nine to twelve inches in diameter; or in rows or drills, their distance apart to be regulated according to the height of the plants when fully grown. When this is done in dry weather, an excellent plan is to fill the furrows with water and allow it to settle before sowing, carefully covering the seeds with the soil removed in the operation, and pressing down firmly with a trowel or flat piece of wood. Such large seeds as Nasturtiums, Lupins, and Sweet Peas may be covered to the depth of an inch; Convolvulus major and minor, not quite so deep; smaller seeds, such as Mignonette, &c., require but a slight covering. Hardy annuals may also be sown broadcast in mixture, in beds or patches, in waste places, shrubberies, &c., and have a very pleasing effect. For early spring decoration such fine varieties as Nemophila insignis and alba, Silene pendula, Limnanthes Douglasii, &c., may be sown in a sheltered position in August or early in September, and transferred as vacancies occur to where they are intended to bloom. Godetias also, in their many beautiful varieties, which are perfectly hardy, bloom much earlier and finer when sown in the Autumn and transplanted early in Spring.

Half-Hardy Annuals.

The great majority of half-hardy annuals require a long period of growth to develop the fine plants and blooms for which they are so much esteemed, and sowing should therefore commence as soon as convenient after the second week in February, and be continued to the end of March, or the middle of April. There are, however, some slight exceptions to this rule, as for instance, in the case of Zinnias and Marigolds, which should not be sown before the middle of March, and Ten-week Stocks, which may be sown as early as the middle of January, or early in February, and indeed treated thus will produce much finer blooms than those sown in March or April; whilst the finest Asters are produced from seeds sown the first and second weeks in April, and which should not, as a rule, be sown earlier. The beautiful Scarlet Flax (*Linum grandiflorum rubrum*) succeeds best treated as a hardy annual, and sown in April.

The most useful soil for raising plants from seeds, under glass, is composed of about equal parts of good rich loam, leaf-mould, and well-decayed manure from an old hot-bed, thoroughly incorporated with a sufficiency of coarse sand to render the whole fairly porous. In filling pots, pans, &c., with soil, it is of the first importance, after providing ample drainage, that the soil should be pressed down firmly before sowing the seeds, which will have the effect of providing a much more even moisture, and certainty of germination, than can be had by sowing on a loose and porous surface. Sow the seeds thinly, distributing as evenly as you can, and cover as lightly as possible with a sprink-ling of fine soil, and after submitting them to a slight pressure from such as the bottom of a flower-pot, give them a careful watering and place in a gentle heat. When the young plants come up, place them as near as possible to the light, and give them on all favourable occasions a fair quantity of air, carefully avoiding, however, their exposure to the keen, drying east winds so often prevalent in Spring. When the plants have reached a size at which they can be handled, the choicer varieties should be carefully pricked out into pots, pans, boxes, &c., and placed in the greenhouse close to the glass, or in frames, &c., where on fine warm days they can have the full benefit of air and sun. This will enable them to make good sturdy plants with plenty of roots, that will transplant well, and produce an abundance of handsome flowers.

The best time for planting out depends very much on the season, and this operation should never be hurried if the weather be unfavourable, or proper attention cannot be given. Where heat is not available for the rearing of half-hardy annuals, they are easily raised by sowing in April, in pans or boxes placed under hand-lights, or in a cool frame close to the glass, the only difference being their blooming somewhat later. We have, indeed, seen a fine Autumn display of half-hardy annuals sown in May on the open border, and of Asters sown so late as the first week in June. We may add, that Lobelias for bedding out, cannot be sown too early in the year, some giving preference to those sown the preceding Autumn.

Hardy Perennials & Biennials.

With the exception of some few sorts, which require a somewhat different treatment, the greater part of these are best raised in the months of May, June, and July, in the manner recommended for hardy annuals, selecting, however, a somewhat cool and shady situation in preference to one exposed to much sun. Sow thinly, and when the plants are large enough, prick out on nursery beds to strengthen, and plant out early in Autumn, or in favourable weather in February and March, where they are intended to flower. Early sowing is decidedly the best, as it gives the plants a far better opportunity of becoming sufficiently strong to resist severe frost in Winter, and to bloom freely and finely in the coming Spring and Summer. This is especially the case in reference to double German Wallflowers and Brompton Stocks, which should not be sown later than the end of May. These being less hardy than most classed as such, should have the benefit of a more sheltered spot when finally planted out, which ought to be done if possible in July. Sweet Williams, unless sown early, will not all bloom the following year.

Greenhouse or Tender Annuals.

The many fine varieties of such valuable plants as Balsams, Thunbergias, Amaranthuses, Celosias, Ipomœas, Cockscombs, &c., are richly deserving of cultivation wherever facilities exist for growing them. Their treatment in the young state closely resembles that of half-hardy annuals, a good light and rich soil with a liberal proportion of sharp sand being nearly all that is required to grow them to perfection. The chief difference in their culture, however, consists in their being sown somewhat earlier and on a stronger heat, and in pricking out the young plants as early as possible, singly into small pots; and as these fill with roots, shifting into larger, and so on, till they are transferred to the size in which it is intended to bloom them. The growth of the plants is very much assisted by occasionally watering with weak liquid manure; but this should be discontinued when the bloom is making its appearance, and tepid rain or soft water only should be used instead. Balsams, although classed as "tender," may be planted out in June, in sheltered positions in the open garden, and will make a fine display.

Every packet of **Flower Seed** supplied by us bears all necessary cultural instructions printed on the envelope.

Gladioli, Hybrids of Gandavensis.

These charming Flowers should be placed in the front rank as decorative plants for the open garden, or for cut flowers. They succeed admirably in almost any soil or situation; and planted three or four inches deep in clumps of three or more, are splendidly effective, whilst if the flower spikes are cut and placed in water the blooms will open to the topmost bud, and retain their beauty for a long period. The colours embrace all the most brilliant and lovely shades of scarlet, rose, crimson, pure white, purple, yellow, &c., and by a few successive plantings from March 10 May a succession of beautiful flowers may be had from July to the end of September.

Daniels' Special Collections of Gladioli—Carriage Free.

WE have much pleasure in recommending the following choice collections of named Gladioli, which will be found to contain a charming selection of the most beautiful and distinct varieties, specially selected for exhibition or decorative purposes.

A. **50 in 50 superb varieties as follows, price 30s.**
Africain, Andre Leroy, Argus, Baroness B. Coutts, Beatrix, Butterfly, Camille, Conqueror, Conquête, Diamant, Dr. Bailly, Dr. Masters, Eclair, Enchanteresse, Eugene Scribe, Figaro, Formosa, Ginevra, Grand Rouge, Harlequin, Horace Vernet, Jubilee, La Candeur, Le Vesuve, Mdlle. Marie Mies, Maréchal Vaillant, Mary Stuart, Meyerbeer, Miltou, Mous. Legouvé, Mount Etna, Murillo, Nereide, Neige et Feu, Ophir, Orpheus, Pactole, Phœbus, Phédre, Primatrice, Psyche, Rayon d'Or, Reine Blanche, Rossini, Rosa Bonheur, Schiller, Shakespeare, Sylvie, Therese de Vilmorin, Virginalis.

B. **25 in 25 superb varieties as follows, price 12s. 6d.**
Africain, Baroness B. Coutts, Beatrix, Camille, Conquête, Diamant, Eugene Scribe, Figaro, Ginevra, Grand Rouge, Horace Vernet, Le Vesuve, Meyerbeer, Mous. Legouvé, Murillo, Neige et Feu, Orpheus. Pactole, Phédre, Reine Blanche, Schiller, Shakespeare, Sylvie, Therese de Vilmorin, Virginalis.

C. **12 in 12 choice varieties as follows, price 6s. 6d.**
Africain, Baroness B. Coutts, Conquête, Grand Rouge, Horace Vernet, Le Vesuve, Murillo, Orpheus, Phédre, Reine Blanche, Shakespeare, Therese de Vilmorin.

D. **12 in 12 fine varieties as follows, price 5s.**
Conquête, Eugene Scribe, Figaro, Ginevra, Le Vesuve, Horace Vernet, Orpheus, Phédre, Therese de Vilmorin, Sylvie, Schiller, Virginalis.

Gladioli in Mixtures from Finest Named and Seedling Sorts.

We can highly recommend our mixtures of these, which are very fine, and contain a great variety of superior flowers of many beautiful and varied colours.
Choicest mixed Seedlings, &c., from the finest sorts per 100, 20s. 0d. per doz. 3s. 0d.

White-ground varieties, extra fine mixed, from named sorts ...	,,	3s. 0d.
Rose and light red varieties, choice mixed, from named sorts ...	,,	3s. 0d.
Brilliant scarlet and dark varieties, choice mixed, from named sorts	,,	3s. 0d.
Yellow-ground varieties, very choice mixed, from named sorts ...	,,	3s. 6d.
Lilac and violet-ground varieties, fine mixed, from named sorts	,,	3s. 6d.
BRENCHLEYENSIS, well-known showy scarlet per 100, 10s. 6d.	,.	1s. 6d.
Snow White. Splendid new pure white ... ... each 9d.	,,	7s. 6d.

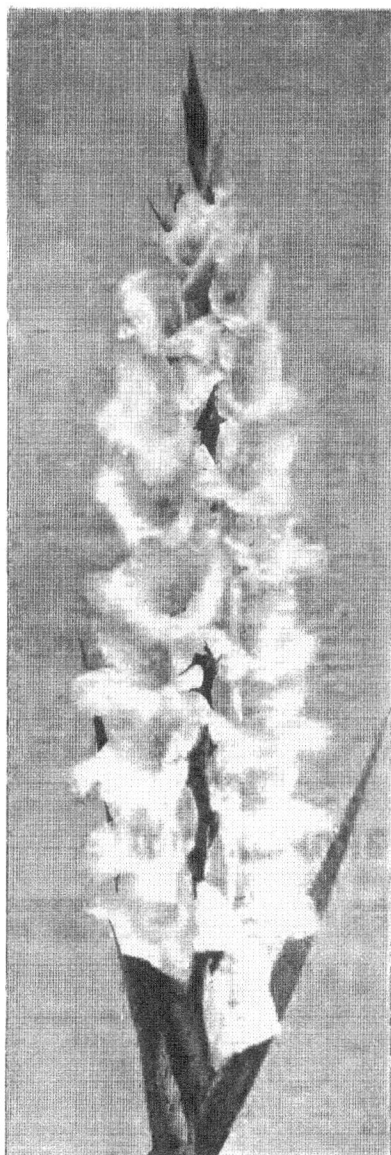

A GRAND GLADIOLUS.
THERESE LE VILMORIN.
(From a Photograph.)

GLADIOLI, HYBRIDS OF GANDAVENSIS.

NEW AND SELECT VARIETIES.

The following List includes what we consider the finest of the exhibition and decorative varieties, and customers making a selection from these may depend on the most satisfactory results.

	each—s.	d.
Africain. Slaty-brown on scarlet ground, streaked scarlet and white, conspicuous white blotch	0	7
Andre Leroy. Fine deep red, white stripe	0	6
Aurora de Feu. Flowers of a bright rose colour, passing to scarlet, with golden-yellow centre	1	0
Baroness Burdett-Coutts. Delicate lilac tinged with rose, flamed rosy-carmine; magnificent variety	1	0
Beatrix. Pure white ground, flushed carmine lilac	0	6
Blanc Frise. Fine creamy white, large, well-expanded flowers, the edges of the petals fringed or crimped	3	0
Buffalo Bill. Large spike of cherry-red flowers with yellow blotch and centre stripe; very fine	1	0
Conquete. Bright cherry-rose, with white blotch	0	6
Cloth of Gold. A fine long spike of well-arranged flowers; colour, a bright golden yellow, slightly tinged with rose, carmine blotch on lower petals; a very fine variety	7	6
Diadem. A charming variety, the flowers are large, well-arranged, and open; colour, a pale yellow, edged with rosy lilac, of exquisite effect	6	0
Diamant. White, streaked with carmine; splendid	0	6
Doctor Masters. Flowers large, bright rose, strongly flushed with dark purple; blotch amaranth	2	0
Eclair. Bright scarlet, with broad white bands	0	6
Enchanteresse. Very large flowers, of a satiny pale lilac-white, streaked violet-red on one or two sepals	1	0
Eugene Scribe. Tender rose, blazed with carmine	0	6
Fantome. Fine spike of enormously large flowers; pure white, slightly streaked at the edges with rosy lilac	1	0
Figaro. Light orange red, large white blotch	0	6
Formosa. Large perfectly shaped spike; flowers of a very delicate satiny rose, thinly striped with carmine on the edges; blotch creamy white	0	6
Gerbe de Feu. Long well-furnished spike of most brilliant and dazzling scarlet flowers, with a large creamy white blotch. A variety of grand effect	0	7
Ginevra. Beautiful cherry-rose, flushed with red, central line of petals pure white; splendid spike	0	6
Grand Rouge. Remarkably fine spike of large flowers of a bright scarlet colour, with small violet blotch. First Class Certificate, R.H.S.	0	6
Grandeur a Merveille. Very handsome spike with immense well opened flowers of a satiny lilac white, very slightly speckled and streaked with rose	2	0
Harlequin. Salmon rose, flaked carmine on a yellow ground, well-shaped flowers	0	7
Le Vesuve. Intense scarlet, magnificent spike	0	6

	each—s.	d.
Horace Vernet. Bright purplish-red, with large pure white stain; a grand variety	0	7
Mademoiselle Marie Mies. Delicate rose, flamed with carmine, blotch rosy purple; magnificent	1	6
Marechal Vaillant. Brilliant scarlet, white stains	0	6
Mary Stuart. White, tinged with rose, and flamed with bright carmine-cherry; very beautiful	0	7
Meyerbeer. Brilliant scarlet, flamed with vermilion	0	6
Michol Ange. Crimson, white blotch	3	0
Mons. Legouve. Bright red, with white lines	0	6
Mont Blanc. Immense pyramidal spike, with very large flowers, creamy white at first, soon changing to snowy white, small violet blotch	6	0
Mount Etna. Brilliant velvety scarlet, white bands	0	7
Mr. Patrick. Splendid spike, with very large and numerous very brilliant scarlet flowers, with violet blotch on a lilac ground; extra fine	2	0
Murillo. Fine cherry-rose on light ground, white stripe down the middle of each petal; beautiful	0	6
Nevada. Long spike of large pure white flowers, with faint amaranth blotch; charming variety	2	0
Orpheus. Rose, blazed with carmine; magnificent	0	6
Pactole. Beautiful yellow, slightly tinged with rose	0	6
Perfection. Pale rose, streaked and banded at the edges with coppery rose, flowers large; splendid variety	3	6
Phedre. Pure white, flamed with cherry-rose	0	6
Phœbus. Brilliant red, with large pure white stain	0	6
Princess May. Very fine compact spike of large well-expanded flowers, white ground, slightly streaked with bright carmine, beautiful colour	5	0
Queen of Summer. One of the grandest of recent introduction, very fine spike of flowers; colour, a pale rosy carmine, streaked with tender rose	4	0
Rayon d'Or. Creamy yellow, flaked rosy purple	0	6
Rosa Bonheur. White, tinged lilac, dark blotch	1	0
Rossini. Dark amaranth red, with white lines	0	7
Schiller. Sulphur yellow, with large carmine blotch	0	6
Shakespeare. White, very slightly suffused with carmine-rose, large rosy blotch; magnificent	0	6
Sylvie. White, edged with delicate cherry-rose	0	6
Therese de Vilmorin. Very fine tall spike of splendid flowers, creamy white passing to pure white, with a few fine purplish rose stripes; superb	0	8
Valkyrie. Brilliant orange scarlet, strangely blotched with slaty-violet, fine spike, a strikingly distinct and original colour	6	0
Virginalis. White, bordered and flamed carmine	0	6

Choice varieties, our selection from the above, per doz. 6s., 9s., 12s., & 18s.; per 100, 60s. & 75s.

NEW HARDY HYBRID GLADIOLI

With Large Stained or Blotched Flowers.

This fine new race of Hybrid Gladioli blooms somewhat earlier than those of the Gandavensis section, and are much more hardy, so hardy in fact, that their bulbs do not need to be lifted in Winter. The flowers are very striking and handsome in appearance, all having conspicuous blotches on the lower petals, whilst the colours are very diversified and beautiful. These will be found splendid alike for garden decoration or for cut flowers.

	each—s.	d.
Alsace. Pale sulphur, with blood red blotch	0	9
Admiral Courbet. Fiery scarlet, side petals blotched velvety red	0	4
Eglantine. Pure white, tinged with rose, tall spike	0	6
Enfant de Nancy. Purplish scarlet, lower petals deep velvety crimson	0	6
E. V. Hallock (new). Sulphur-white, with large blood red blotch on yellow disc; large, well-formed	1	9
Fleur de Lys. Fine compact spike of very large pure white flowers, slightly blotched with violet at the bottom of the throat. The finest of all the whites	7	6
Gloire de Fontainebleau. Tall spike of large, well-opened flowers, bright rosy carmine, with white bands	0	9
Incendie. Purplish scarlet, vermilion rose throat	0	6
Lafayette. Salmon-yellow, with large crimson blotches	0	6
Madame Lemoinier. Pure white, with maroon blotch, spike erect, and very early	0	9

	each—s.	d.
Lemoinei. Creamy white, tinted rose, crimson blotches	0	4
Magnificus. Tall spike of very large flowers, cinnabar red, with white blotch	1	0
Mount Etna. Velvety scarlet, with yellow blotch; very early and effective	1	0
Sceptre d'Or. Chrome yellow, velvet black blotch	1	0
Venus de Milo. Pure white passing to rose, with maroon blotch, flowers large and perfect	1	9
Victor Hugo. Rosy yellow, vermilion blotch	0	9
Voltaire. Violet carmine, with maroon blotch on yellow ground; extra	0	8
W. E. Gumbleton. Rosy purple, striped carmine, velvet blotches on yellow disc	0	4

12 choice varieties, our selection from the above, 6s.
6 „ „ „ „ „ 3s. 6d.

Choice mixed, in beautiful variety, per 100, 24s.; per doz., 3s. 6d.

Lilies (Lilium).

For growing Lilies in pots a compost of about equal parts of sandy loam, leaf mould, and peat, is, perhaps, the best. Fine Lilies may, however, be grown in almost any good light and rich soil, especially those of the Auratum type. For single specimens use pots of about six inches diameter. These will be found very useful for house decoration; but pots of eight or ten inches diameter, with five or six bulbs in each, form grand objects for the conservatory when in bloom. Pot firmly, any time during Spring, with the bulbs about two inches below the surface, and plunge the pots with their rims about six inches deep in some light material, such as ashes or cocoa-nut fibre, in some sheltered position out of doors; and when the stems have pushed their way well through the plunging material, they may be lifted and removed to a cool pit or frame till the flower buds are developed, when they may be removed to the greenhouse or conservatory.

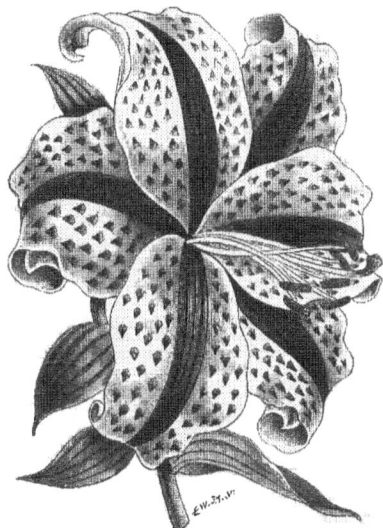

LILIUM AURATUM RUBRO-VITTATUM.

	each—s.	d.
AURATUM (Golden-rayed Lily of Japan). The beautiful large-flowered variety, white with yellow stripes and brownish-red spots; deliciously fragrant, extremely hardy, first-class for pot culture. One of the most useful and beautiful Lilies in cultivation.		
Good flowering bulbs ... per doz. 5s.	0	6
Larger. Very good bulbs ... per doz. 7s. 6d.	0	9
Extra fine. Grand bulbs of splendid size per doz. 15s.	1	6
AURATUM rubro-vittatum. Magnificent variety, immense flowers, petals pure white, with a distinct broad band of deep crimson down the centre 2s. 6d. and	3	6
,, **virginale.** Very large flowers, white, with pale yellow bands; most beautiful variety	3	6
,, **platyphyllum (macranthum).** Gigantic flowers of great substance, very broad petals, white, with yellow bands, slightly spotted; very fine ...	1	6
Chalcedonicum (Scarlet Turk's Cap). Splendid old variety, flowers medium sized, reflexed, and of a deep rich scarlet colour; finely effective per doz. 12s.	1	3
Colchicum (*Szovitzianum*). Pale yellow, spotted with black; finely scented ... ... per doz. 15s.	1	6

	each—s.	d
Croceum. Light orange, spotted black per doz. 5s.	0	6
Davuricum fulgidum. Deep orange red flushed with yellow, very showy ... ... per doz. 7s. 6d.	0	9
Giganteum (the noble Himalayan Lily). White, with broad bands of crimson violet ... 3s. 6d., 5s., and	7	6
Humboldti. A fine species, growing about five feet high, with large golden-yellow flowers, spotted purple ...	2	6
Krameri. Similar to Auratum, but of a beautiful pink colour; deliciously scented ... per doz. 7s. 6d.	0	9
Leichtlini. A rare and interesting species, three to four feet high, and bearing numerous golden yellow flowers spotted with purplish crimson	1	6
Longiflorum giganteum. A fine early flowering, dwarf growing species, beautiful trumpet-shaped flowers, pure white, should be in every garden ... per doz. 5s.	0	6
,, **Harrisii.** Beautiful pure white deliciously scented flowers. Will bloom three or four times in succession without the bulbs being rested. Splendid for pot culture in the greenhouse and for forcing per doz. 7s. 6d.	0	9
Martagon (Turk's Cap). Purple ... per doz. 7s. 6d.	0	9
,, **album.** Pure white-flowered form of the preceding; extremely scarce ... 2s. 6d. and	3	6
,, **Dalmaticum.** A magnificent variety, with deep velvety crimson purple flowers	2	6
Pardalinum. Bright scarlet shading to orange, spotted maroon; large flowers ... ... per doz. 10s. 6d.	1	0
Pomponium verum. An elegant species, with bright scarlet flowers ... ... per doz. 7s. 6d.	0	9
Pyrenaicum (the Yellow Martagon). Deliciously scented flowers, yellow, spotted black per doz. 7s. 6d.	0	9
SPECIOSUM (*Lanceifolium*). A fine hardy class; excellent for pot culture; deliciously scented.		
,, **album.** Pure white, beautiful per doz. 10s. 6d.	1	0
,, ,, **monstrosum.** Flowers produced in large corymbs; very fine ... per doz. 10s. 6d.	1	0
,, **Krætzeri.** Pure white; the finest variety ...	1	0
,, **melpomene.** Most beautiful variety; flowers large; splendid form, and of a lovely purplish crimson colour; heavily spotted ... per doz. 10s. 6d.	1	6
,, **punctatum.** White, rose-spotted...	1	0
,, **rubrum.** White, spotted and shaded crimson	0	9
,, **roseum.** White, crimson-spotted	0	9
,, ,, **multiflorum.** Fine variety ...	1	0
Superbum. A fine yellow Lily with purple spots. Flowers often from 15 to 20 on a stem	0	9
Tenuifolium. Dwarf, glittering scarlet; splendid variety ... ... per doz. 15s.	1	6
Testaceum (*Excelsum*). Nankeen-coloured flowers, delightfully fragrant; four feet high per doz. 10s. 6d.	1	0
Thunbergianum atrosanguineum. Scarlet, spotted black	0	9
,, **aurantiacum multiflorum.** Yellow ...	0	6
,, **fulgens.** Crimson, mottled with yellow ...	0	9
Tigrinum splendens. The finest of the Tiger Lilies. Orange scarlet, black spots ... ... per doz. 5s.	0	6
,, **fl. pl.** Double, spotted brown, very double ...	1	0
Wallichianum superbum. Magnificent variety from the Himalaya Mountains, producing immense long trumpet pure white flowers on stems four feet high; a splendid variety for pot culture 3s. 6d. and	5	0
Washingtonianum. A grand Lily, growing four to five feet high, large white flowers, shaded lilac ...	3	6

We have many other species and varieties of choice Lilies in stock, which from want of space we are unable to enumerate.

Lilies in Collections—our own selection.

Carefully arranged Collections of Lilies, **6s., 9s., 12s., 18s., 24s.,** and **30s. per dozen.**

DOUBLE-FLOWERED ANEMONES.

Superb Double-flowered Anemones.

PRODUCING large, handsome, double flowers of various beautiful colours; some of the varieties are strikingly brilliant and attractive. These are admirably suited for pot culture, and planted in patches of three or five form charming groups for the flower border.

Choice named sorts, our selection per 100, 10s. 6d.; doz. 1s. 6d.
Choicest mixed, from named sorts   ,,   6s. 0d.; ,,   1s. 0d.

Anemones in Mixture.

	per 100.		per doz.	
	s.	d.	s.	d.
Giant French, single. Very fine and floriferous, much superior to the common Dutch varieties ...	5	0	1	0
Choice Seedlings, dbl. blue {Beautiful varieties, producing handsome	10	6	1	6
,, ,, ,, scarlet {double flowers, very	7	6	1	0
,, ,, ,, all colours {superior to the ordinary are mixtures.	6	6	1	0
,, ,, ,, single, very fine and beautiful	4	6	0	8
Dutch, finest mixed, double, fine roots per 1000, 35s.	4	6	0	8
,, ,, single, fine roots ,, 21s.	2	6	0	6
Scarlet, finest double. Fine roots	6	6	1	0
,, ,, single. Strong roots	3	0	0	6
Pure White, single, "The Bride." Splendid	10	6	1	6
Beauty of Cannes. Beautiful double flowers, the centre delicate rose, the outer petals white; charming variety	10	6	1	6
Chrysanthemum-flowered, Double. A distinct and beautiful class. Choicest mixed ...	—		3	6

Anemone Fulgens.

BEAUTIFUL large-flowered varieties with dazzling vermilion scarlet blooms which continue from February to May. Thrive best in a rich loamy soil.

Fulgens. Single scarlet, very fine per 100,10s. 6d.; per doz. 1s. 6d.
Fulgens fl. pl. A fine new double scarlet   ...   ,,   1s. 6d.

Ranunculi.

The Ranunculi are very free flowering and beautiful. They will succeed in almost any soil or position, and planted any time up to the middle of April will bloom abundantly during the Summer; very useful for cutting.

	per 100.		per doz.	
	s.	d.	s.	d.
Turban, Daniels' Giant. A splendid and robust-growing class, very superior to the common Turban varieties; grows to the height of eighteen inches; each plant producing from forty to fifty splendid double flowers	4	6	0	9
French Giant. Very fine	3	6	0	8
Persian, choicest mixed. In beautiful variety ... ... per 1000, 35s.	4	0	0	8
Scarlet. Admirably adapted for filling beds, ribbon borders, or massing	2	6	0	4
Mixed. All colours; a beautiful variety per 1000, 25s.	3	0	0	6

ANEMONE JAPONICA—Lady Ardilaun.

This is unquestionably one of the finest Novelties in Hardy Plants that has been introduced for many years. It is a variety of the old White Anemone Japonica Honorine Jobert, distinct in foliage and growth, producing flowers considerably larger, petals broad and of great substance, like wax, and overlapping almost to the points, forming the most symmetrical flower imaginable, and of the purest white; it is distinct in every way from the old white variety, and will become exceedingly popular when better known   ...   each 2s. 6d.

DANIELS' GIANT TURBAN RANUNCULI.

Miscellaneous Bulbs, Plants, &c.

Amaryllis, Hybrids of Vittata.

A MAGNIFICENT class of almost hardy bulbous-rooted plants, with large lily-like brilliantly coloured flowers, admirably suited for pot culture in the greenhouse, or conservatory, where they are splendidly effective.

Unbloomed Seedlings, choice mixed. These bulbs all of good flowering size, are from a famous collection, and may be relied on to produce some very fine varieties ... per doz. 18s.; each 1s. 9d.

Very Choice Mixed. Including a beautiful variety of the red ground and white ground sorts ... per doz. 24s.; each 2s. 6d.

Choice named varieties, our selection each 7s. 6d., 10s. 6d. and 15s.

Amaryllis (Vallota) purpurea (*The Scarboro' Lily*). Brilliant crimson scarlet flowers. Capital pot plant each 1s., 1s. 6d., and 2s. 6d.

,, **formosissima** (*The Jacobean Lily*). Rich crimson; very showy ... ... per doz. 5s.; each 6d.

,, **lutea (Sternbergia).** Bright yellow, dwarf, hardy, Autumn bloomer ... ... per doz. 2s.; each 3d.

Tropœolum speciosum.

ONE of the choicest hardy climbers in existence, producing a blaze of scarlet flowers in late Summer and Autumn. It grows rapidly, preferring a light alluvial soil, and a somewhat shaded position
per doz. 10s. 6d.; each 1s.

Chinese Sacred Narcissus.

GOODLUCK Lily or "Joss Flower."
EASILY grown in pots of light soil or in bowls containing water, the bulbs being surrounded with pebbles to keep them from falling over
per doz. 5s. 6d.; each 6d.

AMARYLLIS, HYBRIDS OF VITTATA.

Agapanthus—
(The Great African Lily).

FINELY effective plants for the decoration of the conservatory or lawn in the Autumn, *A. umbellatus* with its large umbels of cærulean blue being very striking. It requires potting somewhat firmly into rich, sandy soil, and from one to seven or eight bulbs in a pot according to the size of the latter. Small root-room is conducive of free blooming.

Umbellatus (*Blue African Lily*). Strong roots
per doz. 10s. 6d.; each 1s.

,, **albus.** Fine umbels of pure white flowers
each 1s. and 1s. 6d.

Tuberoses.

Double American "Pearl." Fine new dwarf variety from the United States; deliciously fragrant, with large double flowers, pure white per 100, 17s. 6d.; per doz. 2s.; each 3d.

,, **Extra selected.** Very fine roots
per 100, 21s.; per doz. 3s.; each 4d.

Bravoa Geminiflora (*The Twin Flower*). A hardy, bulbous-rooted plant, bearing erect spikes of rich scarlet cerise, coral-like, tubular flowers; very pretty per doz. 5s.; each 6d.

Colchicum speciosum. Beautiful large-flowered hardy plant from Asia Minor, producing noble, Crocus-like, bright rosy purple flowers in Autumn ... per doz. 8s.; each 9d.

Hyacinthus candicans. Fine strong flowering bulbs
per 100, 12s. 6d.; per doz. 2s.

Schizostylis coccinea. A remarkably handsome, perfectly hardy, evergreen bulbous plant, with beautiful crimson-scarlet flowers ... ... per doz. 2s. 6d.; each 3d.

Sternbergia lutea (*syn. Amaryllis lutea*). A splendid hardy Autumn-flowering bulb, with yellow Crocus-like flowers
per doz. 3s.; each 4d.

Tigridia—Canariensis } (*Tiger*) per doz. 3s.; each 4d.
Pavonia } *Flowers*) per doz. 2s. 6d.; each 4d.
Grandiflora alba. Creamy white, spotted with red, and having a violet centre; a fine novelty, very beautiful; quite hardy ... ... per doz. 4s.; each 6d.

Arums.

Æthiopicum (*Lily of the Nile*). The well-known common or White Arum, excellent as a pot plant for the greenhouse or window per doz. 5s. and 7s. 6d.; each 6d. and 9d.

Little Gem. A charming miniature variety of the well-known Arum Lily, growing only one foot high, and bearing small pretty flowers of a purer white than those of the old variety. Has been awarded a Special Certificate by the Royal Horticultural Society.
Strong Young Plants ... per doz. 10s. 6d.; each 1s.
Strong Flowering Plants ... each 2s. 6d. and 3s. 6d.

Maculatum album. Foliage beautifully spotted, makes a beautiful pot plant; flowers creamy white, very free each 9d.

ARUM ÆTHIOPICUM—LITTLE GEM

Greenhouse and Stove Plants.

STEPHANOTIS FLORIBUNDA.

Achimenes. Very choice mixed ... ... (tubers) per doz. 2s. 6d.
Adiantum cuneatum. Maiden-hair Fern ... 6d., 1s., and 2s. 6d.
  „ **Farleyense.** Very fine variety ... 1s. 6d., 2s. 6d., and 3s. 6d.
Allamanda Hendersoni. Beautiful stove plant ... each 2s. 6d. and 3s. 6d.
  „ **Williamsi.** Very fine variety, flowers rich yellow, very free
          each 2s. 6d., 3s. 6d., 5s., and 7s. 6d.
Aralia gracillima. A very pretty light-looking variety, with very finely cut
  leaves ... ... each 5s.
  „ **Sieboldi variegata.** Beautiful plant ... each 2s. 6d. and 3s. 6d.
  „ **Veitchi.** Very graceful ... ... each 6s.
Araucaria excelsa (*Norfolk Island Pine.*) A fine plant for the conservatory
          each 2s. 6d., 3s. 6d., and 5s.
Aspidistra lurida variegata. A very beautiful and distinct plant, with
  handsomely variegated foliage ... ... each 3s. 6d. and 5s.
Asparagus plumosus ... ... each 1s. 6d. and 2s. 6d.
  „ **deflexus.** A free-growing distinct variety, with coarser foliage than
  Tenuissimus, and has a graceful drooping habit ... ... each 1s. 6d.
Azalea Indica. We offer a choice collection, finest varieties, all in good healthy
  flowering plants, varying in height from about ten inches to sixteen inches from
  the pots. Our own selection, per doz. 24s., 30s., 40s., 50s., and 60s., according
  to size and variety; each 2s., 2s. 6d., 3s. 6d., 5s., and 7s. 6d.
Azalea Mollis. Fine healthy plants well set with flower-buds
          each 1s. 6d., 2s. 6d., per doz. 18s. to 24s.
Begonias, Rex varieties. Well-known beautiful foliaged plants for the
  greenhouse or conservatory ... ... each 1s. 6d. and 2s. 6d.
Begonias, tuberous-rooted. Double & Single-flowered. *See p.* 114, 115.
Bougainvillea glabra Sanderiana. The splendid new high-coloured variety
          each 1s. 6d., to 5s.
Caladiums. The most beautiful varieties ... ... each 2s. 6d. and 3s. 6d.
Carnations, Perpetual or Tree. Established plants in pots
          per doz. 18s., 21s., 24s.
Hoya carnosa. A charming stove climbing plant, producing
  wax-like flowers ... ... each 1s. 6d. and 2s. 6d.
Kentia Belmoreana ⎫ Beautiful Palms
  „ **Fosteriana** ⎬ each 2s. 6d. and 3s. 6d.
  „ **Canterburyana** ⎭
Lapageria rosea superba. Beautiful climber for the cool
  greenhouse ... ... each 2s. 6d., 3s. 6d., and 5s.
Lapageria alba. Lovely pure white, wax-like flowers; very
  beautiful ... ... each 5s., 7s. 6d., and 10s. 6d.
Myrtles (*Myrtus*). Nice young plants each 1s. to 1s. 6d.
Ophiopogon jaburan variegata. Long slender, golden-
  edged, strap-like leaves, with pretty blue flowers each 1s. 6d.
Palms. A nice assortment of choice plants, suitable for the
  dinner table ... ... each 2s. 6d., 3s. 6d., and 5s.
Pandanus Veitchi variegata each 1s. 6d. and 2s. 6d.
Pandanus utilis (*The Screw Pine*). A well known variety,
  very useful ... ... each 2s. 6d.
Passiflora princeps. Lovely stove climber, with large,
  scarlet flowers ... ... each 2s. 6d. and 3s. 6d.
Primula obconica grandiflora (new). A fine variety,
  with handsomely fringed flowers ... ... each 1s. 6d.
Primula obconica. Pretty evergreen species, bearing
  numerous umbels of pale lilac flowers; is in bloom throughout the Winter ... ... each 6d. and 1s.
Saxifraga sarmentosa tricolor superba. Beautiful
  variety, foliage crimson, white and green each 1s. 6d.
Saintpaulia Ionantha. A charming little stove plant,
  bearing lovely deep blue flowers in great profusion. The
  leaves are like those of the Gloxinia but much smaller; and
  an established plant will bloom throughout the whole year
          each 1s. 6d.
Schubertia grandiflora. The best sweet-scented white
  flowered plant for cutting, having larger flowers than
  Stephanotis, equally sweet, and lasts much longer when cut;
  nice plants ... ... each 3s. 6d.
Stephanotis floribunda. Well-known beautiful climber
          each 2s. 6d., 3s. 6d., and 5s.
Swainsonia galegifolia alba. Lovely clusters of pure
  white pea-like flowers; splendid for training up pillar or wall
  in the cool greenhouse, and very useful for cutting
          each 1s. to 2s. 6d.
Swainsona splendens. Fine, showy companion to the
  white variety, bearing in a free manner lovely bright carmine
  flowers ... ... each 1s. 6d. and 2s. 6d.
Tacsonia van Volxemi. Brilliant climber for the greenhouse ... ... each 1s. 6d. and 2s. 6d.
Tacsonia Exoniensis. A fine variety each 1s. 6d. and 2s. 6d.

Camellia Japonica. Our collection of these includes all the
  finest of the English and continental varieties, and our
  plants are amongst the healthiest and best budded we have
  ever seen. The height of plants from the pots varies
  from about a foot to eighteen inches. Our own selection,
  per doz. 30s., 40s., 50s., and 60s.; each 2s. 6d., 3s. 6d., 5s.,
  and 7s. 6d.
Cannas. Crozy's new dwarf varieties ... per doz. 9s.
Clerodendron Balfouri. Useful climber each 2s. 6d.
Coboea scandens variegata. Useful climber for the
  greenhouse ... ... each 1s. 6d. and 2s. 6d.
Coprosma Baueriana variegata. Beautiful greenhouse
  plant, with handsomely variegated foliage
          each 1s. 6d. and 2s. 6d.
Coelogyne cristata. Some fine plants each 10s. 6d. to 42s.
Clerodendron fallax. Lovely bright red panicles of flowers
  thrown well out from the strong broad dark foliage; very
  effective and useful for decoration ... each 1s. 6d.
Crotons. A fine collection of choice sorts in nice young plants
          each 2s. 6d. and 3s. 6d.
Daphne Indica alba. Pure white, deliciously scented
  variety ... ... each 2s. 6d. and 3s. 6d.
Daphne Indica rubra. Very sweet each 2s. 6d. and 3s. 6d.
Dracaena Australis. Fine for furnishing each 2s. to 3s.
  „ **Gracilis.** Very useful for decorative purposes
          each 2s. to 3s.
  „ **Lindeni.** Leaves dark green, traversed their whole
  length by bands of creamy-white and shades of yellow;
  elegantly recurved ... ... each 2s. 6d.
  „ **Terminalis.** Well-known and useful variety
          each 2s. to 3s. 6d.
Eucalyptus citraodora. Deliciously scented each 1s.
Eulalia zebrina. Very handsome each 2s. 6d. and 3s. 6d.
Eulalia gracillima. One of the most elegant grasses,
  splendid pot plant ... ... each 2s. 6d.
Eurya latifolia. Handsome decorative plant, with lovely
  golden variegated foliage; very useful
          each 2s. 6d., 3s. 6d., and 5s.
Ficus elastica variegata. Beautifully variegated with
  yellow, grand novelty ... ... each 2s. 6d., 3s. 6d. and 5s.
Ficus elastica. (*India-rubber Plant*) each 1s. 6d. and 2s. 6d.
Gardenia intermedia. Well-known stove plant, beautiful
  pure white, deliciously scented, double flowers
          each 2s. 6d., 3s. 6d., and 5s.
Gloxinias, grandiflora erecta vars. per doz. 9s. and 12s.
Greenhouse Ferns. A fine selection of the most useful and
  ornamental ... ... per doz. 6s., 9s., 12s., and 18s.

Greenhouse Plants in choice variety, our selection, per doz. 18s., 24s., 30s., and 40s.

Miscellaneous Fruit Trees, &c.

Our Nursery Grounds are especially favourable for the cultivation of Fruit Trees, and to meet the constantly increasing demand amongst our customers, we annually rear many thousands of Apples, Pears, Plums, Cherries, Peaches, Apricots, &c. All are grown hardily, and the plants lift with abundance of fibrous roots, a very essential requirement for their successful transplantation, after-growth, and fruitfulness. A glance at our list will show that we offer a very fine selection of the choicest varieties, and we respectfully invite all who have not yet favoured us with their orders for Fruit Trees to give us a trial, as we feel sure they will be highly pleased with the quality of the plants we send.

The prices quoted per dozen for Apples, Pears, Gooseberries, Currants, &c., are for our own selection of kinds, and are governed principally by the size and strength of the plants supplied.

APPLE—VICAR OF BEIGHTON.

APPLE—Vicar of Beighton.

ONE of the handsomest, most prolific, and best keeping apples in cultivation. The fruit is large and roundish, and when ripe of a deep bright crimson colour, mottled, and striped with yellow and green, giving it the most beautiful appearance, which, if well kept, it retains till April or May; whilst its pale yellow flesh is of fine flavour, juicy, and all that can be desired in a first-class kitchen Apple.

Dwarf Bushes or Maidens, each 2s. Standards, each 3s.

APPLE—Beauty of Bath.

THIS fine new early Dessert Apple, on account of its earliness, extremely handsome appearance, good flavour, and free cropping qualities, will eventually, both for market purposes and private use, take the leading place among first early Apples. The fruit is of medium size, round and flattened, the ground colour a yellowish green, beautifully striped and spotted with crimson toward the sun; the flesh is firm and pale yellow, and it has a brisk, sub-acid flavour far superior to that of other early apples. It is a certain and free cropper.

Strong Maiden Trees, each 1s. 6d. Standards, each 2s. 6d.

NEW APPLE—Chelmsford Wonder.

A VERY fine late keeping culinary variety. Fruit large, skin smooth, deep yellow shaded with brilliant crimson on the side exposed to the sun, and marked with small irregular streaks of deeper crimson. Flesh yellow, tender, rich, and pleasantly brisk, with a delicate aroma.

Strong Maidens, each 2s. 6d. Standards, each 3s. 6d.

The large and steadily increasing demand for all kinds of choice Fruit Trees, &c., furnishes a sure indication that good English-grown fruit is, year by year, becoming more appreciated, and it is clearly shown by the splendid samples being brought to our markets and sold at highly remunerative prices, that by planting only really choice varieties, and with good cultivation, Apples, Pears, and other fruits can be grown in this country of a size, flavour, and quality altogether surpassing those of foreign production.

Wherever space in the garden will admit, fruit of some kind should be grown, as apart from its great usefulness in point of domestic economy, its great value as a health agent cannot be fairly over-estimated where it is freely used in the household.

For small gardens such compact-growing fruits as dwarf or pyramid Apples and Pears, Gooseberries, Currants, Raspberries, and Strawberries are the most useful, and where there is a good south wall a Vine or Peach should be planted, whilst a wall with a westerly aspect will do well for Cherries or Pears, and a north wall is well suited for Currants. In planting in the garden be careful to plant at such a distance apart that the plants get the full benefit of light and air, the result of overcrowding being but too often barrenness or inferior quality.

In very dry weather young fruit-bearing trees of Apples, Pears, Plums, &c., are much benefited by a liberal supply of water, which promotes a healthy growth and prevents cracking of the fruit. Dwarf or pyramid trees are also rendered more fruitful by being partially lifted every other year and having the roots slightly pruned.

The various stocks of choice Fruit Trees we offer include all the best varieties of their respective kinds in cultivation. The plants will be found well grown, strong, and healthy, with abundant fibrous roots, and in the best possible state for removal.

The prices quoted per dozen for Apples, Pears, Gooseberries, Currants, &c., are for our own selection of kinds, and are governed principally by the size and strength of the plants supplied. When the selection is left to us, customers may rely on only the best sorts being sent.

SELECT APPLES.

Our Apples are mostly worked on the ordinary or crab stock, we can, however, supply several of the best varieties in dwarfs on the paradise stock, and shall be happy to furnish a list of these if requested.

Dwarfs or Bushes in fine variety ... ... per 100, 80s.; per doz. 10s. 6d.; each 1s.
Dwarf Trained ... ... each 3s. 6d. to 5s.
Pyramids, our own selection of varieties ... ... per doz. 21s. to 36s.; each 2s. to 3s. 6d.
Standards, our own selection of choice varieties ... ... per doz. 18s., 21s., 24s.; each 1s. 6d. to 2s. 6d.

Special Quotations for Larger Quantities.

General List.

D denotes dessert, K kitchen.

Annie Elizabeth (K.) A very fine late Apple of excellent keeping qualities. Dec. to May.

Blenheim Orange (D.K.) Well-known and splendid variety; large, handsome fruit. Dec. to Feb.

Bramley's Seedling (K.) A large handsome fruit, resembling Blenheim Pippin. Sept. to Jan.

Collini (D.K.) A fine, showy, and handsome Apple of the first quality. Oct. and Nov.

Cox's Orange Pippin (D.) A highly popular and first-rate dessert Apple; fruit, medium-sized, finely coloured, rich, crisp, and juicy, and of delicious flavour. Oct. to Mar.

Cox's Pomona (K.) Large, handsome fruit; excellent bearer. Oct. to Dec.

Court Pendu Plat (D.) A handsome fruit of good keeping qualities; a capital bearer. Nov. to April.

Devonshire Quarrenden (D.) A fine hardy, free-bearing variety of excellent quality; fruit small. Aug. and Sept.

Doctor Harvey (K.) A very fine, large, handsome fruit; first-class for culinary uses. Oct. to March.

Duchess of Oldenburg (K.) Medium-sized, handsome fruit, of good brisk flavour. Sept. and Oct.

Dumelow's Seedling (K.) A large and excellent variety; one of the most useful of culinary Apples; a strong grower, and an excellent bearer. Nov. to May.

Ecklinville Seedling (K.) A large and useful sort; flesh white and tender; a great bearer. Oct. to Dec.

Golden Russet (D.) Fruit medium-sized; an excellent dessert Apple of first-rate quality, but requires a warm situation. Dec. to March.

Gloria Mundi (K.) Very large and excellent kitchen Apple. Oct. to Jan.

Irish Peach (D.) One of the best early dessert Apples. July and Aug.

Jolly Beggar (K.) A first-rate early, and very prolific. Aug. to Oct.

Juneating Red (D.) A very popular early variety. July and Aug.

Kerry Pippin (D.) Small fruit, sweet, crisp, juicy, and richly flavoured; one of the best dessert Apples. Sept. and Oct.

Keswick Codlin (K.) One of the earliest and most useful of kitchen Apples; very prolific. Aug. and Sept.

King of Pippins (D.) Fruit medium-sized; a richly flavoured and excellent dessert variety, in season during Aug. and Sept.

Lady Henniker (K.) Large, handsome fruit; a free bearer, and good keeper. Oct. to Feb.

Lane's Prince Albert (K.) Large, handsome fruit; a great bearer, and one of the very best kitchen Apples. Oct. to March.

Lord Grosvenor (K.) A large and handsome culinary Apple. Sept. to Nov.

Lord Suffield (K.) A fine variety of the *Keswick Codlin* type, on which it is a decided improvement. It is an early and prolific bearer, and one of the very best of early cooking Apples. Aug. and Sept.

Mere de Menage (K.) A handsome and useful culinary Apple; the fruit are very large, and of first-rate quality. Oct. to Jan.

New Hawthornden (K.) A large and excellent variety. Sept. to Dec.

Norfolk Beaufin (K.) A well-known, useful, late-keeping sort; excellent for baking. Jan. to June.

Peasgood's Nonsuch (D.K.) A large, handsome Apple of the *Blenheim Orange* type; excellent for dessert or kitchen. Sept. to Jan.

Ribston Pippin (D.) Well-known splendid old sort, but tree rather subject to canker. Nov. to March.

Stirling Castle (K.) An early and free-bearing Apple; a great bearer, and well-suited for dwarf culture. Aug. and Sept.

Striped Beaufin (K.) Very large, handsome fruit; one of the best culinary Apples; first-class for baking. Oct. to May.

Sturmer Pippin (D.) One of the most valuable of dessert Apples; medium-sized fruit of splendid keeping quality. Feb. to June.

The Queen (K.) A new and most excellent variety. Nov. to Jan.

Warner's King (K.) A very large and splendid Apple of first-rate quality; the tree is a free and vigorous grower, a great bearer, and not subject to disease. Nov. to March.

White Astrachan (Transparent) (D.) Medium-sized handsome fruit of pleasant flavour; a great bearer. Aug. and Sept.

Worcester Pearmain (K.D.) Handsome early variety, suitable for kitchen or dessert; a great favourite in the market. Aug. and Sept.

And many others.

PEARS.

Dwarfs or Bushes in fine variety

	per doz. 10s. 6d ; each 1s.
Dwarf Trained ...	... per doz. 37s. 6d. ; each 3s. 6d.
Pyramids	... per doz. 21s. to 3²s. ; each 2s. to 3s. 6d.
Standards	per doz. 18s., 21s., & 24s. ; each 1s. 6d. to 2s. 6d.
,, Trained ...	... ... each 5s.

PITMASTON DUCHESSE (*see illustration*).

A superb and most valuable variety. The fruit are very large and handsome, and of first-rate quality. The tree is hardy and an excellent bearer. In season from October to December.

Dwarfs or Bushes	... ... each 1s. 6d.
Pyramids ...	... ... each 2s. 6d. to 3s. 6d.
Standards...	... ... each 2s.
Dwarf Trained	... ... each 3s 6d. to 5s.

EARLY AND SECOND EARLY PEARS.

Beurré d'Amanlis, Beurré Giffard, Beurré Superfin, Doyenne d'Eté, Durondeau, Gratioli of Jersey, Jargonelle, Princess, Souvenir du Congrés, Williams' Bon Chrétien, Williams' Victoria.

MID-SEASON PEARS.

Althorp Crasanne, Beurré Clairgeau, Beurré d'Aremberg, Beurré de Capiaumont, Beurré Diel, Brockworth Park, Conseiller de la Cour, Chaumontel, Doyenné du Comice, Duchesse d'Angouléme, Gansel's Bergamot, Hessle, Louise Bonne of Jersey, Magnate, Marie Louise, Marie Louise d'Uccle, Napoleon, Passe Colmar, Triomphe de Jodoigne, Van Mons Leon le Clerc.

LATE PEARS.

Bergamot d'Esperen, Beurré Ranco, Easter Beurré, Josephine de Malines, Knight's Monarch, Ne Plus Meuris, Winter Nelis.

STEWING PEARS.

Catillac ; Uvedale's St. Germain. *And others.*

Cherries—

Archduke, Bigarreau, Downton, Elton, May Duke, Morello, Ohio Beauty, &c., &c.

Dwarf Trained	per doz. 40s. to 54s. ; each 3s. 6d. to 5s.
Standards ...	... ... per doz. 21s. ; each 2s.
,, Trained ...	... ... per doz. 54s. ; each 5s.
Pyramids ...	per doz. 21s. to 36s. ; each 2s. to 3s. 6d.

Chestnuts, Spanish—

Standards ... per doz. 10s. 6d. to 21s. ; each 1s. to 2s.

Mulberries—

Dwarfs	... each 3s. 6d.
Standards	... each 5s. to 7s. 6d.

American Fruiting Blackberry—

Wilson Junr. This magnificent Blackberry is undoubtedly one of the largest, finest, and most prolific in cultivation, producing very large, glossy black fruit, of delicious flavour, in immense quantity each 9d. ; per doz. 7s. 6d.

BLACKBERRY, Parsley-leaved. A very prolific and hardy variety, with finely cut handsome foliage
each 9d. ; per doz. 7s. 6d

Figs—

Strong Plants, in pots	... ... each 2s. 6d.
Fruiting Plants, in pots	... each 3s. 6d. to 7s. 6d.

Walnuts—

Fine Standards ... each 2s. 6d. to 7s. 6d.

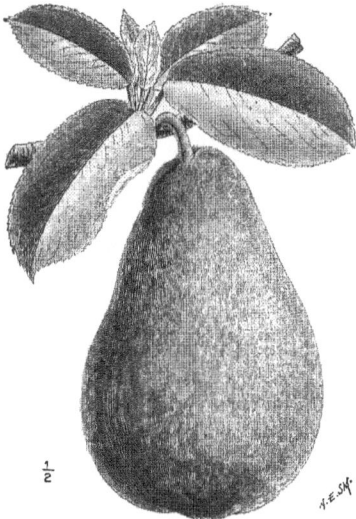

PEAR, PITMASTON DUCHESSE.

Apricots—

Breda, Hemskirke, Kaisha, Large Early, Moor Park, Royal, Shipley's or Blenheim, &c., &c.

Dwarf Trained, very fine	... ... each 5s. to 7s. 6d.
Standard Trained ...	... each 7s. 6d. to 10s. 6d.

Nectarines—

Albert Victoria, Downton, Elruge, Early Newington, Hardwick Seedling, Lord Napier, Pineapple, Pitmaston Orange, Rivers' Orange, Roman, Victoria, Violette Hative, &c.

Dwarf Trained ...	... each 5s. to 7s. 6d.
Standard Trained ...	each 10s. 6d. to 21s.

Peaches—

Alexandra, Barrington, Condor, Dr. Hogg, Early Beatrice, Early Rivers, Grosse Mignonne, Noblesse, Royal George, Stirling Castle, &c.

Dwarf Trained, very fine	each 5s. to 7s. 6d.
Standard Trained, fine	each 10s. 6d. to 21s.

Plums—

Belgian Purple, Coe's Golden Drop, Early Prolific, Golden Gage, Greengage, Huling's Superb, Jefferson's, Kirke's, Magnum Bonum, Orleans, Pond's Seedling, Prince Englebert, Prince of Wales, The Czar, Transparent Gage, Victoria, Washington, &c.

Dwarf Maidens	... ... per doz. 10s. 6d. ; each 1s.
,, Trained	... per doz. 37s. 6d. ; each 3s. 6d.
Pyramids ...	per doz. 21s. to 36s. ; each 2s. to 3s. 6d.
Standards ...	... ... per doz. 21s. ; each 2s.
,, Trained ...	... ... each 5s.

Miscellaneous Fruit Trees, &c. *(continued)*.

Grape Vines.

Our stock of these is a very fine one; the canes have been grown from eyes without bottom-heat, and are remarkably well ripened, short-jointed, and the buds are thoroughly matured and plump.

BLACK HAMBURGH.

The fruiting canes we offer are strong and stout, from eight to ten feet in length; and if cultivated in pots will bear from eight to twelve bunches each next season.

H denotes those varieties that require to be grown in a heated vinery.

C denotes those suitable for growing in a cool vinery.

Strong planting canes, in pots   ...   ...   each 7s. 6d.
Fruiting canes, in pots, very fine ...   ...   each 10s. 6d.

Black Alicante (H.)	Madresfield Crt. Muscat
Canon Hall Muscat (H.)	(H.C.)
Foster's Seedling (C.)	Hamburgh, Black (C.)
Gros Colmar (H.)	Muscat of Alexandria (H.)
Gros Maroc (H.)	Muscat Hamburgh (H.C.)
Lady Downes' Seedling	Sweetwater, Buckland (C.)
(H.)	West's St. Peter's (H.)

Nuts and Filberts.

We have a very fine stock of these in good strong plants, comprising such fine varieties as Cosford, Kentish Cob, Filbert, white, red, purple-leaved and frizzled, Norwich Prolific, &c.

Strong Fruiting Dwarfs or Bushes in first-class condition
for removal   ...   .   per 100, 45s.; per doz. 6s.
Standards   ...   .   each 1s. 6d. and 2s. 6d.

Gooseberries.

WHINHAM'S "INDUSTRY." A superb variety, bearing a wonderful profusion of large handsome fruit, which are of a dull red colour when ripe. This is one of the best and most prolific gooseberries in cultivation, and has proved itself invaluable for culinary and market purposes.
Strong bushes, per 100, 40s.; per doz. 6s.; each 8d.

Keepsake. A very large straw-coloured variety of excellent flavour, and one of the best and earliest for gathering green.
Strong bushes, per doz. 6s.; each 8d.

A good collection of the best Lancashire Prize and other varieties.

Strong Bushes per 100, 21s. to 35s.; per doz. 3s., 4s. 6d., and 6s.

British Crown	Overall
Broom Girl	Pilot
Companion	Red Champagne
Crown Bob	Red Warrington
Drill	Rifleman
Duck-wing	Roaring Lion
Governess	Rough Red
Gunner	Slaughterman
Ironmonger	Snowdrop
Lancashire Lad	Thumper
Leader	Whitesmith
Lion's Provider	Yellow Champagne
London	

And others.

Currants.

VICTORIA BLACK (new). This is the finest and largest black currant in cultivation. The fruit is of great size, splendid quality and flavour; and the plant is a most abundant bearer. A first-rate market sort.
Strong young bushes, per doz. 7s. 6d.; each 9d.

BLACK CHAMPION. A very fine and remarkable variety, bearing large bunches of handsome, globular, richly-flavoured fruit.
Strong young bushes, per doz. 4s. 6d.; each 6d.

FAY'S PROLIFIC. Decidedly the best Red Currant we have. The bush is a strong grower, wonderfully prolific, and comes into bearing early. The fruit is large, bright red, and of excellent flavour   per doz. 6s.; each 8d.

BLACK—	**RED—**
Common	Cherry
Lee's Prolific	La Fertile
Naples	Raby Castle. Fine
Ogden's	Red Dutch
WHITE—	&c., &c.
Dutch	
Transparent White	

Strong bushes   ...   per 100, 21s. to 35s.; per doz. 3s. to 6s.

Raspberries.

2s. to 3s. per doz.   12s. to 20s. per 100.

Fastolf	Red Antwerp
Fillbasket	White Antwerp
Norwich Wonder	

Baumforth's Seedling. A fine variety; fruit very large, of the most beautiful crimson colour; an abundant bearer, of good habit   .. per 100, 21s.; per doz. 3s.

MYROBELLA OR CHERRY PLUM

(Prunus myrobalana).

A GRAND FENCING PLANT.

A Hedge at Four Years Old in Messrs. DANIELS' Nurseries.

ORCHAROMAINS,
TUNBRIDGE, KENT.

Jan 25/93.

Lord Arthur Cecil at the same time wishes to say that the Cherry Plum Fencing is a great success & appears to suit the stiff clay in this part of Kent specially well

This was introduced some few years ago by the late Mr. Ewing of the Eaton Nurseries, and has undoubtedly proved itself to be the very best Fencing Plant ever grown. For rapidity of growth it is unrivalled, and, under fair conditions, will make a capital fence in three or four years from planting. It also grows vigorously in the poorest soils, and is first-class for planting in exposed situations or by the sea coast. It is quite hardy and will stand the severest frosts without injury.

The Myrobella does not often fruit in this country save in the South or West of England and in sheltered positions in the Eastern and Midland Counties, and then only when allowed to grow into trees or large bushes; it, however, forms a capital stock for Plums, and if strong single stems are allowed to grow from the fence at intervals of about twelve feet, they may be budded or grafted with choice varieties of this popular fruit, and in a few years will form a most profitable and ornamental hedgerow.

Bothal Castle,
Morpeth.

8th Oct 1889

*Dear Sirs,
I am very much pleased with the Myrobella or Cherry plum plants which you sent me last Spring, & which have thriven well. I should like to have another 5000 good plants
Yours faithfully,
Tho. Sample*

The best time for planting is in November or early Spring, or it may be done in open weather at any time during the Winter months, but in fairly moist weather successful plantings may be made as late as the middle or end of April. In planting plant firmly, placing the sets from six to nine inches apart according to size. After planting, about the time that growth commences, they should be cut down to eight or ten inches in height. It will bear almost any extent of clipping, and should be cut at least twice a year—about the end of July and in Winter or Spring whilst in a dormant state, and should be fairly trimmed the first year or two after planting to ensure a good bottom for a strong and thick fence, but it may be clipped in to form a fence no thicker than an ordinary garden wall, which will be found quite impenetrable. As the plants advance in age the branches become armed with long, sharp spines, which make the fence impenetrable to cattle, &c. Myrobella will therefore be found splendid for making new or improving old fences, and much superior to Whitethorn or any other fencing plant.

PLANT FIVE OR SIX TO THE YARD.

Extra strong stuff, for immediate planting	...			4s. 6d. per 100;	40s. 0d. per 1000
Fine strong stuff, smaller size	...	...	...	...	3s. 6d. „	30s. 0d. „

Special Quotations for Larger Quantities.

From THE "GARDENERS' MAGAZINE."

"It is one of the best of plants for a close live fence, for it needs but the most simple management to ensure a free growth from the bottom, and this soon becomes so close and so formidable with spines as to be impenetrable by cattle, and equally so against human intruders."

We have selected the favourable testimony, published on this page, as to the suitability of Myrobella or Cherry Plum as a hedging plant from a mass of correspondence, expressing approval of hedges formed by it. We may mention that we have some fine examples of Myrobella hedges in our Nurseries, which we shall be happy to show to any one interested.

DANIELS BROS., Town Close Nurseries, NORWICH.

Hardy Perennial Flowering Plants.

(See Coloured Plate.)

We have a fine collection of these popular, interesting, and beautiful plants, which are daily coming more and more into favour with the Gardening Public. All the varieties are perennial, extremely hardy, and many of them produce flowers of the most exquisite beauty, which are very valuable for cutting, whilst the dwarfer growing sorts are admirably suited for rockeries, or edgings. No special soil or position is necessary, as with but very few exceptions, they will thrive almost anywhere, and with a moderate collection, a charming variety and succession of bloom may be had throughout the Spring and Summer. The plants we offer are all grown in pots, and may be removed at any time or season.

Daniels' Special Collections of Hardy Flowering Plants.

We offer in the following collections a very choice selection of the above, specially arranged for a brilliant and varied display of colour, and a long continuance of bloom in the open garden.

Collection A.	50 in 50 very choice varieties ...	... 25s. 0d.	Including all the beautiful
,, B.	36 ,, 36 ,, ,, ...	... 20s. 0d.	varieties shown on our
,, C.	25 ,, 25 ,, ,, ...	... 15s. 0d.	coloured plate opposite.
,, D.	12 ,, 12 ,, ,, ...	... 9s. 0d.	

ACHILLÆA MONGOLICA (*Plate, No.* 2). Height about 18 inches, pure white flowers in May and June; splendid for cutting ... ... each 1s.

,, **millefolia rosea.** Very useful ... each 9d.

,, **ptarmica—The Pearl** (new). Large double, pure white flowers, similar to *A. ptarmica fl. pl.*, but more than double the size; fine for cutting ... each 1s.

Adonis vernalis. This is a beautiful, early, Spring-blooming plant, with clear golden yellow flowers, known as the "God of Love." The individual blooms are very large comparative to the size of the many-times divided foliage, its general height being six inches. It will thrive in any kind of soil and most situations, and is perfectly hardy per doz. 4s. 6d.; each 6d.

Anemone—Japonica alba. One of the very best Autumn-blooming plants. Flowers produced in great profusion, and of a beautiful pure white per doz. 5s.; each 6d.

,, ,, **Lady Ardilaun.** Fine new, pure white each 2s. 6d.

,, ,, **rosea.** Similar to preceding, but flowers of a beautiful rose colour ... per doz. 9d.

ANTHEMIS TINCTORIA DANIELSI (*Plate, No.* 1.) A very fine new variety, bearing quite a profusion of bright golden yellow marguerite-like flowers; first-class for cutting ... ... each 1s. 6d.

,, ,, **pallida.** An exceedingly beautiful Marguerite, with pale sulphury yellow flowers per doz. 5s.; each 6d.

Anthericum. Beautiful hardy border plants, bearing elegant spikes of pure white flowers in Spring; height about eighteen inches.

,, **Liliago** (St. Bernard's Lily) per doz. 5s.; each 6d.

,, **Liliastrum** (St. Bruno's Lily) per doz. 7s. 6d.; each 9d.

,, ,, **major.** Very fine; pure white; splendid for bouquets ... per doz. 10s. 6d.; each 1s.

ARMERIA GRANDIFLORA (*The Giant Thrift*) (*Plate, No* 3). A distinct and splendid plant, forming tufts of deep green foliage, and throwing up for a long time, on stems eighteen inches high, heads of brilliant rosy-crimson flowers ... ... each 9d.

Asters (*Michaelmas Daisies*). Beautiful Autumn bloomers.

,, **alpinus.** Bright purple, very attractive, neat and dwarf in habit; good for edging, growing only about six to eight inches high ... ... each 9d.

,, **crevis.** A beautiful shade of lavender blue, one of the best of this family. Height two feet ... each 9d.

,, **Dumesus.** Flowers bright purple, 2½ feet high, blooms in September ... ... each 9d.

,, **formosissimus.** A distinct and beautiful species, flowers rosy purple; height four feet ... each 9d.

,, **grandiflorus.** Flowers bluish mauve. The largest of all the Michaelmas Daisies ... each 1s. 6d.

,, **Madame Soyneuce.** A good bright clear rose colour; an exceedingly attractive variety. Height 1½ feet. each 1s.

,, **mirens.** Pure white, very large flowers, which are produced in great abundance. Height two feet each 9d.

,, **Novæ Angliæ.** Large bluish-purple flowers; blooms in October ... ... each 9d.

Aubrietia Hendersoni. A very beautiful and effective plant for Spring bedding, bearing very profusely lovely little flowers of a deep violet purple colour ... each 6d.

Aubrietia Leichtlini. A beautiful dwarf-growing plant, with numerous bright purplish crimson flowers; a gem for dry rockeries, &c. ... ... each 9d.

Centaurea dealbata. Pink, a useful border perennial each 9d.

,, **macrocephala.** A fine ornamental plant, with fine massive foliage produced from the base to the point where the large rich golden flowers issue ... each 1s.

Cheiranthus alpinus. Dwarf neat-growing species; flowers lemon-yellow, borne in great profusion in Spring; very effective, ought to be in every garden per doz. 4s. 6d.; each 6d.

Campanula isophylla. Beautiful dwarf trailing species, bearing large lilac blue salver-shaped flowers; a gem for pots ... ... per doz. 5s.; each 6d.

,, ,, **alba.** A white form of the preceding ... ... per doz. 5s.; each 6d.

,, **grandiflora** } Very fine varieties } ... each 9d.

,, **alba** } { ... 1s.

,, ,, **mariesi.** Very large beautiful dark blue flowers; splendid dwarf-growing variety each 1s. 6d.

,, **persicifolia alba grandiflora.** A fine upright growing variety, with large pure white flowers each 1s.

,, **persicifolia alba grandiflora pl.** Produces spikes two feet high, of pure white double flowers, useful for cutting ... ... each 1s.

,, **pyramidalis** (*The Chimney Campanula*). Long spikes of blue, salver-like flowers, excellent for single specimens in herbaceous border or for pots ... each 6d.

,, ,, **alba.** A white flowering form of the preceding; makes a fine pot plant ... ... each 6d.

,, **turbinata pallida.** A beautiful dwarf compact-growing variety, producing a profusion of beautiful silvery lilac-coloured bells that continue for a long time strong clumps, per doz. 5s.; each 6d.

Chrysanthemum latifolium. A very showy Marguerite, its bold pure white flowers, with yellow centre, are two to three inches across; splendid for cutting, and invaluable for Autumn decoration ... each 9d.

,, **leucanthemum semi-duplex.** A fine novelty, with large pure white semi-double flowers per doz. 10s. 6d.; each 1s.

,, **maximum** (true). A beautiful free-growing plant, only two feet high, and covered with a profusion of large pure white Marguerite-like flowers, that continue for a long period; splendid for cutting per doz. 7s. 6d.; each 9d.

,, **uliginosum.** Strong-growing Autumn-flowering species, with pure white Marguerite flowers each 9d.

Coreopsis grandiflora. This variety is totally distinct from *C. lanceolata*, a 'n far superior plant. It grows about three feet in height, the stems are erect and rigid, flowers 2½ to 3 inches across, and of a bright golden yellow; blooms from June until September ... each 1s.

,, **lanceolata.** The best of the family, and one of the most showy hardy perennials in cultivation. The flowers are large, of a bright golden yellow colour, and produced in the greatest profusion ... per doz. 5s. 6d.; each 6d.

Cypripedium spectabile. The most splendid of this interesting family, growing about two feet high, and producing numerous large delicate rose and white flowers; hardy ... ... per doz. 24s.; each 2s. 6d.

Delphiniums (*see page 125*).

Hardy Perennial Flowering Plants *(continued)*.

Dielytra spectabilis. A beautiful and indispensable plant, with lovely bending sprays of deep rose-coloured flowers and handsomely divided foliage. First-class for shady borders, pots in the greenhouse, &c. It is perfectly hardy and forces well ... ... strong plants, per doz. 6s.; each 8d.

Dodecatheon Jeffreyanum. A beautiful hardy perennial, a native of the Rocky Mountains, producing large umbels of Cyclamen-like blossoms, rose-coloured, with a yellow ring at the orifice of the reflexed corolla ... each 1s.

„ **meadia** (American Cowslip). From the rich woodlands of North America; an elegant Spring-flowering plant worthy of more extended cultivation; flowers purple, inclining to colour of the peach-blossom, in a loose umbel, each blossom drooping elegantly per doz. 5s.; each 6d.

Doronicum austriacum. Bright golden yellow flowers in Spring; very showy ... per doz. 7s. 6d.; each 9d.

„ **Harpur Crewe** (*plantagineum excelsum*). A magnificent variety, growing three to four feet high, bearing bold golden yellow flowers three to four inches across. First-class for cutting, and an almost perpetual bloomer ... per doz. 10s. 6d.; each 1s.

Echinops ritro. A fine perennial, growing three to four feet high, bearing numerous globular heads of blue flowers each 9d.

Erica herbacea (carnea). A procumbent little shrubby evergreen plant; flowers deep flesh-coloured with black anthers ... ... per doz. 7s. 6d.; each 9d.

„ „ **alba.** A pure white-flowering variety of the preceding, very fine ... per doz. 10s. 6d.; each 1s.

Erigeron aurantiacus. A fine new variety, growing about nine inches high and bearing bright orange-coloured flowers as large as a crownpiece per doz. 7s. 6d.; each 9d.

„ **Philadelphicum.** Pink, a very useful variety for cutting ... ... each 9d.

„ **(Stenactis) speciosa superba.** Beautiful border perennial, growing about three feet high, covered for a long time with beautiful large bright purple flowers with yellow centre; very fine ... per doz. 7s. 6d.; each 9d.:

Eryngium Oliverianum. A plant of noble and handsome appearance, with laciniated foliage, and heads of flowers of a lovely amethystine-blue ... ... each 1s.

Funkia, or Plantain Lily. Fine hardy border plants, the flowers of *F. subcordata grandiflora* almost equalling those of the Eucharis. The leaves are large, heart-shaped, and are finely effective for clumps on mixed borders, as edgings to large beds of sub-tropical plants, etc.; is also excellent for pot culture in the greenhouse.

„ **lanceolata.** Dwarf-growing; lilac purple flowers per doz. 5s.; each 6d.

„ „ **marginata.** A form of the preceding, with beautifully variegated leaves per doz. 5s.; each 6d.

„ **Sieboldi.** Glaucous foliage and pink Lily-like flowers; very beautiful ... ... each 9d.

„ **subcordata grandiflora.** A beautiful variety with bright green foliage ... per doz. 5s.; each 6d.

Gaillardias (*see page* 125).

Galega officinalis alba. Produces a profusion of white Pea-shaped flowers; useful for cutting ... each 6d.

Gentiana acaulis. Intense blue, very fine per doz. 7s. 6d.; each 9d.

„ **verna.** One of the most brilliant of all Alpine flowers; one to three inches high, forming dense tufts of intense blue flowers.

Established in pots 1s. & 1s. 6d. each; per doz. 10s. 6d. & 15s.

GEUM COCCINEUM PLENUM (*Plate, No* 6). Height about two feet, bearing a profusion of double, bright scarlet flowers; first-rate for cutting per doz. 8s.; each 9d.

„ **miniatum.** Very showy large orange-scarlet flowers, which are produced in great profusion from Spring until Autumn ... ... each 1s. 6d.

Harpalium rigidum. Rich golden yellow flowers with a black disc, resembling a small Sunflower per doz. 5s.; each 6d.

Helenium pumilum. Beautiful Autumn-blooming plant, eighteen inches high, bearing a profusion of bright yellow flowers ... per doz. 7s. 6d.; 3 for 2s.; each 9d.

„ **autumnale.** Bright yellow flowers; fine for Autumn display ... ... each 9d.

„ **grandiflorum autumnale.** A strong growing Autumn-flowering perennial, bearing large deep yellow flowers, which are very useful for decorative purposes, 1s.

„ **grandicephalum striatum.** Large deep orange flowers, irregularly striped and blotched with crimson; very erect, robust habit, 4 feet in height ... each 1s.

Helianthus multiflorus plenus (*Perennial Sunflower*). Height three to four feet, beautiful golden yellow double flowers in Autumn ... per doz. 8s.; each 9d.

„ **Soleil d'Or.** A fine variety, with deep orange yellow double flowers ... ... each 1s.

„ **(Harpalium) lætiflorus.** Similar in growth and foliage to *Harpalium rigidum*, but with semi-double flowers, and coming into bloom later ... each 9d.

„ **lætiflorus.** Very large flowers of a rich golden-yellow colour, the disc being also yellow instead of purple, as in *H. rigidus*, and the semi-double variety; extremely useful for late cutting ... ... each 9d.

Helleborus (Christmas Rose). *H. niger* and *H. niger maximus* are undoubtedly the finest hardy Winter-flowering plants in cultivation, producing beautiful white flowers through the Winter; useful for potting for greenhouse decoration.

„ **Niger** (*Christmas Rose*). Fine pure white, abundant bloomer ... ... per doz. 10s. 6d.; each 1s.

„ „ **maximus.** A fine variety, large pure white flowers, splendid per doz. 24s.; each 2s. 6d.

„ **atrorubens.** Flowers purplish red, very numerous in clusters; blooms in Mid-Winter per doz. 15s.; each 1s. 6d.

Hemerocallis aurantiaca major (uew). Orange yellow, immense flowers six to seven inches across. First Class Certificate, Royal Horticultural Society each 7s. 6d.

„ **flava.** A beautiful hardy border plant, producing in June and July large umbels of beautiful Lily-like flowers, of a bright yellow colour, and finely scented per doz. 4s. 6d.; each 6d.

„ **fulva.** Bronzy orange, shading to crimson per doz. 3s. 6d.; each 4d.

„ **disticha. fl. pl.** Large, double, bronzy yellow flowers; very fine ... ... each 1s.

„ **Kwenso fl. pl. variegata.** One of the most beautiful hardy variegated plants in cultivation; is admirably suited as a decorative plant for the greenhouse or conservatory ... ... per doz. 10s. 6d.; each 1s.

Hepaticas. These are amongst the most charming Spring-blooming plants we possess, and should certainly be found in every garden.

„ **angulosa.** Sky blue; beautiful per doz. 7s. 6d.; each 9d.

„ **triloba alba.** Single, white ... each 9s. 9d.

„ „ **cærulea.** Single, blue ... „ 1s. 6d.

„ „ „ **fl. pl.** Double, blue ... „ 1s. 6d.

„ „ **rubra.** Single, red ... „ 9d.

„ „ „ **fl. pl.** Double, red ... „ 1s. 0d.

Heuchera sanguinea. Forms a neat compact tuft of deep cordate leaves, crimson tubular flowers per doz. 10s.; each 1s.

Hypericum moserianum. This is the first known hybrid of this family; and its great beauty and distinctive character will command the attention of every one interested in good hardy perennials ... ... per doz. 10s. 6d.; each 1s.

Inula glandulosa. A fine hardy plant, growing about two feet high, and bearing large, single, Helianthus-like yellow flowers ... ... each 6d.

LATHYRUS LATIFOLIUS ALBUS (*The White Everlasting Pea*). Beautiful clusters of pure white flowers; exceedingly useful hardy climber per doz. 10s. 6d.; each 1s.

„ **Drummondi.** Pretty clusters of bright terra-cotta red flowers; very early and quite distinct each 1s. 6d.

Lychnis dioica rubra fl. pl. A plant of great beauty, exceedingly useful for cutting; large double crimson flowers; a first-class border plant per doz. 5s.; each 6d.

„ **chalcedonica.** Height about three feet; brilliant scarlet, very showy ... ... each 9d.

„ **Haageana.** A showy perennial about one foot high, beautiful flowers nearly two inches across, of every shade of colour from brilliant scarlet to white ... each 9d.

„ **VISCARIA SPLENDENS PLENA.** A distinct and splendid variety, growing about eighteen inches high and bearing a profusion of large, double, brilliant rose-coloured flowers per doz. 6s.; each 8d.

Lythrum roseum superbum. Height three to four feet, with fine branching spikes of rose-coloured flowers; very useful for cutting ... ... each 9d.

Matricaria inodora grandiflora pl. Flowers pure white; useful for cutting ... ... each 6d.

Monarda didyma. An erect growing plant, bearing flowers of a bright scarlet colour produced in whorls ... each 6d.

Hardy Perennial Flowering Plants (*continued*).

Œnothera acaulis vera. A beautiful dwarf-growing species, with large white flowers   per doz. 7s. 6d.; each 9d.

,, **macrocarpa.** A fine hardy perennial, forming a trailing mass of foliage covered with large soft yellow flowers ...   .   each 6d.

,, **Youngi.** Height two feet, with deep golden yellow flowers; a first-class hardy plant   per doz. 7s. 6d.; each 9d.

Oxlip, Prince of Orange. A superb variety of Irish origin, bearing immense heads of rich golden yellow flowers on fasciated stems; a fine hardy plant ...   each 9d.

Papaver nudicaule (*Iceland Poppies*). Most useful and beautiful hardy flowers.

,, **nudicaule.** Bright pale yellow per doz. 5s.; each 6d.

,, ,, **alba.** Pure white   ,, 5s.; ,, 6d.

,, ,, **miniatum.** Brilliant orange scarlet   per doz. 6s.; each 6d.

* ,, **bracteata** (true). A charming species, with immense deep blood-crimson flowers ...   .   each 1s.

* ,, **Royal Scarlet.** The flowers are unequalled for size and brilliancy, measuring when fully expanded 12 inches in diameter, and are of a glowing scarlet colour   each 1s. 6d.

* *Large-flowered Perennial Poppies, very showy and splendid flowers, first-class for mixed or shrubbery borders.*

Phlox subulata. (Dwarf Spring-flowering Phloxes). Splendid for rockeries, edgings, or massing.

,, **frondosa.** Dense evergreen foliage, lovely pink flowers, dark centre ...   per doz. 4s.; each 6d.

,, **verna.** A very beautiful trailing species; flowers large, deep rose colour   per doz. 4s.; each 6d.

Phloxes, Perennial (*see page* 125).

Physalis alkakengi (*Winter Cherry*). Bears numerous bright berries, which are most attractive in late Autumn   ...   .   each 6d.

Phyteuma orbiculare. A pretty border plant with very curiously composed round heads of blooms of a lovely blue colour; it is very floriferous   ...   ...   each 9d.

Polemonium Richardsoni. Flowers sky blue with golden yellow anthers; very pretty   ...   ...   each 6d.

,, **cœruleum.** Pale blue; very useful   per doz. 4s. 6d.; each 6d.

,, **Himalaicum.** Vigorous habit of growth, with large branching spikes of azure blue flowers   each 1s.

Potentillas (*see page* 125).

Polyanthus, Gold-laced. Fine seedlings, all good flowers   per 100, 21s.; per doz. 3s. 6d.

Polygala chamæbuxis purpurea. A very pretty dwarf growing plant. Flowers are purple with yellow spots, in shape resembling those of the Pea   ...   ...   each 9d.

Primroses (*Primula acaulis*). A beautiful and indispensable class of brilliant Spring-flowering plants.

Double White   ...   ...   per doz. 6s.; each 8d.

,, **Lilac**   ...   ...   ,, 6s.; ,, 8d.

,, **Yellow**   ...   ...   ,, 6s.; ,, 8d.

,, **Purplish-crimson**   ,, 10s.; ,, 1s.

Single "Harbinger." A superb large-flowered, early blooming variety, with lovely white flowers with an orange centre. Strong plants in pots   per doz. 10s. 6d.; each 1s.

,, **mixed hybrids.** Very fine and brilliant   per 100, 17s. 6d.; per doz. 2s. 6d.

Primula viscosa nivalis. A beautiful dwarf growing species, throwing up numerous heads of pure white flowers   ...   .   each 1s.

,, **japonica.** A fine species, growing two to three feet in height, with whorls of bright crimson flowers   each 6d.

Pyrethrums (*see page* 125).

PYRETHRUM, Mrs. Bateman Brown (*Plate, No.* 7). A magnificent variety. The finest dark single Pyrethrum. First Class Certificate, R.H.S.   ...   each 1s. 6d.

,, **PRINCESS IRENE** (*Plate, No.* 8). By far the finest of all the single whites. The flowers are of medium size, beautifully formed, and of the purest ivory white; splendid for cutting   ...   each 1s. 6d

Rudbeckia Newmanni. A splendid hardy free-flowering plant, height about two feet; flowers golden yellow with black centres   ...   .   per doz. 5s.; each 6d.

,, **purpurea.** Height two feet; large purplish flowers with black centres; very striking   ...   each 1s.

SCABIOSA CAUCASICA (*Plate, No.* 5). Large, handsome, pale lilac-blue flowers, four to six inches across, fine for cutting; good flowering plants   ...   each 1s.

SCABIOSA CAUCASICA ALBA (new). A pure white variety of the beautiful *Scabiosa Caucasica*   each 5s.

,, **elata.** A noble growing species, attaining the height of five to six feet, a grand plant for the shrubbery; the flowers are sulphury yellow, and very beautiful   each 9d.

SENECIO PULCHER. A very fine hardy perennial, flowers large, purplish crimson with yellow centre; three feet high; a fine Autumn bloomer   ...   each 9d.

,, **doronicum.** Large golden-yellow flowers on stems twelve inches in height; a first-class plant   each 6d.

Solidago altissima (*Golden Rod*). A fine hardy perennial, blooming in August and September   ...   each 1s.

Spiræa aruncus. A handsome, stately-growing, border plant, from three to five feet high, with magnificent plumes of creamy white flowers   ...   each 1s.

,, **astilboides.** A beautiful Japanese species, about two feet high, producing dense plumes of feathery white flowers; easily grown in pots or borders   each 1s.

,, **filipendula fl. pl.** Numerous corymbs of double white flowers and pretty fern-like foliage, very hardy and desirable   ...   per doz. 7s. 6d.; each 9d.

,, **palmata** (*Crimson Meadow Sweet*). A very fine border plant, flowers rich crimson. Is well described by its popular name   ...   .   each 9d.

Sidalcea candida. A pretty plant, growing about 2½ feet high, and bearing in great abundance pure white flowers of about one inch in diameter   ...   ...   each 6d.

Silphium perfoliatum. A handsome, tall, stout growing plant with flowers of a lovely clear lemon-yellow; excellent for cutting and decorative purposes, and for massing against a tall background   ...   .   each 1s.

Thalictrum adiantifolium (*The Maiden-hair Thalictrum*). A beautiful plant rivalling the Maiden-hair Fern in the delicacy of the foliage, but hardy and easily grown in any ordinary border, and an invaluable plant for bouquets each 1s.

Tradescantia virginica alba major. A very showy plant, producing its charming white flowers during most of the Summer ...   Strong flowering plants, each 9d.

Trillium grandiflorum (*Large-flowered White Wood Lily*). A very pleasing plant for moist shady nooks, flowers snowy-white on stems about one foot high   ...   each 9d

,, **grandiflora glauca.** One of the grandest of the group; large brilliant spikes of orange red flowers four to five feet long ...   per doz. 10s. 6d.; each 1s.

TROLLIUS EUROPÆUS (*Plate, No.* 4). Beautiful Spring-flowering plant, with large, globular, lemon-coloured and delicately scented flowers   per doz. 7s. 6d.; each 9d.

,, **FORTUNEI FL. PL.** Beautiful semi-double flowers; colour, a bright rich orange   each 1s. 6d.

Verbena venosa. A hardy perennial Verbena bearing a profusion of purplish-blue flowers on long stems   per doz. 6s.; each 8d.

Herbaceous and Alpine Plants in Collections.

WE have a fine collection of these which from want of space we are unable to catalogue. The following collections, which are offered at a very cheap rate, include the most beautiful and useful sorts for border and rockery decoration, and most of the sorts included will be found exceedingly useful for cut flowers. If our customers when ordering will kindly say for which purpose they are required, they may rely on having the very best selection that can be given for the prices quoted.

Popular Collections of Hardy Flowering Plants.

100 in 100 choice varieties		...	40s. 0d.	36 in 36 choice varieties		...	12s. 6d.
100 ,, 50 ,, ,,		...	30s. 0d.	25 ,, 25 ,, ,,		...	8s. 6d.
50 ,, 50 ,, ,,		...	17s. 6d.	12 ,, 12 ,, ,,		...	4s. 6d.

PLANTS AND ROOTED CUTTINGS OF CHOICE FLORISTS' FLOWERS.

PACKAGE AND CARRIAGE FREE AT PRICES QUOTED.

. For new varieties see List of Novelties on coloured paper.

We do not hold ourselves bound by these prices after Midsummer.

GROUP OF SINGLE BOUVARDIAS.

Bouvardias.

THE most beautiful and charming of all flowers to cut for bouquets, button-holes, or table decoration; the colours range from the purest white through the delicate shades of pink and rose to the most intense and brilliant scarlet and crimson. They are easy of cultivation, and grown in the same way as Winter-flowering Pelargoniums will bloom to perfection.

	each—s.	d.
Alba odorata jasminiflora (new). White with under sides of lobes and tubes shaded pink	1	0
Alfred Neuner. Pure white, double	0	6
Angustifolia. Brilliant scarlet, dwarf	0	6
Flavescens. Pale yellow, changing to white	0	6
Flavescens fl. pl. Pale yellow, double flowers	0	6
Candidissima. White, beautiful free growing plant	1	0
Hogarth fl. pl. Double, scarlet, very fine	0	6
Humboldti corymbiflora. Fine white flowers, borne in large trusses	1	0
Jasminoides. Beautiful, pure white	0	6
,, **paniculata.** A magnificent white, flowering in large panicles	0	9
Longiflora flammea. Deep pink	0	9
Lutoola fl. pl. Double-flowered yellow	0	6
Mrs. Robert Green. Clear salmon pink, a most distinct and beautiful variety : very free flowering	0	9
Queen of Roses. Bright rose	0	6
Priory Beauty. Delicate pink	0	6
President Cleveland. A fine sturdy-growing free-flowering variety, bearing lovely trusses of deep crimson-scarlet flowers; splendid	0	9
President Garfield. Delicate rose	0	6
Purity. The finest White Bouvardia yet obtained, flower pure white, with broad lobes and short stout tube, free flowering and very fragrant. Certificate of Merit, Royal Horticultural Society	1	0
The Bride. Beautiful pure white, compact	0	6
Vreelandi. Beautiful pure white, compact, free bloomer	0	6

Choice varieties, our own selection to name

per doz. 4s. 6d. ; 6 for 2s. 6d.　—

Abutilons.

BEAUTIFUL free-flowering plants for pots in the greenhouse, continuing in bloom throughout the Winter. Planted out in May will bloom finely in the garden till killed by the frost; very useful for cut flowers.

New and Select Varieties.

	each—s.	d.
Aurea globosa. Orange red, fine	0	6
Baron Rothschild. Large, beautiful, sulphury-yellow	0	6
Boule de Niege. Pure white, very vigorous	0	6
Cyrus. Orange pink, beautiful	0	6
Esperance. Rosy pink, large flowers	0	6
Grand Duke. Indian red, very fine	0	6
M. Jules Marty. Clear orange yellow flowers; beautiful	0	6
Orange Perfection. Brilliant orange red	0	6
Osiris. Beautiful pink, very large	0	6
Queen of the Yellows. Pale yellow, beautiful	0	6
Sanglant. Deep rich scarlet; splendid	1	0
Souvenir de Bonn. Handsome, bold, variegated foliage with large orange yellow flowers, veined with red	1	0
Thompsoni fl. pl. Flowers double, orange veined with crimson, the foliage beautifully variegated	0	6
White Queen. Large, beautiful pure white	0	9

Beautiful varieties, our own selection to name

per doz. 4s. 6d. and 6s. ; 6 for 2s. 6d. and 3s. 6d.　—

Coleus.

WELL-KNOWN, easily cultivated plants of remarkable beauty, should be grown freely in every greenhouse.

New and Select Varieties.

	each—s.	d.
Ada Sentance. Green, carmine and purple centre	0	6
Beauty of Cambridge. Large, beautiful foliage, crimson splashed with green and gold, all the leaves having a bright gold edge: very handsome	0	6
Cloth of Gold. Clear golden yellow, shaded green	0	6
Conqueror. Leaves cream-coloured at the base, crimson in the centre, surrounded with black, and have a distinct bright green edge	0	6
Countess of Dudley. Large bright green leaves, veins and centre creamy white	0	6
Edith Sentance. Beautiful variety	0	6
EMPRESS OF INDIA (new). Leaves are creamy yellow at the base, suffused with emerald green, with a central band of deep purple, the ground colour of the leaf being a deep magenta crimson, intermixed with maroon, and growing deeper towards the margins until the leaves are almost black	1	6
J. L. Toole. Green, veined and splashed with gold and crimson; fine	0	6
Lord Beresford. Crimson, edged with black	0	6
Lord Rosebery. Leaf black, edged with carmine	0	6
Magenta Queen. Very fine and brilliant	0	6
MRS. F. SANDER (new). The leaf has a central wedge of lovely creamy white, with a clearly defined margin of oxide green, bronze, crimson, and purple. This central wedge occupies the greater part of the leaf, and is sometimes splashed with magenta and porphyry	1	6
Sir E. Birkbeck. Crimson centre, edged black, extreme edge bright green with crimson veins	0	6
Sir Peter 'Eade. Centre of leaf bright carmine surrounded with black, clear green edge; superb	0	6
Pride of the Market. Crimson, green, lake, and cream-coloured; very distinct	0	6
PRINCESS BEATRICE (new). The creamy white veinings of the leaves are intermixed with amber, green and intense crimson; the latter colour is sometimes developed in a most extraordinary degree	1	0
Vesuvius (King). Leaves golden green at base, the upper parts a rich bright crimson, edged golden yellow	0	6

Choice named varieties, our own selection ; rooted cuttings

per doz. 3s. 6d. ; 6 for 2s　—

Chrysanthemums.

The following superb varieties after careful trial have proved to be flowers of exceptional merit, most of them have received high awards at our late shows, and will be in great demand for next season's exhibitions. For Newest Varieties see List of Novelties.

New and Select Varieties, our selection ... ... per doz. 4s. 6d., 6s., and 9s.
Showy and Popular Varieties, our selection „ 2s. 6d., and 3s. 6d.

JAPANESE—New and Select Exhibition Varieties.

Avalanche. One of the grandest white varieties; flowers large without being coarse. Each 6d.

Beauty of Exmouth. The flowers are of the largest size, quite free from coarseness, and of the most lovely pure white. Each 6d.

Charles Blick. Rich golden yellow, result of a cross between *Sunflower* and *Boule d'Or*. Each 6d.

Charles Daniels (Incurved Japanese). Large broad petals, bright orange-red, reverse golden. A splendid Exhibition flower. Each 1s.

Charles Davies. Golden sport from the immensely popular *Viviand Morel*—Canary-yellow, most beautifully tinted rosy bronze. Each 6d.

Col. W. B. Smith. Colour much resembles *L'Automne* lovely old gold yellow, with just a tinge of terra-cotta; Strong dwarf *Avalanche* growth. Each 6d.

Col. Chase. A magnificent flower with long drooping florets of a lovely pale blush tint, the centre shaded slightly; very distinct form. Each 1s.

Duchess of Wellington. A striking variety. The colour is a pure golden yellow; the florets are long, narrow, and beautifully twisted; the outer ones drooping gracefully, and the inner incurving boldly towards the centre. This variety will be in great request for exhibition purposes. Each 1s. 6d.

Duchess of York. The bloom is of great size, massive but graceful; the florets are long and drooping, prettily cut and notched. The colour is a delightfully soft light yellow. Each 2s.

Edwin Molyneux. A fine large flower with rich crimson florets, the reverse of each petal beautiful golden. Each 6d.

Etoile de Lyon. Deep lilac, shaded silvery grey; enormous flowers, sometimes ten to twelve inches across. Each 6d.

Eynsford White. Beautiful pure white, with broad petals; a good exhibition variety. Each 6d.

Florence Davis. Large beautiful flowers with long drooping petals, greenish white, passing to pure white. Splendid habit, and first-class for exhibition. Each 6d.

G. C. Schwabe. Bright carmine rose, gold centre, very full, long, broad, recurving and twisted florets, with gold points. Each 6d.

G. W. Childs. A fine self-coloured crimson variety; flowers massive and of immense size, with broad stiff petals. Each 6d.

Gloire du Rocher. Bright orange amber, flushed crimson. A splendid flower. Each 6d.

Hairy Wonder. This is probably the finest hairy variety yet introduced, and is indispensable to exhibitors. The long spreading florets incurving towards the centre, are of a beautiful bright reddish bronze, passing off to golden bronze. Each 1s.

J. S. Dibben. The colour is a deep yellow, passing, as it ages, to a beautiful clear yellow. Each 6d.

Jean Delaux. Deep velvety maroon; a fine variety. Each 6d.

John Shrimpton. Brilliant crimson-scarlet, with a bright golden reverse. Each 6d.

Lillian B. Bird. Petals long, thin, and tubular, with a tendency to incurve; colour, a delicate pale salmon pink; very striking and beautiful. Each 6d.

Louis Boehmer. Silvery lilac pink, the petals of good substance. Each 6d.

Louise. Large beautiful flowers, pearly white, flushed with pink, dwarf habit. Each 1s.

Madame Carnot. Splendid flower of large size, and of the purest white; long drooping florets. Each 1s. 6d.

Mdlle. Marie Hoste. Pale rose; a very beautiful flower. Each 6d.

Mdlle. Therese Rey. Fine ivory white, very long and graceful petals, a grand exhibition flower. Each 9d.

M. E. A. Carriere. Magnificent flower, white, reverse of petals a delicate blush rose; fine exhibition variety. Each 6d.

Miss Anna Hartshorne (Incurved Japanese). Blush pink, changing to pearly white. A superb double flower. Each 6d.

Mr. A. H. Neve. Very large flower, broad flat drooping petals; colour, a beautiful silvery blush. Each 6d.

Mr. Edwin Beckett. Flowers of fine form; colour a rich golden yellow, richer than *Sunflower*. Each 9d.

Mrs. Andrew Carnegie. Deep bright crimson; a fine flower, and plant of good habit. Each 6d.

Mrs. E. W. Clarke. Deep amaranth purple, reflex silvery rose. Flowers very large. Each 6d.

Mrs G. C. Schwabe. Delicate rose, shaded salmon, points of petals gold twisted, and drooping gracefully. Each 6d.

Mrs. Libbie Allen (Incurved Japanese). Large well-formed flowers, beautiful pure yellow; a fine show flower. Each 6d.

Mrs. E. S. Trafford. Rosy bronze, full flower. A sport from W. Tricker. Each 1s. 6d.

Mrs. C. W. Wheeler. Lovely shade of orange brown; a really grand flower. Each 6d.

Mrs. W. J. Godfrey. The largest, purest, and best white up to date. The florets are of great width, and of good substance, incurving and recurving in the most elegant manner. This variety really belongs to the "hairy" section, as the blooms have a beautiful feathery appearance, but in not quite so great a degree as *Louis Boehmer*. The plant is dwarf and very sturdy in habit, and the leaves are large, leathery, and of dark colour. Each 2s. 6d.

Mutual Friend. Magnificent variety, with broad, long drooping petals, forming a deep flower of the purest white. Each 1s. 6d.

Philadelphia. Creamy white; a fine and distinct flower. Each 1s. 6d.

Robert Owen. Incurved Japanese, colour bright golden bronze, deepening to reddish bronze at the base; thick broad petals, large flower of great depth. Each 9d.

Sarah Owen. Golden bronze, shaded rose, large, florets broad and tipped with gold; a charming bloom. Each 6d.

Stansted White. Purest white flowers, semi-incurved, very long petals, immense size; a magnificent variety for exhibition. Each 6d.

Thistle. Small flowers with very fine thread-like petals, of a lovely pale yellow which changes to pure white. Each 6d.

Viscountess Hambledon. Delicate, silvery blush-pink. large full flower of splendid form. Each 1s.

Viviand Morel. Flower of immense size, with long gracefully drooping petals; colour, a pale rosy pink shading to white; magnificent exhibition variety. Each 6d.

W. H. Lincoln. Immense double flowers, slightly incurved; colour, a beautiful golden yellow. Each 6d.

W. W. Coles. Bright red, long broad flat petals, the brightest and clearest of this colour yet introduced. Each 6d.

White Louis Boehmer. A direct sport from *Louis Boehmer*, and has all the fine healthy vigorous character of its parent. The blooms are very large, and open a delicate primrose, passing to the purest white. Each 6d.

William Seward. A magnificent deep rich blackish crimson, florets exceedingly long and of firm texture. Each 6d.

And many others.

Chrysanthemums.

EARLY-FLOWERING JAPANESE.

Splendid varieties, blooming three to five weeks earlier than other sorts; very useful for cutting.
Our selection, per doz. 4s. 6d.; 6 for 2s. 6d.

Gaspard Boucharlat. A fine dwarf growing variety, bearing large bright Nasturtium red flowers, very striking and distinct. Each 9d.

Grace Attick. Pure white, a very useful variety. Each 9d.

J. Lermont. Large flower, colour a deep chrome yellow veined red at the base of petals, very handsome. Each 9d.

Lady Fitzwygram. The finest early white Chrysanthemum yet raised; abundant bloomer of dwarf habit. Each 9d.

Madame De Chossat. Pure white, extremely valuable on account of its earliness. Each 9d.

Moliere. Large beautifully coloured flowers; bright salmon rose, the reverse of the petals a beautiful golden yellow, a very striking and exceedingly handsome variety. Each 9d.

Mons. G. Grunerwald. Beautiful soft pink, large flowers, very free, and of dwarf habit; a splendid variety Each 9d.

W. Clibron. Very large flower with broad petals, colour a clear garnet red. First class. Each 9d.

Bouquet Estival, Dame Blanche, E. G. Henderson & Son, Ete Fleuri, G. Wermig (*syn.* **Golden Madame Desgrange**), Mrs. Burrell, Madame Desgrange, Mrs. Hawkins, Roi des Precoces, Mrs. J. R. Pitcher, William Holmes. And many others.

INCURVED VARIETIES—New and Select Sorts.

Baron Hirsch (new). Splendid massive bloom of fine form and size, orange cinnamon, inside petals crimson. Four First Class Certificates. Each 9d.

Charles H. Curtis (new). Rich deep yellow, blooms extra large and of good depth, medium height. First Class Certificate. Each 2s. 6d.

George Savage. This is a grand variety, of vigorous free-flowering habit, and is very useful for cutting or exhibition purposes; flowers large, pure white, with broad, strongly incurved petals; good dwarf habit and good doer. Each 1s.

Harry May. Flowers very large and deep, colour deep old-gold, with occasional veins of red, petals broad and thick, spoon-shaped, foliage very luxuriant, thick and leathery, of deep green colour, and quite distinct; one of the most vigorous growers in cultivation. Each 9d.

John Lambert. A sport from *Lord Alcester.* The flowers are of a beautiful light buff, shaded with rose; it has all the grand qualities of the parent, and will take rank as one of the finest incurved varieties in cultivation. Each 9d.

Lord Brook (Japanese Incurved). Flowers very large and deep, broad petals of a beautiful bronze, intermixed with yellow, and carried on stiff stems. It is of a good dwarf habit; is adapted for groups as well as for cut blooms for exhibition, and is considered one of the best varieties of the season. First Class Certificate. Each 9d.

Mrs. Robinson King. A sport from *Golden Empress of India*; of a deep rich yellow. It has been awarded several Certificates. Each 9d.

Miss M. A. Haggas. A sport from *Mrs. Heale*, colour a beautiful light golden-yellow, with all the splendid qualities of the parent. Has received three First Class Certificates. Each 6d.

Miss Violet Tomlin. Beautiful bright purple violet, a sport from *Princess of Wales*. A fine variety, especially valuable on account of its colour. Has been awarded three First Class Certificates. Each 6d.

M. R. Bahuant. The finest seedling incurved that has been raised for years past, and without doubt owes its parentage to the *Queen* family, having just the same style of growth and size of flower, but it is different in colour; it is a lovely carmine rose, shaded cerise, broad smooth petals, beautifully incurved; thoroughly distinct, and a decided acquisition. First Class Certificate. Each 9d.

Mrs. S. Coleman. Bright golden bronze, shaded rose, a sport from *Princess of Wales*; a fine variety, has received six Certificates. Each 6d.

Owen's Crimson (new). One of the brightest crimson incurved Chinese Chrysanthemums in cultivation, florets broad, brilliant dark crimson, five inches in diameter, good habit. Two First Class Certificates. Each 2s. 6d.

Robert Cannell. Quite a new colour in this section, being an exceedingly bright chestnut-red; the reverse of the petals a deep golden-yellow, a beautiful combination, and one of the most effective in the whole of the section. First Class Certificate, National Chrysanthemum Society. Each 6d.

INCURVED—Older Varieties.

Rooted cuttings, our own selection, 2s. 6d., 3s. 6d., and 6s. per doz.; customers' selection, 4d. each; strong plants in May, 6s. and 9s. per doz.

Alfred Salter, Antonelli, Barbara, Baron Beust, Beverley, Bronze Jardin des Plantes, Cherub, Empress of India, Eve, Golden Empress of India, Golden Queen of England (*syn. Emily Dale*), Hero of Stoke Newington, Isabella Bott, Jardin des Plantes, Jeanne d'Arc (*syn. Mad. M. Texier*), John Salter, Lady Hardinge, Lady Slade, Lord Derby, Lord Wolseley, Mabel Ward, Miss Mary Morgan (*syn. Pink Perfection*), Mr. Gladstone, Mrs. George Rundle, Mrs. Norman Davis, Mrs. Heall, Mr. Bunn, Prince Alfred, Princess of Wales, Princess Imperial (*syn. Lord Alcester*), Princess of Teck (*syn. Christmas Number*), Princess Beatrice, Refulgence, Venus, White Venus.

REFLEXED VARIETIES—New and Select List.

Our selection, per doz. 3s. 6d., each 6d.

Mrs. E. D. Adams (Japanese Reflexed). One of the best and most distinct Chrysanthemums in cultivation; flowers very large, measuring ten inches across, and very deep petals very long, the outer ones swirled white, slightly flushed with rose, of dwarf habit and free bloomer, a fine variety for groups as well as a grand exhibition flower. First Class Certificate. Each 9d.

Boule de Niege. Pure white, very fine.

Cullingfordi. Beautiful crimson scarlet.

Chevalier Domage. Deep yellow, fine.

Christine. Peach colour, very good.

Cloth of Gold. Bright golden yellow, splendid.

Dr. Sharpe. Magenta, very fine.

Golden Christine. Very showy.

King of Crimsons. Deep bright crimson.

Mrs. Hope. Pale rose, shaded lilac.

Mrs. Forsyth (*White Christine*). White, pale lemon centre.

Perle des Beautes. Crimson.

R. Smith. A bright mahogany red, sport from *Dr. Sharpe*, which, though one of the oldest, is still one of the best formed flowers of this class, and has the additional advantage of being sweetly scented. Each 9d.

Single-flowered Chrysanthemums.

This beautiful class is becoming very popular. The flowers resemble the Marguerites in form, but vary in colour from crimson pure yellow and rose, to the purest white; all the flowers have yellow centres, which give them the most charming appearance. These should be grown abundantly wherever cut flowers are in demand.

NEW FUCHSIA. PRINCESS MAY.—See page 108.

	each—s.	d.
Admiral T. Symonds. Golden yellow, a large handsome flower, three to four inches across. If disbudded resembles a Sunflower	0	6
Coachman. Beautiful pure white; late	0	6
Ethel Smith. Rosy crimson, distinct and beautiful, a charming flower for cutting	0	9
Exquisite. Pure white, shaded delicate pink; lovely	0	6
Freedom. Bright yellow; very pretty	0	6
Golden Star. Clear yellow, perfect form	0	6
Jane. Pure snow white, most beautiful variety	0	6
Lady Churchill. Terra-cotta, very distinct and beautiful	0	6
Marguerite. Pure white; closely resembling a Marguerite; very pretty	0	6
May Wells. Deep crimson-scarlet	0	6
Miss Ellen Terry. Rosy pink, very pretty	0	6
Miss Cannell. White, first-rate for cutting	0	6
Purity. Pure white, with a single row of broad petals and a bold green eye. Splendid variety	0	6
Souvenir de Londres. Crimson red, very fine	0	6
Yellow Jane. Deep yellow, twisted petals; handsome	0	6

POMPONES AND HYBRIDS.

Our own selection, per doz. 2s. 6d., 3s. 6d., and 4s. 6d., customers' selection, 4d. each.

William Westlake (new). Rich golden yellow, suffused with a reddish tint, fine shaped flowers ...   each 6d.

Amy, Aurora Borealis, Bijou d'Horticulture, Bouquet Fleuri, Crème, Diamant, Eliza Dordan, Exposition de Chalon, Flambeau Toulousain, James Forsyth, La Pureté, Lilacée, L'Orangère, Maid of Kent, Marabout, Maroon Model, Mdlle. Marthe, Mdlle. Martho Golden, Mrs. Cullingford, New York, Osiris, Perle des Beautes, Progne, Reine d'Or, Rubra Perfecta, Sœur Melanie, Soirée d'Eté, St. Thais.

From Mr. W. A. BROOK, Clapham Junction.
April 12th.
"I was highly pleased with the **Chrysanthemums** I received a fortnight ago."

Chrysanthemums.
ANEMONE-FLOWERED—New and Select Varieties.

	each—s.	d.
Delaware. Very large double flowers, white guard petals with pale yellow centre; the finest Anemone-flowered variety yet sent out	0	9
Duchess of Westminster (Japanese Anemone). Long drooping guard petals, silvery blush, centre very full, rosy bronze, a grand exhibition flower, bold and graceful, a distinct and welcome addition to this class. Two First Class Certificates ...	0	9
Gluck. Deep yellow self, fine	0	6
Herald. One of the grandest of this section, flowers large, bright golden-yellow, the centre florets tubular, an inch or more long, notched at the rim, and crowded into a compact head, ray petals very long, arranged in a single row	0	9
J. Thorpe, Jun. Bright yellow, very fine ...	0	6
Lady Margaret. Very large, pure white, splendid flower	0	6
Madame Robert Owen. Pure white, a very fine and distinct variety ...	0	6
M. Charles Lebocqz. Citron yellow, tinted carmine, large flower	0	6
Mrs. Judge Benedict. Flower of good size, a light blush on opening changing to pure white, guard petals very broad, high lemon centre; a charming flower ...	0	6
Prince of Anemones. Lilac blush, fine ...	0	6
Sœur Dorothee Souille. Pale lilac, centre white ...	0	6
And others.		

POMPONE—Anemone-flowered.

	each—s.	d.
Astarte. Amber, shaded gold	0	6
Antonius. Bright yellow, beautiful	0	6
Eugene Lanjaulet. Yellow, orange disc ...	0	6
Madame Sentir. Pure white, charming	0	6
Madame Montels. White, with golden-yellow centre	0	6
Magenta King. Magenta guard petals, yellow disc; fine	0	6

Dahlias—Show and Fancy.

Our collection of Show and Fancy Dahlias includes all the newest and choicest varieties in commerce, and is one of the most complete and finest in the kingdom. We annually raise many thousands of these beautiful flowers, for which we have a very large and increasing demand. Customers wishing to secure special varieties should therefore kindly send us their orders as soon as convenient. Our prices for Dahlias as quoted are for strong plants from single pots, ready in May, carefully packed and sent free by parcel post. Should our customers however prefer to have them sent in pots the charge will be 6d. per doz. extra; when sent in this way we enclose extra plants in part compensation, but do not pay carriage.

PRICES OF SHOW AND FANCY DAHLIAS.

	s. d.			s. d.
New and very choice sorts ... ... per doz.	9 0	Good exhibition varieties ... ... per doz.		6 0
„ „ „ ... ... 6 for	5 0	„ „ „ ... ... 6 for		3 6

Our own selection of popular and beautiful varieties, per 100, 31s. 6d.; per doz. 4s. 6d.; 6 for 2s. 6d.

NEW AND SELECT VARIETIES.

S denotes Show, F Fancy.   *Those not priced 6d. each.*

Alice Emily (S.). Delicate buff yellow, a brighter and purer yellow at the edge of each petal, and toward the centre of the flower, petals beautifully formed, splendid outline, very constant. First Class Certificate, Crystal Palace, 9d.
Arthur Ocock (S.). Reddish orange, a noble flower with every good quality, very large, and of fine form. Three First Class Certificates, 9d.
Buffalo Bill (F.). Buff, striped with vermilion, 9d.
Buttercup (S.). Yellow tinged with red, very fine.
Colonist (S.). Chocolate and fawn, very distinct.
Comte de la Saux (F.). Deep lilac, striped with dark crimson, very fine, dwarf habit, 9d.
Condor (S.). Buff, shaded orange.
Crimson Globe (S.). Crimson, a large deep flower, well up in the centre, good form, very constant and free, 9d.
Dazzler (F.). Lovely pure yellow ground, flaked and striped with bright scarlet; a dwarf and very constant variety, and a valuable addition to the "Fancy" class, 1s.
Diadem (S.). Deep crimson, fine and constant.
Dorothy (F.). Fawn colour, flaked with maroon.
Duchess of Albany (F.). Pale orange, striped with crimson.
Duchess of York (S.). One of the finest show varieties sent out for some years past, being possessed of every good point that is required to make up a good show bloom. In colour it is lemon, veined and edged with a lovely shade of salmon-pink, 2s. 6d.
Duke of Connaught (S.). Dark crimson, large.
Duke of Fife (S.). Fine rich cardinal, large, with great depth of petal, 9d.
Edmund Boston (F.). Orange, striped crimson.
Ethel Britton (S.). Blush white, edged purple.
Flag of Truce (S.). White, faintly flaked lilac.
Gaiety (F.). Yellow, striped red, and tipped white.
General Gordon (F.). Yellow, striped scarlet: very fine.
George Gordon (S.). Bright crimson; this is the largest and finest crimson ever offered, 9d.
Goldfinder (S.). Yellow, tipped with red.
Gloire de Lyon (S.). Pure white, immense flowers.
Grand National (S.). Yellow, very fine.
Harry Keith (S.). Rosy purple, very fine and constant.
Henry Bond (S.). Bright rosy lilac, superb.
Henry Eckford (F.). Yellow, striped scarlet.
James Cocker (S.). Purple, large and good.
James Vick (S.). Purplish maroon.
Jessie Mackintosh (F.). Red, tipped with white.
John Walker (S.). Pure white, a large flower of the finest form, and possessing a splendid centre. It is very constant, every flower coming good, 9d.
John Hickling (S.). Clear bright yellow, of grand form and constant, excelling by far all other yellows. First Class Certificates at Royal Horticultural and Aquarium, 9d.
Joseph Green (S.). Clear bright crimson.
King of Purples (S.). Purple, very fine.
Lottie Eckford (F.). White, beautifully striped with purple.
Maggie Soul (S.). Blush white, edged purple.
Major Barttelot (F.). Orange, heavily striped maroon.

Majestic (S.). White ground, edged and shaded with purple, large, and in every way a fine flower. First Class Certificate at Crystal Palace, 9d.
Matthew Campbell (F.). Buff or apricot, beautifully striped with crimson.
Maud Fellowes (S.). French white, tinted and shaded with purple; a grand show flower, 9d.
Miss Browning (F.). Yellow, tipped with white.
Miss Fox (S.). Blush ground, heavily edged with lake; a splendid variety. First Class Certificate at Trowbridge, 1s.
Mrs. Gladstone (S.) Delicate blush, with white centre; a most charming flower.
Miss Honshaw (S.). Pure white, large.
Mrs. J. Grieve (S.). Yellow, large and fine form.
Mrs. Morgan (S.). Pale ground tinted rosy-purple; the well-shaped petals making up a large flower of perfect form, 1s.
Mrs. C. Noyes (S.). Colour, light fawn, quite a new and very pleasing tint. The blooms are very large, of perfect shape, and produced very freely on a neat dwarf plant, 1s.
Mrs. McIntosh (S.). Old gold colour, very distinct and beautiful, 9d.
Mrs. N Halls (F.). Bright scarlet, tipped with white.
Mrs. Ocock (F.). Pale yellow ground, edges of petals margined with crimson, and distinctly tipped with white; a most beautiful fancy variety, 9d.
Mrs. Stancombe (S.). Canary yellow, tipped with fawn.
Muriel (S.). Clear yellow, a splendid flower.
Nellie Cramond (S.). Purple, shaded cerise, distinct.
Pioneer (S.). Dark velvety maroon, almost black; distinct.
Plutarch (F.). Buff, striped and splashed with crimson.
Polly Sheffield (F.). Lilac striped and speckled with crimson.
Portia (new) (F.). Lilac, striped with purple, good size, splendid form; a variety that will prove to be a great favourite amongst all exhibitors.
Primrose Dame (S.). Primrose yellow, large.
Purple Prince (S.). Rich purple, large and constant.
Reliance (S.). Fawn colour, very prettily shaded with pink, fine form. First Class Certificate at Royal Horticultural, 9d.
Rev. J. B. M. Camm (F.). Yellow, flaked with red.
Richard Dean (S.). Deep purple, splendid form.
Shirley Hibberd (S.). Dark shaded crimson.
Sir J. Bennett (S.). Yellow, scarlet edge, splendid.
Sunrise (S.). Bright magenta, distinct and beautiful, 9d.
Sunset (F.). Yellow, flaked and striped with scarlet; a most telling flower, 9d.
T. W. Girdlestone (F.). Lilac, heavily flaked and splashed with deep maroon, a grand fancy flower, 9d.
Virginale (S.). A lovely blush white flower, suffused and shaded rosy-lilac; very floriferous and dwarf, and will doubtless prove a great acquisition, 1s.
Volunteer (S.). Bright cardinal red, a fine useful flower, with every good property, 9d.
Walter H. Williams (S.). Bright scarlet, splendid.

And many others.

Cactus-flowered and Decorative Dahlias.

The Cactus-flowered Dahlias, with their many brilliant and charming tints and shades of colouring, form a magnificent class either for garden decoration or for exhibition, and certainly no class of flowers has risen so highly in the public estimation of late years as these. The flowers last a long time in water when cut, and apart from their great value as exhibition flowers, they are exceedingly useful to cut for indoor decoration. We have made some splendid additions to our list, and as will be seen below, our collection of Cactus-flowered and Decorative Dahlias includes all the finest varieties.

NEW DECORATIVE DAHLIA, SALISBURY WHITE (*See Novelties*).

each—s. d.

Chancellor Swayne. A splendid bluish plum colour, velvety in texture, perfect in shape, of medium size, and almost every flower fit for exhibition .. 2 6

Countess of Gosford. The florets are long, curled and very narrow; the outer colouring is cinnamon, tinted with gold towards the base of the petals; a lovely flower 0 6

Countess of Pembroke (Decorative). One of the most attractive flowers of this class; of a delicate lilac colour, the base of the florets being deep green ... 0 6

Delicata. Delicate pink, fading towards the centre to a pale yellow. The petals are long, narrow, or twisted, and could be briefly described as a pink "*Juarezi*" .. 0 6

Duke of Clarence. Deep rich maroon crimson with fiery scarlet shading towards the top of petals, dwarf. Awarded two First Class Certificates 0 6

Edmund Weekley. Colour, a pleasing maroon, shading to crimson-scarlet 0 6

Empress of India. Large, splendidly formed flowers; deep crimson and maroon shaded black 0 6

Ernest Glasse. The flowers are of medium size, petals long and twisted, of a rich purplish magenta, and are produced on very long, stiff wiry stems, thus throwing up the blooms well above the foliage 1 0

Fascination (Decorative). Lovely bright lilac-rose, each petal being conspicuously marked with a pure white stripe; charming variety 0 6

GENERAL SELECT LIST.

The Decorative Varieties are intermediate between the Cactus and Show and Fancy.

Strong Plants ready in May.

New and very choice varieties, our selection ... per doz. 9s.; 6 for 5s.

Choice selected sorts, our selection per doz. 6s.; 6 for 3s. 6d.

Showy and popular varieties, our selection per doz. 4s. 6d.; 6 for 2s. 6d.

each—s. d.

Apollo. Grand blooms of a splendid crimson lake colour; the habit of the plant is perfect. 0 9

Beauty of Arundel. Most superb variety. Colour, a brilliant glowing crimson, the tips of the petals shaded bright rosy purple ... 0 9

Bertha Mawley. A magnificent flower, resembling a Japanese Chrysanthemum; the colour is cochineal; an exceedingly attractive, free and beautiful variety ... 0 9

Black Prince. The finest and best dark Cactus Dahlia yet raised. The flowers are large, finely formed, and of a rich purplish-black colour ... 0 6

Blanche Keith. This is an improvement upon all yellows up to date and of the true "Cactus" form. The petals are long and twisted, very full and evenly arranged, and of a uniform rich yellow throughout 1 0

Cannell's Favorite. Quite distinct in colour, which is a charming yellow bronze or old gold. A very fine flower. First Class Certificate 0 6

Centennial. Magenta crimson with side margins of deep maroon, very distinct 0 6

Charming Bride. White, tipped with rosy pink, fine 0 6

Germania Nova (Decorative). A distinct and beautiful variety; colour, a soft mauve-rose; the tips of the petals beautifully laciniated 0 6

Gloriosa. Without doubt, the finest crimson Cactus variety yet offered, and one that will be much admired wherever grown. Every flower is perfect in form, true Cactus in shape, and the petals are very long, narrow, and elegantly twisted 1 0

Grand Duke Alexis. A grand variety. Quite a new departure in this section, each floret being rolled up at the edges so that one side overlaps the other, giving the flower a most beautiful and attractive appearance. The blooms are of great size, a lovely pure white, and in a good light show a glistening silk-like sheen; sometimes the centre and the back of the flower have a very faint tint of lilac, when the effect is extremely beautiful ... ... 3 for 2s. 6d. 1 0

Harry Freeman. Finest pure white Cactus Dahlia yet sent out. Very free-flowering 0 6

Henry Patrick. Beautiful pure white; splendid ... 0 6

Juarezi (*The True Cactus Dahlia*). Brilliant scarlet, large Cactus-like flowers, very showy and effective ... 0 6

Kaiserin. Colour, a lovely sulphur yellow, the tips of the petals shading off to a lemon tint 0 9

King of Cactus. Light crimson red; immense flowers, very showy 0 6

Cactus and Decorative Dahlias (continued).

	each—s. d.
Kynerith. Deep rich vermilion, a lighter shade at the base of the florets	0 9
Lady Marsham. Deep salmon; splendid flower ...	0 6
Lady Penzance. This is unquestionably the finest Cactus Dahlia ever raised. In colour is of the purest yellow; the shape is perfect, and the florets are faultless	1 0
Maid of Kent. Crimson, shading to an intense cherry-red, with pure white tips to each petal	0 6
Marchioness of Bute. Pure white, the petals tipped with bright delicate rose	0 6
Mary Hillier. The petals of this variety are long and twisted, and most beautifully arranged; the flowers are of medium size, of a delightful clear rich salmon colour. There is a grand improvement in the habit, and it possesses many points which render it a very superior variety	1 0
Mikado. Orange buff, very fine and distinct ...	0 6
Miss Barry. Bright rich purple; large splendid flower	0 6
Miss Violet Morgan. A most charming flower, the colour at the base of the petals being a lovely fawn or dull orange, shading towards the edge and point with a delicate tint of pink	0 9
Mr. G. Reid (Decorative). White, tipped with rosy lilac, a beautiful variety of good size and substance ...	0 6
Mrs. G. Marshall. Deep magenta, each petal distinctly edged with velvety crimson	0 6

	each—s. d.
Mrs. J. Douglas. Colour a bright pinkish salmon. A fine flower and free bloomer. First Class Certificate	0 6
Mrs. Hawkins. Soft primrose yellow, shaded delicate fawn on the outer petals; a charming flower ...	0 6
Mrs. Peart. In form it is a *fac-simile* of *Juarezi*, the flowers when opening are of a creamy-white with a sulphury centre fading off, when fully expanded, to the purest white	0 9
Panthea. Reddish salmon, with long graceful petals of the *Juarezi* typo: a superb flower ...	0 6
Prince Albert Victor. Deep rich scarlet	0 6
Professor Baldwin. Brilliant scarlet; splendid ...	0 6
Rayon d'Or. Bright orange with a conspicuous band of white running through each petal; flowers of medium size, broad, stout petals, and very abundant ...	0 6
Robert Cannell. The nearest approach to a blue Dahlia yet raised; the colour is a magnificent magenta, tinted and shaded with blue; it is a true Cactus ...	0 9
Robert Maher. Bright clear yellow, a very free bloomer of good habit. First Class Certificate ...	0 6
St. Catherine. A true Cactus in form, with long, spiral, pointed petals; a cadmium yellow colour, or soft reddish amber; very free flowering	0 6
William Darville. Bright magenta purple, with pointed, recurved petals; very distinct ...	0 6
William Rayner. Beautiful bright salmon buff ...	0 6

Pompone or Bouquet Dahlias.

A brilliant and charming class, of a neat compact habit of growth, with beautifully formed, perfectly double, miniature flowers, which are produced in profusion throughout the Summer and Autumn. The colours vary from deep crimson and brilliant scarlet to the softest primrose, pure white, &c., three colours being sometimes blended in the same flower.

GENERAL LIST.
Strong Plants ready in May.

New and extra choice sorts	per doz. 6s. ; 6 for 3s. 6d.
Our own selection	„ 3s. 6d. and 4s. 6d.
„ „	6 for 2s. and 2s. 6d.

POMPONE DAHLIAS.

SELECT VARIETIES.

	each—s. d.
Bacchus. Bright crimson scarlet; the individual blooms are neat, small and compact, and the plant is dwarf ...	0 9
Boule d'Or. A beautiful clear yellow, very small ...	0 9
Ceres. Rich cream or primrose. Very free-flowering, and of good habit	1 0
Crimson Beauty. The blooms are of medium size, perfect in form, and of the richest crimson colour ...	0 6
Eden. Deep shaded crimson	0 6
Eurydice. Blush, tipped with purple; very pleasing ...	0 6
Fairy Tales. Delicate primrose; fine shape ...	0 6
Gipsy Queen. Deep maroon crimson; the bloom has good petals and outline, and it is very free ...	0 9
Hilda. Deep rose, shaded crimson, tipped and striped white; very free and pretty variety	0 9
Little Ethel. White, often tipped with purple ...	0 6
Lilian. Primrose, deeply edged with peach ...	0 9
Lorna Doone. Rosy purple, dark purple tip, small flowers, remarkably pretty, and good habit ...	0 9
Madge. Soft crimson, distinctly tipped with white; one of the prettiest and most useful for show or decoration	1 0
Mars. A brilliant scarlet, extremely showy, medium-sized flower, exceptionally free, and strong grower ...	0 9
Midget. Soft rose, small and beautifully formed ...	0 9
Midnight. A splendid variety. The colour is a very deep rich crimson, and the plant has a first class habit	1 0
Mittie Wood. Primrose, edged with bronze ...	0 6
Red Indian. Deep coral red; charming ...	0 6
Salmon Queen. Light salmon colour, deepening towards the tips of the petals to a rich reddish salmon	0 6
Sovereign. A very attractive variety of a beautiful bright golden yellow. The flower is small and compact, and is one of the most beautiful of this section ...	1 0
Sunny Daybreak (new). A lovely tint of pale apricot, prettily and regularly edged with rosy red; in shape and size it is simply perfection; very profuse ...	2 0
Whisper. Clear yellow, edged with gold; very attractive	0 6

Also the following varieties:—

Brilliant, Burning Coal, Catherine, Comte von Sternberg, Dandy, Darkness, Don Juan, Dora, Eccentric, E. F. Junker, Fair Helen, Fashion, Favorite, Gazelle, Grace, Gem, Golden Gem, Hector, Iolanthe, Isoult, Janet, Lady Blanche, Leila, Little Arthur, Little Duchess, Little Prince, Miguon, Prince of Liliputians, Profusion, Pure Love, Rosalie, Titania, Virginal, White Aster, White Button, William Carlisle.

Single-flowered Dahlias.

The Single-flowered Dahlias are charming as cut flowers, and splendidly effective when well staged for exhibition. They commence blooming about the end of July, and are resplendent with a profusion of their lovely flowers till killed by the frost in Autumn. The small or medium-sized flowers are the most useful, either for exhibition or decorative purposes, as it is found they retain their beauty for a much longer period when cut than the larger blooms. Our list of these contains the choicest varieties in commerce.

New and very choice varieties, our selection ... ... per doz. 6s., or 6 for 3s. 6d.
Very good sorts, our selection ... ... per doz. 4s. 6d., or 6 for 2s. 6d.

NEW AND SELECT VARIETIES.

each—s. d.

Butterfly. Very bright orange-red colour, the tip of each petal having a heavy blotch of gold, an unusual combination of colour and exceedingly effective, especially for exhibition. 3 feet 0 6

Cleopatra. Deep velvety crimson, very rich and of good substance; flowers medium sized and nicely recurved ... 0 6

Claudia. Medium-sized flowers; reddish salmon, beautifully tipped with delicate mauve, and having a dark crimson ring round the disc; strikingly beautiful ... 0 6

C. S. Daniels. Brilliant orange-scarlet, with golden-yellow centre; strikingly effective and splendid variety 0 6

Dearest. A perfect gem; colour pure white, each floret having a well-defined margin of a clear sulphur yellow; the flowers are carried erect on stiff stems; bushy compact habit. 2½ feet 0 9

Duchess of Albany. An exceptionally distinct variety of quite novel colours, soft mauve, edged with pale buff brown, beautifully recurved, dwarf and free. Two First Class Certificates, R.H.S. and National Dahlia Society 0 6

Duchess of Fife. Beautiful amber, with side edgings of reddish orange. First Class Certificate, National Chrysanthemum Society 0 6

Duchess of Westminster. Pure white, splendid ... 0 6

Eclipse. Beautiful rosy mauve and salmon, with a broad crimson ring round the disc 0 6

Guleilma. Pure white, with broad margins of golden buff; medium-sized flowers of good shape; very distinct. First Class Certificate, National Dahlia Society ... 0 6

James Scobie. Yellow, beautifully striped and flaked with scarlet; one of the finest exhibition flowers. First Class Certificate R.H.S. 0 6

John Downie. Rich scarlet, splendid form; a fine exhibition flower 0 6

Miss Henshaw. Pale primrose, edged with white, beautiful form 0 6

each—s. d.

Miss Jefferies. A most charming variety and one of the grandest exhibition flowers. It has a peculiar combination of colour, rendering it very effective. The colour is a lovely blending of mauve and magenta, with a conspicuous red ring at the base of the petals 0 6

Miss Ramsbottom. Flowers of a lovely pink colour, shaded cerise, quite new and distinct, medium size and perfect in form. First Class Certificates, National Dahlia Society and National Chrysanthemum Society 0 6

Miss Louisa Pryor. Deep velvety crimson, with golden yellow disc, a splendid flower 0 6

Mr. Riley. Deep carmine-crimson, with golden disc, splendid form 0 6

Mrs. Barker. Pale buff, shaded red, and sometimes edged with gold; fine 0 6

Mrs. Charles Daniels. Sulphury white, edged with crimson; a very distinct and showy variety ... 0 6

Mrs. J. Coninck. Pure white, shaded with pale mauve, very beautiful form and colour 0 6

Nellie. One of the best and most distinct yet raised, the colour is an intense crimson-maroon with a bright golden-yellow disc around the centre; the flowers are large, slightly reflexed, and most symmetrically formed. Splendid show flower ... 0 6

Northern Star. Bright red, margined with deep golden yellow; small, well-formed flowers on stiff wiry stems; very showy and distinct. Has been awarded three First Class Certificates 0 6

Paragon. Deep maroon, edged with crimson ... 0 6

W. C. Harvey. A striking novelty, and one that must become a favourite. It is a bold, handsome flower, with petals of great substance and slightly reflexed, and of a rich yellow, shaded with orange, having a distinct red ring at the base. First Class Certificate, National Dahlia Society 0 6

And others.

SINGLE DAHLIA—"Marguerite."

THIS very pretty and useful variety was recently introduced by us, and named "Marguerite," in consequence of its striking resemblance at a short distance to the Marguerite Daisy. The flowers are white with a yellow disc, the petals long and pointed, and when the blooms are made up into bouquets, &c., they have the most charming appearance. This will be found a welcome addition to the white flowers now used for decorative purposes, and valuable alike for decorating the church or home; it is also exceedingly useful in the making of memorial wreaths and crosses.
Each 9d.; 3 for 2s.

NEW DOUBLE MIGNONETTE—Bush Hill White.

A BEAUTIFULLY compact growing variety, with pretty spikes of almost pure white, deliciously scented, double flowers. It is admirably suited for growing in pots, and will be found exceedingly useful for bouquets. The flowers being very double, it can only be propagated from cuttings.
Strong young plants, each 1s.; 3 for 2s. 6d.

Fuchsias.

OUR list of these has been carefully revised, and includes only really good sorts that can be highly recommended. These beautiful flowers are not only admirably suited for pot culture indoors, but if planted out in May they will form beautiful objects in the garden, and bloom profusely throughout the Summer and Autumn.

NEW AND SELECT VARIETIES.

Those marked (*) are double-flowered.

	each—s.	d.
Beauty of Clyffe Hall. Tube and sepals blush white, corolla rich bright carmine pink; beautiful	0	6
BEAUTY OF EXETER. One of the largest and handsomest Fuchsias; immense bright salmon rose blooms, most abundantly produced on a plant of a vigorous habit; most charming variety	1	0
Beauty of Lavington. White tube and sepals, rosy carmine corolla; very fine	0	6
*Compacta superba. Beautiful dwarf compact habit; tube and sepals light crimson, corolla violet blue	0	6
*Colonel Domine. Sepals a bright rich scarlet, corolla a beautiful creamy white veined with pink; superb	0	6
COUNTESS OF ABERDEEN. A beautiful dwarf-growing, free-flowering variety. Both the sepals and corolla being white, it is quite unique and totally distinct from any other Fuchsia, whilst its elegantly formed flowers and neat habit will make it a general favourite	1	0
Diadem (Lye). Delicate blush tube and sepals, pale magenta corolla, broadly edged with brilliant carmine	0	6
*Duchess of Edinburgh. A superb variety bearing large well-formed flowers; the tube and sepals which are well reflexed, are of a rich crimson-scarlet colour; the corolla a charming creamy-white. A decided improvement on "Molesworth"	0	9
Earl of Beaconsfield. A splendid hybrid variety, flowers over three inches long, carmine, with deep carmine corolla	0	6
Emily Bright. White tube and sepals, corolla bright carmine	0	6
Ernest Renan. Large, beautiful flowers, tube and sepals waxy white, well reflexed; corolla rosy crimson	0	6
*Esmeralda. Light crimson tube and sepals, corolla lilac blue, heavily splashed with red; very distinct	0	6
Final. Tall and graceful growing variety; tube and sepals crimson; corolla rich violet	0	6
EXCELSIOR (new). Long finely recurved crimson-scarlet sepals, with very large bell-shaped bluish purple corolla; distinct and fine	2	6
*Frau Emma Topfer. A remarkable dwarf-growing variety, with extraordinarily large flowers, tube and sepals bright rosy coral, corolla rosy blush	0	6
General Gordon. Very large well-formed flowers; corolla a bright purple, tube and sepals scarlet	0	6
Gem of Lavington (Lye). White tubes and sepals, very delicately tinted with the palest pink, very stout carmine corolla, flushed with soft violet	0	6
General Garfield. Rich crimson, carmine corolla	0	6
Jason. Deep crimson tube and sepals, corolla dark purple; fine and distinct	0	6
*Joseph Rosaine. Scarlet, purple corolla; very fine	0	6
Jupiter. Large, beautiful double flowers; sepals well reflexed, brilliant scarlet; corolla, a deep purple violet	0	9
Loveliness (Lye). Creamy tube and pale blush sepals, very long and stout, pale violet pink corolla	0	6
Lye's Excelsior. Creamy tube and sepals, tinted with emerald, stout and well reflexed; rich deep rosy magenta corolla flushed with carmine	0	6
*La France. Large handsome double flowers of beautiful form; the sepals a bright rich scarlet, the corolla a bright light violet	0	6

	each—s.	d.
Lady Doreen Long. White tube and sepals; deep pink corolla	0	6
*Le Cygne. Crimson tube and sepals, corolla white	0	6
MADAME BRUANT. Immense flowers; tube and sepals a rich scarlet, corolla a beautiful lilac-mauve veined with rosy red. The blooms are very double and of splendid effect	1	6
Madame Millet Robinet. Immense flowers; tube and sepals waxy white; corolla rosy crimson	0	6
*Madame Jules Chretien. Large well-shaped flowers, tube and sepals crimson, corolla beautiful white, veined red	0	6
Madame Rozain. A truly grand variety, bearing immense flowers of the most elegant form; the tube and sepals a deep rich scarlet crimson colour, the corolla a charming creamy white; most beautiful, and distinct from all others	0	9
*Magnificent. A grand variety, bearing immense double flowers. The sepals are well reflexed, of a bright rich crimson colour, the corolla deep violet blue	0	9
*Merope. Fine double flowers, rich crimson scarlet, with dark purple corolla	0	6
Miss Lizzie Vidler. Red, lilac corolla; fine	0	6
*Molesworth. Tube and sepals a bright deep carmine-crimson colour; full double white corolla	0	6
*M. Berraud Massard. Tube and sepals light scarlet, well reflexed; the corolla very double, lilac-coloured, scarlet at base of petals. Splendidly-formed flowers	0	6
*MRS. E. G. HILL. This magnificent Fuchsia is one of the most splendid ever sent out. The plants are short-jointed and sturdy in growth, with beautiful dark green foliage. The flowers are of an immense size, the tube and sepals being of a deep rich scarlet colour, the corolla a beautiful creamy white, veined with pink; grand variety	1	0
P. RADAELLI. Enormous double corolla of a rich bluish-violet colour, striped and stained with lovely carmine. The tube and sepals are of a rich red, the sepals well recurved. The plant is of compact habit, and a very free bloomer. A grand variety of exceptional merit	1	0
*President Gunther. Corolla double, of a bright reddish purple colour, sepals light crimson	0	6
PRINCESS MAY. A most charming variety. The tube and sepals are of lovely creamy white, the corolla a brilliant carmine-rose colour. The plant is of a dwarf, compact habit of growth, a wonderfully profuse bloomer of beautiful effect	1	6
*Raphael. Immense double flowers, tube and sepals crimson, corolla violet splashed with red	0	6
Rose of Denmark. White, pink corolla; beautiful	0	6
Star of Wilts. White, rosy crimson corolla; splendid	0	6
Sunray. Foliage handsomely variegated	0	6
Trailing Queen. Tubes and sepals bright rosy scarlet; corolla a deep rich violet-purple, changing to a fine shade of crimson; a very free bloomer; vigorous	1	0
Walter Long (Lye). Bright pale coral-red tube and sepals, clear violet corolla	0	6
Wiltshire Giant (semi-double). Stout broad tube and sepals of a beautiful pale orange-carmine, distinct; corolla a lovely deep magenta	1	0

New and very choice sorts, our selection	...	...	per doz. 6s.; 6 for 3s. 6d.
Twelve choice named varieties, our own selection	...	...	... 3s. 6d. and 4s. 6d.
Six „ , „	...	...	... 2s. 0d. and 2s. 6d.

Single-flowered Zonal Pelargoniums.

WE have a grand collection of these superb flowers, including all the finest of recent introduction. A great improvement has been made in those of late years, and the flowers and trusses of some of the varieties attain an immense size. The individual blooms of many of the specimens grown at our Nurseries during the past season measured upwards of seven inches in circumference, being at the same time of the most perfect form, and of the most exquisite colours.

ZONAL PELARGONIUMS.

NEW VARIETIES OF 1894. ENGLISH AND CONTINENTAL.

	each—s. d.
CANDACE. Rich deep crimson, almost as dark as *H. Jacoby*, but much finer and better in form than any previous introductions in this colour	1 6
DR. ERNEST RAWSON. Deep purple velvety crimson, flowers exceptionally fine in form, the single pips being upwards of two inches in diameter	1 6
E. BIDWELL. Bright vermilion scarlet, with conspicuous white eye: a beautifully formed flower	1 6
ENID. Clear bright rosy red, large well shaped pips, 2½ inches in diameter, forming huge compact trusses	1 6
GERTRUDE PEARSON. Pure rose pink, with conspicuous white blotch on two upper petals; the flower is beautifully formed, and the largest in this colour	1 6
JOHN FORBES. Rich crimson scarlet, flowers very large, 2½ inches diameter, plant dwarf and very free	1 6

	each—s. d.
MADAME JULES CHRETIEN. Clear rosy scarlet, centre of flower white; at the junction of the two colours the flower is richly shaded with brilliant purple, a scheme of colour quite unique among Zonals	1 0
MONS. CALVAT Rich crimson scarlet, with very conspicuous clear white eye, very showy and attractive	1 6
MRS. FRANK ROTHERA. Clear salmon, shading to nearly white round the eye, a lovely delicate colour, and one of the most perfectly formed flowers	1 6
OLIVIA. Bright rosy cerise, the upper petals being suffused with a rather darker shade, a most charming colour	1 6
WINTIE. Bright cherry red, with distinct white eye, flowers large and of beautiful shape	1 6

SELECT VARIETIES—General List.

	each—s. d.
Alex. Albrecht. Rich dark scarlet	0 6
Aline. Pure white, splendid flower	0 6
Amy Amphlett. Purest white; blooms well shaped	0 6
Ayesha. Salmon, suffused with orange	0 6
Benoit Rozain. The largest flower in existence, and the whole bloom is perfect in form. The centre of the flower and the upper petals are orange, whilst the lower petals are a lovely salmon, delicately veined with orange	1 0
Cato. Bright orange scarlet, very large	0 6
Chas. Mason. Brilliant vermilion, perfect shape	0 6
Clara Palethorpe. Blush white, suffused with pink	0 6
Conde. Deep crimson scarlet, plum colour	0 6
Cyclops. Very dark rich crimson	0 6
Dr. S. Grey. Deep rich crimson; splendid	1 0
Dr. Nansen. Finest pure white; the flower large and beautifully formed	1 0
Dr. Rothera. Rich dark glowing scarlet; splendid	1 0
Eccentric. Salmon, shaded with orange	0 6
Eleanor. Clear bright orange	1 0
Ellen Clarke. Bright orange salmon	0 6
Eric. Purple scarlet, beautifully shaded, white eye	0 6
Ethel Lewis. Rose pink, white blotch on upper petals	0 6
Etna. Rich crimson scarlet, suffused with plum colour	0 9
Falstaff. Rich plum colour, shading to scarlet	0 6
Flamboyant. Brilliant scarlet; flowers very large	0 6
Flamingo. Scarlet, shaded with orange	0 9
Florence Farmer. White ground, veined and tinted with rosy salmon	1 0
Galatea. Delicate salmon-rose, with white blotch on the upper petals; large truss, very free	0 9
G. Dore. Mottled salmon	0 6
Grace Harvey. Pale rose, lighter centre	0 9
Guinevere. Creamy white; splendid truss and pip	0 6
Hecla. Crimson scarlet, immense truss	0 6
Herminius. Scarlet, shaded magenta, fine	0 6
International. White, very large and fine form	0 6
James Douglas. Rich dark crimson, superb	0 6
Jno. Lorraine Baldwin. Scarlet, white eye	0 6
Juliet. Ground colour salmon pink, shaded rosy pink	0 6
Kaiser Frederick. Rich plum-purple, very distinct	0 9
Katherine Moreton. Salmon, light edge; very large	0 6
Lady Chesterfield. Salmon, suffused with orange	0 6
Lady Francis Russell. Clear rose pink	0 6
Livy. Rich orange-scarlet, upper petals veined	0 9
Lord Chesterfield. Crimson magenta, magnificent	0 6
Lord Tredegar. Scarlet, suffused with plum	0 6

	each—s. d.
Lucreece. Clear bright rosy pink, with large white blotch on two upper petals	1 0
Lucy Mason. Mottled salmon, large and distinct	0 6
Mary Caswell. Delicate pink, beautiful form	0 6
Mary Clarke. Salmon, shaded with pink and red	0 6
Mercedes. Salmon, tinted orange	0 6
Midsummer. Pale salmon, lighter edge	0 6
M. Myriel. Crimson scarlet, white eye	0 6
Mrs. David Saunders. Pale lilac pink	0 6
Mrs. Gordon. Rich crimson, white eye	0 6
Mrs. H. F. Barker. Dark rose	0 6
Mrs. Holford. Salmon, large and splendid	0 6
Mrs. Johnson. Rosy lilac, beautiful	0 6
Mrs. Norris. Scarlet, with white eye	0 6
Mrs. Robertson. Bright deep pink, white eye	0 6
Mrs. E. Rawson. Rich orange-scarlet	0 9
Mrs. Wilders. Bright scarlet, white eye	0 6
Mrs. Wright. The nearest approach to a blue yet raised, being several shades nearer that colour than any other variety	1 0
Nerissa. Orange cerise, beautiful	0 6
Norah. Delicate rosy salmon	0 6
O. W. Holmes. A beautiful shade between orange and salmon, and is one of the most lovely tints	1 0
Œnone. Salmon, flushed orange	1 0
Opal. Beautiful shaded salmon	0 6
Orestes. Carmine rose, beautiful	0 6
Perdita. Salmon, shading off to white at the edge	0 6
Phœna. Scarlet, shaded magenta, white eye	0 6
Phryne. Cerise, shaded plum colour	0 6
Plutarch. Bright orange scarlet, with white eye	0 6
Proserpina. Salmon, shaded orange	0 6
Puritan. White ground, shaded salmon	0 6
Rev. R. D. Harries. Salmon scarlet, soft shade	0 6
Rhodope. Bright orange, flushed with pink	0 6
Rhada. Rose colour	0 6
Rosy Morn. Delicate rosy pink	0 6
Shirley Hibberd. Rich scarlet, shaded plum	0 6
Sir Percivale. White; flowers large and well shaped	0 6
Soulary. A charming clear shade of orange-salmon with a beautiful white eye	1 0
Souvenir De Mirande. Rosy carmine	0 6
Stella Massey. Blush pink; beautiful flower	0 6
T. Hayes. Dark crimson; fine pip and truss	0 6
Th. de St. Vinox. A most distinct and novel shade, a lively slaty-rose, veined and striped carmine	1 0
Tristrain. Crimson scarlet, with white eye, very fine	0 6

PRICES OF SINGLE ZONAL PELARGONIUMS.

New and select varieties, very choice	6 for 5s.; per doz. 9s.	
Twelve in 12 superb varieties, our selection	4s. 6d. and 6s.	
Six in 6 superb varieties, our selection	2s. 6d. and 3s. 6d.	

DOUBLE-FLOWERED IVY-LEAVED PELARGONIUMS.

No class of plants has been so highly improved within the past few years as these. The flowers of some are as double and well-formed as the most perfect Rose or Camellia, and the colours range from pure white to the most intensely brilliant magenta, crimson, scarlet, delicate rose, lilac, mauve, &c. Magnificent for pots or hanging-baskets in the greenhouse or conservatory, or for garden decoration, whilst as cut-flowers they are charmingly beautiful.

IVY-LEAVED PELARGONIUM.

From **Miss ROBLIN**, Narberth.

"I have taken three Prizes, two First and one Second, for the **Dahlias** I received from you."

	each—s.	d.
QUEEN OF ROSES (new). A splendid variety, with very large perfectly double flowers of the most brilliant rosy crimson colour; a first-class variety for hanging baskets, &c.	1	6
Abundance. Deep rosy lilac, fine	0	6
Alice Crousse. Violet purple, tinged crimson	0	9
Beauty of Castle Hill. Soft pink, free bloomer, dwarf	0	9
Bernardo Marone. Deep rosy pink	0	9
Cardinal Lavigerie. Beautiful bright scarlet	0	9
Cuvier. Beautiful rich violet purple, very fine	0	6
De Quatrefages. Deep bright rosy purple; very fine	0	6
Edmund About. Brilliant cerise; very double	0	6
Francisque Sarcy. Rosy crimson, splendid	0	6
Future Fame. Brilliant amaranth purple	0	6
Galileo. Bright rosy pink; large, beautifully formed	0	6
General de Negrier. Scarlet carmine	0	6
Giroflee. Rich bright purplish crimson	0	6
H. Cannell. Clear amaranth, shaded madder	0	9
Jeanne d'Arc. White, suffused with lavender	0	6
Louis Mayet. Very large bright rosy purple	0	9
Madame Crousse. Delicate rose, large flowers	0	6
Madame Sylvain May. Cerise pink	0	6
Madame Thibaut. Brilliant crimson cerise	0	6
Mdlle. Marie Fabre. Splendid carmine cerise	0	6
Mdlle. Laura Daix. Charming rosy crimson	0	6
Mignonne. Delicate bright rose, splendid form	0	6
Murillo. Large, deep crimson flowers	0	6
Robert Owen. Large, deep rosy carmine	0	6
Ryecroft Surprise. It has a fine bold vigorous upright habit, producing the largest truss ever seen; it is wonderfully free, blooming at nearly every joint, individual pips of immense size, being large enough for a gentleman's buttonhole. Colour a lovely salmon-pink. Award of Merit	0	9
Sir Richard Wallace. Lovely rose-carmine	0	9
Soleil Couchant. Bright rosy mauve	0	6
Souvenir de Charles Turner. Splendid variety, large, well-formed flowers; beautiful deep rose	0	6

New and select varieties per doz. 6s. 0d.; 6 for 3s. 6d.
Choice varieties, our selection „ 3s. 0d.; 6 for 2s. 0d.

DOUBLE-FLOWERED ZONAL PELARGONIUMS.

DOUBLE PELARGONIUM, PERLE BLANCHE.

Splendid double and massive flowers of the most charming and brilliant colours; in many of the varieties the flowers are beautifully formed, whilst they are all much more durable than those of the single-flowered varieties. The following list includes the finest varieties in the different colours.

New and select varieties ... per doz. 9s.; 6 for 5s.
Choice varieties, our selection
per doz. 4s. 6d. and 6s.; 6 for 2s. 6d. and 3s. 6d.

SELECT VARIETIES.

	each—s.	d.
VIOLET DANIELS. A remarkably fine variety, and the individual blooms are of immense size. The colour of the flowers is a beautiful transparent salmony-gold with a delicate fleshy tint. This is one of the finest varieties that has been offered for several years	1	6
Attraction. Light lilac pink, beautiful	0	6
Californian Gold. Brilliant orange scarlet	0	6
Candidissima plena. Pure white, large and good	0	6
Contraste. Carmine purple, washed with orange, a distinct and beautiful flower of exceptional merit	0	9
Fille d'Honneur. Pure white, the centre tinted slightly with rose	1	0
Fratelli Cavelli. Brilliant scarlet, fine form and truss	0	6
Hong-man-hao. Clear violet rose, of perfect shape and great size	0	6
Hermine. White, large and perfect in shape	0	6
L. Contable. Beautiful clear rose; free	0	6
Le Pilote. Brilliant scarlet, beautifully formed flowers	0	6
M. Adrien Corret. Lovely cerise	0	6

Double-Flowered Zonal Pelargoniums (*continued*).

	each—s.	d.
M. Alois Frey. Delicate salmon rose	0	6
Madame Buchnor. Pure white, one of the largest double Zonals ever raised	1	0
Madame Despans. Large semi-double white flowers, the centres shaded with bright rosy-flesh	1	0
Madame Grillet. Rose shaded purple, beautiful ...	0	6
Madame Guilbert. Lovely bright fresh rose ...	0	6
Madame Thibaut. Shaded blue, abundant bloomer	0	6
Madame van Houtte. Delicate rosy pink, beautiful	0	6
Madame Rozain. A very fine double, pure white; plant dwarf, and free blooming	1	6
Marquise de l'Aigle. Brilliant carmine pink ...	0	6

	each—s.	d.
Mignon. Lovely orange shaded rose ...	0	6
Perle Blanche. Pure white flowers, perfectly double and of the most perfect form	0	6
P. Mercadier. Upper petals scarlet, lower ones magenta; very effective	1	0
Raspail Improved. Bright rich scarlet; large flowers, very free	1	0
Secretaire Daurel. Deep carmine cerise, splendid ...	0	6
Souvenir de Grenoble. White, centre rosy apricot	0	6
Surpasse E. Barker. Vermilion rose, splendid ...	0	6
Vesuvius. Intense vermilion scarlet	0	6

GERANIUMS—Show, Fancy and Regal.

WE have a very choice collection of these beautiful and highly popular flowers, which we offer in fine healthy plants, well set with flower-buds, at prices as below. Our collection includes such fine varieties as Beauty of Oxton, Captain Raikes, Duchess of Edinburgh, Duchess of Teck, Gold Mine, Kingston Beauty, Masterpiece, Pink Perfection, Prince Arthur, Prince of Novelties, Prince of Wales, Princess of Wales, Queen Victoria, Triomphe de St. Mande, Rob Roy Improved, and many other new and beautiful sorts. These being offered as established plants in pots are not sent carriage paid.

SHOW AND REGAL GERANIUMS.

New and Select Varieties.

	each—s.	d.
Achievement. Lower petals bright orange-scarlet, upper petals dark edged scarlet, the centre of the flower pure white	1	6
Blue Beard. Very large light purple flowers, with white eye	1	6
Bush Hill Beauty. Beautiful soft pink and white; a charming variety	1	0
Duchess of Albany. Deep rich carmine; handsomely fringed	1	0
Duchess of Fife. Clear lake, shaded with white margin and centre; splendid	1	6
Duke of York. Crimson, shaded with rosy purple, edged with white, veined with maroon, light centre ...	3	6
Dorothy. Carmine-rose with white centre, beautifully fringed petals, margined white ...	1	0
Emperor of Russia. Petals dark maroon, surrounded with crimson-purple, margined with blush white ...	1	0
Fimbriatum Album. Pure white semi-double flowers, the petals beautifully crimped on the edges ...	1	6
H. M. Stanley. Bright rosy crimson, upper petals shaded scarlet, and beautifully blotched; very free flowering	1	6
Scarlet Gem. Bright rosy-scarlet, with white centre; beautiful and attractive flower; quite distinct ...	3	6
Volonte Nationale Alba. Beautiful pure white; fringed	1	0

New and select vars., fine plants	per doz. 15s. and 18s.
Very fine sorts, good plants ...	„ 9s. „ 12s.
Very fine sorts, smaller plants	6 for 3s. 6d.; per doz. 6s.

Sweet-scented Geranium.

Lady Plymouth. Handsomely divided silver-variegated foliage, deliciously scented ... ... 3 for 2s.; each 9d.

HELIOTROPES.

THE delicious fragrance of this popular class of plants renders them great favourites in the greenhouse, conservatory, or flower garden.

Beautiful varieties to name ...	6 for 2s. 3d.; per doz. 4s.

	each—s.	d.
Bouquet Blanc. Large umbels, flowers pure white, and very odoriferous	0	9
Madame de Bussy. Dwarf plants, very large bloom, deliciously scented; colour, a beautiful blue with large white eye; a variety to be highly recommended ...	1	0
Queen of Violets. Dark violet with white eye, very free-flowering and of good habit ... per doz. 3s. 6d.	0	4

	each—s.	d.
Madame Arthur Gue. Large umbels, flowers violet with white centre; dwarf plants of good habit, branched, very free-flowering; an excellent variety for growing in pots, and for massing or bedding ...	0	9
White Lady. Fine variety for bedding, and potted may be had in bloom in the greenhouse throughout the Winter; deliciously scented ... per doz. 3s. 6d.	0	4

TROPÆOLUM "COMET."

Tropæolum "Comet."

each—s. d.

An extremely beautiful, free-flowering, and graceful-growing variety; splendid for pots or hanging-baskets in the greenhouse or conservatory. The blooms, which are elegantly formed, are of the most intense deep brilliant scarlet colour, and form an admirable contrast with the rich glaucous green foliage of the plants. It blooms profusely throughout the Summer and Autumn months, and with a moderate warmth will bloom freely throughout the Winter and Spring
3 for 1s. 3d.; per doz. 4s. 6d.   0   6

Fuchsia procumbens.

An exceedingly pretty trailing species from New Zealand, with small round leaves and bearing small erect flowers with yellowish tube, the upper portion reflexed blue. Capital plant for suspended baskets or pots in the greenhouse   ...   .   3 for 1s. 3d.   0   6

Fuchsia triphylla.

A beautiful and very distinct Winter and Spring flowering species for the warm greenhouse. The neat foliage is of a dark bronzy green, and the flowers are of the most lovely brilliant orange scarlet colour; very attractive and striking in appearance   3 for 2s. 6d.   1   0

Campanula isophylla.

each—s. d.

Beautiful dwarf trailing species, bearing large lilac blue salver-shaped flowers; a gem for pots   3 for 1s. 3d.   0   6
Alba.   A white form of the preceding   3 for 1s. 3d.   0   6

Crassula jasminoides.

Beautiful pot plant for the cool greenhouse, growing about nine inches high, and bearing heads of pure white Jasmine or Bouvardia-like flowers   per doz. 5s.   0   6

Impatiens Sultani.

(THE SULTAN'S BALSAM.)

This is without doubt one of the most brilliant and beautiful plants of recent introduction. Its flowers, which are single, are of a beautiful bright magenta rose colour, and are produced in the greatest profusion throughout the year, forming a splendid plant alike for the greenhouse, conservatory, or the dinner-table. It is a fine perennial, easily cultivated, and should be in every greenhouse   ...   ...   3 for 1s. 3d.   0   6

Mimulus.

Daniels' Large-flowered Hybrids.   In beautiful variety   ...   ...   per doz. 2s. 6d.; 6 for 1s. 6d.   —

Musk.

Harrison's Giant.   Splendid variety of a robust habit of growth, fine for pots   ...   per doz. 2s. 6d.   0   4
New Double-flowered.   Beautiful double yellow flowers quite as large as those of the old single form, but bearing no seed.
Strong young plants in April; 3 for 2s.   0   9

Pentstemons.

Beautiful showy plants, with graceful spikes of brilliant and delicately coloured flowers, resembling the Fox-glove somewhat in form of flower and habit of growth; height about two feet. Splendid for garden decoration and for cut flowers.

Choice named sorts, our selection
per doz. 3s. 6d.; 6 for 2s.   —

Streptosolen (Browallia) Jamesoni

A beautiful cool-greenhouse plant, growing to the height of three to five feet, bearing at the extremity of its branches dense panicles of thirty to forty flowers; in colour a pale orange at first, but changing to a bright cinnamon. It is a free and vigorous grower, and makes nice compact specimens if stopped from time to time. Strong young plants   ...   ...   3 for 2s.   0   9

Swainsona galegifolia alba.

Beautiful plant for the greenhouse, with clusters of pure white pea-like flowers   ...   ...   3 for 2s.   0   9

Francoa ramosa.

(THE BRIDAL WREATH PLANT.)

Beautiful half-hardy plant, throwing up long sprays of pure white flowers   0   6

Miscellaneous Bedding Plants, &c.

READY FOR SENDING OUT DURING MAY AND JUNE.

The prices quoted are for fine strong plants from single pots. All orders for these will be executed in the same rotation as received. Not less than 50 supplied at the rate per 100.

BEDDING GERANIUMS (Pelargoniums).

	per doz.—s. d.			per doz.—s. d.
Crimson, Henry Jacoby	per 100, 30s. 4 0	Silver Tricolor. Lass o' Gowrie, Mrs. John		
Pink, Master Christine	„ 24s. 3 6	Clutton, Mrs. Laing ... ... each 6d.		5 0
Salmon, Mrs. G. Smith...	„ 24s. 3 6	Silver-leaved. Avalanche. Pure white flowers ...		6 0
Scarlet, Vesuvius. Splendid bedder	„ 21s. 3 0	„ Charming Bride		6 0
White, Queen of the Belgians	„ 24s. 3 6	„ Flower of Spring ... per 100, 24s.		3 6
Verona. Golden foliage, pink flowers	... ... 6 0	„ Happy Thought ... „ 30s.		4 0
Crystal Palace Gem. Beautiful	per 100, 24s. 3 6	„ May Queen		6 0
Golden Tricolor. Lady Cullum	per 100, 30s. 4 0	„ Mrs. Mappin. White flowers ...		6 0
„ Sophie Dumaresque	„ 30s. 4 0	Bronze-leaved. Black Douglas „ 30s.		4 0
„ In fine variety to name ...	... each 9d. 8 0	„ Marechal McMahon ... „ 30s.		4 0

	per doz.—s. d.		per doz.—s. d.
Ageratum. Dwarf. Blue ... per 100, 17s. 6d.	2 6	Heliotrope. White Lady. Fine for bouquets ...	4 0
Alternanthera amœna. Bright red foliage		Mixed sorts ... ... per 100, 21s.	3 0
per 100, 17s. 6d.	2 6	Hollyhocks. Fine double, Seedlings 4s. 6d. and	4 0
„ aurea nana. Clear golden yellow foliage	3 0	Lobelia. Blue Stone ... ... per 100, 17s. 6d.	2 6
Alyssum (Koniga) Silver-variegated per 100, 17s. 6d.	2 6	King of the Blues. Dark blue, with conspicuous	
Arabis lucida variegata. Dwarf, yellow variegated		white eye ... ... per 100, 18s. 6d.	3 0
foliage; capital edging plant ...	4 0	Pumila grandiflora ... ... 17s. 6d.	2 6
Calceolaria. Golden Gem ... ... per 100, 21s.	3 0	White Perfection ... ... 17s. 6d.	2 6
Canterbury Bells. From single pots ...	3 6	Cardinalis Victoria. Splendid scarlet ...	4 0
Centaurea candidissima. Beautiful silvery foliage,		Marguerites or Parisian Daisies per 100, 24s.	3 6
dwarf ... ... per 100, 21s.	3 0	Mesembryanthemum cordifolium varie-	
Coleus Verschaffelti splendens. Fine and effective		gatum. Splendid bedding plant ...	2 6
variety for bedding ... ... per 100, 25s.	4 0	Pentstemons. In beautiful variety ... 4s. and	4 0
Diplacus Californicus. Flowers orange buff ...	4 0	Petunias. Fine mixed Seedlings per 100, 17s. 6d.	2 6
Echeveria secunda glauca ... per 100, 21s.	3 0	Pyrethrum. Golden Feather ... 7s. 6d.	1 0
Funkia lanceolata marginata. Handsome varie-		Salvias, Scarlet, Blue, White. Beautiful showy plants	3 0
gated foliage, a good edging plant ...	5 0	Verbenas. Scarlet ... ... per 100, 21s.	3 0
Gazania splendens. Beautiful golden yellow flowers,		Pink, purple, and white ... ... each „ 21s.	3 0
dwarf ... ... per 100, 21s.	3 0	In twelve beautiful varieties to name „ 30s.	4 6

OUR GUINEA HAMPER OF CHOICE BEDDING PLANTS, &c.,

CONTAINS THE FOLLOWING LIBERAL ASSORTMENT:—

30 Geraniums, assorted	12 Petunias, mixed	6 Phloxes, choice perennial
12 Verbenas, assorted	12 Pansies or Violas	6 Heliotropes
12 Calceolarias, yellow	6 Chrysanthemums, choice named	4 Pentstemons
24 Pyrethrum, Golden Feather	6 Dahlias, named	12 Hardy Flowering Plants
18 Lobelias, dark blue	6 Fuchsias, named	

Half the above quantity 11s. 6d.; double quantity 40s.

No Charge for Hampers or Packing.   *Ready for delivery in May.*   *Orders executed in same rotation as received.*

PLANTS IN POTS FOR GREENHOUSE DECORATION, &c.

		per doz.—s. d.
BEGONIAS. Single-flowered hybrids. Strong growing plants		6s. and 9 0
„ Double „ „ Strong growing plants		9s. and 12 0
CHRYSANTHEMUMS (JAPANESE, &c.). Choice named sorts		6s. and 12 0
COLEUS. New and choice sorts		6s. and 9 0
GERANIUMS (PELARGONIUMS), ZONAL. Single-flowered. New and choice sorts ...		9s. and 12 0
„ „ „ „ Choice named sorts ...		4s. 6d. and 6 0
„ „ „ Double-flowered		6s. and 9 0
„ Ivy-leaved. Splendid for baskets or vases. Choice named double-flowered varieties ...		4s. 6d. and 6 0
PELARGONIUMS (GERANIUMS). Show and Regal. Choice named sorts		9s., 12s., 15s., and 18 0
FUCHSIAS. Single and double-flowered. In beautiful variety to name		4s. 6d., 6s., and 9 0

Seedling Plants of Choice Florists' Flowers, &c.

POST OR CARRIAGE FREE.

READY FOR SENDING OUT IN MAY.   **READY IN JULY AND AUGUST.**

	per doz.	per 100.		per doz.	per 100.
	s. d.	s. d.		s. d.	s. d.
Asters, Pæony-flowered and Victoria	1 0	6 0	Calceolarias. Very choice strain ...	1 6	10 6
Balsams, Improved Camellia-flowered	1 6	10 6	Carnations. Choicest double ...	1 6	10 6
Carnations, Margaret ...	1 6	10 6	Cinerarias. From a grand strain ...	1 6	10 6
Hollyhock. Choicest double ...	3 6	—	Primulas, Crimson King ...	2 6	—
Gloxinias. Very choice strain ...	3 6	—	„ Alba magnifica ...	2 6	—
Pansies, Prize Blotched. Splendid ...	1 6	10 6	„ Blue. Very fine strain ...	2 6	—
Petunias, Large-flowered. Single ...	1 6	10 6	„ Choicest mixed ...	1 6	10 6

Tuberous-rooted Begonias.

SINGLE-FLOWERED VARIETIES.

We have much pleasure in offering tubers of our grand strain of Tuberous-rooted hybrid Begonias, which have been grown and selected at our Nurseries during the past season, and which for form, size, and substance of flower, and beauty and variety of colouring will be found second to none.

The individual blooms of many of the single-flowered varieties are of immense size—often measuring over six inches across—of splendid form and substance, and the colours range from the most intense dark crimson through all the shades of scarlet, salmon, cerise, and yellow to the purest white, the plants being of a fine, dwarf, sturdy habit of growth. They will be found splendid for pot culture and for bedding out; much superior to Geraniums, as they continue in full bloom through the wettest season and late into the Autumn, when Geraniums have but a poor appearance.

Their treatment when grown in pots is the same as that recommended for the doubles. When bedded out, however, they will thrive in almost any wet or other soil, if fairly good, but a good rich soil with the addition of some leaf mould and well-decayed manure suits them best. The tubers should be started in March, in boxes or small pots of light rich soil, placed in a gentle heat, or they may be placed in a cool frame. Keep moderately dry till they have started into growth, when they may have more moisture and plenty of air on warm days. About the first week in June they will be ready for planting out. Plant out nine or twelve inches apart, and give the beds a good top-dressing of some well-decayed manure, keeping them well supplied with water if the weather sets in dry. As soon as cut down by the frost they should be taken up, dried, and stored for the Winter, as recommended on opposite page.

SINGLE-FLOWERED BEGONIA.

CHOICE NAMED VARIETIES.

Specially selected when in bloom, none but really first-class varieties are included.

	each—s.	d.
Alice Hampson. Bright glowing salmon; perfectly erect, well-formed flowers of grand substance	3	0
Aurora. Very bright glowing fiery-scarlet; very free...	2	0
Bexley White. The grandest white single Begonia ever sent out; blooms of immense size, perfect form, and of the purest white. First Class Certificate	2	6
Black Knight. Very dark crimson, flowers of great substance	2	0
Champion (new). Deep rich bronzy yellow, a lovely colour; flowers very large, superb variety. F.C.C.	4	0
Challenger. Dark crimson, fine substance	2	6
Goliath. Rich golden bronzy yellow, darker in the centre; a lovely flower. First Class Certificate	3	6
Heroine. Brilliant vermilion; a bold flower and a grand bloomer	2	6
Leonora. Beautiful bright pink; very attractive	2	6
Marginata. Flowers large, pure white, with a fine pink line on the margins of the petals	2	6
Minnie Cleave. Rich rosy scarlet, very large; splendid exhibition flower	4	0
Paragon. Beautiful salmon rose, peculiar and pleasing shade	2	6
Perfection. Dark orange yellow; a grand flower	2	6
Purity. A grand white, having beautiful round symmetrical flowers. One of the best flowers	2	0
Rosea superba. Beautiful rose, splendidly formed flowers	2	6
Sovereign. The best yellow, large, brilliant, deep-coloured flowers of great substance; magnificent variety	2	6
Superba. Brilliant orange scarlet, exquisitely beautiful	2	6
Valkyrie (new). A pretty shade of salmon, will become a great favourite	2	6
Vigilant. Rich glowing crimson; perfect flowers of immense size	4	0

Choice named sorts, our selection from the above list per doz. 21s. and 30s.

Single-flowered Begonias.

Extra choice Exhibition varieties. A very fine selection indeed, the flowers which are of the most perfect form, are of immense size and of the most brilliant and charming variety of colour, equal to the finest named flowers. Highly recommended   *per doz.*—s. d.   18 0

For Greenhouse and Conservatory. A very fine mixture of choice selected flowers, mostly equal to the named sorts, the flowers being perfect in form and of the most beautiful colours   9s. & 12 0

For Pot culture. A capital mixture of beautiful colours, the varieties all being carefully selected and really good. Considering the high-class quality, we consider these remarkably cheap   per 100, 40s.   6 0

BEDDING VARIETIES.

		per doz. s. d.	per 100. s. d.
Crimson and Scarlet	Distinct and beautiful colours, highly effective for bedding out. All in strong flowering tubers that will produce a charming display. Should be kept well supplied with water during dry weather.	4 0	30 0
Rose and Carmine ...		4 0	30 0
Pink and Salmon ...		4 0	30 0
Primrose and Citron		4 0	30 0
Orange and Bronze		4 0	30 0
Pure white ...		5 0	35 0

Choice mixed seedlings. In beautiful variety, all approved flowers from our fine collection   3 6   25 0

Tuberous-rooted Begonias.

DOUBLE-FLOWERED VARIETIES.

The Double-flowered Begonias, with their grand massive blooms, and their wonderful variety of exquisite colours, ranging through all the most beautiful shades of scarlet, crimson, salmon, rose, and yellow, to the purest white, are eminently suited for pot culture. They are easily grown, and when in bloom form magnificent objects for the greenhouse or conservatory.

The best soil for growing Begonias in pots is a good compost of turfy loam, leaf mould, and some coarse sand. Pot the tubers, any size, as early as convenient in Spring, in rather small pots with good drainage, and place in a warm greenhouse. Keep fairly moist, and take care that the heat is not too forcing. As growth advances, keep near the glass, and give plenty of air on warm days. Shift into larger pots as the plants require, and give them a watering with liquid manure about twice a week. When blooming is over in Autumn, the tubers should be gradually dried off, and when quite dormant, they should be placed in dry soil, and put in any dry cellar or cupboard out of the reach of frost till again wanted for starting.

DOUBLE-FLOWERED BEGONIA.

From Mr. J. BULLOCK, Nantwich.

Aug. 7th.
"I have pleasure in sending you word about the **Begonias** I had from you. I won First Prize for a collection of Begonias, and I exhibited a Begonia which was three feet across it both ways, and covered with a mass of beautiful white flowers"

SUPERB NAMED VARIETIES.

	each—s.	d.
Alba fimbriata plena. Beautiful pure white, with prettily crimped edges; very attractive	3	6
Alba Rosea. Pink, with pure white centre	2	0
Beauty of Belgrove. Beautiful rose, resembling in form and colour the Rose *La France*	2	6
Bexley Gem. Rich dark rose colour, of perfect form; a splendid flower	5	6
Bridesmaid. Large, beautifully formed flowers; colour, a lovely blush pink	2	6
Brilliant. Bright scarlet, flowers of immense size; one of the very finest	5	0
Claribel. Salmon pink with white centre; an exquisite flower	3	0
Doris. Delicate rosy pink, shading to white in the centre, a superb flower of grand form	2	0
Dr. Masters. Rather small flowers, freely produced on a sturdy compact growing plant; colour, a soft creamy white; a gem for cutting	2	0
Duchess of Teck. Golden yellow, large, beautiful, well-formed flowers, and handsome dark green foliage	4	0
Duke of Teck. The finest double crimson in cultivation, large, well-formed flowers of the most distinct glowing crimson-scarlet colour	4	0
Elegans. Salmon with white centre; beautiful variety for button-holes or bouquets	5	0
Henshaw Russell. Brilliant scarlet, splendidly formed camellia-like blooms, very distinct and splendid. F.C.C.	4	0
Manora. Dark rose, well-formed and capital exhibition flower	2	6
Miss Jennie Fell. A charming camellia-shaped flower, of a deep rosy crimson colour; fine dwarf habit. F.C.C.	5	0
Phœbus. Large golden yellow flowers; one of the best	3	6
Picotee. Large, beautifully-formed, camellia-like flowers; colour, a lovely white, edged with bright pink; most charming variety	6	0
Princess May. Beautiful pure white camellia-shaped flowers, with handsomely crimped edges; superb variety. First Class Certificate	7	6
Salmonea. Rich salmon, splendid flowers borne on gracefully drooping flower stems; well adapted for hanging baskets	2	0
Venice. Pure white, grand, beautifully-formed flowers on straight, erect stems; a vigorous grower ...	4	0

Choice named varieties, from above list, our selection ... per doz. 30s., 36s., 40s., 45s., and 50s.
Six superb varieties, including Duke of Teck, Duchess of Teck, and Princess May ... ... 20s.

Double-flowered Begonias.

IN CHOICE MIXTURE.

per doz.—s. d.
Extra choice varieties for exhibition. All carefully selected fine double flowers of the most splendid form and colour. A grand selection ... 24s. & 30 0
Mixed Doubles for Bedding. A capital variety of large, full, double flowers, in beautiful variety of colour ... ... per 100, 40s. 6 0

per doz.—s. d.
For Pot culture. A superb selection of choice sorts equal to named varieties, the flowers being of the most perfect form, and of the most varied and beautiful colours. Highly desirable for conservatory decoration ... ... 9s., 12s., & 18 0

Mixed Double and Semi-double. Good showy sorts for bedding out, &c. ... per 100, 25s.; per doz. 3s. 6d.

Grand New Carnations for 1896.

The varieties named below are of exceptional merit, and highly recommended.

CARNATION, PRIDE OF GREAT BRITAIN, was awarded First Class Certificates at Manchester, Regent's Park, Crystal Palace, Forestry Exhibition, Earl's Court, and an Award of Merit by the Royal Horticultural Exhibition.

CARNATION, PRIDE OF GREAT BRITAIN, was awarded First Class Certificates at Manchester, Regent's Park, Crystal Palace, Forestry Exhibition, Earl's Court, and an Award of Merit by the Royal Horticultural Exhibition.

CARNATION, PRIDE OF GREAT BRITAIN.

PRIDE OF GREAT BRITAIN (Fry). This is undoubtedly the largest and finest yellow border Carnation ever raised, and may fairly be described as a yellow Malmaison, although the foliage is not so broad, it is quite as strong growing; wonderfully free blooming with pure yellow flowers of immense size. A grand novelty ... ... strong plants, each 2s. 6d.

COUNTESS OF SEFTON. An exceptionally fine variety that will be highly appreciated. The flowers are large, slightly fringed at the edges, and the colour is a lovely soft shade of pink. It is a very free bloomer, very hardy, and one of the very best for cutting purposes ... ... each 2s.

MRS. CHARLES DANIELS (Ware). A sterling novelty, one of the finest of this season's introduction, and which we can with every confidence recommend. It is remarkably free flowering, a strong robust grower, producing plenty of grass. The flowers are full, of fine form, and very sweet scented, the colour being a deep flesh pink; splendid for cutting ... . each 2s.

MISS MINNIE CLARKE. Deep yellow ground, edged and slightly striped with crimson. A strong grower, and very free flowering ... . each 2s.

YELLOW QUEEN (Improved Pride of Penshurst). A fine strong grower, bearing flowers of a lovely soft yellow colour, deliciously scented, and never bursts its calyx. The blooms being well formed and of good substance .. .. each 2s.

One of each above five superb varieties, 9s.

Carnations and Picotees.

Our Grounds are peculiarly well suited for the cultivation of these charming and highly popular flowers, and we have much pleasure in stating that our stock for the present season, consisting of many thousands of the choicest varieties in commerce, is in unusually fine condition, the plants being thoroughly healthy and well-rooted. As we have a very great demand for Carnations and Picotees, we respectfully beg that, to prevent disappointment, our Customers will kindly favour us with their orders as early as convenient.

NEW AND VERY CHOICE SORTS.

	each—s.	d.
Alice Ayres. Pure pearly white, the centre petals delicately marked with carmine, most beautiful form	1	0
Ambassador. Light purple, very compact; a large and remarkably fine flower	1	0
Anna Benary. White, beautifully striped with carmine; very dwarf, requiring no sticks	1	0
Cantab. Deep bright scarlet self, as powerfully scented as the Old Clove	1	6
Cara Roma. A beautiful glowing maroon with a soft blending of mulberry; a large flower of fine substance	1	6
Countess of Paris. Delicate flesh colour, fine	1	6
Duc de Raqeuse. Velvety-crimson, compact flower	1	0
Duchess of Fife. A quite distinct and most beautiful variety. The flowers are of good size and perfect form, with broad petals of great substance, the colour being a most lovely shade of delicate rosy-pink	2	0
Duke of Fife (new). Clear soft salmon-scarlet, one of the largest and finest ever introduced	2	0
Duke of York. Flowers large, of excellent form, and of the richest blood-crimson colour	1	6
Empress. Beautiful pure white, with shell-like petals, a large smooth flower of first-class quality	1	6
Favourite. White ground, edged rose; a good flower	1	0
Germania. Large, bold, perfectly formed flowers, with broad flat petals; colour, a soft pure yellow. First Class Certificate, R.H.S. ... 3 for 2s. 6d.	1	0
Gertrude Teigner. Rich pink; of medium size, fine shape, and heavy petal; a great favourite	1	0
Gloire de Nancy. Large pure white clove-scented...	0	8
Hon. W. Lowther. Brilliant clear scarlet, the edges of the petals slightly serrated. The plant is of sturdy compact growth, and a most profuse bloomer. The flowers do not burst the calyx, and owing to their splendid and striking colour will prove of great value for cutting ... ... 3 for 3s. 6d.	1	6
Lady Wantage. The finest white Carnation yet raised. The plant is of strong vigorous growth, of excellent habit and marvellously free-flowering	3	0
Lucy. White, beautifully striped, edged pink	1	0

	each—s.	d.
Leander. Intense deep yellow self, a fine heavy shell-like petal, especially useful in wet seasons	2	0
L. H. Pomeroy. Deep crimson; an extra fine and large flower; strong grower	1	0
Miss Joliffe (Perpetual). Pale pink, dwarf habit, very fine flowering, splendid for Winter blooming	1	6
Montague. Rich deep scarlet, a very large flower of splendid form and substance; said to be the finest scarlet variety ever offered to the public	2	0
Mr. Dennis. Primrose yellow self, medium size	1	0
Mrs. Frank Watts. Flowers very large and full, smooth edge, beautiful pure white, very fragrant	1	6
Mrs. Muir. Fine pure white; medium-sized flowers; very free and dwarf	1	0
Mrs. Reynolds Hole. Quite a novel shade of colour, salmon-apricot; producing a great quantity of flowers	1	0
Mrs. Thornhill. Beautiful bright salmon-pink, delicately fringed; does not split the calyx	1	0
Pride of Penshurst. Deep clear yellow; a large flower of beautiful form, and strong free habit	1	0
Purity. Beautiful pure white, dwarf and free blooming	1	6
Raby Castle. Clear soft salmon-pink, neatly fringed...	1	0
Redbraes (Picotee). White ground, edged with purple	1	0
Rose Celestial. Clear soft rose; a large full flower, one of the very best of this particular shade	1	6
Sandringham White. Splendid for cutting	1	0
Sir Beauchamp Seymour. Orange buff, edged with carmine, extra free. First Class Certificate...	1	6
Souvenir de la Malmaison. Well known grand old variety with very large delicate pink flowers	1	6
Souvenir de la Malmaison, New Crimson. A grand novelty, bearing immense rose-like flowers; colour, a deep velvety crimson-scarlet, splendid variety	2	0
Terra-Cotta. Terra-cotta ground colour, beautifully edged with bright pink, large, full, and of perfect form	1	6
The Coroner. Rich scarlet, early and free ...	1	6
Uriah Pike. Rich clear crimson self, smooth, very fragrant, and a vigorous hardy grower. The best Winter and Spring-flowering variety	2	6

Carnations and Picotees in Collections.

50 in 50 choice named sorts	**40s.**
25 in 25 extra choice sorts	**21s.**
25 in 25 standard varieties	**17s. 6d.**
12 in 12 extra choice sorts	**12s.**
12 in 12 good sorts	**9s.**
12 in 12 popular varieties	**6s.**

PERPETUAL or TREE CARNATIONS in Pots—
A good collection of choice sorts per doz. 18s., 21s., 24s., & 30s.

YELLOW AND YELLOW-GROUND CARNA-TIONS AND PICOTEES—
Including all the leading varieties, our selection per doz. 18s.

SELECTED BORDER CARNATIONS (Seedlings)—
All good double flowers, and in fine variety; strong plants
per doz. 4s. 6d.

CRIMSON CLOVE. The fine old spice-scented variety ... ... per doz. 5s.; each 6d.

White Clove. Pure white, deliciously scented per doz. 5s.; each 6d.

Garden Pinks.

	each—s.	d.
Annie Boleyn. Deep rose; dark centre; large and free flowering	0	6
Alice Lee. Creamy white; neat and compact	0	6
Clove Pink. Deep rose; flowers full, fringed, and clove scented	0	6
Derby Day. Deep pink, heavily laced purple	0	6
Eclipse. Heavy dark red lacing	0	6
Early Blush. Blush pink, large double fringed flowers per doz. 4s. 6d.	0	6
Her Majesty. The finest and best White Garden Pink in cultivation. Has been awarded nine First Class Certificates ... per doz. 5s.	0	6

	each—s.	d.
Mrs. J. M. Welsh. Large entire pure white flowers, lacking the green centre and the tendency to burst which is sometimes exhibited in the case of *Mrs. Sinkins* per doz. 5s.	0	6
Mrs. Sinkins. Large pure white, dwarf free habit, very hardy ... per doz. 5s.	0	6
Mrs. Waite. Rosy red	—	—
Old double white fringed. Very sweet per doz. 2s. 6d.	—	—
Paddington. Deep rose, dark centre, edge fringed	0	6
Scarlet Gem. Dark red	0	6
Choice named varieties. Including the most beautiful laced sorts, our selection ... per doz. 4s. 6d.	—	—

Miscellaneous Spring-flowering Plants.

BEDDING PANSIES AND VIOLAS.

THE Pansies and Violas are amongst the very best of our Spring and Summer flowering bedders. They are wonderfully free-flowering and pretty, and will thrive in almost any soil, but should not be planted in a hot dry position. A spot where they are shaded from strong sunshine for some part of the day, a north or west border, suits them admirably, and a fair supply of weak liquid manure in dry weather will keep them in splendid flower.

Ardwell Gem. Sulphur yellow, dwarf habit. A profuse bloomer ... ... per doz. 4s. 6d.; each 6d.

Blue King. Magnificent variety, producing an abundance of large deep ultramarine blue flowers, which continue from early Spring till late in Autumn; should be in every garden ... ... per 100, 16s.; per doz. 3s.; each 4d.

Cliveden Purple. Fine large flowers of a rich bright purple colour, a constant bloomer
per 100, 15s.; per doz. 2s. 6d.; each 3d.

Cloth of Gold. Beautiful bright yellow with dark centre, very effective for Spring gardening
per 100, 16s.; per doz. 3s.; each 4d.

Duchess of Fife. Large flowers of a delicate primrose yellow shade, neatly edged with mauve; the centre is slightly shaded with orange; a very pretty variety per doz. 6s.; each 9d.

Golden Gem. Deep golden yellow, a free grower and first rate bedder ... ... per doz. 3s., each 4d.

Holyrood. Deep indigo-blue, with dark blotch, one of the finest ... ... per doz. 6s.; each 9d.

Jeffrey's White. Pure white, dwarf per doz., 6s.; each 8d.

Max Kohl. Dark purplish maroon „ 4s.; „ 6d.

Mont Blanc. White, very free „ 4s.; „ 6d.

Mr. Bennett. Large, beautiful pure white flowers, with a lovely blue blotch in centre per doz. 4s. 6d.; each 6d.

Souvenir. Rich lavender „ 4s. 0d.; „ 6d.

Virginale. Pure white, a very fine bloom
per doz. 6s.; each 9d.

Our own selection, per 100, 21s.; per doz. 4s.

Show and Fancy. A splendid collection of choice named sorts, our own selection ... per doz. 6s. and 9s.

PRIMROSES AND POLYANTHUSES.

A BEAUTIFUL and indispensable class of brilliant Spring-flowering plants, blooming at the same time as Narcissi and many other bulbs; many of the single-flowered varieties are exceedingly handsome.

Double White ... ... per doz. 6s.; each 8d.
„ **Lilac** ... „ 6s.; „ 8d.
„ **Yellow** ... ... „ 6s.; „ 8d.
„ **Purplish-crimson** ... „ 10s.; „ 1s.
Single "Harbinger." A superb large-flowered, early blooming variety, with lovely white flowers with an orange centre ... ... per doz. 10s. 6d.; each 1s.

Single, mixed hybrids. Very fine and brilliant
per 100, 17s. 6d.; per doz. 2s. 6d.
Polyanthus, Gold-laced. Fine seedlings, all good flowers
per doz. 3s. 6d.
Oxlip, Prince of Orange. Large trusses of rich orange-coloured flowers, very fine and effective each 1s.

Alpine Auriculas. The Alpine Auriculas in their many beautiful varieties are eminently suited alike for Spring flowering, in pots in the greenhouse, or the open border. The flowers from our improved strain are exceedingly brilliant and varied in colour.

Choice Named sorts per doz. 12s., 18s., and 24s.
Selected Seedlings. Strong plants, from our very fine strain per doz., 4s. 6d.
„ „ Smaller plants „ 2s. 6d.

Myosotis dissitiflora (Forget-me-not).
Exceedingly valuable Spring-flowering plant, producing a great profusion of bright sky blue flowers; a fine bedding variety, the best of all Forget-me-nots
per doz. 3s. 6d.; each 4d.

Double Daisies. Well known beautiful and brilliant little plants for edgings of beds or borders, which continue in bloom throughout the months of April and May; the dark crimson and pure white are very handsome.

Large crimson, double ... per 100, 16s.; per doz. 2s. 6d.
Large white „ ... „ 16s.; „ 2s. 6d.
Large pink „ ... „ 12s.; „ 2s. 0d.
Wallflowers. Old Double yellow. A fine plant for Spring decoration ... ... 3 for 2s.; each 9d.
Old Double dark red or purple. Very useful and fine old sort ... ... 3 for 2s.; each 9d.
Single, blood red per 100, 7s. 6d.; per doz. 1s. 0d.
„ **yellow** „ 7s. 6d.; „ 1s. 0d.
Double German „ 10s. 6d.; „ 1s. 6d.

PENTSTEMONS.

A VERY beautiful class of Summer and Autumn-blooming plants that should be extensively grown. They form neat-growing bushes, and throw up graceful spikes 1½ to 2½ feet high, covered with large, handsome Gloxinia-like flowers, and when planted in beds or masses have a grand effect. They include almost every shade of colour, from the purest white to the deepest crimson, shades of rose, scarlet, purple, &c.; are easily grown in any garden border, and are best planted out in April or May. By pinching out the leading shoots after blooming in Summer, the plants will start into fresh growth and furnish a beautiful display of flowers quite into the Autumn. For the general adornment of the garden, or for cut flowers, these cannot be too highly recommended.

NEW AND SELECT VARIETIES.

Our own selection, from the following list, per doz. **6s.** Customers' selection, per doz., **9s.**

Agnes Wickfield. White, edged and shaded with rosy lilac: extra fine spike.

Alliance. Clear French white; a good spike.

Andrew Hunter. Rosy scarlet, pencilled throat; a pleasing shade, and very effective.

Constance. Deep crimson rose, throat pencilled with light carmine; a noble spike.

F. Burnaby. White throat, and lovely carmine rose flower; very fine.

General Nansonby. A kind of mulberry colour, throat striped with chocolate; fine large spike.

Little Pet. Dark rose, white throat; very pretty variety.

Lord Byron. Large violet purple flower, white throat, very slightly blotched; good flower and spike.

Lord Hillingdon. Rich rosy lilac, with a clear white throat; large noble spike, very effective.

Madame de Faydeaux. Rich purplish violet; a fine, distinct variety.

Madame Antoinette Sterling. Rich coral red, with fine pure white throat; an extra large spike.

Miss Alice Gomez. Pleasing shade of salmon-rose, throat pencilled with magenta; a bold spike.

Mrs. Sterry. Lovely bright rosy peach, clear white throat; a fine variety.

Mr. Peggotty. Bright salmon pink, light pencilled throat; of good habit.

Norma. Fine bright rose, pure white throat; large spike, very pretty.

Hybrid Perpetual Roses.

This magnificent and beautiful class of Roses is better than any other adapted for garden and pot culture, and for exhibition. They continue in flower from the early part of June to the end of October, and are by far the most desirable for general cultivation. Our stock of these comprises many thousands of the newest and choicest varieties in standards and dwarfs, and the past season having been very favourable to their growth, the plants we offer will be found unusually well grown and vigorous, and may be expected to produce a fine display of bloom next season.

Hints on Cultivation.—Generally speaking the Rose will thrive in any good garden soil, but as it has a decided preference for that which inclines to the clayey or loamy, it is advisable in planting, where the soil is not of a suitable nature, to make for each plant a hole of about eighteen inches diameter, removing a sufficient quantity of soil to admit of about a bushel of good rough loam with the addition of a fair quantity of well-decayed stable manure incorporated, in which to place the roots. If planting be done in dry weather in Autumn or in Spring, the roots of the plants should be well watered before filling in with soil, and at all times the standards should be firmly staked and tied to prevent their disturbance by the wind. To ensure a vigorous growth, Roses should be cut back the first season from planting to two or three eyes or buds on each shoot. The best time to do this is about March, but a longer succession of bloom may be had by pruning some at intervals from the new year to the beginning of April. November is perhaps the best month for planting, but it may be done with perfect safety any time from October to March.

NEW H. P. MARCHIONESS OF LORNE. Dwarfs 2s. each.

Hybrid Perpetual Roses in Collections.

These collections are carefully made up to ensure a fine variety, and customers ordering may depend on their giving the most unqualified satisfaction. In all cases good healthy plants will be sent, and in the best variety of colour, &c., that can be included in the number given, but in all instances the selection must be left to ourselves.

CARRIAGE FREE. IMPORTANT NOTICE.

To meet the requirements of many of our numerous customers, we send all these collections Carriage Free to any part of the British Isles at prices quoted, and we make no charge for packing.

	Stds. & Half-Stds.	Dwarfs.
12 in 12 of the most select varieties	£1 10 0	£0 10 6
12 in 12 good and popular varieties	1 4 0	0 7 6
25 in 25 of the most select varieties	2 10 0	1 0 0
25 in 25 good and popular varieties	2 0 0	0 14 0
50 in 50 of the most select varieties	4 0 0	1 10 0
50 in 50 good and popular varieties	3 10 0	1 7 6
100 in 50 of the most select varieties	7 10 0	3 0 0
100 in 50 good and popular varieties	7 0 0	2 10 0

Daniels' Special Collections of H. P. Roses.

We have much pleasure in recommending the following collections of Hybrid Perpetual Roses, which contain the very best selection of varieties that can be included in the quantities given, and which are guaranteed to give the highest satisfaction. We shall feel obliged if customers when ordering these collections, will kindly name two or three other varieties which may be sent in case of our being sold out of any of those specially named.

Abel Carriere	† * Duke of Edinburgh	Jean Liabaud	† * Merveille de Lyon
† * Alfred Colomb	Dupuy Jamain	John Bright	† * Mrs. J. Laing
Alphonse Soupert	* Earl of Dufferin	* John Hopper	Pride of Waltham
† * Baroness Rothschild	† * Eclair	† * La France	* Prince Camille de Rohan
* Beauty of Waltham	† * Etienne Levet	Madame Gabrielle Luizet	* Raoul Guillard
† * Captain Christy	General Jacquiminot	Madame Lacharme	* Silver Queen
* Charles Lefebvre	† * Grand Mogul	Madame Victor Verdier	* Ulrich Brunner
† * Comte de Mortemart	* Heinrich Schultheis	† * Marie Baumann	* Violette Bouyer
* Countess of Oxford	* Hippolyte Jamain	Marquise de Castellane	* Xavier Olibo

Thirty-six splendid varieties, as named above, in fine dwarfs or bushes £1 6 0
Twenty-five choice sorts, as marked (*) ,, ,, ... 0 18 0
Twelve very choice varieties as marked (†) ,, ,, ... 0 10 6

Carefully packed and sent Carriage Free at prices quoted.

Roses—Tea-scented and Noisette.

This beautiful class is distinguished by the peculiar and delightful fragrance of the flowers, and the many charming tints and shades of yellow, rose and salmon colour, not to be found amongst the hybrid perpetuals. The individual blooms are of exquisite form, and invaluable for button-holes or bouquets. They are especially suited for pot culture in the conservatory, and planted outside on slightly raised beds in a sheltered position, and given a slight protection in Winter, they will furnish some beautiful flowers throughout the Summer and Autumn. The following list contains a very choice assortment.

	Dwarfs—s.	d.
Adam. Rose, shaded salmon, large, globular, and very sweetly scented ...	1	6
Amazon. Deep lemon yellow; a very useful sort for cutting	1	6
Anna Olivier. Flesh-coloured rose	1	6
Belle Lyonnaise. Deep canary yellow	1	6
Bouquet d'Or (Noisette). Deep yellow, coppery centre	1	6
Caroline Testout (Hybrid Tea). Bright satin rose with brighter centre, large, full, and globular, very free and sweet; a charming rose ...	2	6
Catherine Mermet. Flesh-coloured rose ...	1	6
Celine Forestier (Noisette). Pale yellow ...	1	6
Cleopatra. Creamy flesh shaded rose; a superb variety	1	6
Comtesse de Nadaillac. Bright rose, with coppery yellow...	1	6
Comtesse Riza du Parc. Salmon rose, shaded with copper	1	6
Devoniensis. White, tinted yellow, beautiful ...	1	6
Ernest Metz. Soft carmine rose with brighter centre; very large, and of fine form; handsome bud ...	1	6
Ethel Brownlow. Salmon pink, shaded yellow at the base of petals, flowers of perfect form ...	2	0
Etoile de Lyon. Fine saffron yellow, large fine form	1	6
Francisca Kruger. Copper yellow, shaded peach, large and full ...	1	6
Gloire de Dijon. Buff, with orange centre. A well-known old favourite 1s. 6d., 2s. 6d., 3s. 6d., 5s., and	7	6
Grace Darling. Creamy white, shaded peach; very pretty...	1	6
Homero. Rose, centre salmon ...	1	6
Hon. Edith Gifford. White, centre flesh colour, large, and full, fine form; very free flowering variety	1	6
Innocente Pirola. Pure white, slightly rosy	1	6
Isabella Sprunt. Sulphur yellow	1	6
Jean Ducher. Salmon yellow, shaded with rose	1	6
La Boule d'Or. Bright golden yellow, large and of exquisite form ...	2	6
Lady Castlereagh (new). Soft rosy yellow, very large ...	2	6
L'Ideal (Noisette). Yellow and metallic red, streaked and tinted golden yellow; a charming variety of indescribable beauty	1	6
Ma Capucine. Nasturtium yellow, tinted copper; small but charming bud ...	2	0
Madame Bravy. Creamy white ...	1	6
Madame Charles. Deep apricot yellow; fine long buds and large flowers ...	1	6
Madame Cusin. Rosy purple, with pale yellow at base of petals, exquisitely formed ...	2	6

	Dwarfs—s.	d.
Madame Falcot. Apricot yellow, very distinct	1	6
Madame Lambard. Bright red, a fine variety	1	6
Madame Margottin. Deep yellow, centre rosy peach ...	1	6
Madame Plantier (Noisette). Pure white, free bloomer, beautiful and full; the finest of all pure white Roses for massing	1	0
Madame de Watteville. Salmony white edged with bright rose and pink; beautiful and distinct variety ...	2	0
Marechal Niel (Noisette). Beautiful golden yellow. Well known 1s. 6d., 2s. 6d., 3s. 6d., 5s., and	7	6
Marie Guillot. White, slightly tinted with yellow ...	1	6
Marie van Houtte. Lemon yellow, edged with lively rose, medium size, good form, beautiful 1s. 6d. and	2	6
Medea (new). Lemon colour, with canary yellow centre; very beautiful ...	2	6
Mrs. James Wilson. Deep lemon yellow, margined rose, very fine ...	2	6
Niphetos. Pale lemon, changing to white 1s. 6d. and	2	6
Perle de Lyon. Deep yellow; splendid ...	1	6
Perle des Jardins (Climbing). Straw colour; very fine for climbing	2	6
Perle des Jardins. Straw colour	1	6
Primrose Dame. Primrose yellow, apricot centre, fine form; very free flowering	2	6
Princess of Wales. Rosy yellow, centre deeper	1	6
Reve d'Or (Noisette). Deep yellow	1	6
Safrano. Bright apricot; beautiful...	1	6
Souvenir d'Elise Vardon. White, centre pale yellow	1	6
Souvenir d'un Ami. Salmon and rose ...	1	6
Souvenir de S. A. Prince. The finest Tea Rose offered in late years; flowers of the purest white 1s. 6d. and	2	6
Souvenir de Therese Levet. Deep red, shaded with scarlet, large, full, and a free bloomer	1	6
Sunset. Rich tawny saffron colour 1s. 6d. and	2	0
The Bride. A pure white sport from *Catherine Mermet;* most valuable for cutting purposes	2	0
Vicomtesse Folkestone. Lovely delicate creamy pink ...	2	6
W. F. Bennett. Crimson, large and double	2	6
Waban. A sport from *Catherine Mermet;* carmine pink splashed with madder red; flowers borne on long straight stems; very fine and distinct ...	2	6
William Allen Richardson (Noisette). Fine deep orange yellow, very showy and distinct; a gem for buttonholes and bouquets 1s. 6d., 2s. 6d., 3s. 6d., and	5	0

Our own selection, in choice variety, plants mostly established in pots, per doz. 15s., 18s., and 21s.

NEW POLYANTHA ROSE—TURNER'S CRIMSON RAMBLER.

This remarkable Rose, sent out last season, was originally received from Japan. The plant is of very vigorous growth, making shoots from eight to ten feet in height during a season, and is consequently a most desirable climbing variety, and when pegged down or grown as a bush, a marvellous head of bloom is the result, the two year old wood producing trusses of flower on every growth. It is also exceedingly hardy, having successfully withstood the test in exposed situations of two very severe winters in England.

The bright green glossy foliage with which the plant is covered very early in the Spring, forms a pleasing and striking contrast to the flowers which are produced in large trusses of pyramidal form, and of the brightest crimson colour, the blooms remaining on the plant for a great length of time, without falling or losing their brightness. The foliage is also retained to a great extent during the winter, making the plant almost an evergreen.

Three Gold Medals, as well as numerous **First Class Certificates**, have been awarded to this Rose.
Strong Plants, 2s. 6d., 3s. 6d. and 5s. each.

Climbing Roses, Hardy and others.

The following list of Climbing Roses includes the most useful and beautiful varieties in cultivation. For pillars, walls, or arches in exposed positions the fine old varieties of Ayrshire, Evergreen, Banksia, Boursault, Cheshunt Hybrid, Gloire de Dijon, and Aimee Vibert are the most desirable; whilst for greenhouse work the beautiful Marechal Niel, Climbing Niphetos, and Climbing Devoniensis are the best.

WILLIAM ALLEN RICHARDSON.

	s.	d.
Aimee Vibert (Noisette). Small pure white flowers in large clusters; very hardy	1	0
Ayrshire, Dundee Rambler. White, edged pink	1	0
,, **Queen of the Belgians.** Pure white ...	1	0
Banksia alba, or white. Pure white	1	6
,, lutea, or yellow. Fine yellow	1	6
Boursault (Rosa alpina), Amadis, or crimson	1	0
Cheshunt Hybrid. Bright cherry carmine, large open flowers; a very hardy and strong grower; fine 1s. and	2	6
Climbing Devoniensis (T). Magnificent strong-growing variety, flowers creamy white with blush centre; deliciously scented		
1s. 6d., 2s. 6d., 3s. 6d., 5s., and	7	6
Climbing Niphetos. A fine new, rapid growing, climbing tea-scented variety; blooms of a purer white than those of the old variety, not showing the pink tinge, and even more delicately scented. First Class Certificate, Royal Horticultural Society		
2s. 6d., 3s. 6d., 5s., and	7	6
Evergreen, Donna Maria. Pure white ...	1	0
,, **Felicite Perpetuelle.** Creamy white	1	0
,, **Leopoldine d'Orleans.** White, tipped red	1	0
,, **Myrianthes.** Blush, edged rose ...	1	0
,, **Rampant.** Pure white ...	1	0
Gloire de Dijon (T). Buff, with orange centre, well known, superb variety		
1s. 6d., 2s. 6d., 3s. 6d., 5s., and	7	6
L'Ideal (Noisette). Yellow and metallic red, streaked and tinted golden yellow; a charming and distinct variety of indescribable beauty ... extra strong plants 5s.	1	6
Marechal Niel (Noisette). Beautiful golden yellow of the most lovely form and delicious fragrance; well known, superb variety 1s. 6d., 2s. 6d., 3s. 6d., 5s., and	7	6
Perle des Jardins (Climbing). Straw colour; capital climber	2	6
*****Waltham Climber, No. 1.** } Light crimson	2	0
*****Waltham Climber, No. 3.** } Dark crimson	2	0
William Allen Richardson (Noisette). Fine deep orange yellow, very showy and distinct; a gem for buttonholes and bouquets; a capital variety for the greenhouse: a very strong grower		
1s. 6d., 2s. 6d., 3s. 6d., and	5	0

* Seedlings from the well-known Gloire de Dijon.

Miscellaneous Roses.

AUSTRIAN COPPER. Distinct and beautiful, golden terra-cotta colour, flowers single ... ... each 1s.

AUSTRIAN BRIER. Deep golden yellow, full, double flowers ... ... each 1s.

PERSIAN YELLOW. The deepest yellow, fairly full, the most double of this class ... ... each 1s.

PROVENCE OR CABBAGE ROSES—
Old Provence. Rose colour, very fragrant ... each 9d.
White Provence. White, beautiful bud ... each 9d.

ROSA RUGOSA, Japanese Roses. Beautiful varieties, bearing very large single blooms, followed by handsome fruit in Autumn; highly ornamental.
Alba. Pure white, very large and sweet ... each 1s. 6d.
Rubra. Bright rose, very sweet scented ... each 1s. 6d.

CRIMSON CHINA. Dark crimson, dwarf and pretty; an old favourite ... ... each 1s.

MOSS—Blanche Moreau. Perpetual Moss, pure white flowers in clusters, well mossed Standards 2s.; Dwarfs 1s.
  ,,   **Celina.** Rich crimson, shaded with purple Dwarfs 1s.
  ,,   **Colonel R. Lefort.** Purplish red, shaded with bright red ... ... Dwarfs 1s.

MOSS—CRIMSON GLOBE (New Hybrid Moss). Buds nicely mossed, flowers deep crimson, large, full, and globular, growth very vigorous. This magnificent Rose will be a great acquisition to the Moss Roses, as it possesses the qualities of a show flower combined with the true Moss characteristics. First Class Certificate, Royal Horticultural Society ... ... Dwarfs only, each 2s.

  ,,   **Common Moss.** Rosy blush, mossed well up the bud. Standards, each 2s.; Dwarfs, each 2s.; Dwarfs, each 10s. 6d.; each 1s.

  ,,   **Crested.** Rose, beautiful, large and full Dwarfs 1s.

  ,,   **Little Gem.** A miniature Moss Rose, forming compact bushes, densely covered with small double crimson flowers, beautifully mossed. It is of charming effect in the garden, and most valuable for bouquets or vases Dwarfs, 1s. 6d.

  ,,   **White Bath.** Paper-white; beautiful, large, and full ... ... Dwarfs 1s.

  ,,   **White Moss.** Pure white, beautifully mossed Dwarfs only, per doz. 10s. 6d.; each 1s.

Perle d'Or (Polyantha). Nankeen yellow with orange centre; small and very beautiful buds ... ... each 1s.

Clematises.

These magnificent hardy climbers are highly popular amongst amateur growers, and considering their great beauty, freedom of blooming, and the facility with which they may be trained on any kind of wall, trellis, verandah, or pillar, and in almost any aspect, it is surprising that Clematises are not found in abundance in every garden. The plants we offer are established in pots, and can be removed at any time of the year. The sorts blooming after June are the best for bedding purposes; they flower on the young wood, and therefore require before growth commences in Spring, to be cut down to within six or twelve inches of the ground, as likewise do all the late-flowering kinds; and early sorts, flowering from May to July on the old wood, should be pruned similarly to Roses. When the selection of sorts is left to ourselves, customers may rely on our sending a really good variety.

	Months of Flowering.	s.	d.
Albert Victor. Deep lavender	My Jy	1	6
Ascotiensis. Azure blue, large	Jy Sp	1	6
Barillet Deschamps. Double, brilliant mauve, with yellow stamens, distinct	Ju Jy	2	6
Beauty of Surrey. Greyish blue	Jy	2	6
Beauty of Worcester. Large and handsome, producing double and single flowers on same plant, lovely bluish violet, pure white stamens ...	Ju Oo	2	0
Belle Nantaise. Lavender blue, very large flowers, extra fine	Jy Oc	2	6
Belle of Woking. Silvery grey, double	Ju	1	6
Blue Gem. Pale cerulean blue	Jy Oo	2	0
Countess of Lovelace. Bluish lilac, double ...	Ju Jy	2	0
Duke of Edinburgh. Rich violet purple	My Jy	1	6
Duchess of Edinburgh. The best of all the double whites, deliciously scented	Ju Jy	2	0
Duchess of Teck. Pure white, mauve bar ...	Jy Oo	1	6
Earl of Beaconsfield. Rich royal purple ...	Jy Oo	2	0
Enchantress. White, flushed with rose ...	Ju Jy	1	6
Fair Rosamond. Blush white	My Ju	1	6
Flammula. Sweet-scented. White	Jy Oo	1	0
Fortunei. Creamy white, rosette form, sweet-scented	Ju Jy	1	6
Gipsy Queen. Dark velvety purple ...	Jy Oo	1	6
Henryi. Beautiful large creamy white, most hardy variety	Jy Oo	2	0
Jackmani alba. Fine white, very distinct ...	Jy Oo	2	0
Jackmani. Intense violet purple	Jy Oo	1	6
Jackmani, snow white (new). Beautiful pure white, very free flowering ...	Jy Oo	2	6
Jackmanii superba. Similar to "Jackmanii," but later than that variety, and the colour more intense ...	Jy Oo	2	0
Jeanne d'Arc. Greyish white	Ju Oo	2	0
La France. Deep violet purple, dark anthers, large and robust	Jy Oo	1	6
Lady Bovill. Greyish blue, cupped	Jy Oo	2	6
Lady Caroline Neville. French white ...	Jy Oo	2	6
Lanuginosa. Pale lavender	Jy Oo	2	6
Lanuginosa candida. Tinted greyish white ...	Ju Oo	2	6
Louis van Houtte. Bluish purple ...	Ju Oo	2	6
Lucie Lemoine. Double, white	Ju Jy	2	0
Madame Edouard Andre (new). Beautiful bright velvety red, very distinct and free flowering ...	Jy Oc	3	0
Madame van Houtte. White, mauve tint ...	Jy Oo	2	0
Miss Bateman. White, red anthers ...	My Jy	1	6
Mrs. S. C. Baker. French white	My Ju	1	6
Purpurea elegans. Deep violet purple ...	Jy Oo	2	0
Robert Hanbury. Bluish lilac	Jy Oo	2	0
Sir Garnet Wolseley. Slaty blue ...	My Jy	1	6
Star of India. Reddish plum	Jy Oo	1	6
Symeans. Delicate lavender blue, deeper bars	Jy Oo	1	6
Venus Victrix. A fine double-flowered variety, delicate lavender blue, beautiful form	Jy Oo	2	0
William Kennett. Deep lavendor ...	Ju Oo	2	0

GROUP OF CLEMATISES.

From the Honble. F. P. BOUVERIE, Bradford-on-Avon.

Mar. 27th.
"The Honble. F. P. Bouverie has received from Messrs. Daniels Bros. the **Rose Trees**, &c., which are most satisfactory."

From Mr. W. COVEY, Alton.

Oct. 23th.
"I received the **Roses** and **Clematis** quite safe, and am very pleased with them."

	Months of Flowering.	s.	d.
Mrs. Baron Veillard. Distinct light lilac rose; very free bloomer, vigorous grower ...	Jy Oc	2	0
Mrs. Hope. Satiny mauve	Ju Au	2	6
Mrs. Geo. Jackman. Satiny white, beautiful	Ju Oo	2	0
Othello. Dark velvety purple	Ju Oo	2	6
Princess of Wales. Deep bluish mauve ...	Jy Oo	2	0

Choice named varieties from the above list, our own selection, per doz. 18s., 21s., and 24s.

Clematis indivisa lobata.

WE offer fine plants of this beautiful evergreen greenhouse species. The foliage is of a dark olive green and of great substance; the flowers are of the purest white, very fragrant, and produced in wonderful profusion. Highly recommended as a greenhouse climber. The flowers are very neat and exceedingly useful for cutting. Fine strong plants, each 2s. 6d.

Clematis montana.

A BEAUTIFUL early, free-flowering variety, blooming in May and June, and producing a profusion of small, pure white starry flowers, somewhat resembling those of the white wood Anemone. Splendid for covering trellises, porches, &c. Very hardy and highly recommended. Each 1s.

Hardy Climbing and other Plants

SUITABLE FOR TRAINING ON WALLS, &c.

These are mostly grown in pots, and can be supplied and planted at any time of the year with perfect safety.

	each—s.	d.
Akebia quinnata. Purplish brown flowers	1	6
Ampelopsis (*Virginian Creepers*).		
Veitchi. Small-leaved, very beautiful variety. Clings to walls with great tenacity ... 1s. and	1	6
purpurea. A beautiful dark-leaved variety ...	1	6
Hederacea. Common Virginian Creeper	1	0
Sempervirens. Evergreen	1	6
Hoggi. Large-leaved, fine variety ...	1	6
Aristolochia sipho. Deciduous	1	6
Azara microphylla. Beautiful plant for walls ...	1	6
Berberidopsis corralina. Evergreen 1s. 6d. and	2	6
Bignonia radicans (*Trumpet Flower*)	1	6
Buddlea globosa. Orange globose flowers ...	1	6
Ceanothus. Gloire de Versailles. Sky blue ...	2	0
Azureus. Pale blue	2	0
Divaricatus. Very pale blue	1	6
Chimonanthus fragrans. Very sweet-scented ...	2	0
Cotoneaster microphylla ⎱ Very handsome with berries	1	0
Simmondsi ⎰ in Autumn	1	0
Cratægus pyracantha. Well-known white-flowered variety, having bright scarlet berries in the Autumn	1	6
Pyracantha Lælandi. Red-berried and splendidly effective plant in Autumn and Winter 1s. 6d. and	2	6
Garrya elliptica. Beautiful for the wall 1s. 6d. and	2	6
Escallonia macrantha. Evergreen, with bright rosy crimson flowers, very pretty ... 1s. 6d. and	2	6
Ivies (*Hedera*)—		
Cavendishi. Silver-margined	1	6
Clouded Gold. Fine	1	6
Irish. Strong-growing, very useful per doz. 10s. 6d.	1	0

	each—s.	d.
Ivies (*Hedera*)—*continued.*		
Madeiriensis variegata. Fine robust-growing variety, beautiful silver-edged foliage 1s. 6d. and	2	6
Maculata. Very handsome	1	6
Palmata. Handsome variety	1	0
Rœgneriana (*The Giant Ivy*). Very large ...	1	6
Tricolor. Very pretty	1	6
Jasminum (*Jasmine*)—		
Nudiflorum. Yellow, blooms in December ...	1	0
Officinale. White, very sweet-scented	1	0
Kerria Japonica fl. pl. Double yellow flowers	1	6
Lonicera (*Honeysuckle*)—		
Aurea reticulata. Golden-veined foliage ...	1	6
Flexuosa. Evergreen	1	6
Halli. Pure white, evergreen, fine	1	0
Early White ⎱ Well-known deliciously-scented	1	0
Late Red Dutch ⎰ varieties	1	0
Scarlet Trumpet ⎰	1	6
Magnolia grandiflora. Exmouth variety 2s. 6d. to 10		6
Passiflora cærulea. Common blue Passion-flower ...	1	0
"Constance Elliott." Flowers pure white ...	1	6
Periploca græca. Rapid climber	1	0
Pyrus Japonica. Valuable early Spring-flowering plant, rich scarlet, exceedingly handsome 1s. 6d. and	2	6
Maulei. Very beautiful plant, bearing bright light red flowers in Spring and handsome golden yellow fruit in the Autumn	1	6
Wistaria sinensis. Large clusters of lilac mauve coloured flowers ... ... 1s. 6d. and	2	6
alba. White flowers	2	6

Choice Hardy Climbers, our own selection, including Roses and Clematises,
per doz. 10s. 6d. and 15s.; per 100, 75s. and 105s.

Hardy Flowering & Ornamental Foliaged Deciduous Trees & Shrubs.

Some fine effects may be produced in the garden or the shrubbery border by the judicious planting of the following ornamental trees and shrubs. Such graceful plants as Weeping Willows and Mop-headed Acacias are well suited for planting amongst dwarf-growing shrubs, and will also form nice specimens on the lawn, whilst a back ground or line of such choice subjects as Double Scarlet Thorn, Acer negundo variegata, Prunus Pissardi, Laburnums, Purple Beech, planted alternately, produce the most exquisitely beautiful effects when in full bloom and leaf in May and June.

Acer negundo variegata. Beautiful silver-edged leaves. Dwarfs, each 1s. to 1s. 6d.

Half-standards, each 1s. 6d.; standards, each 2s. 6d. to 3s. 6d.

Ailanthus glandulosa. Per doz. 8s., 10s., and 12s.

Arbutus unedo. Strawberry-tree, each 2s.

Ash, Weeping. Fine standards, each 3s. 6d. to 7s. 6d.

Aucuba Japonica (*mas. et fæm.*). Each 1s. to 3s. 6d.

Beech, Copper. Each 1s. 6d. to 5s.

,, **Fern-leaved.** Each 2s. to 3s. 6d.

,, **Purple.** Each 1s. 6d. to 5s.

Berberis aquifolia. Per doz. 1s. to 6s.

,, **Darwini.** Elegant evergreen shrub, each 6d. to 3s. 6d.

,, **Purple-leaved.** Handsome, each 1s.

Bird Cherry (*Cerasus padus*). Each 1s.

Catalpa Kæmpferii. Each 2s. 6d.

,, **syringifolia.** Each 1s. and 1s. 6d.

Cherry, Double-blossomed. Dwarfs, each 1s. 6d.; standards, each 2s. and 2s. 6d.

Chestnut, Horse. Per doz. 9s.; each 1s.

,, ,, **Larger trees, each 2s. 6d. and 3s. 6d.**

,, ,, **Scarlet.** Standards, each 2s. 6d. and 3s. 6d.

Elm, Golden-leaved. Very handsome, each 2s. 6d. to 5s.

Elder, New Golden-leaved. Each 1s.; per doz. 9s.

,, **New Silver-leaved.** Very handsome. Each 9d.; per doz. 7s. 6d.

,, **Scarlet-berried.** Each 1s.

Genista Andreanus. A beautiful variety of the common Broom; golden-yellow flowers, with a crimson keel, each 1s. 6d.

Halesia tetraptera (*Snowdrop tree*). Very pretty, each 1s. 6d.

Holly, Gold-variegated ⎱ Beautiful varieties, each 2s. 6d.

,, **Silver Queen** ⎰ to 10s. 6d.

Japanese Maples. Beautiful varieties, quite hardy. Each 2s. 6d., 3s. 6d., and 5s.

Kalmia latifolia. Pretty free-flowering shrub. Each 1s. 6d.

Laburnum, English or Common. Each 1s. and 1s. 6d.

Liquidambar styraciflua. Each 1s.

Lilac, Marie Legraye. Pure white deliciously-scented flowers. Dwarfs, each 1s. 6d. and 2s. 6d.

,, **Charles X.** Numerous clusters of deep purple flowers, very fine variety. Dwarfs, each 1s. and 1s. 6d.

,, **Common.** Each 1s. and 1s. 6d.

,, **Madame Lemoine.** Pure white double flowers, very fine. Each 2s. 6d.

,, **Souvenir de Louis Spath.** Rich mauve purple flowers, splendid variety. Each 1s. 6d.

Lime, Red-twigged. Each 1s. to 3s. 6d.; per doz. 10s. 6d. to 30s.; extra large 5s. each

Mountain Ash. Common. Each 6d. to 1s. 6d.

Oak, Scarlet. Each 1s. to 2s. 6d.

,, **Turkey.** Variegated, standards. Each 2s. 6d. and 5s.

Philadelphus (*Syringa* or *Mock Orange*). Each 1s. and 1s. 6d.

Poplar, Golden-leaved. Each 1s. to 2s. 6d.

Prunus Pissardi (*Japanese Plum*). Dark crimson-purple foliage, very beautiful in Autumn. Dwarfs, each 1s.; standards, each 2s.

Rhus cotinus (*Sumach*). Slender panicles of flowers in Summer forming hairy tufts; curious. Each 1s. 6d.

Ribes sanguinea. Red-flowered American Currant, each 1s. and 1s. 6d.

Robinia inermis (*Mop-headed Acacia*). Standards, each 2s. 6d., 3s. 6d., and 5s.

,, **hispida** (*Rose Acacia*). Dwarfs, each 1s. 6d.; standards, each 2s. 6d. and 3s. 6d.

Spiræa ariæfolia. Large panicles of white flowers, very fine. Each 1s. and 1s. 6d. And other varieties.

Sumach, Stag's Horn. Each 9d. to 1s. 6d.

Thorn, Double Scarlet (Paul's). Splendid dwarfs, each 1s.; fine pyramids and standards, each 1s. 6d. to 2s. 6d.

Willows, Weeping. Fine standards, each 2s. 6d. and 3s. 6d.

Choice Hardy Coniferous Plants.

	each—s. d.	s. d.

Abies canadensis (*Hemlock Spruce*). Very graceful ... 1 0 to 1 6
  „ **Douglasii.** Very ornamental ... 1 6 „ 2 6
  „ „ **glauca.** Beautiful glaucous-green foliage ... 3 6 „10 6
  „ **Engelmanni.** Fine variety ... 3 6 „10 6
Araucaria imbricata (*Chilian Pine*) ... 5 0 „10 6
Cedrus Atlantica. Very hardy ... 2 6 „ 5 0
  „ **deodara.** One of the most graceful and useful ... 1 6 „10 6
Cryptomeria elegans. Very hardy and useful ... 1 6 „ 7 6
  „ **Japonica.** Very ornamental ... 2 6 „ 5 0
Cupressus—
Lawsoniana. Very useful ... 1 6 „ 5 0
  „ **alba spica.** Very handsome ... 2 6 „10 6
  „ **argentea.** Very distinct ... 3 6 „10 6
  „ **erecta viridis.** Beautiful up-right-growing variety, dark green foliage 1 6 „ 5 0
  „ **lutea.** Beautiful golden foliage ... 2 0 „10 6
  „ **pyramidalis alba spica.** Very handsome and distinct ... 3 6 „10 6
Juniperus Chinensis aurea (*Golden Juniper*) ... 2 6 „21 0
  „ **Virginiana** (*Red Cedar*)... ... 1 0 „ 3 6
Picea lasiocarpa. Fine for single specimen 5 0 „10 6
  „ **pinsapo.** Handsome and distinct 2 6 „10 6

Picea Nordmanniana. Very handsome 2 6 to 10 6
Pinus cembra. Beautiful variety ... 2 6 „ 5 0
Retinospora plumosa. Very ornamental 1 6 „ 5 0
  „ **argentea** } Extremely handsome ... 1 6 „ 5 0
  „ **aurea** } ... 1 6 „ 5 0
  „ **squarrosa.** Fine glaucous foliage... 2 6 „ 5 0
Taxus baccata (*Common Yew*). Fine young plants ... 1 0 „ 5 0
  „ **elegantissima.** Beautifully variegated ... 2 6 „10 6
  „ **fastigiata** (*Irish Yew*). Very distinct, upright-growing ... 1 6 „10 6
  „ **aurea variegata** ... 3 6 „10 6
Thuja Lobbi. Very hardy and ornamental... 1 0 „ 5 0
  „ „ **aurea.** A beautiful golden-leaved conifer; should be in every collection 2 6 „ 7 6
  „ **occidentalis** (*American Arborvitæ*) 1 0 „ 8 6
  „ „ **Vervæneana.** Beautiful golden variety ... 1 6 „ 5 0
Thujopsis borealis. Fine dark green foliage 1 6 „ 5 0
  „ „ **lutea.** A grand new golden Thujopsis; perfectly hardy ... 2 6 „ 7 6
  „ **dolabrata.** Very handsome ... 2 6 „ 7 6
  „ „ **variegata.** Beautiful silvery foliage ... 3 6 „ 7 6
Wellingtonia gigantea. Nice young plants 2 6 „ 7 6

Hardy Evergreen Shrubs & Coniferous Plants.

WE have a fine collection of these in sturdy, healthy young plants, all of which were transplanted during the past season, and are in splendid condition for removal.

Our own selection of sorts, in good variety { ... ... height 1 to 1½ ft., per doz. 9s.; per 50, 30s.; per 100, 55s.
  „ 1½ to 2 ft., „ 12s.; „ 40s.; „ 75s.
  „ 2 to 3 ft., „ 18s.; „ 65s.; „ 120s.

RHODODENDRONS—Garden Hybrids.

THE cultivation of these beautiful hardy evergreen flowering shrubs has been greatly on the increase since the discovery that peat soil is not absolutely necessary for their successful growth. Sandy peat free from stagnant moisture probably suits them best, but they will do well in sandy loam or even clayey loam, if free from calcareous matter, whilst we have seen many beautiful specimens growing in ordinary light garden soil. The colours of the flowers range from the richest and most intense crimson to the most delicate shades of rose and pure white, the masses of beautiful bloom having a charming appearance with the rich dark green foliage.

Choice named varieties. Strong young plants, well set with flower buds. Our own selection, according to size
   each 2s. 6d., 3s. 6d., and 5s.; per doz. 24s., 30s., and 40s.
   Standards and half-standards each 7s. 6d. to 21s.
Unnamed Hybrids. Good kinds, producing a beautiful variety   per doz. 12s., 18s., 24s. and 30s.
Ponticum ... ... each 1s. to 2s.; per doz. 9s. to 21s.

Iris Germanica.

THESE beautiful hardy plants are very easy of cultivation, and will thrive and bloom freely in almost any soil or position, and always have a fresh and pleasing appearance. We have a fine collection of these, including upwards of fifty of the most distinct and beautiful sorts. The best time for planting these, and the *Kæmpferi* varieties, is in March or April.

Germanica albicans. Pure white; the largest and purest in colour of this group ... 0 9
  „ **Darius.** Upper petals chrome yellow, lower ones purple, margined with yellow and reticulated white; very distinct ... 1 6
  „ **Flavescens.** Light primrose yellow; a large and beautiful flower ... 0 9
  „ **Madame Chereau.** White, edged and feathered violet and pale blue; a charming variety ... 1 0
  „ **Pallida Dalmatica.** Lavender, faintly touched with purple; a very fine, large flower ... 2 0

Germanica, Queen of May. Delicate rosy lilac; the lower petals are veined with yellow. A distinct and attractive variety ... 1 0
  „ **Rowlandiana.** White, slightly purple-veined upper petals; the lower ones strongly marked with purple. A beautiful flower ... 1 0
  „ **Victorine.** Upper petals white, blotched with purplish blue; the lower ones purple, delicately veined with white. One of the most lovely of this section ... 1 6
Choice named varieties, our selection   per doz. 6s. and 9s.
Very choice mixed ... per doz. 3s. 6d. per 100, 24s.

Select Hardy Florists' Flowers.

Delphiniums.

SINGLE AND DOUBLE-FLOWERED.

THESE fine hardy plants are deserving a place in every garden, they continue in bloom for a long time in Summer, many of the varieties producing spikes of bloom one foot to two feet in length, and of the most intense and delicate colours.

	each—s.	d.
Alopecuroides. Double, rich blue, splendid variety...	1	6
Autolycus. Bluish violet, shaded bronzy-blue ...	1	6
Belladonna. Single. Very pale blue, a lovely shade ...	0	9
Brittanicus. Azure blue, shaded mauve :.. ...	1	6
Conspicua. Bright blue, white and orange eye ...	1	0
General Urich. Bright blue, white centre ...	1	6
Mrs. James Helme. Silvery blue, long spike ...	1	6
Nudicaule. Bright orange scarlet flowers ...	0	9
Thomas Tilbrook. Rich blue, grand spike ...	1	6
Ustane. Light blue, inner petals rosy mauve, dark eye	1	0

Strong established plants, in choice variety to name, our selection ... ... per doz. 6s. and 9s.

Perennial Gaillardias.

SPLENDID hardy perennials. The very large and beautiful flowers are almost unique in their charming blendings of the many rich shades of brown, maroon, and golden yellow, and being of good substance are first-class to cut for indoor decoration, as the blooms will last a week in water. The plants, which are of a bushy habit of growth, attain about 2½ feet in height, will thrive in any soil, and produce a profusion of their lovely flowers from June to October.

	each—s.	d.
Addison. Crimson, edged with gold ...	1	0
Attraction. Intense vermilion, golden margin ...	1	0
Banquo. Orange, red centre, fine	1	0
Bethcar. Crimson, gold edge, quilled and tasselled ...	1	0
Diana. Deep crimson with golden edge ...	1	0
Distinction. Dark crimson and yellow, quilled ...	1	0
Hercules. Yellow, large flower	0	9
James Kelway. Very fine flower, sometimes 5½ inches in diameter; dazzling scarlet with golden edge ...	2	6
Lutea. Very fine yellow	0	9
Magnifica. Golden yellow, carmine band round the disc	1	0
Maxima. Blood crimson, edged golden yellow ...	1	6
Perfection. Brilliant scarlet, edged with yellow ...	1	0
Superba. Deep crimson, with broad yellow edge ...	1	0
Vivian Grey. Yellow, a grand flower ...	1	6

Choice named varieties, our selection
per doz. 9s. and 12s.
Choice mixed seedlings, will produce some beautiful flowers ... ... per doz. 4s. 6d.; 6 for 2s 6d.

Perennial Phloxes.

MAGNIFICENT hardy plants, in bloom from July to November. The flowers, which are produced in grand spikes, are of the most beautiful form, and the colours range from the most intense crimson and scarlet to the purest white, and white with delicately coloured eyes. Will succeed well planted out in Spring and grown as Chrysanthemums. We have a fine collection of these, including the most charming flowers in cultivation.

EARLY-FLOWERING—Bolle Pyramidale, Clipper, Forerunner, John Beaton, King of Purples, Madame Rendatler, Mr. Fraser, Mrs. Miller. Nemo, Nettie Stewart, Pengo, Rose of Castile, Sanspareil, Thos. E. Glover, &c.

LATE-FLOWERING—Aurora, Brutus, Coccinea, Comtesse de Suresnes, Decius, Delicatum, Gipsy Queen, Gloire de Poiteau, Jessie Laird, Independence, J. K. Lord, Jeanne d'Arc, Le Vengeur, Lothair, Louis Schwartz, M. Gardener Brewer, M. Hugh Low, M. Jules Roche, Mdlle. Coppenheim, Mdme. Autin, Mdme. Verschaffelt, Mrs. Dombrain, Mrs. Kerr, Peerless, Richard Wallace, Roi des Blancs, Souvenir de Berryer, The Queen, The Me Newman, W. Kilgour, White Lady.

Strong Plants established in pots, our own selection, in beautiful variety to name
per doz. 4s. 6d., 6s., and 9s.; per 100, 30s. and 40s.
Strong Plants, Customer's selection per doz. 6s. & 9s.

Double-flowered Pyrethrums.

THESE fine plants produce a great variety of beautiful flowers in all the shades of crimson, carmine, rose, to pure white. The individual blooms are as double and finished as those of good Asters, which they resemble, and are extremely useful for cutting.

	each—s.	d.
Aphrodite. The purest white variety ever seen; very free bloomer	1	6
Captain Boyton. Carmine, edged white ...	1	6
Carl Voget. The earliest of all whites. A beautiful variety with large, grandly-formed flowers ...	1	6
Celia. Very fine pink, of good habit. F.C.C. ...	1	6
Cleopatra. Yellow and white; novel and distinct ...	1	0
Delicatum. Lilac peach, changing to almost pure white	1	0
Dr. Livingstone. Delicate flesh colour; very showy	1	0
Empress Queen. Blush; a fine flower. F.C.C. ...	2	0
Floribundum plenum. Rosy pink very fine ...	1	0
Gloire d'Italie. Rosy red; finely-cut blooms ...	1	6
King Oscar. Crimson scarlet, tipped white ...	2	0
Magician. Lovely bright pink; gold tips ...	1	6
Melton. Intensely bright crimson scarlet; free and vigorous, the brightest Pyrethrum ever raised. F.C.C.	1	6
Pericles. Peach guard-petals with lovely golden centre; the yellowest variety in existence. F.C.C. ...	2	6
Rev. J. Dix. Rosy carmine; a fine deep, full flower	1	0
Sambanburgh. A good, fine, free-flowering pure white	1	6
Solfaterre. Beautiful creamy sulphur guard-petals, golden centre	1	6
Toison d'Or. A first-class yellow. It is really a dwarf "Solfaterre," but freer bloomer, and a shade deeper	3	0

Strong established Plants in pots in choice named variety. Our selection ... per doz. 6s., 9s. and 12s.

SINGLE-FLOWERED.

	each—s.	d.
Mrs. Bateman Brown. The finest dark single variety in existence; of a rich carmine crimson beautifully blended; the flower is of extraordinary size and perfect form. Has been awarded a F.C.C. ...	1	6

Our selection of sorts, beautiful varieties to name ... ... per doz. 6s. and 9s.

Potentillas.

DOUBLE AND SINGLE-FLOWERED.

VERY free-flowering and useful hardy perennials, growing about two feet high. The flowers are of a rich velvety texture, and vary in colour from crimson and maroon to orange and golden yellow.

12 in 6 choice varieties, our selection 9s.; 6 for 5s.

Herbaceous Pæonies.

DOUBLE-FLOWERED.

WELL-KNOWN, magnificent, hardy, herbaceous plants for the shrubbery border, &c., will thrive in almost any soil or situation, but to be grown well should be planted in an open position and not disturbed for several years. We have a splendid named collection of these, including the newest and best sorts, the flowers ranging in colour from pure white to the deepest crimson and purple. Cut when just expanding, the blooms will last a long time in water.

	each—s.	d.
Duchess de Sheba. Lovely flesh white ...	1	6
Excellent. Delicate rose guard petals, centre sulphur	1	6
General Havelock. Deep rosy pink, shading lighter	1	6
Madame Paternoster. Rosy crimson; a showy variety	1	6
Lilacina superba. Delicate lilac; a charming colour	1	6
Pio Nono. A fine purple; very attractive ...	1	6
Officinalis rubra plena. Beautiful rich crimson	1	6
Whitleyi. This variety, when it first opens, has often a sulphury tinge of colour, but this soon fades away to pure white. It is a very free bloomer ...	1	6
Tenuifolia plena. A distinct variety with elegantly-divided Fennel-like foliage, and full, large double flowers of a deep rich crimson; it is a dwarf compact grower, an early bloomer, and very beautiful ...	2	6

Our selection of choice named varieties
per doz. 12s., 18s., and 21s.

LILY OF THE VALLEY.

Lily of the Valley.

For early forcing single crowns of these should be planted about twelve in a five-inch pot, with the buds well above the surface. Cover the crowns with a little moss or an inverted flower pot for about ten days, and place them in a good heat of say 85 or 90 degrees; water frequently with tepid water, and if judiciously looked after they will bloom in four or five weeks from the time of potting. Good single crowns are much the best for the purpose. Clumps or single shoots can be supplied up to the end of April.

Selected Single Shoots, German. Produce splendid heads of bloom, much superior to the Dutch ... per 100, 6s.; per doz. 1s.

Spiræa Japonica.

Perhaps the most elegant and useful of all plants for early forcing. Lovely and chaste spikes of elegant white inflorescence, and is singularly adapted for pot display, table or hand bouquets, &c., and by judicious forcing may be had in abundance at Easter. It will last well in almost any situation when in bloom. It is besides perfectly hardy, and can be grown on the open border.

Strong clumps for forcing ... ... per doz. 5s.; each 6d.

Japonica multiflora compacta. A fine free-flowering dwarf-growing variety; splendid as a pot plant or for cutting
per doz. 6s.; each 9d.

Spiræa astilboides.

This fine new variety is one of the most handsome of hardy herbaceous perennials, and has been certificated both by the Royal Horticultural and the Royal Botanic Societies on account of its great merit. The stems grow from two to three feet high, and are terminated by compound feathery branches of elegant white flowers, which are produced in the greatest profusion. A charming and effective plant for pot culture.

Strong plants ... ... each 1s.

Violets—Sweet-scented.

These deliciously-scented and ever welcome favourites, so extremely useful as cut flowers for bouquets, button-holes, &c., may, with a little management, be had in abundant bloom throughout the Winter and Spring months—a time when they are especially valuable. The stock Plants should be divided in April or early in May and planted out in rich soil in a partially shaded position, the doubles in rows one foot apart, and nine inches apart in the rows, the singles one foot apart each way. As growth commences, the young shoots or runners should be removed and the plants should be watered in the evening in dry weather, whilst if extra fine plants are required, they should have a mulching of well-decayed manure from an old mushroom bed or cucumber frame. Towards the end of September the plants may be lifted and planted into specially prepared frames placed in a south aspect, and partially filled with stable litter, leaves, &c., with about six or eight inches of soil on the top. The plants should be placed sufficiently close together to fairly fill the space without crowding, and should be as near the glass as the foliage will admit. When planted, give a thorough watering and keep close for a few days, after which admit air freely at every opportunity through the Winter. The glass may be entirely removed in sunny weather when there is no frost, and in all mild weather plenty of ventilation should be given. *Marie Louise, Count Brazza's,* and *Neapolitan* are the best of the doubles to be grown in this way, and when treated as recommended above will produce some grand flowers.

DOUBLE-FLOWERED VARIETIES.

each—s. d.

Belle de Chatenay White. New double; pure white, tipped with bluish purple; very double   per doz. 6s.   0 9

Count Brazza's Neapolitan White (*syn.* Swanley White). Magnificent variety; large, double, pure white flowers, deliciously scented; the finest of all double white Violets; splendid for bouquets   per doz. 5s.   0 6

De Parme. Deliciously fragrant flowers of a delicate pale lavender purple, in great profusion   per doz. 6s.   0 9

Mademoiselle Bertha Barron (new). Flowers beautiful indigo blue, deliciously scented
per doz. 7s. 6d.   0 9

Marie Louise. A fine variety, large double flowers, rich lavender blue, with white centres ...   per doz. 5s.   0 6

Neapolitan. Lavender blue, flowers very large and double, profuse bloomer ... ...   per doz. 4s.   0 6

SINGLE-FLOWERED VARIETIES.

each—s. d.

California. A fine vigorous-growing, free-blooming variety from the United States. The flowers are very large, of a deep, clear violet purple colour, deliciously fragrant, and are borne on stems ten to twelve inches in length, making it especially valuable for florists' work, bouquets, &c. Highly recommended   3 for 5s.   2 0

Odoratissima. Similar to *Victoria Regina*   per doz. 6s.   0 8

Princess of Wales (new). Large, beautifully-formed flowers of a deep violet blue colour and deliciously scented, borne on long stems. A most vigorous grower, and a splendid variety ...   per doz. 15s.   1 6

Rawson's White. A very free-flowering and beautiful variety, producing immense quantities of deliciously fragrant pure white flowers   per doz. 7s. 6d.   0 9

The Czar. An almost constant bloomer   per doz. 3s.   0 4

Victoria Regina. Large, fragrant, fine shaped flowers, on strong flower-stems ... ...   per doz. 3s. 6d.   0 4

Wellsiana. Very large, deep rich purple, superior to *Victoria Regina* ... ...   per doz. 7s. 6d.   0 9

Strawberry Plants—Prepared Runners.

Strawberries when well-grown are wonderfully prolific, and constitute one of the most profitable crops, really good fruit always meeting with a ready sale at high prices. These delicious and wholesome fruit should be grown freely in every garden where there is room for them. As will be seen, our collection of choice Strawberries, a select list of which we offer below, contains all the finest varieties in cultivation.

The best system of culture for the production of really fine and richly-coloured fruit is to plant in good deep rich soil, in rows 2½ feet apart and 18 inches apart in the row; keep the plants free of runners and give a liberal top dressing of well-decayed manure in Winter.

GRAND VARIETIES OF RECENT INTRODUCTION.

ROYAL SOVEREIGN (Laxton). This fine variety ripens a few days after *King of the Earlies*, and in the open air the first fruits are ready with *Noble*. It may be fairly looked upon as the long sought early, highly-flavoured, and improved *Sir Joseph Paxton*, and just the fruit wanted to precede that popular variety.   Per 100, 20s.; per doz. 3s. 6d.

SENSATION (Laxton). An enormous second early or mid-season variety of good flavour, and probably the largest Strawberry ever introduced. *First Class Certificate, Gardening and Forestry Exhibition, 10th May, 1893.* Per 100, 10s.; per doz. 1s. 6d.

COMPETITOR (Laxton.) A very large, handsome, and luscious early fruit. A good doer in every respect, and will probably displace *Nicaise* for forcing purposes.   Per 100, 7s. 6d.; per doz. 1s. 6d.

LAXTON'S No. 1. The Earliest of all Strawberries. This precocious Strawberry is a seedling from *Noble*, fertilized by *May Queen*, and is unquestionably the earliest in the market.   Per 100, 20s.; per doz. 3s. 6d.

GENERAL LIST.

		per 100—s. d.			per 100—s. d.
A. F. Barron (Laxton)	...	per doz. 1s. 0d. 7 6	La Grosse Sucree	...	5 0
Auguste Nicaise	...	... ... 5 0	LORD SUFFIELD (new) ...	per doz. 1s. 6d. 10 6
Black Prince ...	...	... ... 3 6	LATEST OF ALL (Laxton) ...	per doz. 1s. 6d. 10 6
British Queen ...	...	... ... 5 0	Loxford Hall Seedling ...	... 5 0
Commander (Laxton)	...	per doz. 1s. 0d. 7 6	Lucas	... 5 0
Duke of Edinburgh	...	... ... 5 0	NOBLE (Laxton) ... per 1000, 40s.; per doz. 1s. 5 0
Elton (*syn. Elton Pine*)	...	... ... 5 0	President	... 5 0
EMPRESS OF INDIA (new)		per doz. 1s. 6d. 10 6	SCARLET QUEEN (Laxton) ...	per doz. 1s. 6d. 7 6
Filbert Pine (*syn. Myatt's Seedling*)		... ... 5 0	Sir Charles Napier ...	... 5 0
GUNTON PARK (new)		per doz. 1s. 6d. 10 6	Sir Joseph Paxton ...	... 5 0
John Ruskin	...	... 7 6	The Amateur	... 5 0
James Veitch	... ...	5 0	The Countess ...	... 5 0
Keen's Seedling	... ...	5 0	Vicomtesse Hericart de Thury ...	4 0
King of the Earlies	... ...	5 0	Waterloo	per doz. 1s. 6d. 7 6
Kitley's Goliath	... ...	4 0		

1000 in 10 choice varieties, our own selection	...	**35s. 0d.**
100 in 10 choice varieties, our own selection		**5s. 6d.**

Forest Trees—Transplanted.

The following Forest Trees, &c., are all well grown, healthy stuff, and nearly all having been carefully transplanted within the past twelve months, they are splendidly rooted, and in the best possible condition for removal.

Alder	...	... 3 to 4 ft. 7/- per 100 ; 60/- per 1000		Fir, Scotch. Very good	1½ to 2 ft. 8/- per 100 ; 70/- per 1000
Ash	...	... 2 „ 3 „ 6/- „ 50/- „		„ Spruce. Fine stuff	1½ „ 2 „ 15/- „ 100/- „
„	...	... 3 „ 4 „ 8/- „ 60/- „		„ „	2 „ 2½ „ 20/- „
Beech, Common	... 1½ „ 2 „ 5/- „ 40/- „		Hazel	...	2 „ 3 „ 5/- „ 40/- „
„ „	... 2 „ 3 „ 6/- „ 50/- „		„	... 3 „ 4 „ 7/- „ 60/- „
„ „	... 3 „ 4 „ 12/- „		Hornbeam	... 2 „ 3 „ 6/- „ 50/- „
Birch, Common	... 2 „ 3 „ 6/- „ 50/- „		Limes per doz. 12 - to 30/-	
„ „	... 3 „ 4 „ 7/- „ 60/- „		Maple	... 2 „ 3 „ 7/- „ 50/- „
Chestnut, Spanish	... 2 „ 3 „ 7/- „ 60/- „		Oak, English	2 „ 3 „ 8/- „ 70/- „
„ „	... 3 „ 4 „ 10/- „ 90/- „		„ Turkey	2 „ 3 „ 14/- „
„ Horse	... 3 „ 4 „ 20/- „		Poplar, Black Italian	2 „ 3 „ 7/- „ 60/- „
„ „	... 4 „ 5 „ 25/- „		„ „	6 „ 8 „ 20/- „
Elm, Common	... 3 „ 4 „ 6/- „ 50/- „		„ Lombardy	3 „ 4 „ 14/- „
Fir, Austrian	... 1 „ 1½ „ 6/- „		Sycamore ...	2 „ 3 „ 6/- „ 50/- „
„ „	... 1½ „ 2 „ 26/- „		„ „	3 „ 4 „ 7/- „ 60/- „
„ Larch ...	... 1½ „ 2 „ 4/- „ 30/- „		Willow, of sorts	4 „ 5 „ 10/- „
„ „ ...	... 2 „ 3 „ 5/- „ 40/- „			

Choice Bouquets and Cut Flowers.

WE grow many thousands of Plants specially for our supply of **Choice Cut Flowers**, which we furnish in season from the following superb assortment:—

Abutilons, in variety	Chrysanthemums, Pure White,	Lily of the Valley
Arum Lilies	&c.	Narcissi, of sorts
Azaleas, Pure White and	Deutzia gracilis	Orange Blossom
others	Heaths, of sorts	Orchids, in variety
Begonias, Greenhouse and	Heliotropes, Sweet-scented	Primulas, Double White
Stove varieties	Hyacinths, White Roman and	Roses, Tea-scented and others
Bouvardias, the most beau-	others	Spiræa japonica
tiful sorts	Lapagerias, Rose, White	Stephanotis floribunda
Camellias, in variety	Lilacs, Pure White (forced)	Violets, Sweet-scented
Cyclamens, of sorts	Lilies, Pure White	

And many other Choice Greenhouse and Stove Flowers.

MEMORIAL WREATHS AND CROSSES. Made up with choicest pure white natural flowers and Maidenhair Fern, arranged in the most beautiful style, and guaranteed to give the highest satisfaction

each 7s. 6d., 10s. 6d., 12s. 6d., 15s., 21s., 31s. 6d., and 42s.

BRIDES' SHOWER BOUQUETS. Exquisitely made up with choicest pure white flowers only each 7s. 6d., 10s. 6d., 16s., and 21s.

BRIDESMAIDS' BOUQUETS. Made up with pure white and delicately tinted flowers, or to order each 5s., 7s. 6d. and 10s. 6d.

BUTTON-HOLE BOUQUETS. White or coloured flowers ... ... each 1s. and 1s. 6d.; per doz. 10s. 6d. and 16s.

LADIES' DRESS BOUQUETS OR SPRAYS. Beautifully made up to order ... ... each 2s. 6d., 5s., and 7s. 6d.

LOOSE CUT FLOWERS AND FERN. For table and other decorations supplied in liberal quantity in boxes

each 2s. 6d., 3s. 6d., 5s., 7s. 6d., 10s. 6d., 15s., 21s., 31s. 6d., and 42s.

By our careful and perfect system of packing, the Wreaths, Bouquets, &c., we supply, will stand a journey of fully two days if necessary, and then reach their destination in beautifully fresh condition.

All orders are despatched promptly on receipt, if required, but customers residing at a distance should give, if possible, at least two days' clear notice before the flowers are required, and full particulars for forwarding.

Index.

NORWICH: FLETCHER AND SON, HORTICULTURAL PRINTERS AND LITHOGRAPHERS.

✦ THE ✛ ROYAL ✛ NORFOLK ✛ SEED ✛ ESTABLISHMENT, ✦

NORWICH,  ENGLAND.

TERMS OF BUSINESS, &c.

☞ All orders from unknown Correspondents must be accompanied by a sufficient Remittance or satisfactory References; and to save cost and trouble of Booking, a Remittance should in all cases be sent with Orders under 10s. in value.

ACCOUNTS—DISCOUNTS.—All accounts are due net in three months, we however allow a discount of 1s. in the pound on all orders of 20s. and upwards when accompanied by a remittance, or when paid within fourteen days of date of invoice.

CHEQUES, MONEY ORDERS, AND POSTAL ORDERS.—Please make payable to DANIELS BROS., and cross "GURNEY & Co.," Norwich.

POSTAGE-STAMPS AND COIN.—All letters containing postage-stamps should be registered before being posted. The registration fee is now only 2d., and this ensures a safe delivery. Letters containing coin *must* be registered.

VEGETABLE SEEDS, CARRIAGE FREE TO ANY PART.—We send all Vegetable Seeds Post or Carriage Free to any part of the United Kingdom.

SEED POTATOES CARRIAGE FREE.—All general orders for Garden Seeds (including Seed Potatoes), to the value of 10s. and upwards, Free to any Railway Station on the **Great Eastern** System; and of the value of 20s. and upwards, Carriage Paid to any Railway Station or Steam Port in the United Kingdom.

FLOWER SEEDS.—All orders for Flower Seeds we send Post or Carriage Free to any part of the United Kingdom; and all orders of 10s. value and upwards we send free to any part of the World.

CARRIAGE OF ROSES, FRUIT TREES, MUSHROOM SPAWN, &c.—We do not undertake to pay carriage on general orders for Roses, Fruit Trees, Ornamental Shrubs and Plants, but continue to enclose extra plants free of charge to partially meet the cost of carriage; nor can we undertake to pay carriage of horticultural requisites such as Mushroom Spawn, Silver Sand, &c. All Fruit Trees, Roses, and Shrubs, will be so packed as to stand a journey of a week or ten days without injury. Should the packages arrive at their destination during a severe frost, it will be advisable not to unpack them, but keep them cool and moist out of the reach of the frost, until a change of weather takes place.

CO-OPERATION IN SENDING ORDERS.—Allotment holders, Cottagers, and others requiring but small quantities of Seeds and Seed Potatoes, by joining together in sending their orders, can have the advantage of our terms of Free Carriage, and will be allowed a special discount of ten per cent., taken in seeds, besides the usual discount of five per cent. for cash, thus:—for every 20s. remitted 23s. worth of seeds may be ordered. No order can be recognised under these terms unless over the net value of One Pound, and accompanied by prepayment in full. Every care will be taken to pack each lot of goods separately, according to order, and they can all be despatched in one parcel. Full name and address of each customer ordering under this arrangement should be sent, so that copies of future editions of our *Illustrated Guide* may be posted to each as published.

EMPTY PACKAGES.—All packages are charged at the lowest cost price, and are not returnable unless sent back in good condition, and Carriage Paid, within fourteen days after receipt of goods. Customers are particularly requested to have their name and address on each package, and to advise us by post when returned, or they cannot be credited.

CHANGE OF RESIDENCE.—We shall esteem it a favour if our customers, on changing their residence, will kindly favour us with their new address, that we may be able to send them our Catalogues as usual.

RECOMMENDATIONS.—The many kind recommendations to new customers with which we have been honoured during the past season have been very gratifying. Should any of our customers have friends requiring Seeds, Bulbs, &c., and to whom a copy of our *Illustrated Guide* would be acceptable, we shall feel much obliged for intimation of the fact.

IMPORTANT NOTICE.—We are extensive growers of many years' experience, and take the greatest possible care to supply only reliable seeds of the finest stocks and quality; we however wish it to be distinctly understood, that we give no warranty expressed or implied as to description, quality, or productiveness, or any other matter relating to the seeds or plants we supply, and will not in any way be held responsible for any failure of crop.

SPECIAL NOTICES.

CORRESPONDENCE.—Our customers having occasion to write to us respecting any order previously sent by them, would much facilitate attention to their letters if they would kindly state the date on which the order was sent, and name amount remitted with it; this would enable us the more readily to identify their orders on reference to our Registers.

ADDRESSES.—Full Name and Address should be sent with every communication, and both Postal and Rail Address should accompany all orders, as much time is thereby saved to us, especially in our busiest season, when we are receiving from 1200 to 1500 letters daily.

PACKETS.—Will our customers kindly note that, in all cases where Seeds are quoted by the "Packet," that is the minimum quantity supplied; less quantities or half-packets are not sold.

ORDER EARLY.—All orders are executed in the rotation which they are received, and we beg our customers to send us their orders as soon as possible after receiving this Catalogue. Waiting for favourable weather, or until seeds are urgently needed for sowing, may involve a rush and accumulation of orders with an excessive strain upon our large staff of executants, and delay and disappointment will be avoided by attention to our appeal.

TELEGRAPHIC ADDRESS:—DANIELS, NORWICH.

Price

Estd. 1844.

Entd Sta Hall

DANIELS BROS'

Illustrated GUIDE

for

ROYAL · NORFOLK · SEED · ESTABLISHMENT

SPRING 1896.

AMATEUR GARDENERS

* 9 7 8 3 7 4 1 1 9 6 0 1 0 *